SPORTS COACHING

A Reference Guide for Students, Coaches and Competitors

Edited by Anita Navin

THE CROWOOD PRESS

First published in 2011 by
The Crowood Press Ltd
Ramsbury, Marlborough
Wiltshire SN8 2HR

www.crowood.com

British Library Cataloguing-in-Publication Data
A catalogue record for this book is available from the British Library.

ISBN 978 1 84797 193 7

Disclaimer
Please note that the authors and the publisher of this book do not accept any
responsibility whatsoever for any error or omission, nor any loss, injury, damage,
adverse outcome or liability suffered as a result of the use of the information
contained in this book, or reliance upon it. Since some of the training exercises
can be dangerous and could involve physical activities that are too strenuous for
some individuals to engage in safely, it is essential that a doctor be consulted
before training is undertaken.

Typeset by S R Nova Pvt Ltd., Bangalore, India

Printed and bound in Singapore by Craft Print International Ltd

Contents

Acknowledgements

The editor, authors and publishers would like to thank the following for their help in the production of this book: David Griffiths, Northumbria University and Team Northumbria for kindly providing photographs; Human Kinetics for the table and diagram in Chapter 1; Prozone for an illustration in Chapter 14; Coachwise for the illustration in Chapter 30; Keith Russell for tables and diagrams in Chapter 6; Cengage Learning for the diagrams in Chapter 25; Steven Pope (ICPE & FIT) for the model in Chapter 26; Kirsty Hay and UK Sport for illustrations in Part IV; Youth Sport Trust for illustrations in Part III; Karl Wharton for providing us with the tables and diagrams in Chapter 6; Su Stewart for a photograph in Chapter 6; Mick Wilkinson for two photographs in Chapter 11; Joanne Davison for allowing us to reproduce a photograph that appears in Chapter 14; Daniel Morand of DARTFISH for granting us permission to reproduce 'screen dumps' that appear in Chapter 18; John Parsons for allowing us to publish images of Raising the Bar resources in Chapter 22; John Porteous for supplying three photographs that appear in Chapter 24; and Jeanette Pointon for allowing us to reproduce a photograph that appears in Chapter 28.

Thanks also go to the School of Psychology and Sport Sciences at Northumbria University for supporting the whole project in terms of resource allocation. Thanks also to Helen Bushell for her support of the chapters written by Frederic Pivotti.

Finally, the authors are truly grateful to all athletes who have allowed their profiles and performance issues to be shared in the book, knowing that the review of real-life issues offers the reader useful insights and enhances learning.

Contributor Profiles

EDITOR: ANITA NAVIN

Anita is currently the Head of Department for Sport Development, Management and Coaching at Northumbria University in Newcastle-upon-Tyne, and is a lead member for the development of the undergraduate, postgraduate and professional doctorate programmes in sport coaching. Alongside her academic role Anita is an experienced coach and coach educator, and serves as a consultant for England Netball; she is also involved in tutor development and programme reviews for other sports with a consultancy group. Anita is also a technical commentator for netball on Sky television.

Anita has been involved with England Netball for over twenty-five years as a player, coach, scout, tutor and technical expert for the development of the UK coaching certificate. She has coached at International level with the Northern Ireland Netball Association, and is involved in both the England coaching programme for talented athletes and the Netball Super League programme at Northumbria. Because of her expertise in coaching and in the professional development of fellow coaches she has recently been appointed to the International Federation Coaching Advisory Group for Netball. Anita is also a member of the UK Centre for Coaching Excellence Higher Education Advisory Group.

DR LES ANSLEY

Les lectured at Kingston University for four years before moving up to Northumbria University in 2007. He graduated with a BSc (Hons) in Sport and Exercise Science from the University of Birmingham. In June 2003 he was awarded his PhD (Physiology) from the University of Cape Town. His early research focused on pacing strategies and fatigue during exercise, and at his first international conference in 2004 he was a finalist for the Young Investigator Award. In 2005 he was awarded a HEFCE Promising Young Researcher grant for an international collaborative project. More recently, Les has developed a research interest in exercise-induced bronchoconstriction.

DR PAULA ROBSON-ANSLEY

Paula was appointed as a Reader in the School of Psychology and Sport Sciences at Northumbria University in 2007. Her current research is focused on the role of the immune system in fatigue and recovery from exercise. Paula graduated from the University of Brighton in 1996, and completed her PhD at the University of Birmingham in 1999 where she investigated the impact of exercise on immune system function. She was a research fellow in South Africa at the University of Stellenbosch and the University of Cape Town, where she formulated and tested a range of nutritional supplements to maintain immune function in endurance sports people, as well as working with a range of athletes on strategies for avoiding overtraining syndrome.

KELVIN BEECHING

Kelvin Beeching graduated with a BA (Hons) degree in Applied Sport Science and Coaching in 2005, and has more recently undertaken a postgraduate degree in his specialist field of coaching science. Kelvin currently works as a Lecturer in sport coaching at Northumbria University. Prior to his appointment there, he worked as a Sport Lecturer in further education. He has a range of coaching experience from working in both participation and performance levels of sport in both football and cricket. He has experience of both coaching and sport science support in professional settings, working with a range of athletes from footballers to ice hockey players.

CLAIRE BRUCE

Claire Bruce is a Senior Lecturer and the programme leader for the Sports Development with Coaching programme at Northumbria University. Having obtained a BA (Hons) in Sport and Recreation Management from Sheffield Hallam University in 1994, Claire went on to work in the business sector. She has over ten years of experience in business management in industry, at both regional and national levels. In 2005 she completed an MSc in Sport Management, her research focusing on an evaluation of the Talented Athlete Scholarship Scheme in England. She is currently engaged in research, addressing the impact of computer gaming technology on the sustainability of youth sport participation.

EMMA COCKBURN

Emma was appointed a Graduate Tutor at Northumbria University in 2005. She was herself a successful graduate from Northumbria University, obtaining a BSc (Hons) degree in Applied Sport and Exercise Science in 2003. She is involved in teaching in the fields of sports physiology, sports nutrition, and the application of sports science to coaching and research methods. Currently, Emma is in the final year of her PhD investigating 'the effects of milk-based protein-CHO supplementation on the attenuation of exercise-induced muscle damage'. Other research interests include the reliability of performance tests, the use of milk as a sports drink, and recovery methods. She is also BASES accredited for physiological support, and coaches at England Hockey Centres.

DENISE EGAN

Denise is currently an Assistant Head Teacher at St Anthony's School in Sunderland, and has been involved in the coaching and mentoring of trainee teachers and newly qualified staff at the school. She has also been instrumental in the review of teaching strategies to support staff in managing behaviour. Denise was recently awarded a government qualification following her involvement in the national programme for Specialist Leaders of Behaviour and Attendance. She is a successful World Championship and Commonwealth Games coach in netball. She is renowned for putting forward successful teams in National Schools Netball competitions, and her notable achievements include eight players from the school gaining a place in the England squads. Currently Denise is an active Coach Educator and Assessor, as part of the UK Coaching Certificate programme in netball.

DR LESLEY FISHWICK

Lesley is a Principal Lecturer at Northumbria University. She graduated with a BSc (Hons) in Sport Science from Liverpool Polytechnic, and an MA in Physical Education from Dalhousie University in Canada. She was awarded a PhD from the University of Illinois in the USA. Her specialist subject is the sociology of sport, and her current research interests include gender equity, sporting identities, health discourses and sports ethnography. She has written several distance learning modules for the National Coaching Foundation, and was a course tutor. She was a hockey coach at Liverpool Polytechnic, and assistant coach for the women's soccer team at Dalhousie University.

JANE LOMAX

Jane graduated from Loughborough University with a BSc combined honours degree in Physical Education and Sports Science, and a postgraduate certificate in Education in Physical Education. Jane was a secondary school teacher for seven years, and was a Head of Department and Deputy Head of Sixth Form, before returning to Loughborough University to complete an MSc degree in Sports Psychology and Management Studies. Jane entered into higher education first at Brunel University, moving to her current post at the University of Chichester in 1994. Jane is a BASES-accredited sports psychologist, and has worked as a consultant with performers and coaches from a range of sports. Jane is also involved in coaching the English Universities netball team. She is a Sports Coach UK tutor and is currently working with England Netball as a Tutor and Assessor.

DR DAVID MORLEY

Dr David Morley taught physical education in a number of secondary schools for nearly ten years, and recently held the position of senior lecturer in physical education and sport pedagogy at Leeds Metropolitan University. In his time at Carnegie he led the national strategy for talent development in PE, and was involved in Teacher and Coach Education. David continues to act as a consultant, adviser and project director for PE, sports and educational agencies on projects ranging from multi-skills delivery and curriculum development to talent development in PE and sport. Most recently he has worked with the Rugby Football League and Scottish Football Association on their player development strategies.

He has published extensively in these areas, developed resources, delivered CPD for coaches and teachers, and presented his work at National and International conferences. His latest involvement in nurturing movement competencies is in developing multi-skills within the playground, and he heads a multifaceted, international initiative with ESP (Education and Special Projects) in a bid to make a difference to every child's involvement in PE, and sport and physical activity.

DR ELIZABETH PARTINGTON

Liz is a Senior Lecturer in Sport and Exercise Psychology at Northumbria University. Liz is a chartered psychologist and a full member of the British Psychological Society (BPS), and also an accredited sport and exercise psychologist with the British Association of Sport and Exercise Sciences. Liz has conducted sport psychology consultancy with various national and international performers from a range of sports. She spent two years working with the English Badminton Development squad based at Bath University High Performance Centre. Liz was involved in the design of the sports psychology curriculum for the Badminton Association of England World Class Start and Potential programmes, and was a major contributor to the England Badminton mental skills handbook for national coaches.

DR SARAH PARTINGTON

Sarah is a Principal Lecturer in the Department of Sport and Exercise Sciences at Northumbria University. She is a chartered sport and exercise psychologist, and a full member of both the British Psychological Society

(BPS) and the British Association of Sport and Exercise Sciences (BASES). Sarah is accredited by BASES for psychological support, and has worked with a variety of athletes competing at both national and international level. Her key work has been with England Badminton. She provided regional support for development and performance players based at Bath University High Performance Centre, helped design the sports psychology curriculum for badminton's World Class Start and Potential programmes, contributed to badminton's Long-Term Athlete Development Model and co-wrote their mental skills handbook for national coaches.

FREDERIC PIVOTTI

Frederic Pivotti obtained a Master's Degree in Physical Education and Sports Science at the University of Leuven (Belgium), and specialized as a gymnastics coach. After working as a PE teacher and club coach, he moved on to work for the Belgian Gymnastics Federation as coach education specialist. In 2006 he moved to the UK and became coach education manager for British Gymnastics. He currently works as the coaching system co-ordinator for Welsh Gymnastics, responsible for coaching, workforce development and the development of coach education, mentoring and CPD programmes in gymnastics in Wales.

JOHN PORTEOUS

John Porteous has worked in the sports industry for the past thirty years both lecturing in higher education at Northumbria University (1992–2002 and 2007–the present day), and working in the public and private sport sectors. His latest work experience involved being the National Performance Lifestyle Adviser for the English Institute of Sport (2002–07), where he worked with world-class pathway athletes and national governing bodies of sport to ensure a balanced lifestyle for identified athletes. His research interests focus on sport development, élite athlete transitions and junior golf development. John has worked as a consultant for a range of National Governing Bodies, and also the Youth Sport Trust.

DR EMMA STEVENSON

Emma Stevenson was appointed as a Lecturer in the School of Psychology and Sport Sciences at Northumbria University in October 2006. She completed her BSc (Hons) in Physical Education and Sports Science at Loughborough University in 2002, and stayed to complete her PhD in sports nutrition under the supervision of Professor Clyde Williams. Following this, Emma worked in the School of Biomedical Sciences at Nottingham University. She has also worked as a consultant sports nutritionist for a number of international athletes and squads, including the

England women's football squads, Great Britain ice-skating squads and England Netball.

DR SU STEWART

Su is a Senior Lecturer in Sport and Exercise Science at Northumbria University; her work and research is in the area of sports biomechanics, and sports medicine and rehabilitation. She teaches various modules including sports medicine and rehabilitation, biomechanical profiling, and the fundamentals of sports science. Su's main research and consultancy interests are in the sports science support of élite athletes, in particular international fencers and golfers. She has undertaken consultancy work with a number of élite GB squads and individuals, and works closely with manufacturers on the design and testing of new products.

MELANIE TUCKWELL

A Senior Lecturer at Newport University, Mel is involved in the delivery of a range of sport modules of study, and is programme leader for the MSc Sports Coaching. Previously at Northumbria University, Mel was involved in the development of the undergraduate coaching degree. She was employed with the Welsh Sports Council, where she managed several Olympic sports in terms of policy and coach development. Mel has also coached netball to an international level in Wales, and has contributed to a range of sports in terms of performance analysis. Mel completed a PGCE and MSc at UWIC.

KARL WHARTON

Karl is programme leader for sport coaching, and a Senior Lecturer in the School of Psychology and Sport Sciences at Northumbria University. He joined the university in September 2008, having previously worked for eight years as a national coach for British Gymnastics. He was a teacher of physical education for fifteen years, and was a head of department. Karl's involvement in coaching contributed to his recent appointment to the International Federation of Gymnastics Coaching Academy as a world expert in coaching pedagogy. He has coached at international level with British Gymnastics, and has produced more than fifty world and European medallists, including three world and four European champions.

DR MICK WILKINSON

Mick is a Senior Lecturer in Sport Sciences at Northumbria University; his area of expertise is the physiology of exercise. His main research area is the physiology of high intensity intermittent exercise, an interest he actively pursues with other members of the Sport Performance and Exercise Regulation research group. His PhD examined the physiological determinants of fitness and performance in squash. Part of this work involved the design and validation of squash-specific fitness tests that have been adopted by England Squash and the England Institute of Sport for the testing of the England national squads. Mick has worked with national and international squash players, and a range of other endurance athletes. He is also an advanced level squash coach, and has worked with players from beginner to professional standard.

PART 1: PEDAGOGICAL ISSUES IN SPORTS COACHING

1

Effective Coaching Behaviour

by Anita Navin

The coach is significant in determining the success and overall impact of an athlete's experiences in sport (Williams *et al.*, 2003), yet the definition of effectiveness remains inconsistent amongst sport practitioners and organizations. The majority of sport coaches will measure their effectiveness in terms of the 'value added' to the performance of a team or an individual, and all coaches will try to encompass behaviours that promote success and personal development. Coaching is often referred to as a complex activity, and in order to be successful a coach must possess both the coaching process knowledge and sport-specific knowledge (Abraham and Collins, 1998). Effective coaching behaviour is often associated with positive outcomes for the performer – for example enjoyment, self-esteem and perceived ability. Bowes and Jones (2006) refer to coaching as 'comprising endless dilemmas and decision making, requiring constant planning, observation, evaluation and reaction' (p. 235), and this ability to identify, analyse and control variables that affect athlete performance is central to effective coaching (Cross and Ellice, 1997).

Early research into coach effectiveness suggested that the successful coach provided more feedback in practice; also indicated is the notion that this successful coach used more training and instruction behaviours than the less successful coach (Markland and Martinek, 1988). Research by Tharp and Gallimore (1976) involved the observation of John Wooden the legendary basketball coach from the University of California (UCLA), and used a category-coding system to identify the use and frequency of behaviours. Wooden had a proven ability to consistently produce winning teams, and it was his ability to communicate information, pass on knowledge, detect and correct errors in performance and reinforce behaviours, and his capability to motivate individuals, that received considerable attention when defining effectiveness. Observations of Wooden over

Figure 1.1 A coach engaging in the feedback process. (Courtesy of David Griffiths)

fifteen practice sessions revealed that over 50 per cent of behaviours were categorized under verbal instruction, with other notable behaviours being hustles (12.7 per cent), praise (6.9 per cent) and scolds (6.6 per cent). Based on this early research, coach effectiveness was believed to encompass:

- Constructive feedback
- Prompts and praise
- Detection of errors and corrective measures employed
- High proportion of questions
- Numerous explanations and clarifying of a task and technique
- Vast proportions of a session engaged in instruction
- Management of the learning climate (Becker and Wrisberg, 2008).

Smoll and Smith (1989) proposed a model of leadership behaviours in sport, which has been applied to the study of sport coaches and their effectiveness. Figure 1.2 outlines the model, which assumes the following:

- The coach behaves in a certain way
- The performer perceives and recalls the coach behaviours
- Based on this perception and recall, the performer has an evaluative reaction to the coach behaviours (_see_ the solid arrow lines on the diagram)
- Situational factors along with the individual differences of the coach and performer determine the coach's actual behaviour (_see_ the broken arrow lines on the diagram) and the performer's perception, recall and evaluation of the behaviour
- The effectiveness of the coach is therefore determined and dependent upon the dynamic interactions of all variables presented.

This model of leadership behaviour has been tested using the Coach Behaviour Assessment System (CBAS: Smith, Smoll and Hunt, 1977), which involves the observation of coach behaviour in competition and training. The observations were made using categories noted under either 'Reactive Behaviours' or 'Spontaneous Behaviours' (_see_ box/panel on p. 16).

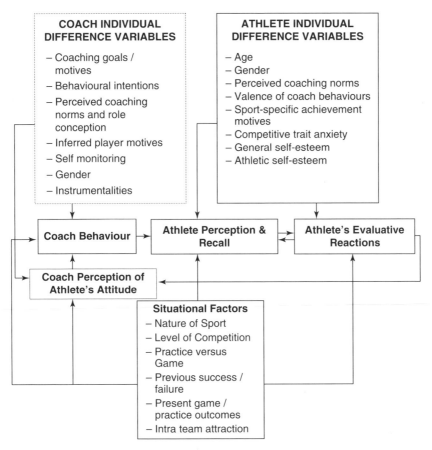

Figure 1.2 Model of leadership behaviours in sport. (Small & Smith, 1989)

While research studies using the CBAS have indicated that the use of instruction varies between coaches, it still appears as the highest scoring category. Lacy and Darst (1989) carried out some early research into coaching effectiveness and noted that skill-related instruction occurred three times more than any other behaviour. Claxton (1988) further confirmed this finding when reviewing the behaviours of tennis coaches. Age has been noted as a significant variable, and when a coach is delivering a session to young performers, Claxton (1988) noted a greater praise-to-scold ratio.

Gallimore and Tharp (2004) have since revisited some of the earlier research cited above, and while using the CBAS in the famous study of coach Wooden, other informal notes recorded during that study have since been made available. Other emerging behaviours of the coach identify the organization of practices and time on task to be important features of an effective session. Performers were often moving fluently between one practice to another, and transition time was kept to a minimum, ultimately maintaining the intensity of training within a session.

Categories of Coaching Behaviours

Class 1: Reactive Behaviours

Responses to Desirable Performances

Reactive Behaviours

- Reinforcement (a positive verbal or non-verbal reaction to good effort or performance)
- Non-reinforcement (no response to good effort or performance)

Responses to Mistakes

Mistake-contingent encouragement (encouragement given to the performer after a mistake)

- Mistake-contingent technical instruction (instruction or demonstration on how to correct a mistake)
- Punishment (a negative reaction, verbal or non-verbal, following a mistake)
- Punitive technical instruction (technical instruction that follows a mistake given in a hostile manner)
- Ignoring mistakes (no comments or action taken by the coach)

Responses to Misbehaviour

- Maintaining control (reactions to maintain order among the team or group)

Class 2: Spontaneous Behaviours

Game-related

- General technical instruction (spontaneous, and not given following a mistake)
- General encouragement (spontaneous, and not given following a mistake)
- Organization (assigning duties, organizing space and groups)

Game Irrelevant

- General communication (interactions not related to the game) (Weinberg and Gould, 2007, p. 214)

The research study also noted the coach consistently modifying practice to ensure that skill execution became more automatic and fluent. Wooden did not believe that drill-like practices were the end, but promoted the notion that drilled practices opened up the opportunity for a performer to apply individual creativity and apply their own initiative. Emerging out of the early studies on coach Wooden was a perception that planning and detailed reflection of individual coach, performer and team performances led to a successful coaching programme.

Becker and Wrisberg (2008) outline the importance of feedback, and revealed that a performer is undoubtedly influenced by the feedback given by the coach. Higher levels of satisfaction are correlated to a high frequency of positive coaching behaviours, which include training and instruction, praise, encouragement, social support and democratic behaviour (Allen and Howe, 1998). Also noted is the notion than a performer's perceptions of competence appear to correlate to the levels of praise and instruction received in response to a successful performance outcome. It is therefore assumed that the effective coach will ensure equity in levels of feedback to the individuals in a coaching session.

Becker and Wrisberg (2008) looked to extend the research findings linked to the CBAS observation tool, and carried out a research study that addressed the systematic coaching behaviours of Pat Summitt, a successful collegiate female coach (NCAA Division 1) in the United States of America. In this study another observation tool was utilized, namely the Arizona State University Observation Instrument (ASUOI: Lacy and Darst, 1984). This instrument contained thirteen behavioural categories representing three behaviours as outlined below:

- Instructional: pre-instruction, concurrent, post-instruction, questioning, manual manipulation, positive and negative modelling
- Non-instructional: hustle, praise, scold, management and other
- Dual codes: statements directed to an individual.

The findings of the study revealed that a significant amount of time was devoted once again to instruction, but the amount of questioning was also a significant finding when addressing the coach behaviours.

Coach Summitt's Behaviours (per cent) after 504 Minutes of Observation

Instructional Behaviours

Instruction	48.12 per cent
Questioning	4.61 per cent
Manual manipulation	0.06 per cent
Positive modelling	2.09 per cent
Negative modelling	0.58 per cent

Non-Instructional Behaviours

Hustle	10.65 per cent
Praise	14.50 per cent
Scold	6.86 per cent
Management	9.34 per cent
Other	3.19 per cent

The study also compared the frequency of the categories directed to either the group or an individual. In contrast to pre- and concurrent instruction, the post instruction was directed mainly to individuals, with hustles, praise and management emerging as being directed mainly to the group. Findings in this study were consistent with the previous investigations, with instruction once again emerging as the highest score (48 per cent). Concurrent instruction appeared as the highest sub-total in this category, and highlighted how much support was being verbalized as players were carrying out a skill.

The study highlights that the expert coach will provide pre-instruction to the group, and post-instruction to the individual to promote greater benefits and confidence in the feedback process. The study also outlines that effective feedback should be brief and concise for an individual. Summitt also identifies the need for high levels of praise to motivate and promote perceptions of competence within a performer. Intensity of training was another feature emerging, and the expert coach is deemed to be someone who is able to replicate the game intensity in a training session, and ensure that all performers 'practise like they compete'. It is the hustle behaviours that were used by Summitt to ensure that players remained on task and maintained the correct level of intensity.

The literature using the quantitative observation tools did convey some significant behaviours of a successful coach; however, limitations point to the need for future research to use qualitative data. Through gaining the perspectives of players, assistant coaches and the coach himself, the data obtained would have been enhanced.

The context a coach operates within is known to require different approaches and coach behaviours. Participation coaching will focus on the positive affective outcomes, including perceptions of competence and enjoyment, and may also be defined as being episodic, having loose membership and including transient participation. Smoll and Smith (2001) outlined the need to utilize the following behaviours when coaching a young performer:

- Use demonstrations frequently to support instruction and explanations
- Encourage and praise effort along with performance
- Provide feedback immediately after mistakes, and outline initially what was successful
- Remove any punishment strategies from the coaching session
- Provide positive reinforcement after any positive behaviour
- Ensure that expectations and codes of practice are clearly communicated.

In contrast, performance coaching has a higher level of commitment, fosters strong athlete-coach relationships, and will incorporate a significant planning regime for the mid- to long-term control of performance factors (Lyle, 2002). As a result of the complexity of the coaching process for a high performance coach, the literature offers some clarity in terms of coach effectiveness at this level. Gilbert and Trudel (2004) identified that several high-performance coaches were measured on effectiveness, simply in terms of competition outcome and by the number of their athletes selected on to national squads.

There remains a debate as to what control a coach has over the performance outcomes, and a review of the effectiveness of the high performance coach required a close examination of the coach–athlete relationship in action at this level. When assessing coach effectiveness it is vital to assess the impact of the interactions between the coach and the athlete, rather than reviewing the outcomes of performance.

Cote *et al.* (1999) developed *The Coaching Behaviour Scale for Sport (CBS-S)*, which attempted to provide evidence of the élite coach behaviours conveyed in a training session, in competition and in any organizational setting. The CBS-S contained seven dimensions of effective coaching behaviours linked to the élite (high performance) coach.

The Dimensions of Élite Coaching Behaviours

- Physical training and planning for competition
- The identification, development and monitoring of athletes' goals
- Mental preparation strategies, for example, focus under pressure, confidence building and performing under pressure
- Technical skills, including coach feedback, demonstration, and cues given
- Rapport with the athletes, for example, approachability
- Negative personal rapport, for example, yelling at a performer
- Competition strategies concerned with coach-athlete interaction during competition (Cote *et al.*, 1999)

COACHING EFFICACY

Coaching efficacy (Feltz *et al.*, 1999) is described as a multi-dimensional construct, which encompasses the dimensions of motivation, game strategy, technique and character building. The dimensions that were devised based upon the effective coaching behaviours noted in the coach education literature are defined in the box [below].

Dimensions of Coaching Efficacy

Motivation efficacy: The confidence that a coach possesses to influence the psychological state and skills of the athlete

Game strategy efficacy: The confidence of the coach to lead the team to success in competition

Technique efficacy: A coach's belief about their instruction and ability to detect and correct errors in performance

Character-building efficacy: A coach's belief in their ability to influence the personal development of an athlete

A coach displaying high levels of coaching efficacy is identified as being highly committed to coaching, and someone who will promote greater athlete satisfaction, performance outcomes and more sportsmanlike behaviours in their athletes. Performers coached by high efficacy coaches in basketball, softball and soccer reported higher satisfaction with their coach, and performance success was notably higher (Myers *et al.*, 2005).

Boardley *et al.* (2008) carried out a study with male Rugby Union players (mean age 26.5) to establish whether their own levels of effort, commitment, enjoyment, self-efficacy, pro-social and antisocial behaviour in rugby were associated with their perceptions of the coach's effectiveness through the efficacy dimensions. As expected, athlete perceptions of the coach through all efficacy dimensions have a positive correlation with experiences in rugby.

Within the coach–athlete relationship Lent and Lopez (2002) presented the theory of *relational efficacy*, of which there are two types: the first is other-efficacy, which relates to 'an individual's beliefs about his or her significant other's ability to perform significant behaviours' (Lent and Lopez, 2002, p. 264); and the second is relation-inferred self-efficacy (RISE), which is concerned with the notion of questioning how confident is the significant other in my ability? Jackson *et al.* (2009) investigated the coach–athlete relationship in six élite dyads in an attempt to highlight the factors that contribute to an effective partnership.

The findings indicated a relationship between efficacy perceptions and relationship formation, and where the relationship was effective both parties held strong beliefs about the other's capabilities. Interestingly, athletes in the study who exhibited high levels of other-efficacy and RISE were deemed more likely to persist with a coach partnership. Individuals who were confident in the coach's ability were also more effective in communication and would show higher levels of attention, initiate communication, communicate more frequently, and report a greater closeness to their coach. The coaches in the study also highlighted that they would set more challenging goals when they held a high level of confidence in their athletes.

SUPPORTING THE ATHLETE-CENTRED APPROACH

Adopting an athlete or person-centred approach involves coaching the individual, not the skill, always ensuring that the needs and interests of the individual are met. This approach seeks to empower the individual towards achieving personal goals, and educates them to take ownership of learning and solving problems for themselves. This athlete-centred approach places the sporting experience in context as being only one part of the athlete's life. This holistic approach is set in context from the outset of all coaching, with the other important human experiences being considered – for example education, career, family and health. The coach therefore assumes a holistic view of the individual, and this requires a facilitative inter-personal relationship between athlete and coach.

A successful coach will make the transition through three stages in terms of their behaviour in order to empower the individual and promote self-responsibility. In stage one the coach will coach skills, ensure safety and communicate procedural information, and as a result the environment is coach dependent. In stage two the coach begins to offer collaborative opportunities for the individual which build upon self-management and self-determination skills. At this stage there is a gradual transition from coach dependence to a shared decision-making context. In stage three there is greater athlete-dependence and personal autonomy in the learning process. This coaching approach accepts that experience is defined individually and that to succeed the coach must create a mastery (or task-oriented) climate for learning.

According to Arai (1997), empowered athletes move through four stages: of becoming self-aware, connecting and learning, taking action, and contributing to their own learning. The effective coach will adopt the following strategies to empower a performer:

- Ask meaningful questions
- Promote an understanding of why the athlete must be part of their own learning
- Provide support and be an information source for athletes to add personal choice to the tasks
- Support an athlete's ideas, and question and support self-expression
- Be a facilitator, and encourage the growth of the athlete in the final stage.

(Kidman, 2005)

Coaching is a complex system, and literature highlights the need for coach education to focus more closely on the 'interactive and social nature of coaching' (Bowes and Jones, 2006, p. 243). In summary, early research indicated a number of factors which related to coaching effectiveness, namely:

- A high frequency of feedback
- High levels of detection, correction and reinstruction
- High levels of questioning
- The ability to manage and maintain order in the training and competition environment.

Effective coaching is also related to the coach's ability to react to the needs of the individuals in a session. The ability to plan and reflect upon individual coaching sessions has frequently been cited as a tool that would contribute to coach effectiveness and therefore should be encouraged in all coach education programmes. Trends in coaching in the last decade appear to conflict with the earlier notion of drill and repetition, and critics do believe that this approach should 'take second place to assisting learners to construct meaning and understanding' (Gallimore and Tharp, 2004, p. 133). Certainly the empowerment approach to coaching has emerged as a priority in more recent years, but the need for coach instruction, modelling and performance-related feedback must not be underestimated, particularly in the early stages of learning.

2
Exploration of the 'How to Coach' Skills

by Anita Navin

CREATING A POSITIVE ENVIRONMENT

The 'how to coach' skills – often referred to as the 'coaching process' or 'craft-based skills' – provide a set of guiding principles for the delivery of an effective coaching session. To be successful a coach must know about the technical and tactical components that impact upon performance, and have the necessary communication and interpersonal skills. A coach might be the technical expert or the most conscientious and effective in the planning phase, but he will only succeed if he can apply the craft-based skills in the delivery of the coaching session. Effective organization of the working environment, together with good communication skills, contribute to individual satisfaction and performance improvement within the sports setting. It is the 'how to coach' skills that provide the strategies and an essential 'tool kit' for the coach. The 'how to coach' skills reviewed in this chapter provide guidance on creating a positive climate, the organization of resources, presentation of information, and coach relationships/interventions with the participants.

The 'How to Coach' Skills

- Safety
- Build rapport
- Fun
- Organization
- Explanation
- Demonstration
- Observation
- Analysis
- Feedback

Figure 2.1 The coach in action. (Courtesy of David Griffiths)

SAFETY

Initially, the coach must ensure that the working environment is free from hazards and risks. According to Rink (1993), safety takes precedence over all other concerns. Martens (2004) presents a step-by-step guide to represent the risk management process. First, the coach should assess the risks within the coaching environment by considering the participants, the intended activity, the equipment, coaching methods and the working environment. An evaluation and overall assessment of the risks should take place, and often a risk assessment proforma utilized by the coach would identify the impact of the risk in terms of a low, medium or high rating. The rating relates to the likelihood of the risk leading to an injury, and how frequently the coach believes this could occur. The coach is required to make a decision in relation to the intended action, and most often he will eliminate the risk from the coaching environment.

If the risk cannot be eliminated, the coach must accept the risk and implement an approach to safeguard all participants. A coach will decide either to avoid the activity due to the high risk factor with a particular group and associated environment, or to accept the risk and work to the safe practice principles outlined in this chapter. Reinforcing the safety issues with participants, and conveying the code of behaviour for them to work to, will support the coach in ensuring safe and effective practice.

Figure 2.2 The swimming coach operates in a high-risk environment.

Risk Assessment

Step 1: Identify the risks
Step 2: Evaluate the risks
Step 3: Select an approach to manage the risk
Step 4: Implement the approach

The Environment

The coach should check the working space; the following guidelines identify the specific aspects a coach should consider before, during and after the coaching session:

- Check for any debris on or around the working area
- Ensure there is access to a telephone in case of emergency
- Know the first aid procedure at the venue
- If outdoors, monitor the temperature
- The weather can affect the outdoor working area, so check the ground surface, particularly if there has been rain or frost, or if there are fallen leaves
- Secure all fixed equipment, and store equipment not in use
- Ensure that the lighting is adequate
- Check that emergency exits are not obstructed, and that fire procedures are known
- Ensure that participants know how to carry equipment safely
- Always check any equipment that has been assembled by others prior to using it

- Always clearly demonstrate the working area and boundaries to those taking part in the session
- Ensure that the equipment to be used is appropriate to the age and ability level of the group
- Store equipment intended for use in a safe place during the session
- Distribute all equipment in a safe and systematic way, making sure that large numbers of people do not all descend on an equipment store or one location to collect equipment at any one time
- Ensure that equipment is put away safely at the end of the session, and that participants follow the routines as communicated by the coach.

Participants

A coach should carry out a check with all individuals in terms of their readiness to participate. It is essential that the coach is briefed and informed of any injuries or illness a participant may have sustained, and that asthmatic participants have their inhalers with them at all times. Participants should remove all jewellery and tie long hair back, and they should be wearing appropriate clothing and footwear for the session. They must not be allowed to chew gum during the session, but all should be encouraged to have water bottles with them, and to drink to help rehydration. A coach must ensure that no young person leaves the session unsupervised.

All planned activities and progressions should be appropriate to the individuals in a session, and to promote a safe and productive working environment the coach should establish and reinforce rules and safe practice routines with the participants.

Safety Checks

- Assess risks associated with the participants, environment and equipment
- A coach should perform the same checks throughout a session
- Ensure participants remain 'on task' and in the correct area
- Ensure the learning activities and progressions are appropriate

---

BUILDING RAPPORT

Interpersonal skills are of paramount importance, given the complexities of human interaction that should feature within the coaching environment. As Lyle (2002, p. 151) indicates: 'The danger of focusing on performance and performance outcomes, and the potential for emphasizing organizational rewards and goals above individual interests, have highlighted the human and interpersonal aspects of coaching as areas of concern.' A coach should get to know the participants, should appreciate their needs and

SMILE AND MAKE EYE CONTACT WITH EACH PARTICIPANT

ADOPT A PERSON-CENTRED APPROACH

LEARN AND USE PARTICIPANT NAMES

SHOW INTEREST AND RESPECT THE NEEDS OF ALL PARTICIPANTS

Figure 2.3 Guidelines for building rapport. (Courtesy of David Griffiths)

individual differences, acknowledge their efforts, and be an active listener. According to Weinberg and Gould (2003), active listening enhances communication, and the coach should pay full attention to the speaker, make eye contact with the participants and use a nodding gesture to demonstrate understanding. A coach who actively listens may summarize what has been said with lead-in questions to the speaker: for example, 'What you are telling me is ...'.

A coach should make every effort to speak with all participants in a session, and show respect to everyone irrespective of their ability level. The power of non-verbal communication – a smile, for example – must not be underestimated, and a coach who smiles and engages with the participants is more likely to create a supportive climate for learning. A coach must also consider that up to 70 per cent of communication is often defined as non-verbal.

FUN

The *fun* factor must not be underestimated within a coaching session, and whilst a productive and safe environment must be maintained, fun practices and activities will motivate and engage participants. To make a session fun, the coach should apply the good practice principles outlined below:

Ensure participants are active quickly:

- Know your session plan
- Equipment should be organized and easily accessed
- Plan explanations, and use cue words to reduce talk time
- Participants should have all they need for the session (kit, drinks bottle and any personal equipment required).

Learning activities should be varied and challenging for all:

- Differentiate in planning for all performance levels
- Avoid repetition of the same warm-up, practice and groupings
- Make a conscious effort to offer a novel idea or different task in each session planned.

Promote activities so that all participants can be actively involved:

- Keep group sizes small to reduce any waiting time in long queues
- Plan for odd numbers in the practices
- Equipment should be organized for the numbers in the session
- Make adaptations if an individual is repeatedly over- or under-challenged on a task.

Feedback should be positive, and should reward effort along with performance outcomes:

- Praise individuals who commit fully to the task and always give of their best in a session
- If there is an error in terms of performance offer corrective feedback or questions to tease out what the individual should do.

Figure 2.4 A fun environment will promote learning and enhance participant motivation. (Courtesy of Northumbria University)

ORGANIZATION

A coach must be an effective organizer of all resources, and this is a vital consideration within the planning phase. The coach must plan how they will support the participants, and manage the working area and equipment. An effective coach will also have a contingency or back-up plan should there be fewer or more participants, a reduced working area, or indeed problems with equipment. When organizing individuals into groups and allocating working areas, the coach should strive for smooth transitions between practices and regroupings. Effective organization will address the following issues:

Planning:

- Know the number of participants, and note how you will run a practice with a greater or lesser number of participants
- Clearly note how the working area will be sectioned, and try and maintain a similar set-up, therefore maximizing the time spent in a learning activity
- Plan the process for allocating or collecting equipment in a session
- Complete any organizational steps prior to a group arriving for the session if possible.

Safety considerations:

- Complete a risk assessment for a coaching venue
- Check the working area before commencing delivery of a session
- Do not use faulty equipment
- Reduce the area of work if there are hazards close by.

Grouping participants:

- Organize groups randomly or by ability
- Be sensitive when grouping by ability, and set realistic challenges for each group accordingly
- Plan groups in advance, and progress logically (for example twos to fours, threes to sixes).

Group size:

- Consider the intensity and involvement of all participants
- Smaller groups maximize involvement
- If the activity is intensive a larger group offers more recovery/rest time, thus encouraging high quality practice
- Smaller groups contain fewer communication channels between participants, therefore discussion is easier.

EXPLANATION

Success as a coach is manifested in the art of communication, and a coach must understand how to send an effective message to participants.

A breakdown in communication is often the result of too much or too little information, or because of misinterpretation, or as a result of the coach not communicating sufficient information. The content of the message should be appropriate to the age level of the participants, and conveyed in user-friendly language. A coach should plan what is to be communicated, and should ensure that all participants are attentive and free from distraction. Explanations should be simple, brief and direct, and a coach should use appropriate questions at the end of an explanation to check that everyone has understood. Exemplar questions might be:

- What will you now focus upon in the practice?
- How many in each group?
- Where will players stand to start the practice?

A coach should avoid asking the question 'Do you understand?' as this will often prompt individuals to respond with a 'yes', even though they require more information. Participants often feel reluctant to expose their lack of understanding in the whole group context, and a coach should avoid such exposure by appropriately worded questions.

DEMONSTRATION

Demonstrations present a visual picture of the task organization/practice context and the technical/tactical information to be learned. A demonstration and a concise explanation will often be connected together, and can be used before participants practise a skill, intermittently throughout the skill development phase or as a conclusion to a particular practice or phase in the session.

The explanation when combined with a demonstration should be concise and incorporate learning cues, often referred to as a key word or phrase that summarizes and identifies the main features of a skill or task. The learning cues presented must be appropriate to the age and experience of the participants, and be concise and accurate in order to assist the individual in the learning process. A coach may decide to break down a skill into the three phases of preparation, execution and recovery in order to identify the key learning cues. Using action words or verbal labels can assist a performer and support the retention of key information.

Bandura (1977) outlined the importance of 'vicarious experiences' – also known as modelling or demonstration in conjunction with the theory of self-efficacy. Self-efficacy is associated with an individual's perceptions of their own ability to perform a task successfully, and can be referred to as a situation-specific form of self-confidence. The demonstration is deemed to be one of the most important sources of self-efficacy information for a novice or intermediate performer. Observing a fellow participant complete a demonstration of a difficult task can reduce anxiety in others.

In order to understand fully the importance of demonstration, a four-stage process has been outlined in literature (Bandura, 1974; McCullagh, Weiss and Ross, 1989); a summary is presented below:

Attention

- Ensure that all participants can see and hear, and are free from distraction (they are not facing the sun, not involved in other activities)
- Introduce the skill to focus the participants and gain interest
- As the coach, direct attention to the key elements of the skill
- Focus upon one or two key points or cues.

Retention

- The demonstration should be observed more than once and from different angles if required
- Question participants on the key points/cues given, to check that they have understood
- A coach should repeat the same cues with each demonstration to improve retention.

Reproduction

- A coach must plan appropriate progressions following a demonstration to support the performer
- Individuals may not be able to perform the skill being demonstrated because they have not developed the prerequisite skills
- A coach must continue to reinforce the key points, and allocate ample time to practise the skill immediately after the demonstration
- Slow motion demonstrations may be useful in the early stages of learning
- Observing a demonstration of someone performing as a non-expert may prompt observational learning and allow the observer to engage in the problem-solving processes the performer would be experiencing.

Motivation

- Individuals may lack the motivation to learn a new skill, but if the demonstrator has a high level of skill, social status and competence the participant is likely to be attentive
- A coach should praise participants and communicate the importance and relevance of the skill being demonstrated
- The demonstration should where possible use individuals from the peer group to present the skill.

When planning a demonstration the coach must carefully consider how the participants will be organized. Often a coach will ensure that all equipment and the working areas for each group have been set up before the demonstration. A coach may elect to use one of the following arrangements to deliver a demonstration, ensuring that all participants can see from the same angle:

- Semi-circle formation
- Group stand at the sideline of the pitch or court area
- Group position around a key area of the court, for example the key in basketball.

Consideration must be given to the viewpoint that participants should observe, and the positioning of the coach in relation to the group can impact upon the clarity of the demonstration to some participants. A coach who stands close to a group may reduce the visibility of the demonstration to some participants. When arranged in a semi-circle, the coach who stands close to the group will be viewed from the side by participants standing at the end of the semi-circle, compared to the front view for those standing in the middle.

When evaluating the success of a demonstration, the coach should use the following review questions to prompt accurate self-reflections:

- Were the organizational issues related to equipment, participant groupings and the working areas covered prior to the demonstration?
- Was the purpose of the demonstration communicated clearly?
- What were the coaching points communicated in the demonstration?
- Was the organization also communicated in the demonstration?
- Was the demonstration a good model of the movement? Why?
- How was the group arranged to view the demonstration?
- How did the coach conclude the demonstration?
- Was the transition time between demonstration and practice time minimal? Why?

OBSERVATION

Following a demonstration a coach must facilitate the learning process, and this is an essential skill required in order to eventually provide quality feedback. Effective observation relates closely to movement analysis, and a coach should plan how to observe (from different angles, thus see the action more than once), make a decision on what to observe, and identify the critical features and understand the factors that impact upon one's ability to observe – for example, skill level, the number of participants, the size of the working area, fear and personal knowledge (Barrett 1983).

Observing performance with a large number of participants can prove challenging, and a coach is encouraged to focus on one coaching point or learning cue as they move around the group. The learning cue or coaching point selected should be one covered in the demonstration and explanation of the skill. The coach must have a mental picture of the perfect model of the skill or task, and will use this to form the basis of any observations; they will be non-judgemental at this stage and will build up an overview of what is being observed. Once this information has been obtained the coach is able to diagnose the performance.

Effective Observation

- Break down the action to focus on one phase, body part, coaching point or learning cue presented
- Observe several times
- Observe from different angles
- Observe the outcome (Did the participant score a goal? Did the pass reach the intended recipient?)

ANALYSIS

Following the observation stage, a coach must now evaluate the extent to which the skill execution matched the perfect model of the skill or task. Here the coach will also identify aspects of the skill that were performed incorrectly, and will establish the root cause of the error. Factors affecting the error rate of a performer could be a result of primary factors connected to technique, psychological factors (for example, low levels of confidence or high levels of anxiety) or perceptual or decision-making errors, and a coach should strive to identify the root cause.

At this point the coach must make a decision either to take action to remedy the situation, or not to take any action. A coach may decide not to take any action to change the performance because of the time in the season – for example, in basketball, correcting a player's shooting action just before a competition would not be sensible, and it should be put right in the off season.

Following the diagnosis or analysis stage, the coach is suitably placed to begin the feedback and guidance process.

PROVIDING FEEDBACK

Feedback will provide the participant with knowledge, motivation and reinforcement, and will often promote adherence and full commitment to the learning process. Congruent feedback maintains a focus on the learning cues initially presented to a participant, and limiting feedback to these congruent cues ensures that the learner is not overloaded or presented with additional information not provided at the outset. Only when differentiating for an individual would the coach be expected to offer other cues. This type of feedback offers specific and qualitative information to guide the performer, and is more powerful in terms of learning than the general feedback often used, such as, for example, 'Good work'. While the general comments are sometimes used for motivating or ensuring that a group remains on task, the general comments do not provide a clear focus for the individuals when engaged with a learning activity.

Feedback should be positively phrased, and while there may be a need to identify what is being executed incorrectly, the coach should strive to ensure that a supportive comment is also provided. This is often where positive, negative and corrective components are integrated; for example, a coach may say: 'You are trying hard, John, but having problems at the release point of the pass; try extending the arm further forwards, and release the ball in front of the body.'

Giving Feedback

- Initially prompt the performer to engage in self-analysis
- Give congruent feedback in a simple and supportive manner
- Focus on only one or two key points
- Check for understanding at the end of the dialogue with the participant

---

The expertise required to be successful in the coach role is extensive, and a coach must not only possess the capacity to execute the 'how to' coach skills but also display effective inter-personal social skills. The range of expertise for the coach role is extensive, and a coach must not over-emphasize the need for technical and tactical knowledge in a sport at the expense of developing the skills overviewed in this chapter.

3

Athlete-Centred Coaching

by Kelvin Beeching

Being athlete-centred (or empowering one's athletes) is a common theme in modern-day coaching practices, and has been used successfully in the business world. It is a leadership style that encourages recipients to make decisions and take responsibilities for his/her contribution, as greater understanding is developed through solving problems. A relationship is formed between the athlete and coach (or in business, between the manager and employee) where the power, in terms of decision-making and goal-setting, is shared between them. This form of leadership is used more and more as coaches seek to gain the utmost from their performers. Coaches create a culture within their sessions that focuses on the development of the athlete and facilitates self-reliance. This chapter explores the concept of athlete-centred coaching by first defining it, and then discussing the notion and the benefits associated with such an approach. As in other texts, the terms 'athlete-centred coaching' and 'an empowering approach' will be used interchangeably throughout this chapter.

Athlete-centred coaching is an empowering approach to coaching, sometimes referred to as 'humanistic coaching'. It is an ideology that refers to the development and growth of the ability of performers to make decisions and think for themselves. Athlete-centred coaching develops awareness and enables athletes to take responsibility for their own knowledge, development and decision-making, which will help them achieve performance success. In a business context, Nutbeam (1998) and Davis and Broadhead (2007) propose that empowerment is a process by which employees take control over the decisions that affect their working lives. In a sporting context, these are the decisions that affect and define a performer's athletic career, both in training and in general lifestyle.

Athlete-centred coaching goes beyond the reaches of merely requiring an input: it is about increasing the ability and effectiveness of the individual. Gibson (1991) stated that empowerment, or indeed athlete-centred coaching, is where people take control over the factors that influence their lives. It requires the coach to provide the appropriate tools, resources and environment (Hawks, 1992). In this sense, coaches create an environment

Figure 3.1 The participants take responsibility on and off the court in 'High 5' (Junior) Netball. (Courtesy of Team Northumbria)

that facilitates the aims of athlete-centred coaching, where workers have an input, an opportunity to shape their future direction, and are given freedom in which to exercise. Thus within athlete-centred coaching the coach attempts to develop an environment where the athlete is involved in their learning, indeed an environment that allows for self-government of the athlete's learning (Hawks, 1992; Usher, 1997).

Athlete-centred coaching has been depicted as a process of recognizing and enhancing people's abilities to identify needs, solve their own problems, and organize the necessary resources in order to feel in control of their own lives (Gibson, 1991): that is, the performers learn the ability to solve problems for themselves. The coach empowers the athletes to make informed decisions and then take appropriate actions (Morgan, 2004), and so the power of choice lies with the athletes (Arai, 1997).

The converse of athlete-centred coaching is coach-centred coaching, which is a more traditional approach where the power is held by the coach: the coach has taken the choice and control away from the athletes, and as such, athletes have been socialized into a process where they are told what to do (Kidman, 2005). This coach-centred form of coaching follows the established autocratic and command styles of leadership.

THE CONCEPT OF ATHLETE-CENTRED COACHING

Developing the decision-making skills of athletes is crucial in implementing successful performance, as it is the athlete who will be competing and not the coach (Kidman, 2005). The athlete needs to be able to make the informed decision, as he/she is the one who will be in the competitive environment that will force the decision to be made.

Coaches must know the athletes before an athlete-centred approach can be implemented. Lather (1991) proposed that by increasing one's awareness and knowledge (which is a major benefit of athlete-centred coaching), a coach runs the risk of disempowering their athletes, as awareness can lead to a feeling of hopelessness and fear. Consequently, before deciding to implement athlete-centred coaching, a coach must decide whether their athletes are ready for such a process, and whether the potential gain will outweigh the risk. Hogg (1995) cites an evolving coaching practice, where a more directive relationship between athlete and coach develops into a more sharing relationship as the performer grows into his or her sport. Accordingly, Hogg promotes the use of athlete-centred coaching, but only when the athlete is ready for it. The need for a more directive relationship in the early years stems from a safety point of view, and is also due to the fact that the athlete is still learning valuable routines and habits that are important to their sport (Hogg, 1995; Lyle, 2002).

Athlete-centred coaching is a long-term process and therefore results cannot be expected overnight. Developing the thought processes of an individual does take time, and often these are skills that are neglected within the practice of learning. Nevertheless, athlete-centred coaching will provide benefits in the long run, and so both the coach and hierarchy need to be patient and supportive of the process if they want to reap the rewards (Stamatis, 2002; Gill, 2006). In addition, there is a lot expected of a coach in order to implement an empowering approach; besides which Capozzoli (1995) declares that not all managers are suited to athlete-centred coaching as they need to have excellent skills in facilitation and information-sharing. Some managers do not have these skills, and indeed do not wish to have them.

The Benefits of Adopting an Athlete-Centred Approach to Coaching

The practice of athlete-centred coaching improves decision-making among athletes (Rink *et al.*, 1996; Jones, 2001; Jones, 2006). Athletes are given the opportunity to make mistakes for themselves and to learn from their mistakes, which in turn improves their decision-making skills. Gill (2006) states that being able to make mistakes for oneself is essential in developing decision makers. Involving athletes in the decision-making process is fundamental in producing successful performance, as they are the people who have the most up-to-date experience of the subject. It is the athletes who are the ones working in the environment; hence they understand the problems that they face (Hoyle, 1986). By being empowered, individuals (and indeed athletes) feel that they are more involved with the running of the business or team, which results in the individual feeling more important to the organization (Bayham, 1988; Turney, 1993). Through greater involvement in their development, individuals' intrinsic motivation is increased (Krane *et al.*, 1996; Kidman, 2001; Hollembeak and Ambrose, 2005). Since athletes are more involved, they have a greater desire to learn and improve. Kidman (2001) expands on this when stating that athlete autonomy results in greater retention and understanding of skills, and thus greater performance outcomes.

It is documented that individuals who are exposed to an athlete-centred coaching environment take greater responsibility for their own performance and that of their team (Bayham, 1988; Turney, 1993; Morgan, 2004). The individual takes greater responsibility as they are involved in the decision-making process and thus are more accountable. Whitmore (2002) develops this concept when declaring that raising awareness and responsibility are two qualities that are essential for achieving and sustaining high levels of performance. Empowering people produces higher levels of productivity, which in turn leads to greater effectiveness, and so managers and coaches who employ such an approach are amongst the most effective leaders (Tannenbaum, 1968; McCleland, 1975; Kanter, 1979; Krazmien and Berger, 1997).

It is well documented that employing athlete-centred coaching strategies leads to increased self-efficacy and growth in satisfaction in the athletes (Gibson, 1991; Blinde *et al.*, 1993; Turney, 1993; Lindgren *et al.*, 2002). Self-efficacy is the belief one has in one's own ability of successfully performing a particular task (Bandura, 1986), and is effectively one's own judgement of one's personal skills. Accordingly, if an individual's belief in their ability increases, so will their self-confidence, and this increase in

Figure 3.2 The coach and athlete define the shooter training programme in netball. (Courtesy of Anita Navin)

self-confidence will be of assistance in both their sporting existence and in general life (Lindgren *et al.*, 2002).

Athlete-centred coaching techniques play a crucial role in group development and teamwork (Beckhard, 1969; Blinde *et al.*, 1994). As athletes become happier with their role in the team, the team environment will become more cohesive. Kidman (2001) and Jones (2006) enhance this statement by stating that the increase in teamwork and cohesion will result in greater on-field success, and thus empowering techniques are crucial in producing successful performance.

Common Barriers to Implementing an Athlete-Centred Approach

Within current coaching culture, coaches have a strong desire to take charge of every situation, besides which they have been encouraged to take control and lead from the front (Seaborn *et al.*, 1998; Cassidy *et al.*, 2004; Jones, 2006). As a result, in order to implement athlete-centred coaching successfully, coaches need to contradict and challenge everything they have been taught, and indeed been exposed to themselves as athletes. They need to be able to release their control, and to give the athletes the chance to make decisions for themselves. However, it is documented that managers and coaches fear the loss of power and so are reluctant to let go (Lowe, 1994; Capozzoli, 1995; Quinn and Spreitzer, 1997). This is due to the fact that it is the coaches and managers who are ultimately accountable for their team, and so one can understand their fear (Lyle, 2002).

Relinquishing power can create a danger for the coach and scepticism among peers. As they are seen to be going against the grain, the sharing of power may have a negative impact on reputation and subsequently future job prospects (Jones, 2006). Consequently, the coach has to be willing to accept this risk. Lowe (1994) explains that it is the desire to not take this risk that has stopped athlete-centred coaching being implemented on a far grander scale. By taking the risk, coaches may worry about their job security as a consequence of how they have handled the task of leadership, and also people's perception of that role (Gill, 2006). In addition, coaches fear making themselves redundant, because when the coach increases athlete autonomy, where is the need for the coach? (Gill, 2006).

By adopting an athlete-centred approach to coaching, athletes may perceive the coach to not be doing their job properly, as an abandonment of power, as they are adopting an approach that does not fit into their perception of the coach's role (Capozzoli, 1995; Jones, 2006). As a result, the athlete may lose confidence in the coach's ability because they perceive a lack of leadership. In order to implement athlete-centred coaching successfully, athletes need to be aware of, and to understand the process: they need to understand why it is being implemented and the benefits associated with it. Coaches should therefore take time to explain the process, showing understanding to the concerns of the athletes so they feel understood and accepted (Deci *et al.*, 1994; Deci and Ryan, 2002). Gill (2006) explains that by empowering people, one also gives them the right to say 'No' – the players have the right to reject the opportunity. The athletes may not wish to be empowered, as they may not wish to take on further responsibility. In addition, some performers may abuse the power by not using it in the way that it was intended (Capozzoli, 1995; Wallace, 2001; Jones, 2006).

If coaches are empowering athletes, then they need to support the decision an athlete makes: they cannot criticize their performers for making errors, but must support them for making a decision and using initiative (Morgan, 2004). Once the coach begins to criticize the athlete for the decisions he/she makes, the athlete attempts to make the decisions that they think the coach wants, and so are no longer making the decisions for themselves: they are therefore no longer empowered. In this situation, a coach needs to be able to remain true to their principles and help the athlete reflect on the situation and to develop their decision-making skills for the next time this situation arises. Coaches also need to be mindful that the poor execution of a decision is very different to a poor decision, and they need to differentiate between what requires development of the decision-making skills, and what requires technical correction.

It is not just the coach and athlete who provide barriers to applying an athlete-centred coaching approach. Argyris (1998) states that athlete-centred coaching is notoriously difficult to implement, and often feels resistance at every level from athlete to chairman. Quinn and Spreitzer (1997) and Mills and Ungson (2003) imply that bureaucratic factors can have an impact on the implementation of athlete-centred coaching. The team/organization needs to have an openness to new ideas, and to be willing to undertake them. There is a need for honesty, and a need to remove the 'blame' culture that is often rife. Everyone needs to be working towards the same goals and to have the same wants, as every member needs to be pulling in the same direction (Lowe, 1994; Quinn and Spreitzer, 1997; Gill, 2006). Time constraints also play a significant part in preventing athlete-centred coaching taking place (Quinn and Spreitzer, 1997): it is much quicker and easier to tell someone what to do than to let them guide themselves through the discovery. The coach needs to be able to facilitate this discovery, and so may resort to the command style of leadership for ease and to provide instant results.

QUESTIONING

Kidman (2001) proposes that in order to become empowering, coaches need to be able to apply an effective questioning technique to enhance athlete learning. By asking meaningful questions and analysing the responses given, coaches learn what action the athlete intends to make, as well as the reasons behind the action (Whitmore, 2002). Accordingly, questions help develop decision makers and develop those thinking processes associated with making decisions (Kidman, 2005). Asking questions and then asking meaningful, effective questions are two very different concepts. Meaningful, effective questions ask the athletes to develop their thinking at a far deeper level and thus help develop a deeper level of understanding. A deep learning approach encourages the comprehension of ideas and demonstrates an intrinsic motivation and interest in the studies. A deep approach results in better understanding and a higher calibre of learning. Conversely, a surface approach to learning is for the purpose of completing the task, but with as little understanding of the concept as possible. The focus is on being able to recall information and to reproduce it as required within the task.

Questions that encourage deep level thought have been termed 'high order' questions, and those that encourage surface level thought are 'low order' questions (Kidman, 2005). Low order questions are those that generally have just one answer, where the performer is either right or wrong. High order questions enhance the performer's ability to make decisions by developing their enquiry and thought processes, and are generally a starting point for discussion with the coach. The coach will listen to the response provided, and then probe and develop the discussion with further questioning. Low order questions usually begin with the words 'What' and 'Where', whereas high order questions begin with 'Why' or 'How'; this simple adaptation of terminology encourages far deeper thought and thus understanding by the performer.

Coaches must take a number of considerations into account in order to make the questions as effective as they can be. They should use open questions, as these produce more detailed answers and encourage thinking at a deeper level (Whitmore, 2002). The objective of the question must first be understood so that the coach can decide between high order and low order questioning, and then construct their questions accordingly. The questions should be specific for the athlete and the environment they are in. They should be planned beforehand, and coaches should be flexible as to when they ask the questions, as the questions should fit the situation (Kidman, 2001).

Effective questioning is a difficult skill to master, but it does aid the athlete-centred coaching process and the athlete's learning considerably. Consequently, questioning is a skill that is well worth the time invested in its development. Whitmore (2002) postulates that the detail involved in the question can help maintain the focus of the athlete. If it is too detailed or not detailed enough, their mind will begin to wander; hence the coach needs to know their athlete and pitch their questions accordingly.

SUMMARY

Empowerment is a powerful tool for coaches. It can help them get the most from their athletes through raising their awareness and knowledge, and by helping to improve decision-making. These are skills that are not just valuable in sport, but are transferable into general everyday life. It takes a skilled practitioner to be able to implement an athlete-centred approach to coaching. Not every practitioner has the skills or the time to implement such an approach, but for those that do invest, the rewards are evident.

4

The Coaching Climate for Learning

by Anita Navin

Creating a positive climate is a key consideration for any coach, and by providing a supportive environment the motivational level and overall attitude to learning of all participants will inevitably increase. A coach should ensure that he/she is purposeful and in control of their approach, have knowledge of what they want to coach, and also check participant learning regularly, taking positive action should progress not be occurring in the session. Being sensitive to the reactions of individuals and engaging the individual in the learning process will undoubtedly contribute to the creation of an effective climate for learning. A coach must influence the motivation of a participant, which is often interpreted as the direction and intensity of one's effort (Sage, 1977). The coach must therefore create a climate to encourage the individual to attend, and put maximum effort into developing skills and overall performance.

Motivation is a phenomenon that has been extensively researched in the area of sports psychology, and is defined as 'a theoretical concept that accounts for why people ... choose to engage in particular behaviours at particular times' (Beck, 2000, p. 3). Through identification and an understanding of the influences on human behaviour a coach can improve an individual's performance, participation and overall learning in the sporting context. The negative effects of poor practice in the learning environment which discourage an individual from physical activity could then be eliminated (Deci and Ryan, 1985).

THE MOTIVATIONAL CLIMATE

Three theories are proposed within the field of achievement motivation: achievement goal (Duda and Hall, 2001; Nicholls, 1984); Need Achievement (Atkinson, 1964; McClelland, 1961); and Attribution Theory (Heider, 1958; Weiner, 1985). All of the proposed theories inter-relate and predict how high and low achievers differ in terms of their goals, task choices, performance and attributions for success and failure. The impact of this

Figure 4.1 A swimmer will always measure success against a previous personal best time. (Courtesy of David Griffiths)

approach has been extensively reviewed, and its impact on the motivational climate well documented.

Achievement goal theory is a key consideration in providing a suitable climate for learning, and the focus here is on the individual and the goals they set or strive to achieve, along with their expectations about the actions required for achieving such goals (Nicholls, 1984). To understand a participant's behaviour it is vital to know what success and failure mean to the person. There are two contrasting achievement goal orientations, namely task- or mastery-, and ego- or performance-orientated goals (Duda, 1989). Task-involved goals include seeking a challenge, skill development, an acquisition of mastery, and a learning orientation. An individual here

Task- and Ego-Orientated Individuals

Task-orientated individuals like:

- Learning new skills
- Making progress
- Solving problems
- Understanding something in detail
- Working to the best of their ability

Ego-orientated individuals like:

- Performing better than others
- Performing as well as others with less effort
- Hiding their incompetence
- Not showing their inadequacies or errors to others

would place a high priority on effort and on learning from mistakes, and would seek mainly to learn and develop skills or knowledge, and would define success in terms of personal improvement. In contrast, an individual who adopts ego-orientated goals focuses on comparing performances with others, and defines success in terms of winning, and preferably with less effort, so as to enhance their social status (Carpenter and Morgan, 1999).

Therefore, it is important for a coach to understand achievement goal theory, and to recognize that the motivational climate set by the coach could aid interactions and learning with all participants. Research by Treasure (1994) highlights that a participant who perceived a climate set by their physical education teacher to be mastery orientated reported a positive attitude to learning and feelings of satisfaction. In contrast, participants who perceived the climate to be high in performance orientation reported a negative attitude towards the class and a sense of boredom. A coach must therefore consider the tasks that are delivered in a session, the coaching style adopted, recognition or reward processes, participant ability groupings, evaluation processes, and the time allocated to perform planned activities (Ames, 1992).

Epstein (1989) uses the acronym TARGET to outline six important structural features for coaches to consider for an effectual motivational climate. It is the perception of these structural features that constitutes the motivational climate. These features have the following characteristics:

T   **Tasks** should be designed that promote diversity, are novel and varied. They should involve personal goal setting and be challenging. Feedback should be given from multiple sources, and peer reviews of performance should be part of the tasks. Standards for measuring progress should be self-referenced.

A   **Autonomy** should be promoted through individuals taking control in the learning environment. Choices should be given within the sessions, and leadership roles should play a part in some tasks. The individual should take some ownership in performance profiling and the overall monitoring of performance.

R   **Rewards** and **recognition** should avoid comparative performance outcomes such as winning or rankings. Praise and reward should be based upon individual performance improvements and effort.

G   **Grouping** should be varied, and sessions should contain multiple grouping arrangements. The coach must foster an environment where individual differences are tolerated.

E   **Evaluation** should be based upon self-referenced criteria and mastery. It should be private and meaningful, with the individual contributing fully to the evaluation process.

T   The **timing** of events in a session should be considered in relation to the ability, volume and intensity in which an individual can perform in practice, attentional capabilities and rates of learning.

Research by Ntoumanis and Biddle (1999) has indicated that a mastery- or task-orientated climate set by the coach will inevitably ensure participants display a more positive attitude to learning and make more effort, and more effective approaches and strategies for learning are notable differences when compared to the performance- or ego-orientated climate. Newton and Duda (1999) outline key factors for mastery- or task-orientated climates, stating that a coach should value and recognize personal improvement, working hard and helping peers to learn, and should value the contribution of all members in the session. In the ego-involving climate a coach will punish poor performance and errors, give more attention and recognition to the higher level performers, and encourage competition between all members of the group.

Research by Smith (2005) identifies the relationship between a participant's perception of the task-orientated climate and their positive motivational responses in the learning/performance environment. Participants who have perceived the climate as task- or mastery-orientated report greater enjoyment and effort, more team satisfaction and more positive relationships with their coach and support staff. In summary, this individual is less likely to miss a session, and would not experience worry or tension in relation to expectations and performances. If a participant perceives an ego- or performance-orientated climate they are more likely to experience negative reactions from coaches, higher levels of worry and boredom, and a reduced level of enjoyment and satisfaction within the session.

Roberts (1992, p. 166) outlines some key considerations and suitable responses for a coach to consider in relation to the climate set for learning:

- *How is success defined?* By individual progress/improvement
- *What is valued?* Effort
- *How is the participant evaluated?* Through effort and progress
- *How are mistakes viewed?* As an inherent part of learning
- *Why is the participant engaging in the activity?* To develop new skills
- *Why does a participant feel satisfied?* Because he achieves successful effort, challenge and personal bests
- *What should the participant focus upon?* Learning and the development of skills
- *What are you, the coach, focusing on?* Development and learning.

Need achievement theory stipulates that a participant will have two motives for achievement: the need to achieve success, and the need to avoid failure. Gill (2000) defines the first as 'the capacity to experience pride in accomplishments', and the second as 'the capacity to experience shame in failure' (p. 104). The high achiever is therefore not concerned with thoughts of failure, and is highly motivated to achieve success. A low achiever, by contrast, desires to avoid failure and will display anxieties and negative thoughts concerning failure.

A coach must therefore take the time to understand the motives of an individual here, and create appropriate learning activities. The coach must provide a supportive climate and recognize the needs of all individuals.

Adapting practices to suit an individual's performance level and needs will lead to greater levels of motivation.

Attribution theory is concerned with how a performer explains their success and failures, and three attribution categories summarize the many explanations. The categories proposed in this theory are stability (a relatively permanent or unstable factor), locus of causality (internal or external to the participant), and locus of control (either in or out of the participant's control). A coach must ensure that all performers attribute success and failure in a session or in a competition to stable, internal causes and factors within one's control. For example, a tennis player who has just won a competition would be encouraged by the coach to attribute success to their own ability (a stable factor), the effort put into the performance (an internal cause) and their game plan (in one's control).

In contrast, a coach would decrease motivation if the win were attributed to an unstable factor (for example, luck), an external factor (an inexperienced performer) or to a factor out of a performer's control (poor technical skills displayed by the opponent). Adopting good practice principles from this theory will ensure that a coach encourages greater expectations of success and increased levels of motivation in the performer, and overall promotes an increase in the level of pride or shame in the performer. Scanlan (1988) outlines three stages in the development of achievement motivation:

1. Autonomous competence
2. Social comparison
3. Integration.

Stage 1 is where an individual thought to be around the age of four will focus on mastering skills within the environment; the emphasis is on self-testing for evaluative purposes, therefore in this stage there is no reference to others for comparison. In stage 2, which would commence at around the age of five, the individual will focus on comparing performances to those of others, and is keen to outperform their peers. In the final stage there is a combined approach, where social comparison and self-referenced standards are used for evaluation. However, in this stage the individual is able to recognize when it is appropriate to self-reference and compare to others. This latter stage is the most effective, but not all individuals reach it. A coach must therefore strive to promote learning in relation to this integrated stage and highlight clearly in their sessions when it is appropriate to compete and compare with others, and when it is appropriate to apply self-referenced standards for comparison and evaluation.

Weinberg and Gould (2007, p. 70) outline some key considerations for a coach to consider in their practice:

- The participants' stage of achievement motivation
- The participants' goal orientation
- The attributions the participant applies to their performances
- Situations the participant will approach or avoid.

A coach should therefore encourage the mastery- or task-orientated climate for coaching, and ensure that they know exactly when competitive goals are appropriate. The coach can increase motivation by correcting inaccurate attributions that foster a decline in motivational behaviours, and ultimately should endeavour to promote positive feelings and perceptions of competence.

LEARNING PREFERENCES

The climate set by the coach for any session should account for a range of learning preferences exhibited by the participants. There is evidence to suggest that individuals can be characterized by a dominant preference, and that they are either a visual, auditory or kinesthetic learner. Although an individual will use all of the senses to receive information, it is vital that a coach is aware that one of the preferences will often dominate. This dominant style conveyed by an individual will be the best method for receiving new information. However, it must be noted that the preference could be dependent upon the nature of the task, and the individual may have varying preferences depending on the context of the session.

Visual Learners

There are two types of visual learner: the visual-linguistic learner, and the visual-spatial learner. The visual-linguistic learner will prefer reading and writing tasks, and a great deal of information in written form will be retained in memory, even if it is only read once. The visual learner would prefer to have notes on the subject matter and also write information down in a session. The visual-spatial learner prefers a chart, demonstration, video and other picture material.

Auditory Learners

This preference indicates that an individual would prefer to talk through a situation and would not enjoy reading and writing tasks.

Kinesthetic Learner

This individual would prefer to learn new skills by movement, and they will lose concentration if movement is not interlinked to a learning situation.

A coach is most likely to plan and deliver a session using their own preference; for example, if he were coaching the lay-up shot in basketball, the coach with a visual preference would use demonstration, photographs and/or video clips of the perfect model. In comparison the coach displaying an auditory preference may only explain the skill and use key words and sounds to replicate the perfect model. The coach with a kinesthetic preference will simply ensure that individuals get active quickly and experience the action by lots of practice.

A coach must utilize a range of activities that place emphasis on the different learning preferences in order to set a suitable climate for all involved.

Should an individual not grasp the skill through a selected method, the coach should apply his/her knowledge of learning preferences and try an alternative sense, for instance, demonstration rather than only explanation.

LEARNING STYLES

Honey and Mumford (2006) identify four learning styles which will allow a coach to reflect thoroughly on the methods used within the learning context.

The Four Learning Styles

- Activists
- Reflectors
- Theorists
- Pragmatists

The activist would involve themselves fully in new experiences and they are extremely open-minded, not skeptical which is often reflected in their enthusiasm for new tasks or skills being introduced by the coach. This individual will thrive on the challenges placed on them in a new task and will want to be active immediately in the task. This individual is gregarious, and would constantly get involved with others and is always seeking to centre the activity on themselves. A coach who is an activist would often structure the learning climate with group discussions and tasks, games, and involve peer group coaching. The activist coach would expect the participants to think out loud, respond eagerly to questions and be willing to try new skills and tasks. The coach must be aware of the activist, and ensure a climate which supports the following:

- Learning of new skills and tasks
- Offers a variety of activities
- Mistakes are seen as an inherent part of learning
- The climate supports a 'have a go' value.

A coach who displays this style may encounter the following problems when coaching:

- Move the group too quickly into a task
- May struggle to manage time effectively
- May focus on too many aspects in a learning activity
- May miss the detail out of a demonstration.

The reflector would prefer to stand back and observe a situation or new task carefully from many different perspectives. In a learning situation they would prefer to think the situation through before arriving at any decisions. A careful analysis of all possible information and scenarios would be required before any decisions are made in a task or situation. The reflector is cautious and thoughtful, and would enjoy observing others in action. In group discussions the reflector would listen to others before arriving at their own views, and would often take a back seat in any group task. The coach who is a reflector would allow time for individuals to think through a particular task (through observation or reading notes), hence allowing more time prior to getting involved in the actual practical performance. A coach should ensure the following issues are addressed in the learning climate:

- An appropriate time period is allowed for preparation before practice
- Time is allowed to gather relevant information related to a task
- Opportunities are given to listen to other individuals and their viewpoints.

This coach may face the following problems when structuring and delivering a session:

- May keep groups waiting too long prior to starting an activity
- May not organize their session logically
- Can be distracted from the focus of a learning activity if other issues appear
- May not be assertive when working with individuals or in terms of disciplinary issues.

The theorist would want to integrate observations into theoretical information ensuring they think a problem through in the most logical format. This individual is a perfectionist and will not rest until the task has been accomplished. Questions frequently asked by this type of learner could be: 'How does this skill fit with that tactical play?' Or 'What are the game principles behind this attacking move?' Overall the theorists' approach is extremely logical and they would feel very uncomfortable with subjective judgments and lateral thinking. The coach who is predominantly a theorist will structure a session to allow for discussion and answers to be identified prior to engaging in the learning activity. Tasks involving analysis, a clear correct answer and solo exercises will be planned and delivered. The coach should also consider the following when structuring the climate to meet the needs of this learner:

- Time is set aside for questioning
- Communicate the content of the session and the intended pathway
- Ensure there is a sound basis for learning a new skill or completing a learning activity
- Grouping based on similar abilities is preferred.

The theorist would be guilty of the following when structuring and creating the learning climate:

- Reluctant to try a new strategy for learning a skill
- Tendency to structure more individual tasks
- Does not open up discussion on the problems encountered in the learning activity
- Structures activities that do not always contain the appropriate level of challenge, and remains over-cautious.

Figure 4.2 The pragmatist will value the time to practise, experiment and arrive at a solution. (Courtesy of David Griffiths)

Pragmatists would be keen to try out new ideas and skills in practice, and they would always seek out new ideas or strategies to solve specific problems. The pragmatist is keen to get on with the task, and would act quickly and confidently on ideas that are attractive to them. Often this individual would be impatient with open-ended discussion as they are essentially practical individuals. A philosophy adopted by the pragmatist would centre on there always being a better solution, and if something works well in training it must be a good strategy to apply in the game. The coach who is a pragmatist will structure the session to allow for discussions about the tasks, and will often set group tasks. There will be many problem solving-type tasks covered in the session, but the coach will ensure that the relevance of the skill or strategy is initially communicated and understood. The pragmatist would also value the following in the learning climate:

- Time to practise and experiment with new tasks and skills
- Learning cues and tips are frequently communicated
- The chance to arrive at solutions related to learning activities and challenges posed.

The disadvantages for the coach would centre around:

- Being impatient when individuals share their thoughts and views in a session
- Believing there is only one method to achieve in a particular task
- Tending to lack imagination and use the same practices repeatedly
- Not always working well with other support coaches in a team coaching approach
- Cutting corners when structuring and delivering progressive practices.

In summary it is vital that any coach structures the learning climate to accommodate the individual needs and preferences of all individuals.

CONCLUSION

The fundamental role of a coach is to promote and maximize learning. Through careful consideration of the concepts discussed in this chapter the coach has a sound base for ensuring the climate meets the needs of all individuals in a session. Positive self-reflection after each coaching session will ensure that a coach can continue to increase the likelihood of learning taking place. A coach should therefore establish a professional working relationship with all participants, and create a suitable climate for learning that will in turn support and promote effective learning.

5
Planning the Coaching Session

by Anita Navin

A successful coaching session is planned and relates closely to the overall annual plan, and it goes without saying that those coaches who fail to plan will undoubtedly plan to fail. The coach must always adopt a player-centred approach, and in doing this ensures that the needs of the participants are put first rather than the activity, parents, coach goals and ambitions. Each individual (whatever their age, ability or disability) in a session must be viewed as an individual with unique needs, interests and goals. A coach who knows how a session should be structured will be able to deliver a session that contains appropriate progression, and ultimately achieves its purpose.

The Content of a Session

- Introduction and warm-up
- Skill development section
- A competitive element (full game or modified game)
- Cool-down and conclusion

The session plan outline assists the coach in structuring and designing a session, and it is recommended that all coaches complete one of these for each session delivered.

SESSION GOALS

It is essential that the coach states clearly what the participants should be able to do by the end of a session, and that the intentions are stated as session goals on the plan. There should not be too many goals to achieve, and the goals must be measurable – for example, to be able to execute a shoulder pass at the appropriate time.

Coaching Session Plan

Date		Venue		Duration		Number		Equipment	
Session Goals						Personal Coaching Goals			

Content	Time	Task and Group Management	Coaching Points
Introduction/ warm up			
Skill development / practices			

Content	Time	Task and Group Management	Coaching Points
Game / modified game / conditioned activity FOCUS:			
Cool down / wrap up			
Other comments			

Figure 5.1   A coaching session plan proforma.

A coach should use the SMART acronym to ensure that the goals set are accurate:

- **S**pecific: for example, use a change of direction to get free at the appropriate time
- **M**easurable: for example, always look to pass forwards for the first option
- **A**djustable: the goal may not be achievable, but monitoring of progress will allow the coach to make necessary adjustments
- **R**ealistic: a goal should be challenging but within reach for a performer
- **T**ime-based: goals should be set for the session (short term), and they should link closely to the intermediate and long-term goals for the participants.

A coach should also set personal goals for the session which relate to his/ her own coaching skills and performance. These personal goals allow a coach to continue in their own professional development by continually reviewing their performances.

Equipment

A coach should know what equipment is available in order to plan for the session, and this should be appropriate for the group. For example, Under 11 participants will use size 4 as opposed to size 5 balls in football and netball.

Duration

It is vital that the coach is aware of the duration of the session in the planning stages. The length of a session should take account of the playing level and stage of development of the individuals: for example, a ninety-minute session should be the maximum time for a potential player, whereas an open age group player will often train for a two-hour period. In the planning stage a coach should ensure that time will be maximized by planning smooth transitions from one activity to another. Once the content of the session has been decided, the coach should allocate a period of time to each phase of the session, acknowledging the transition time between activities.

Number of Participants

A coach should know how many participants will be at the session, and should also give consideration to the different ability levels, development and training ages. Any individual medical or health issues should also be considered in the light of the content.

SESSION CONTENT

Figure 5.2 Session content should reflect the different ability levels. (Courtesy of Northumbria University)

Warm-Up

The warm-up should prepare participants mentally and physically for the subsequent activities by incorporating dynamic mobility activities and ball work if the activity is basketball, football, etc.

Top Tips for the Warm-Up

- Start slowly and gradually increase the intensity
- Activities should be relevant to the focus of the skill section
- Include dynamic mobility, not static stretching
- Vary the activities and make them fun

Dynamic Movement Skills for a Warm-Up

The following dynamic movement activities are examples of what should feature in the early stages of the warm-up; once these are completed, the sport-specific work can begin:

- Sidestepping, leading with right and left leg
- Skipping with a low knee lift
- Skipping with a high knee lift, adding arm swings
- Stretch calf muscle in the lunge position and simultaneously swing one arm in a spiral pattern, repeating on the other leg
- Carioca stepping, followed by wide leg squats (lead left then right leg)
- Lunging forward in a variety of directions, simultaneously reaching the arms to various directions
- Ankle rolls for 10m (30ft), heel flicks for 10m (30ft), ankle rolls followed by a two-footed jump
- Falling start, then sprint forwards with three quick steps and repeat
- Hamstring stretch in standing position whilst turning trunk to either side; repeat with the other leg
- Sprint forwards for five strides, stop, return backwards with diagonal stepovers to the right. Repeat, but then diagonally back to the left. Repeat to complete three in each direction.

There are several factors that could impact upon the content of a session, such as the stage in the season, previous performances in competition, and training, lifestyle issues and player motivation. A coach should select the practices, progressions and game activities required to achieve the session goals. Progressions should be carefully planned to ensure an appropriate increase in complexity. All progressions should begin in a closed practice situation – no defenders, limited movement and a small number of participants – and gradually increase in terms of complexity, pressure situations and level of decision-making expected from the participants in the practice.

Figure 5.3 The practices in a session should simulate the game. (Courtesy of Northumbrian University)

Progressions for Passing Practices

- Static participants
- Participants on the move
- Increase the number of participants for passing options
- Add direction to the practice (moving to goal)
- Reduce the space available
- Add defenders (passive – active)
- Set play situations (goal kick in football, side line throw in, and so on)
- Small side game

It is also important to be able to adapt any practice planned should the number of participants change – for instance, if you have planned for an even number and one player does not attend the session. Some participants may find a practise easier or more difficult than others, and so alternative tasks or targets will need to be planned should this happen.

For each practice the coach should ensure that one or two coaching points are stated on the session plan to ensure that the participants have clear points to focus on in order to improve their performance.

Adapting an Activity

Activities will need to be adapted to suit all individuals within a session, as there may be individual differences related to ability, experience, developmental level, physiological aspects and attention span. The following are tips for adapting an activity:

- Modify equipment – for example, use a smaller ball
- Adapt the rules – for example, in rugby no tackling to ensure certain skills are practised
- Modify the practice by making the area smaller if the practice focus is on getting free from an opponent, or increase the area if the practice has a defending focus. Increasing the number of participants in a practice means the ball carrier has more decisions to make
- Individuals with special needs must not be neglected. Participants with visual impairments will require a coach to use their name more frequently; using a ball with a bell inside is a useful aid. Individuals with speech or hearing impairments will need more time to convey their thoughts, and the coach should use visual cues where possible: for example, the official may have a flag to raise if the whistle cannot be heard when an infringement has occurred.

Volume and Intensity

A coach must ensure that there are a sufficient number of hydration breaks within the session, and also that participants have appropriate work-to-rest ratios. If a practice involves sprinting (for example, sprinting to receive a pass over 10m (30ft)) a player must ensure that the appropriate work rate is maintained otherwise the practice effect cannot be achieved. When working on a practice involving short sprints, an individual on average will be able to complete between six and eight repetitions before performance levels deteriorate. This period of work should be followed by a rest period giving time for the body to recover (work to rest = 1:2 or 1:3, depending on fitness levels).

TASK AND GROUP MANAGEMENT

When planning the session a coach must ensure that all space is used effectively and groups have clear boundaries within which they will practise. The session plan should identify the areas within which the groups will work, and often a coach will use court markings in a sports hall or cones to communicate the working areas to the group.

Grouping is also a key consideration when planning, and a coach can group according to ability, friendship or developmental level, or randomly. Ensuring that individuals are challenged in the group activities is a paramount concern and so ability groupings may be more beneficial. A coach should vary the groupings within and between sessions to ensure that individuals are able to work with a range of other individuals as the season progresses.

The session plan should contain brief information, and if required a diagram to show how many individuals there are in a group, and the allocated working space. Any coach should plan for fewer or more participants by planning practices which can be adapted for different numbers.

The timings for each task should be noted in the appropriate column as a guide to the coach, and these should be evaluated on completion of a session.

Coaching Points

The coaching point column of a session plan will contain one or two key points for the learning activity. The coaching points listed here will be the key points the coach identifies when presenting the activity or skill, and they will form the basis of all observations carried out by the coach. The information listed here will guide the analysis carried out in the session by the coach and serve to remind the coach of the components of effective performance. A coach may also list the types of question they may ask at various stages of the session, and also note the intended response.

THE COOL-DOWN

This component of the session comes at the end and allows time for participants to carry out exercises to assist the body in returning to its normal resting level in terms of heart rate, blood pressure, adrenalin levels and temperature. The cool-down will rid the body of waste material (lactic acid) as the legs will have a build-up of this waste following a training session or game. Participants should gradually reduce the intensity of the exercise in this phase, and move from an upright position to a position of rest on the floor, with the legs elevated to remove waste products. The cool-down should encompass five to ten minutes of aerobic exercise, stretching exercises that work on improving flexibility, and a player must refuel and rehydrate in this phase.

COACHING STYLE

In the final stage of preparing the session plan a coach must identify the most appropriate coaching style for each activity. Often a coach will need to introduce new skills or tactics, and to adopt a 'tell and show' approach; however, if a task includes decision-making, the coach may wish to use a questioning style to encourage self analysis and reflection. A coach may also wish to set up a practice and stand back to observe, allowing participants to take greater responsibility for learning and the correction of errors.

Top Tips for Planning

- Ensure progression from session to session
- All practices are appropriate for the level of participant
- Safety aspects have been considered
- Allow sufficient time on task for participants to practice
- Reduce transition time between activities
- Vary the practices and activities
- Session content relates to the session goal(s)

SESSION EVALUATION

The success of future coaching sessions depends on the effectiveness of the evaluation of the previous sessions. The evaluation stage should be focused and should initially be written, based and reflecting upon the personal and session goals set in the planning phase. The self evaluation can consider all areas of coaching performance, namely: the content, climate, organizational features and overall coach presentation, or it can focus specifically on key aspects of delivery. The categorized questions below can be used as a guide when completing an 'all embracing' evaluation:

Content

How well did the participants achieve the learning objectives?
Did the session build on previous learning and experience?
Did the coach allow sufficient time for the tasks?
Were the progressions effective and logical?

Climate

How well did the coach promote a TARGET climate?

Organization

Were groupings effective and easy to manage?
Did any tasks take longer to organize than anticipated?
Did the participants behave?
Were there any instances of misbehaviour, and were your strategies effective?

Presentation

Were tasks explained clearly, or was there confusion at any time?
Did the coach use a variety of coaching styles, and if so, when?
Were demonstrations used, and if so, when?
Was rapport developed, and if so, how?
Was feedback provided to the group, and what impact did the information have on the participants?

The ability of a coach to self-reflect and to address issues that were effective and least effective in a session contributes to the success of any individual in the coaching role. It is vital that a coach does not continue to do what they always have done, and consequently always achieve the same results. The coach should engage in two types of critical reflection: reflection in action, and reflection on action.

Reflection in action occurs during the coaching and is best described as 'thinking on your feet'. A coach will change his or her approach following the judgement that a task is not working, or could be organized and coached better. Then at the end of all coaching sessions the coach must reflect on action, which involves looking back at the session and is a retrospective contemplation. The coach must self reflect and analyse critically the impact of their coaching behaviour. Through a structured comparison of the desired and actual behaviours utilized, the coach should identify aspects of delivery that require change.

A Framework for Guiding Reflection

Borton (1970) offers a framework for guiding reflection, and this follows a process of responding to the questions 'What?', 'So what?' and 'Now what?'

'What?': The focus is on the description of aspects in the session and a self-awareness level, for example: What happened? What did I do? What did the participants do? What was I aiming to achieve? What worked well?

'So what?': This stage represents a deeper evaluation and analysis of the coaching experience, for example: So what do I need to do about this? So what have I learned from this approach/content? So what more do I need to do or know about this aspect of delivery? What are the implications of this for me as a coach?

'Now what?': This stage is the detailed synthesis, and represents a way forwards for improvement and change. The questions posed here to oneself consider alternative courses of action, and highlight what a coach will do next, for example: Now what do I need to do next time? Now what might be the consequences of this action and different approach? What will I do differently as a result?

In the reflection stage the coach may seek support from a mentor, or access sources of information to guide and inform this change process. The coach will then ensure that an action plan is in place to make necessary changes for subsequent sessions. The cyclical nature of this reflection process continues with the monitoring of progress and reanalysis.

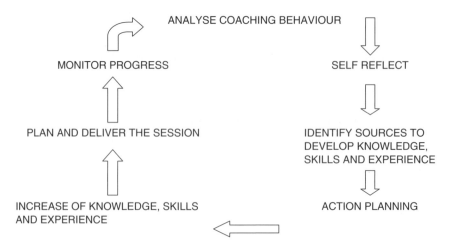

Figure 5.4   The reflective coaching cycle.

The coach is involved in a cyclical coaching process whereby they will plan, deliver and review a coaching session. All stages are important and should be valued equally by all coaches to ensure success. The coach should therefore always *reflect*, ensuring that there is a clear description of what happened and notes are made on personal feelings following the coaching session. The next stage is to *connect* by relating to previous actions and experiences in coaching, and make comparisons and note the new insights. Ultimately, the coach must *apply* this new insight and learning, noting what will be done differently in subsequent sessions, looking forward and setting an action plan for a change in coaching practice.

6

Coaching the Individual Child Athlete in Performance Sport

by Karl Wharton

The child in performance sport is likely to have superior athletic talent, is subjected to long, arduous training programmes and early, intense competition schedules involving great sacrifice, effort and in many instances social isolation; he/she receives expert coaching, and in many cases is exposed to training camps and international travel away from family and friends. Children in performance sport are a unique athlete population with different emotional, physical and social needs, which vary depending on the athlete's particular stage of development and maturation. They demand specific and appropriate training programmes, expert coaching and support from a variety of services, and appropriate competition schedules that ensure a safe and healthy athletic career, thus promoting a healthy lifestyle and future well-being.

WHAT IS NEW IN THE WORLD OF PERFORMANCE SPORT?

Development in high performance sport has led to a situation that is characterized by the following factors:

- Early talent identification and specialization is now more prevalent and structured in many sports, where children from an early age are faced with demanding training programmes involving long hours of intensive, repetitive training and in some cases strict dietary regimes
- The age of athletes has decreased dramatically in many sports
- In some sports, instead of adults we now have children at élite level
- Skill levels and mechanical loads have increased considerably
- Flexibility and strength levels have increased dramatically in many sports
- Training time has increased substantially

- Major competition commitments have increased, and sometimes over-competition
- Children are now doing more and more repetitions of skills
- Pressure has increased, as too have expectations from coaches, parents, schools, governing bodies of sport and from themselves to succeed.

Associated with major athletic achievement, many coaches may encounter problems of 'burn-out', over-use injury, substance abuse, sometimes financial inequality between performers, and a loss of enjoyment in sport amongst their young athletes. In some medical, scientific and educational communities, the child in performance sport is often used as an example to illustrate excessive and undesirable coaching practice. Consequently, it is a duty of all coaches who are working in a performance environment to be aware of the potential negative health implications (physical, physiological and psychological), and the impact on the young athlete's socio-cultural life of performance sport and the potential strategies and support structures that can be put in place to minimize such risks.

This chapter aims to develop knowledge of key issues that coaches face when dealing with young athletes, and how they may address these when coaching in a performance environment.

MATURATION AND GROWTH ISSUES

It is important that we make a distinction between the adult performance athlete and the child in performance sport. At this level, many factors come into play, most of which centre on the fact that a young athlete is not a miniature adult athlete, but an individual with specific needs that are unique to children in performance sport.

Many sports still use age-based standards for performance levels and squad selection – for example, U11, U13, U15; however, these do not account for the considerable individual variability in maturity status of young athletes at a given chronological age, nor are they concerned with the social, psychological, physical, emotional or intellectual consequences for children of intense participation. Therefore, coaches should not use an individual's chronological age either as the sole measure of maturation or to plan an athlete's training programme, as it may put excessive demands on late-maturing individuals or leave early-maturing athletes uninterested and unchallenged. For these reasons, coaches need to be aware of the distinction between the following three ages:

- **'Chronological' age:** the number of years and days elapsed since birth
- **'Skeletal/biological' or 'developmental' age:** a measure of the maturity of the skeleton determined by the degree of ossification of bone structure
- **Training age:** the number of years an athlete has been specializing and training in a particular sport. This will affect an individual's level of fitness and work capacity.

The table [below] demonstrates the importance of considering chronological, skeletal and training ages:

Chronological Age	Skeletal Age	Training Age	Implications for the coach
12	14	1	The athletes have the same chronological and skeletal age but the coach must take into consideration the difference in training ages when devising each individual's training programme
12	14	4	
11	13	2	The athletes have different chronological ages but the same skeletal and training age. Therefore, these two individuals could have similar training programmes
14	13	2	
13	10	4	These athletes have the same chronological and training age but a big difference in skeletal age. This will affect the training load and strength/ conditioning capacities of each athlete
13	15	4	

Figure 6.1 *The importance of the different ages of development on the planning of training.*

Normal growth in children after twenty-four months is steady until puberty, with height increasing by approximately 5cm (1.9in) and weight by 2.5kg (5.7lb) per year, with a great intensity during the adolescent growth spurt, or peak height velocity (PHV) (Wilmde & Coshill, 2004). In order for coaches to fully individualize training for every young athlete it is essential that they identify each athlete's PHV to help establish the individual's level

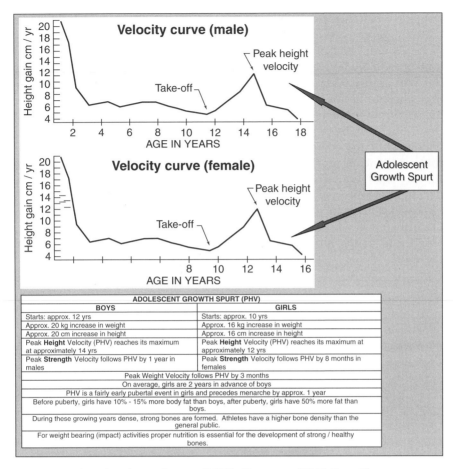

Figure 6.2 The pubertal growth spurt (PHV). (Courtesy of Keith Russell).

ADOLESCENT GROWTH SPURT (PHV)	
BOYS	**GIRLS**
Starts: approx. 12 yrs	Starts: approx. 10 yrs
Approx. 20 kg increase in weight	Approx. 16 kg increase in weight
Approx. 20 cm increase in height	Approx. 16 cm increase in height
Peak **Height** Velocity (PHV) reaches its maximum at approximately 14 yrs	Peak **Height** Velocity (PHV) reaches its maximum at approximately 12 yrs
Peak **Strength** Velocity follows PHV by 1 year in males	Peak **Strength** Velocity follows PHV by 8 months in females
Peak Weight Velocity follows PHV by 3 months	
On average, girls are 2 years in advance of boys	
PHV is a fairly early pubertal event in girls and precedes menarche by approx. 1 year	
Before puberty, girls have 10% - 15% more body fat than boys, after puberty, girls have 50% more fat than boys.	
During these growing years dense, strong bones are formed. Athletes have a higher bone density than the general public.	
For weight bearing (impact) activities proper nutrition is essential for the development of strong / healthy bones.	

of readiness for various training regimes and motor abilities (speed, strength, endurance, flexibility and skill) and corresponding training loads (volume, intensity, duration). Coaches need to exploit the onset of PHV as it is considered the second motor learning window, and provides a great opportunity to increase physical literacy.

Early Versus Late Maturation

Even though every child passes through the same stages of development, the tempo and timing passing through each stage is highly variable, and there may be a five- to six-year difference in maturity in a typical group of children of the same age. For example, if we take a typical group of ten-year-olds, there is a potential difference in skeletal age of seven to thirteen years, which has obvious consequences for coaching practice and training regimes.

Every coach has seen the early-maturing child who tends to be several years in advance of average and in many cases produces outstanding performances for their chronological age in the short term, but who may struggle when their peers increase in size and strength. In contrast, the late maturers tend to be many years delayed from average and consequently have a lower level of performance. However, coaches should be patient with these late developers, who may be overwhelmed in some activities but will improve rapidly later. It is worthy of note that Michael Jordan, acclaimed to be the greatest basketball player of all time, was cut from his sophomore varsity team because he was only 1.75m (5ft 9in) at that time. But over the next two years he grew 20cm (8in) and developed enough skill and co-ordination while on the junior varsity squad to be on the varsity team as a senior in high school. Imagine if he had been so disillusioned with the sport when he was cut from the team that he decided to stop!

Coaches need to nurture and in some cases protect the small, late-maturing child who is exceptionally skilled but lacks the physical characteristics to match more mature athletes so that he/she will continue in the sport.

Maturation Differences

One of my colleagues, Su Stewart, works with British Fencing and took this photograph.

Boy X   **Boy Y**

The two boys are the same chronological age (16 years) but there is an obvious difference in their skeletal age. Su stated that there was more than 50 centimetres difference in height and 45 kilograms difference in weight between the two boys.

When there is considerable disparity in terms of the physical make up of two athletes this will have a direct implication for coaching practice in terms of specific individual training programmes, psychological and social support and competitive success (Martens 2004). In contact and collision sports, such as Rugby, it is obvious that the boy on the right would be at considerable risk playing against the boy on the left. In sports where speed, strength and power are more likely to determine the outcome it is obvious that the boy on the left would have a greater advantage. In contrast, young athletes with a smaller stature are likely to have more success in sports such as diving and gymnastics.

Figure 6.3 Maturational differences. Boy X and Y.

Coaches involved with development programmes need to be aware that the differences in the rate at which youngsters mature can have a significant impact on optimal training loads and an individual's competitive career. The growing child and adolescent can be divided into pre-pubertal, pubertal and post-pubertal stages. In each stage the young athlete will have different physiological characteristics, and therefore training loads and competition exposure must be planned very carefully and in accordance with current knowledge of the growing athlete (Wilmore and Costill, 1994).

Research suggests that early-maturing individuals are more likely to be selected through talent identification programmes than late-maturing players (Davids, *et al.*, 2000; Malina, *et al.*, 2000), which means there is an inherent bias towards stronger, more cognitively developed athletes. This can lead to late-maturing athletes missing out on performance coaching and/or dropping out of the sport at an early age. With this in mind, coaches should accommodate such differences by providing developmental programmes that permit both early and late entry into performance sport. This could involve competition 'age banding' of two to three years, and selection on to development programmes based on skill and future potential rather than just on physical ability. In addition, athletes should be monitored for improvement rather than against a baseline score.

The timing of selection events can also be a limiting factor in selection. I know from my years in teaching that many of the boys selected on to the school soccer teams were born in the early part of the academic year, and their selection was related to their physical maturation. Thus some of the boys had up to eleven months advantage on their peers born at the end of the academic year.

In my experience, quite often late maturers are not only superior performers, but because they have not been involved in high pressure competitive situations with the associated psychological pressures for as long as their early-maturing counterparts, they tend to have a longer competitive 'shelf life' and a more positive outlook to their sport (*see* table on p. 68).

Injury Issues and Maturation

As a senior athlete myself I was very aware when I had an injury, but when I moved into coaching I found that on many occasions young athletes do not tell you when they have a niggle or strain – they put up with a lot of pain and feel as if they have few limitations. As a coach you must be aware of this, and dealing with child athletes is very different from dealing with adults – not only because of an adolescent's physical immaturity, but also because of their emotional and psychological needs. When you discuss injuries and training with a twelve-year-old it is very different from talking with a twenty-five year-old. The attitude of 'win at all costs, and try to work through your injuries' is unacceptable coaching practice and should be avoided at all times.

EARLY MATURITY	LATE MATURITY
Generally taller than their peers.	Small stature.
Generally heavier than their peers.	Narrow hips.
Succeed at an earlier age in sports that require power and strength.	Low adiposity.
	High strength to weight ratio.
Early developing children should be restrained or controlled in their training progress. The coach should ensure that their skill learning and development is not neglected or minimised in view of the relative success achieved by virtue of their advanced development.	Catch up to early maturers in height too in late adolescence, but they do not catch up in weight.
Tend to have a shorter competitive career.	Tend to have a longer competitive career.

Figure 6.4 Characteristics of early versus late maturity.

Why Are Child Athletes More Vulnerable?

The difference in the rate of growth between bone and soft tissue places the child athlete at a greater risk of over-use injury; especially vulnerable are the apophyses, the articular cartilage and the physes (growth plates). The growth plate is the area of growing tissue near the ends of the long bones in children and adolescents.

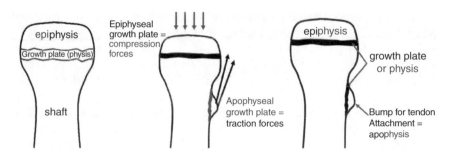

Figure 6.5 Bone growth. (Courtesy of Keith Russell)

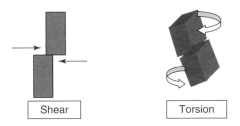

Figure 6.6 Shear and torsion. (Courtesy of Keith Russell)

It should be noted that the growth plate is an interruption in the structural integrity of bone and is considerably weaker than the rest of the bone. These are the weakest areas of the growing skeleton, weaker than the surrounding ligaments and tendons that connect bones to bones and muscles, and therefore they are vulnerable to injury. Growth plate injuries can be caused by the following:

- A fall or a blow to the limb
- Maturity mismatches between performers in terms of size, strength and power
- A sudden explosive contraction of a major muscle group
- Over-use
- Concentric contractions, for example a swimmer's shoulder
- Shear and torsion forces on the bones (*see* Figure 6.6)
- Eccentric contractions such as landings in gymnastics (a pull on the tibial tuberosity by an eccentric contraction of the quads).

Coaches must be aware that growth plates are widest and most vulnerable to damage during the adolescent growth spurt, and that the type of training that coaches set for their young athletes may result in injuries to the epiphyseal and/or apophyseal growth plates.

Coaches must be even more careful when working with late-maturing athletes as they have growth plates for a longer period of time and are therefore more vulnerable to such injuries.

DISORDERED EATING IMPLICATIONS

Young performance athletes, especially girls, are more vulnerable to the onset of eating disorders than are people in society at large, due to the very nature of what makes for athletic success (Ryan, 1999). The required commitments to intense training, with its physical demands combined with the prospect of achievement, invariably attracts individuals who are competitive and often perfectionist by nature. In almost every sport, as the athlete progresses to performance levels of competition, they will experience an increasing emphasis from coaches, trainers and other support staff on the recording of personal data. Physical factors such as weight, the dimensions of the body, physique and percentage of body fat become increasingly

---

Epiphyseal and Apophyseal Growth Plate Damage

Epiphyseal (end of the long bones):

- Vulnerable to compression forces
- Damage can be acute or chronic
- Damage can result in premature fusion (ossification) of that growth plate and the possibility of that bone being shorter

Apophyseal (tendon pulling):

- Apophysis is the generic name for bony bumps that have tendons (muscles) attached
- The growth plate is between the apophysis and the shaft (*see* Figure 6.5)
- Apophyseal growth plates are subjected to tensile forces (traction). Muscles contract and pull on the apophysis, which in turn puts shear force on the growth plate
- These are mainly damaged by chronic use (over-use)
- Occasionally a severe pull can be sufficient to avulse the apophysis – pull away a piece of bone – especially in children (this is rare in adults because once the bones are fully ossified they are strong, and a tear of the muscle and/or tendon is more likely to occur)

---

important as the 'competitive edge' is sought. This pressure to sometimes meet unrealistic weight goals may lead to problems associated with disordered eating, including anorexia and/or bulimia nervosa. These disorders may affect the growth process, influence hormonal function, cause amenorrhoea, low bone mineral density and other serious illnesses, any of which may be life-threatening.

Eating disorders in an athlete are serious and can become life-threatening if left untreated. Anorexia and bulimia nervosa are a serious health concern, and it generally requires someone close to the athlete – a coach, team mate or family member – to recognize the warning signs and seek professional help (*see* Figure 6.7).

KEY WINDOWS OF OPPORTUNITY FOR PHYSICAL AND SKILL DEVELOPMENT

For many activities, such as ice-skating, diving, gymnastics and swimming, establishing a broad repertoire of skills at an early age is vital, partly due to the fact that world class careers in those sports are often over by the age of twenty-six. Many other sports also require an early acquisition of technical ability, and this broad repertoire of skills should be taught

Anorexia nervosa	Bulimia nervosa	Physical problems	Psychological problems
Pursuit of a thin body shape through strict dieting, which leads to a drastic weight loss.	Strong desire for thinness.	Cavities and gum disease, osteoporosis	Feeling of low self-worth
Obsession for thinness is accompanied by a fear of being fat.	Interrupted by episodes of binge eating.	Gastrointestinal disturbance and dehydration.	Social withdrawal.
Obsessive about food intake.	Feelings of guilt and lack of control.	Hair, nails and skin problems.	Depression.
Compulsive about exercise. Wearing layered clothing.	Eating is followed by efforts to avoid calorie absorption by vomiting, laxative abuse, excessive exercise or extended periods of fasting.	Kidney damage, swollen salivary glands. Electrolyte imbalance, irregular heart beat, dizziness, fainting, headaches.	Inability to identify or cope with feelings.
Excessive self criticism.		Absence of menstruation.	Mood swings and irritability.
Unrealistic expectations.		Water retention and bloating.	Guilt and shame.
Sleep disorders.		Extreme sensitivity to cold.	

Figure 6.7 The signs of an eating disorder. (Courtesy of Keith Russell)

correctly and appropriately from the start – how many times have you seen a talented athlete with ingrained poor technique?

Before the first major growth spurt for any young athlete there is a key period of skill acquisition and technical refinement. If there is a prolonged period of poor practice during this stage with little correction of errors, then poor technique will result and changing it will be almost impossible. Gone are the days of passing your talented performers from the Level 1 coach to the Level 2 coach and so on until they reach the high performance coach several years later. We must adopt a more structured approach to the technical development of young high performance athletes, and the most valuable contribution that high performance clubs and coaches can contribute to the development of talented young athletes is the deployment of their best coaches to work with these young athletes from the start, and a focus on key windows of opportunity for physical and skill development.

Key Windows of Development

These are critical periods that refer to a point in the development of a specific behaviour or characteristic when training or practical experience has an optimal effect on development. The same experience introduced at an earlier or later time has no effect on, or may hinder, later skill acquisition. It should be pointed out that all the energy systems are always trainable to some extent, but during the 'key windows' accelerated adaptation will take place if the appropriate volume, intensity and duration of training are implemented (*see* Figure 6.8).

The belief by many coaches that we must 'catch them when they are young' has been supported by a philosophy that in order to achieve success at senior level it is necessary to start intensive training well before puberty (Baxter, Jones and Mundt, 2007). At the 2008 Beijing Olympics, gymnast Oksana Chusovitina (GER) took a silver medal on vault at the age of thirty-three, and said 'I want to go to London in 2012 – I will only be thirty-seven!' Coaches should reflect on both statements and contemplate if either do, or should, impact on coaching practice.

I would like you to consider the following question: do children need to specialize in one sport early in their athletic career, and will this give them a head start?

Element	Age and associated issues	
	Girls	**Boys**
Speed 1	Age 6–8 (SAQ Development)	Age 7–9 (SAQ Development)
Speed 2	Age 11–13 (Anaerobic Alactic Power)	Age 13– 6 (Anaerobic Alactic Power)
Strength	Immediately after PHV and at the onset of menarche	12–18 months after PHV (testosterone spike)
Flexibility	Develop early and maintain	Develop early and maintain
Endurance	General training before PHV – the optimal trainability for endurance occurs during PHV	General training before PHV – the optimal trainability for endurance occurs during PHV
Skill	Age 8–11	Age 9–12

Figure 6.8 Key windows of opportunity for physical and skill development. (Courtesy of Keith Russell)

PSYCHOSOCIAL ISSUES AND GOAL SETTING

Coaches must be aware of the risks of 'burn-out' from physical and emotional stress, missed social and educational opportunities, and disruptions to family life. Since performance sport is mostly a phenomenon that occurs during late childhood and early adulthood, it is important to put this into a total life perspective. I remember one of my international gymnasts telling me that 'my performance is more important than anything else in my life'. While his commitment has to be applauded and is a prerequisite of exceptional performance – what would happen if he failed?

As coaches we must be aware of the impact that performance sport has on young athletes and their personalities and motivational state. To be constantly put into competitive situations with resulting highs and lows associated with success and failure should be of major concern to coaches. Young athletes are under constant scrutiny, and their performance achievements are highly visible to many others of significant standing, sometimes on the world stage. These experiences will obviously have a great impact on an athlete's feelings of self-worth and confidence, and will need careful nurturing by coaches and support staff.

We must remember that as coaches we have a massive impact on the young athletes we coach: they are so impressionable that what we say and do can often 'make or break' them. It is therefore imperative that the quality of these interactions is of the highest standard, and we must be aware that the enthusiasm generated can be a crucial developmental force in a young athlete's career. The promotion of a 'win at all costs' ethic has both short-term and long-term detrimental effects on impressionable young athletes.

Goal setting is an extremely powerful technique for enhancing performance, but it must be implemented correctly. Coaches and athletes must set the right kinds of goal, which provide direction and enhance motivation. We must help each individual athlete learn how to stick to and achieve goals by setting effective goals and designing a programme to accomplish them. Be aware that:

- Crucial early years of successful training help develop physical and mental competence
- The achievement of early goals increases commitment to future goals, and confidence in present ones
- Coaches help increase confidence by being positive and having realistic expectations.

If coaches can make their training sessions enjoyable and give each individual the opportunity to succeed, then there is more chance of athletes having a 'good' time! I have seen young athletes accepting pain, tolerating demanding coaching sessions and fatigue, and being unaware of the length of the session just because they were enjoying themselves. This should prompt coaches to reflect on their coaching practice and session planning – is it fun, enjoyable, varied and athlete-centred?

In terms of letting your young athletes have some form of childhood and social life, coaches must remember that young athletes are still children/adolescents and have the needs of such! If you always ban them from going out with their friends, attending parties and so on, it is likely to cause resentment and start to affect training. Coaches should be more athlete-centred in their awareness of the individual's needs, and flexible when designing training programmes, and should discuss issues such as the scheduling of sessions with their athletes so that a balance can be negotiated between training and having some sort of a social life. Thus effective and performance training regimes necessitate the availability of interconnecting disciplines and processes in order to form a complete system to meet the sporting, social and emotional needs of the child in performance sport.

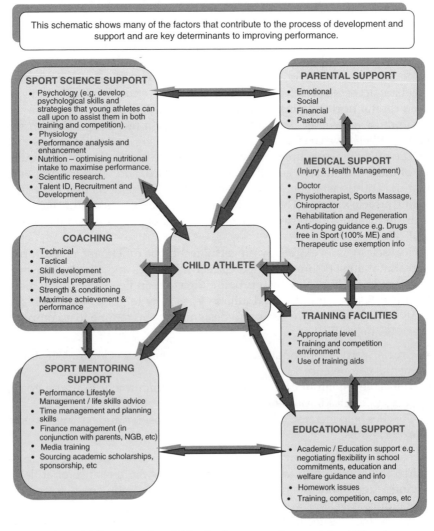

Figure 6.9 Multi-dimensional model for development and support for children in performance sport.

FORMING A COMPLETE SYSTEM FOR THE CHILD ATHLETE

Practical Implications for the Coach

- Keep a regular check on athletes' weight and height so that you can identify growth spurts and restructure training programmes accordingly
- Regularly test and monitor individual athletes' performance and physical capabilities to keep you informed of progress (or lack of it) – remember, early success is no guarantee of later success
- Group athletes in terms of skeletal age rather than chronological age when taking part in physical conditioning and other related fitness work
- Consider the effect of training age when grouping athletes
- Physical and performance characteristics associated with growth and maturation are important, but they are not the only determinants of successful performance. There is a very complex matrix of bio-social-psychological characteristics related to the demands of each sport
- Be prepared to change and adjust the training loads, methods and practices to fit the physical, psychological and performance outcomes as the athletes develop along the performance pathway
- Develop a skill development plan for each of your athletes that is discussed and agreed by both you and the athlete. In conjunction with this, you will need to devise a specific and individualized training programme for each athlete, which needs to be under constant review
- Remember that the social development of your athletes is just as important – there needs to be a balance of social as well as physical development. This may require some discussion and flexibility between you and your athletes in terms of altering training times/sessions occasionally so that your athletes can also socialize with their non-sporting peers
- Coaches should experience, exchange and apply advanced training and coaching methods
- Coaches should use specialist expertise (coaches, doctors, physiotherapists, performance analysts)
- Coaches should simulate various situations in the course of competition preparation
- Coaches should create a positive psychological environment to increase the compatibility of team members
- To help young athletes achieve their dreams, coaches need to be prepared to 'go the extra mile'
- Think about the language that you use, especially with regard to poor competitive performance and weight issues. Remember – you are a 'significant' person in your athlete's life
- Do not take extreme decisions to 'drop' athletes from your squad before the age of sixteen years old. Remember, big changes occur during PHV.

Rest and Rehabilitation

Rest and sleep are the most natural physiological ways of recovery.

- We can differentiate between the pedagogical, psychological, medical and physiotherapeutic means of recovery
- The pedagogic means of recovery are in the hands of the coach. In all sports, a professional programme should accommodate the individual training needs. For example, the density, load or volume of training would reflect the current position in the training cycle of the individual. Fast and efficient recovery using psychological and physiotherapeutic means should be available via rehabilitation – for example, physiotherapy, massage, sauna. This type of rehabilitation plays an important role in preventing injuries. Regular screening and monitoring of the young athlete also makes it possible to identify the physical condition of an athlete, to detect, in appropriate time, a deviation of one or more indications from the normal.

Training Facility and Equipment

- Equipment available should be of NGB-approved standard and specific to particular age groups
- Auxiliary and additional equipment should be available – training aids should be used when appropriate to suit individual athletes.

Nutrition

- The amount and quality of food consumed should compensate for energy losses made (measured in kilocalories)
- The age and maturational level of the athlete must be taken into consideration as it is necessary to ensure not only compensation for energy losses, but also for physical development and growing of overall dimensions of the body
- May be necessary to provide additional meals/hydration during training sessions
- Access to a nutritional support as and when required.

Education

The combination of education and training in performance sport is a very acute problem.

- When designing training programmes, coaches must also consider academic demands on the child athlete. Programmes should take into account academic loads, timing of exams and school-based physical activities. A good idea is to get a copy of the athlete's school/college timetable and any forthcoming examination dates or work deadlines. This will allow you to plan ahead and limit or resolve any potential conflicts between the athlete's sporting and other commitments well in advance

Case Study

Tom Daley (age 15) became Britain's first world diving champion in July 2009. However, he has had some difficult moments since he qualified for an Olympic final in Beijing. Daley was forced to move schools after being subject to bullying and is now settled on a scholarship at Plymouth College, Daley said "Everything is going well because there are 50 other elite athletes there who understand the pressures of high-level competition so it's great to be among them and not stick out like a sore thumb" (BBC Sport website).

Plymouth College offer a flexible academic programme and timetable for international athletes, access to support services, smaller class size and individual support.

Figure 6.10 Case study: Tom Daley.

- Negotiate with schools for athletes to be excluded from certain aspects of the curriculum or to have a diluted curriculum and extend this over a longer period of time
- Wherever possible, training camps and additional training sessions should compliment, not conflict with major academic events at school
- Coaches should be in regular contact with the school, the athlete and their parents to establish and maintain an effective support structure.
- Most schools will have a policy for dealing with gifted and talented students, and this will outline how the school will support the additional demands made on child athletes. This may include a flexible approach to curriculum delivery, homework, examinations, distance learning, and so on
- With knowledge of the above, coaches and athletes can set realistic goals and plan more effective training programmes to reduce the pressure that many child athletes feel between school and sport.

CONCLUSION

Coaches must remember that there is a great variability in the rates of child athletic development. Most of the talented athletes that I have worked with were multi-talented across a range of sports and transferred their skills and physical capabilities, some in less time than the 'ten year rule'. Therefore, coaches must not be restricted by historical viewpoints on talent development of child athletes, but remain open-minded to any opportunities that can manipulate the talent development pathway and actually keep athletes on it long enough for them to reach their true potential. It is the coach's job to maximize a child athlete's development by focusing on their physiological, psychological, technical, educational and social development in association with the athlete's support structure by providing a holistic training environment that is coach-driven and athlete-centred.

Remember, be patient and careful with young child athletes – they are first and foremost children/adolescents and have the needs of such – they are not miniature adults.

7

Inclusive Coaching and Differentiation

by Anita Navin

Responding to the diverse needs of a range of participants in a coaching session is a key priority for any coach, and sessions should be planned to reflect the individual needs and differences exhibited within a coaching session. Some of the following factors may affect an individual's approach and performance within the sport domain:

Factor	Example
Abilities	Endurance, trunk strength
Attitudes	Open to new experiences
Body type	Tall, lean, muscular
Cultural background	Religion, race
Emotional make-up	Fear, joy, excitement
Fitness level	High or low
Learning style	Theorist, pragmatist
Learning preference	Visual, auditory
Maturational level	Above or below actual age
Motivation	Intrinsic, extrinsic
Previous social experiences	One to one, large group tasks
Prior movement experiences	Competitive, recreational

(adapted from Schmidt and Wrisberg, 2000, p. 27)

In order to adopt an inclusive approach the coach must therefore consider the following three ages:

Chronological: actual age from birth.

Developmental: physical, social, emotional, cognitive development in comparison to individuals of the same age.

Training: the number of years they have been specializing and training in a sport.

By considering all ages the coach will reduce the likelihood of injury, ensure that individuals have a better chance of reaching their potential, and ultimately will promote enjoyment and adherence to the sport. Individuals can be up to four years apart in terms of their maturation levels, and so the development age is a key consideration when planning training and performance programmes.

LEARNING

The fundamental role of any coach at any level is to facilitate learning, and the effective coach will be able to distinguish between performance improvement and learning. Learning is not simply the acquisition of knowledge or skills, but is best characterized by the performer who can adapt or apply the knowledge or new skills to other situations. Learning has occurred when a performer can make connections to other areas or sports, and can relate and compare this new information to previous experiences. In contrast, performance improvement is a short-term response to training, and over time the performer is unable to replicate such an improvement.

The following statements outline the *truths* about learning:

- Individuals learn in different ways
- Learning and knowledge can be differentiated
- Individuals should take responsibility for their own learning
- Learning is being able to apply knowledge and skills to novel situations
- Learning involves a shift in one's mindset
- Learning in one situation can be transferred to other situations
- Learning is evidenced by a relatively permanent change in behaviour or performance.

In order to promote learning a coach will use a variety of coaching styles. Coaching styles are best described as patterns of behaviour, and also represent a range of methods used to promote learning. Three approaches are advocated, and these are best described as 'tell and show', 'set up and stand back', and 'question and empower':

Tell and show: the coach uses explanations and demonstrations; players are told or shown what to do.

Set up and stand back: learning is promoted by the individual experiencing the activity. The coach should stand back and observe. This is more player-centred than the previous style.

Question and empower: the coach uses questions to promote awareness, and encourages the player to take responsibility.

The effective coach will use a range of these styles, and will determine the most suitable style given the participant's stage of learning, characteristics, and the task to be delivered. The 'tell and show' style is often used with inexperienced performers, large groups and when safety is an issue. The 'set up and stand back' style is used to encourage learning by doing, and promotes thinking and decision-making. The questioning style is used with more experienced players, when the coach adopts a more facilitative role.

The Stages of Learning

Cognitive theories are often used to explain learning, and the three-stage model produced by Fitts and Posner (1967) and Gentile (1972) accounts for the three stages of learning a coach should understand in order to support the learning process: the verbal-cognitive stage, the motor or associative stage, and the autonomous stage.

The Verbal-Cognitive Stage

The model refers to an initial stage, known as the verbal-cognitive stage, in which a novice begins to grasp what the skill looks and feels like, and what it involves; any performance depends on step-by-step cognitive or thinking processes demanding a vast amount of attention. A performer in this stage will spend time talking to themselves, as the title of the stage suggests. The individual will learn by observing demonstrations, and the coach must support them by identifying cues that will help to improve them further. Improvements occur on a large scale in this phase and over a short period of time. Skill execution is at times uncertain, and does not always take the external environment into consideration.

The Motor or Associative Stage

After a certain amount of practice, the player reaches the motor or associative stage where he/she has mastered the general idea of the skill, and the cognitive effort being applied is reduced. Now the player can execute the action, and the focus is on refining the skill so as to be more consistent and effective. If the skill requires a fast action – for example, a forehand drive in tennis – the player will begin to formulate a movement programme; with a movement involving slow movements – such as balancing on a beam in gymnastics – the individual can use self-generated feedback during the movement execution. The skill becomes smoother and the player can make better use of internal (kinesthetic) feedback as well as the augmented feedback from the coach.

A performer in this phase knows what the skill looks like, but requires ample time to practise for greater consistency; his/her decision-making capabilities are improved in this stage, and the timing of a movement and overall anticipation of external influences develops. This stage is longer in duration when compared to the initial stage, and the coach will respond to the performer by offering feedback on the components of the skill the individual is attempting to refine.

The Autonomous Stage

Following extensive practice, some performers will reach the autonomous stage where the skill execution is automatic with minimal thought processes. In this phase the skill is now well learned and can be performed with minimal amounts of conscious effort. The skill execution of the performer in this phase will be highly fluent, and the performer can attend to other environmental factors, tactics and decision-making aspects relative to executing the skills in open situations and under pressure. In this phase the performer will detect their errors, and overall performance improvement is more difficult to observe as competence is almost at its peak.

Applying the Stages of Learning

The effective coach will understand the stages of learning and evaluate each individual's current stage and subsequently plan and adapt practices to ensure all participants are engaged in relevant and appropriate learning activities. The coaching style adopted may also vary across the three stages, and the following recommendations would support good coaching practice:

Verbal-Cognitive Stage:

- 'Tell and show' style dominates
- Demonstrations are frequent
- Coach explanations and feedback dominates.

Associative Stage:

- The 'set up and stand back' style of coaching dominates
- The number of demonstrations and explanations is reduced
- Practices should be designed in a variety of contexts
- Performer-generated feedback is applied.

Autonomous Stage:

- The 'questioning and empowering' style is adopted to raise awareness
- Demonstrations or explanations are rarely needed
- The performer works out solutions themselves.

Learning Preferences

The inclusive coach will at all times consider the learning preferences of each performer in a group, and each individual will have a dominant learning preference, either visual, auditory or kinesthetic. Although a player receives information through the eyes, ears and from senses in muscles and joints, evidence suggests that one of these receiving modes is normally dominant, and defines the best way for that person to learn new information, by filtering what is to be learned. This style may not always be the same for some tasks, however. These preferences may be defined as follows:

- The visual learner will want to see the skill being performed, or indeed will picture the skill in memory prior to performance
- The auditory learner may recall and listen to key cues or coaching points, and will rehearse these in their mind prior to performance
- The kinesthetic learner will grasp a feel of the movement and rehearse the skill by attending to the body parts and associated actions prior to performance.

The performer may prefer one style of learning for one task and a combination of others for other learning activities. The learning preference of a coach may dictate the structure and content of a coaching session, hence it is vital that the coach attributes time to consider a careful match of activities and tasks to the range of preferences within a group.

Working out your preference as either a performer or coach is easy to do, and the following descriptions will help you evaluate your dominant preference:

Visual Learners:

Visual-Linguistic Learners:

- Learn through written language, such as reading and writing tasks
- Remember what has been written down, even if only seen once
- Write down directions.

Visual-Spatial Learners:

- Have difficulty with written language and do better with charts, demonstrations, videos and other visual materials
- Easily visualize faces and places by using their imagination
- Seldom get lost in new surroundings.

Auditory Learners:

- Talk to themselves
- Move their lips as they read out loud
- May have difficulty with reading and writing tasks
- Are better talking to an individual and hearing what was said.

Kinesthetic Learners:

- Learn best while touching and moving
- Tend to lose concentration if there is little or no external stimulation or movement
- Like to scan first when reading, and then focus in on the details (get the big picture first)
- Typically use colour highlighters and take notes by drawing pictures or diagrams, or by doodling.

While an individual will operate using a combination of all three preferences, there will always be one that will dominate within a learning environment. Similarly a coach is likely to coach in the way he or she prefers to learn: thus if they are a visual learner, they will probably use plenty of demonstrations and images to support the coaching session; an auditory learner may predominately use verbal information, words and sounds; and a kinesthetic learner will expect a performer to want to get involved and perform the action immediately and grasp the 'feel' of the skill.

A coach must take care not to select the coaching methods in line with their own preference, rather than giving consideration to the participants. Within a session a coach will inevitably have all preferences represented, so must adapt the methods they use. When coaching one player or a small group, they need to tune into the player's preferred style to accelerate their learning.

Learning Styles

Honey and Mumford (1986) identified four learning styles: activists, reflectors, pragmatists and theorists.

Activists: learn by doing, by trial and error, and will always be prepared to 'have a go' at any activity. The activist is open-minded, enthusiastic in a learning environment, and will thrive on any challenge presented to them. This learning style often leads an individual to think out loud, and promotes a desire to answer questions posed by the coach. The activist is often creative in any cognitive and decision-making activity.

Reflectors: contemplative learners who will always want to think through a task prior to performing. Reflectors will often stand back and watch others and become a listener in the learning process. This individual will often take time to consider options, he takes a back seat and appears very tolerant in a learning situation.

Figure 7.1 A coach who is a reflector will stand back and take time to consider the options. (Courtesy of David Griffiths)

Pragmatists: problem solvers, and will focus on methods to resolve immediate difficulties. When new information is presented the pragmatists will need to see the application, the relevance of the new information or skill, and where it would be effective in the sport. Pragmatists will test out new ideas, but in a learning situation can become impatient if a task becomes time-consuming.

Theorists: like to work problems out in a logical and analytical format, and would be best represented as the 'perfectionists' in a coaching session. The theorist will often mistrust creativity, and prefers to know the underlying theory before taking part.

Once again the coach must be prepared to devise tasks that encompass the needs of all learning styles, and must be mindful of the influence of their own dominant style on their planning and subsequent delivery. The effective coach must be prepared to utilize a range of coaching strategies, styles, tasks and organization in order to address the differing needs of the performers in any one session. This process of adapting tasks to suit individual needs is termed 'differentiation'.

DIFFERENTIATION

Differentiation can be defined as a process whereby the needs of individuals within a coaching session are recognized, planning by the coach takes place to meet those needs, and appropriate activities are delivered in order to maximize learning and attainment for all individuals. Differentiation can be distinguished in terms of differentiation by task – for example, where a coach plans a range of tasks of varying levels of difficulty – and by outcome – for example, when a range of challenges is set within the same activity, and individuals respond according to their performance capability and level.

Differentiation Strategies

Bailey (2000) offers a model for differentiation, and recommends that this model is used in the planning phase by any coach. The model offers differentiation strategies related to the organization (the context of the session), the presentation of a coaching session (how the material is presented to a group or individual), and the content (the actual skills or strategies being delivered), the components of which are as follows:

- Organization: Grouping, space, roles and interaction
- Presentation: Coaching style, response, resources and support
- Content: Task, pace, level and practice style.

Organization
Grouping: The size of group can impact upon the effectiveness of the interactions and communication between members. A novice performer would benefit from smaller group activities where the communication channels and

intellectual challenges are reduced. Smaller groups present a less pressurized situation for the novice, and will enable the individual to engage in a learning activity with limited social comparison between group members.

Space: a coach can reduce or extend the working area for individuals in a session; for example, if a basketball coach is working on an offensive task in a two-versus-two situation, the space can be reduced to increase difficulty for the offensive players: with a reduced working area the offensive pair must get free from their opponent under greater pressure. If a coach witnesses a group struggling to succeed in getting free from their defence in this two-versus-two practice, then the space can be increased. Restricting a performer to a set area or zone can aid decision-making, and often ensures all players have a greater involvement.

Roles: within a game situation there is the opportunity for an individual within a coaching session to take on varying roles – for example, positional roles can vary in complexity within a game. In basketball the more capable performer may take the lead role in calling a change in a defensive formation or strategy. Alternatively, more able individuals may engage in the officiating or coach role within a session to promote greater understanding of the game.

Interaction: a novice will be more successful if they are allowed to practise a new skill in a cooperative environment. When placed in a competitive situation – for example, the execution of a lay-up shot in basketball in a game situation – the novice is placed under immense pressure, and this should initially be avoided.

Presentation

Coaching style: as previously noted, the more direct 'tell and show' style would be more suitable with a novice; as the performer moves into the next stages of skill learning they can be exposed to a more empowering and questioning approach. The empowering style will allow the more able performer to engage in greater decision-making, and to identify a range of possible solutions to a task.

Response: individuals within a coaching session can demonstrate their understanding and learning through demonstration, writing or through explanation. The more able performer may be comfortable in demonstrating a skill or their solutions to a task to a group, whereas the less competent and confident performer may prefer to perform as part of a group. Individuals may also find it easier to explain their ideas rather than to perform them in a practice situation.

Resources: equipment can be modified or adapted to increase success and provide the appropriate challenge. Thus, for example, in tennis a novice may perform with a smaller racket and/or a larger ball, and also the coach could lower the net. Many games have a junior version of the game (for example 'kwik' cricket or 'tag' rugby), with a smaller working area and modified rules. The height of the apparatus in gymnastics can be adapted for the level of performer, such as when practising skills for the beam. In swimming, the performer can use floating aids for support in the water.

Support: a novice performer or an individual who has a low attention span in a session would benefit from increased support from a coach or assistant. A novice in gymnastics may require manual guidance on a task. The effective coach should deploy an assistant to work with the groups requiring this extra attention.

Content

Task: here a coach would devise variations of a task for the participants of her/she might introduce different tasks in a session. For example, in gymnastics group prepare a sequence of movement containing different equipment or different music. In basketball participants could be taking part in a 2 v 2 game and be implementing man–man defence only or may be mixing their defence between man–man ad zone (more able).

Pace: individuals working on learning activities in a coaching session may take varying amounts of time to complete a task, and often a coach working with a large group of performers may use work cards to support this strategy. If a coach groups performers by ability, then the number of challenges or tasks presented to each group can be increased or decreased according to the performance level. Thus the less able performers in a group should be given more time or a reduced number of options on a task to practise and achieve the outcome.

Level: a coach can set varying levels of challenge by devising a range of team sizes in a game situation. For example, the less able performers will be more successful in a three-versus-three game rather than a five-versus-five.

Practice style: a novice performer will need to engage in practices that are less complex and involve the repetition of the same skill in a closed situation. A more able performer can cope with practising combinations of skills in a practice, and is also able to cope in a range of, and in more open, contexts.

Further Differentiated Approaches

Differentiated activities represent one of the approaches outlined in an 'inclusion spectrum' (Black and Haskins, 1996), and four other approaches have been highlighted to address the varying needs of a group. While initially devised for physical education, the spectrum should be understood and applied by the coach: the approaches are as follows:

- Mainstream activities: total inclusion of all in a session
- Differentiated activities: modified tasks
- Parallel activities: same activity, but ability grouping
- Adapted activities: all play adapted game
- Separate activities: all perform separately.

A coach may implement one or a range of the approaches in any one session in order to ensure that inclusive coaching takes place. Varying the strategies to meet the needs of individuals in a group is recommended to promote greater challenge, learning and motivation. The effective coach will therefore coach the individuals within a session, and not merely coach the sport.

CONCLUSION

To conclude, it is essential that the coach always puts the player first, and this means placing the needs of players before all other issues, such as a competition, parents, and the coach's own individual goals and ambitions. The coach should recognize individuals, and ensure that all participants, whatever their age, ability or disability, are treated as individuals, with their own specific needs, interests and goals. The coach must empower individuals, and as a result ensure that they become responsible for their own learning and development.

8

Management of Participant Behaviour

by Anita Navin and Denise Egan

This chapter is designed to provide a coach with information and strategies for positive behaviour management; however, it must be emphasized that the effective coaching strategies previously discussed should, if used appropriately, promote good behaviour.

The Coach's Responsibilities

It is a coach's responsibility to ensure the following:

- That tasks are interesting and achievable
- To engage the individual in decision-making, and to promote responsibility
- To be well organized and plan differentiated activities
- To adopt a range of styles, strategies and tasks for each learning preference
- To set clear objectives for the coaching session
- To use praise and rewards to engage individuals
- To apply consistent rules, routines and rituals

According to Cohen, Mannion and Morrison (1996), discipline is viewed as a 'built in' not a 'bolt-on' extra of effective teaching. Bailey (2001) draws attention to previous stereotypes of the physical educator, and states they were perceived as a bully, always shouting, threatening, teasing, punishing and ridiculing the less able. There appears to be a number of individuals that look back upon their experiences in sport and as a result possess very negative attitudes to physical activity. It is vital that participants feel valued in a coaching session whatever their ability, and essential that positive experiences are advocated to promote a healthy lifestyle and continued participation (Lambirth and Bailey, 2000).

Positive behaviour stems from good relationships, positive role models and clarity in communication, and associated with effective behaviour is one's perception about oneself. A participant will learn how to behave by copying others, from demonstration, from explanation, with rewards for good behaviour, with modelling from peers and adults, through practice and receiving reminders on their actions from the coach.

THE IMPORTANCE OF RELATIONSHIP BUILDING

The importance of high quality relationships between the coach and participant must not be underestimated in promoting positive behaviour. Stress and conflict will inhibit learning, and it is vital that the participant has a relaxed and positive 'learner state'. The coach must therefore create an appropriate learning climate, as discussed in Chapter 4, for the participant to feel valued as an individual, have a sense of belonging, and believe they can be successful in the session. The following attitudes on the part of the coach will help him/her foster effective coach-participant relationships:

- Being willing to spend time with the participants
- Respecting the participants and their individuality
- Knowing that any relationship involves 'giving and taking'
- Respecting the value of generating feedback to others
- Knowing that positive action is often rewarded with a positive response
- Recognizing that an individual will not always behave as you would like them to.

Raising Self-Esteem

The coach must ensure that tasks set in the sessions are challenging yet achievable, and as a result they should serve to raise the levels of self-esteem in the participants. Participants displaying low levels of self-esteem may exhibit any of the following behaviours: withdrawal from the task, displaying avoidance tactics, shouting out, being annoying to others, and criticizing others. Differentiating for the needs of all participants is therefore essential in order to minimize any misbehaviour that may result from low levels of self-esteem and perceptions of incompetence. Accounting for individual differences in learning will support the formation of an effective working relationship between the coach and participant, as will respect, empathy and praise as explained below:

Respect: as a constituent part of a person's behaviour, respect makes others feel valued and important. This can be evidenced in the following coach behaviours: allowing participants time to talk with each other, valuing participant responses and not speaking over them, active listening, recognizing the value of their point of view, recalling details about the participant, giving appropriate choices, and sharing in the decision-making within a session.

Empathy: is demonstrated by a coach through reflecting back feelings that are picked up from individuals within the group, sharing appropriate and related experiences of their own, and communicating their belief that every member of the session has something to contribute. Being genuine is critical within a session, and if the coach is consistent in practice, clear about the boundaries, prepared to admit their mistakes and not defensive, an appropriate working relationship will be established.

Praise: a coach must plan to be positive, and by praising the participants who are behaving well through descriptive praise (for example, 'I liked it when …') the coach will encourage positive responses. Using names, complimenting individuals within the group, being warm and positive, knowing the participants and enjoying their conversations, are strategies that will promote positive behaviour. A coach must remember that praise is effective when it is personal (use the person's name), specific (it states what is pleasing) and genuine (there is no need to use excessive superlatives). Proximity praise is praising one participant in the hope that others in the immediate area of work will also consider replicating the positive behaviour.

   Ineffective praise is often witnessed with a developing coach, and statements such as 'Well done', 'Good job' and 'That was brilliant' are some examples of worthless statements. Participants will often interpret this ineffective praise as being false, or even excessive, hence it is rejected and devalued.

The Effective Use of Language

Our own personal skills can have a positive impact on participant behaviour, and a coach must be aware of the impact of certain words within communication. The language employed by a coach can be motivating and encouraging or at times diminishing and hurtful – it is never neutral! Language must be used positively to help participants understand how they should conduct themselves within a session, and to avoid confrontation and argument. The following are some common phrases that should be avoided by a coach, with suitable positive alternatives:

Common phrases	*Could become …*
Don't speak like that to me	Speak to me in a polite manner as I do with you – thanks
You have left your equipment out again	James, put your equipment away – thanks
How dare you argue with me?	I require you to listen to my instructions
You really are annoying me	I feel annoyed when I am interrupted
When you interrupt	Please wait your turn to speak

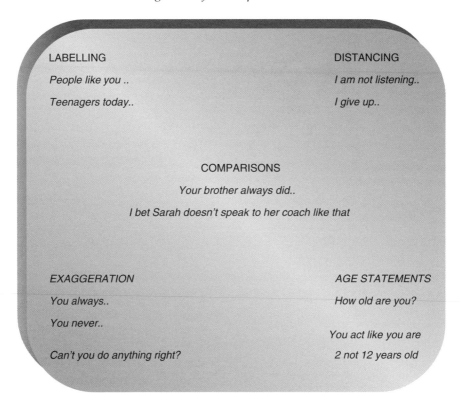

Figure 8.1 Language to be avoided in the coaching situation.

The language utilized by a coach should at all times remain positive, and Figure 8.1 outlines some statements that would lead to difficult situations.

Effective instructional strategies have been explored in previous chapters; to summarize, the coach should make sure they observe the following linguistic parameters:

- Give direction
- Use the participant's name or the group name
- Establish eye contact
- Use pauses
- Give reminders
- Offer their thanks (this will imply the instruction will be carried out).

SELF-RESPONSIBILITY

Physical activity and sport provide suitable environments for the development of positive values and good citizenship. Hellison and Templin (1991) devised a 'responsibility model' as support to those attempting to develop and practise self-responsibility. The model embraces the types of responsibility a young adult may encounter; it is not meant to show a progressive pathway, although it is often interpreted in this way.

Figure 8.2 A coach can deliver citizenship education through sport. (Courtesy of Northumbria University)

The model proposes a set of hierarchical levels of self-responsibility presented as Level 0 through to Level 4, as follows:

Level	Characteristic	Behaviours
Level 0	Irresponsible	Unmotivated, ill disciplined, makes fun of others; abuses peers and the coach, interrupts the coach
Level 1	Self-controlled	Controls behaviour so they do not interfere with others, does not show improvement
Level 2	Involved	Shows self-control and is fully immersed in the coaching session, accepts challenges and practice
Level 3	Shows self-direction	Participates without direct supervision, takes responsibility for their actions. Plans and executes their own practice and identifies their own needs
Level 4	Helpful	Participants wish to extend their sense of responsibility by supporting and co-operating

A coach should take account of the levels of self-responsibility, and should look to implement some of the strategies outlined by Hellison (1991) by observing the following parameters:

- Make reference to the levels of responsibility in a coaching session
- Model the levels through their own coaching behaviour
- Give participants time to reflect on their own behaviours.

Bailey (2001) also offers the following strategies in an attempt to promote positive social values and citizenship:

- Offer co-operative tasks and challenges
- Allow discussion and debate
- Give a participant choices and offer shared decision-making activities.

The long-term strategy for any coach is therefore to provide opportunities to create a learning environment where participants show respect, support others, and are given opportunities to develop their levels of responsibility to build positive relationships and be well informed of appropriate social attitudes and citizenship values. However, even though the coach may utilize all of the aforementioned strategies, has a well planned programme with clear rules and routines, and effective management strategies – nevertheless acts of misconduct can still arise.

MISBEHAVIOUR AND CONTROL ISSUES

Citing potentially difficult situations is essential in the coach education process, and any developing coach must realize that all coaches will at times in their career encounter such situations. The inexperienced coach is most likely to encounter discipline and control issues when working with large groups of young participants, and therefore it is critical that a range of behaviour management techniques are known and employed in the practical situation.

Within a sport environment the most common acts of misbehaviour are minor and irritating, such as participants who, for example, persist in the following misdemeanours:

- Refuse to co-operate on a given task
- Refuse to listen, and talk over you
- Interfere with the performance and work of others
- Refuse to participate in the task set
- Misuse equipment.

A research study in physical education (Hardy, 1999) found that the most frequently cited acts of misbehaviour in lessons were as follows (presented with the highest scoring first):

- Not paying attention to instructions, and talking to another participant
- Not completing the task as directed to do so
- Disrupting others
- Refusing to co-operate in a team or group task
- Not abiding by procedures (for example chewing, or wearing jewellery or incorrect kit)
- Seeking attention, and pulling faces or misusing equipment.

Managing Difficult Situations

In order to manage the difficult situation the coach should model the behaviour they wish to observe. Making the behaviour unacceptable, and not the person, allows the person to change, and this approach acknowledges that all individuals make mistakes sometimes. The coach should remain calm, should not become involved in the argument, and should not compete for the last word, and ultimately this will help to diffuse the situation. The following represent some techniques for remaining calm in a difficult situation when coaching:

- **Broken record:** be clear about your needs, and do not become angry, uncomfortable, loud or irritated (for example, be firm in body language when conveying the issue)

- **Fogging:** where a coach does not fuel the argument, but absorbs it (for example, accepts the other person's point of view and feelings)

- **Expressing feelings:** a coach can communicate their anger without demonstrating it (for example, be angry without shouting)

- **Defer:** a coach may want to wait before dealing with the issue.

Figure 8.3 A coach must always remain calm when managing misbehaviour. (Courtesy of Northumbria University)

A coach must ensure they do not overreact to what are known as *secondary behaviours*: responses from participants when they have received information about inappropriate behaviour. Secondary behaviour is often displayed as either non-verbal responses – tutting, sighing, arm-folding – or verbal responses – 'It wasn't me', or 'The other coach allows us'. The coach must realize that the secondary behaviour is simply making the participant feel better, and it is vital he remains focused on correcting the primary behaviour issue.

Bailey (2001) outlines some of the strategies which can be employed to deal with the difficult behaviours outlined above; these are described below.

Maintaining an Overview

A coach should maintain a good overview of the participants in the group by scanning the working space: he should look around each working space at regular intervals, and should ensure a position is adopted for obtaining a view of the whole working area. A coach may be working closely with an individual on performance feedback, but it is vital that he obtains the best positioning in order to view the whole space, and by periodically offering comments to the whole group he maintains control. Constantly moving around the working area promotes greater control, and allows the coach to note potential problems and to diffuse them before the incidents turn into major problems.

Maintaining Eye Contact

Keeping eye contact on the misbehaving individuals shows awareness of the act, and maintains coach control. This is a common strategy, and is often accompanied by a coach stopping talking and using non-verbal actions such as folding the arms or raising an eyebrow. Such a strategy does not prevent others in the session from working on the task, and disruption to them is therefore minimal.

A participant may become aggressive (when their eye contact is of long duration and challenging), or they may engage in a staring competition, thus it is vital that the coach shifts the eye contact to the side. The coach should not change the focus to a downward position, as this would imply a submissive response.

Proximity Control

A coach may decide to move physically closer to a participant in order to attempt to correct their behaviour, and this is often carried out without any disturbance to others in the group. A coach may move closer to the misbehaving individual or group, and question the performers on the task and expectations.

Desists

A coach using this approach will simply ask the offender to stop the action, and it is vital that this strategy is not overused. If the coach has to ask the same offender to stop several times, then it is appropriate to try another strategy. Taking the individual aside and directing the reprimand at them privately and not in view of the whole group is the most effective method in this context, in order to avoid additional confrontation. The coach must be firm in their approach, but should not shout or be humiliating. Acknowledging positive behaviour is essential, and where possible the coach should redefine the code of conduct and procedures.

A Questioning Style

Using a questioning style will often promote positive behaviour, and will remind the participant of what is expected of them.

Relocating the Offender

In some working areas individuals can become distracted, and in this instance the coach would identify another space for the individual or group to work in. A coach may decide to move any misbehaving individuals away from the boundaries of the working space – for instance near walls, windows and storage areas in a sports hall – and place them in the centre of the hall. As the coach changes position and moves around the groups, he/she will pass through the centre area more frequently and their proximity to the misbehaving individuals may promote an improvement in their behaviour.

Punishment

Punishment is often considered to be the final strategy, and must only be applied when dealing with repeated acts of misbehaviour or when a participant is not making any attempts to improve. It may include temporary withdrawal, and a meeting with parents; however, note that some punishments would be deemed inappropriate to use in the coaching situation:

- Punishing all participants in the session as a result of a small number misbehaving
- Physical punishment
- Forms of psychological punishment, such as ridicule and sarcasm
- Sending a participant out of the working area, or home (note there are child protection issues here if the child is under eighteen).

CONCLUSION

Dealing with inappropriate behaviour can be emotionally tiring for a coach, and often discussing the incident with fellow coaching staff may allow a more rapid recovery from such a negative event. Occasionally a coach may bring unnecessary personal emotions into the session, and the consequences can impact upon how difficult behaviour is managed. A coach may have prejudices, their personality or style may affect the response, they may have professional insecurities, work stress and home pressures – or they may just be having a bad day!

A coach should reflect upon the behaviour and his/her response to it in order to prevent it happening in the future. The following questions may support the coach in his reflection:

- Have I followed club policy, and their procedures for reporting the incident?
- What aspect of the participant behaviour was difficult to manage?
- What are the reasons for this misbehaviour?
- What behaviour strategies have I tried with this individual or group?
- What will I do differently next time?
- How do I care for myself during and after the incident?

Every sports club should have a policy for dealing with inappropriate behaviour, and expectations should be stated clearly in a participant code of conduct. Ensuring participants have ownership of the code of conduct is essential, and such practices are advocated at the start of any season or coaching phase. It goes without saying that 'prevention is much better than cure', and 'being proactive rather than reactive' is a key message in this chapter.

Decision Training as a Coaching Method

by Anita Navin

Decision training will ensure a performer can cope with the pressure of competition, as a coach will have implemented a range of practice scenarios that simulate the competitive environment. Decision training will build confidence and enhance the cognitive processes of a performer by developing attention, problem-solving skills and anticipatory components.

Skilled performance is often measured by the consistency of the response demonstrated by a performer, and will display the following features:

- It is task orientated and goal directed
- It involves some neurological activity and cognitive processes
- It is dependent upon practice and learning
- It can be modified and regulated to adapt to varying contexts.

Skilled performance therefore has a specific objective and purpose, it incorporates decision making, it requires a commitment to practise, and it can be modified to suit internal (for example, effort) and external (such as opponents) conditions.

In every sport an individual will be forced to make a range of decisions; for example, this might be before the execution of a pass, such as when and where to pass the ball, and the weight and type of pass required. The decisions requiring attention relate closely to what are called 'perceptual factors'; for example, an attacking player in any invasion game would consider the following factors before executing a movement to free themselves from an opponent:

- The free space and where to move
- Timing: when to move and when to break free
- The speed and pace required to free oneself
- The direction and angle of the movement.

This processing of information can be broken down into stages, and is best represented using Figure 9.1.

A defender approaches in football

Identify stimulus

Select a response

Programme response into action

The attacker passes the ball

Figure 9.1 The information processing stages.

The stages of processing relating to the decision making between input (the individual receives environmental information) and output (the final action) are identified as stimulus identification, response selection and response programming. In the stimulus identification stage an individual will analyse the environmental information using their senses (auditory, visual and kinaesthetic), and will assimilate the information and detect movement, speed and the direction of any objects or opponents, for example. At the end of this initial stage the performer will have a clear overview of the information presented for the second stage: response selection.

Once the nature of the environment has been determined, the performer must make a decision as to what, if any, action is required. If a response is required, the individual must at this point select an appropriate movement from a range stored in memory from previous experiences. For example, a basketball player may have a choice to pass or dribble, and given the space in front and no approaching defender, the player would choose the latter.

Once this decision has been made, the information is passed to the response programming stage: the plan of action is formed, and through a range of cognitive processes the muscles are directed to contract in a certain sequence, with appropriate force and timing.

Figure 9.2 The rugby player plans the response and executes the pass in the final output stage. (Courtesy of Team Northumbria)

The output stage represents the end result of all information processing. Decision making is governed by a performer's reaction time, and this is best defined as the time gap between the presentation of the stimulus and the start of the response. Reaction time can therefore serve as a time measure of the three stages outlined above. The shortest reaction time is when there is only one stimulus and one response (simple reaction time); when there are numerous stimuli with several possible responses (choice reaction time) the time taken to react increases. Thus to succeed, a performer must deceive their opponents and increase the number of actions: for example, using a variety of shots in badminton with similar preparatory stages would effectively delay the information processing.

Figure 9.3 'Selling a dummy', or deception, is vital in outwitting an opponent. (Courtesy of Northumbria University)

A coach must therefore apply this notion of information processing to ensure that the practices planned for a session incorporate opportunities to make decisions in environments offering a range of stimuli at the input stage.

TRADITIONAL VERSUS DECISION-MAKING COACHING METHODS

Vickers (1996) accounts for two distinct methods of coaching. The first is known as the traditional or technical method of coaching, and possesses the following features:

- Technical and physical emphasis
- Progressing from simple to complex practices
- Large amounts of coach feedback
- Repetitive (blocked) practice

- Low levels of questioning
- Low levels of athlete detection and correction of errors
- Low levels of performer cognitive effort.

A coach utilizing this method would only implement competitive situations as the season progressed, and although the resultant effect of this method would produce a well drilled and successful performer early in practice, they would fail under the pressure of competition.

The second method is the decision-making approach, where the following features are identified by Vickers (1996):

- High levels of cognitive effort
- Combined skill (random) practice
- Competition scenarios
- High levels of questioning
- Reduced and delayed feedback
- Athlete detection and correction of errors
- Use of video feedback
- High variability in activities.

A coach employing this method will see an increased amount of performer error in the early stages of practice, but information will be retained more effectively, and performers will achieve a higher level of ability later in the season or phase: as a result of this independent thinking being an integral part of this coaching method, the performer is better equipped to cope when novel and challenging situations are presented in competition.

It is therefore essential that a coach continuously reflects upon the methods employed within their coaching programmes. Coaching sessions should be planned to allow a performer to experience the following:

- Game contexts providing the 'big picture' and game scenarios
- Modified, simulated and real contexts
- Combined sessions of technical and physical skills.

Figure 9.4 A coach presents the game scenarios for players to identify appropriate strategies. (Courtesy of David Griffiths)

DECISION-TRAINING METHODS

Decision-training methods may be summarized as follows: (Vickers, 1996)

- Random practice
- Variable practice
- Hard first instruction
- Video analysis
- Modelling
- Bandwidth feedback
- Questioning.

Random Practice

Practices using this approach are designed to combine a range of skills from the same sport in game-like practices. Vickers (1996) refers to the skills selected as 'smart combinations' (page 20), and the two or three skills are placed within the same practice, along with interlinked tactical information.

Often a coach will plan logical progressions, moving from simple to more complex practices following the philosophy that the fundamental skills must be mastered prior to the more advanced skills being introduced. This practice design is referred to as 'blocked' practice, and is characterized by repeated practice of the same skill. However, with safe practice, and the inclusion of decision-making and smart combinations of skills, the random design is deemed most appropriate in terms of psychological and physical preparation.

The differences between blocked and random practice are outlined below in the following example:

Scenario: A coach in hockey is planning a practice session for three passing skills (A = the hit, B = the push pass and C = the scoop), and should this be delivered adopting a blocked design, each skill would be practised in isolation and would therefore involve repeated rehearsal of the same skill until competence is achieved. If the coach is adopting a practice design that is random, then there would be no particular order to the practice, that would incorporate the execution of the different passes in what is known as the 'smart' combinations outlined earlier.

Practice Designs

Blocked practice: Repeated rehearsal of the same task – for example, the hit (AAAAAAAAAAAA).

Random practice: No particular order to the practice of different tasks – for example, the hit, push and scoop pass, in no particular order (ABCAACBBCABC).

Variable Practice

A coach will strive to incorporate a range of practices that offer variations of the same skill, for example when sprinting to get free from an opponent the coach should ensure this can be practised using a variety of directions and in varying locations and amounts of space on the court. By varying the conditions, the performer must use different tactics to get free and this impacts differently on the attention and on the cognitive effort demanded for each repetition. When using this design a performer will engage in a great deal of problem solving, and will be constantly retrieving information from memory.

In a blocked practice design the performer would practise the sprint to get free within the same environmental conditions; he/she moves into an automatic state and simply executes the movement with very little thought and planning. The resultant impact of such a practice design is a performer who moves into a mindless state after the first two or three repetitions.

In the short term the effects of blocked practice are higher, but in the long term the benefits of random practice are significantly higher.

Hard First Instruction

The traditional coach has in the past been guilty of promoting technical practice in isolation, with no reference to tactical or strategic thinking skills. Hard first instruction encourages a coach to present a range of tactical information interlinked with technical practice early in the season. The performer is subjected to a range of tactical and competitive situations where decisions are required, thus ensuring that the underlying knowledge is experienced. Initially a performer will make mistakes, but ultimately their ability to act on external stimuli in a competitive situation is enhanced. A performer's retention of information is significantly higher when compared to a performer who follows a more traditional delivery style.

The novice performer would be exposed gradually to more complex tactical models and decision-training contexts, whereas the more experienced performer would cope with hard first instruction in terms of the physical and the conceptual.

Video Analysis

A coach is able to enhance a performer's ability to appraise their performance and begin to recognize matches, and mismatches in relation to the perfect model. The video method enables a performer to confirm their strengths and also to note the aspects of their performance requiring development. It will raise the performer's own awareness, and help him develop the ability to engage in self analysis and intrinsic feedback opportunities. Over time the individual is less dependent on coach feedback, and can engage in the learning process unaided.

Using video analysis can serve to confirm that the performer's goals are being met through the practices employed by the coach: such a process will provide a record of progress and therefore help motivate the performer. It enables a performer to view movements repeatedly, from a range of angles and at various speeds, and also the video can be stopped at critical points of an action to view isolated aspects more closely.

The benefits of video analysis can be identified, but a novice would require education and guidance in order to master the process of observation. A coach should work with the novice, and provide key areas for observation; he should also draw attention to specific aspects of the performance, often called 'cueing'.

Video should also be utilized for tactical analysis, and often a team can observe and identify the tactical strengths and weaknesses of the forthcoming opponents in order to make decisions as to the game plan to be practised and executed. For example, in rugby a coach may record a number of lineouts executed by the forthcoming opponents, and the performers can then view these repeatedly, discuss the tactics required, and ultimately take ownership of the decision-making process in relation to formulating a suitable game plan.

Bandwidth Feedback

Traditional coaching methods would support the notion of more feedback equalling a better learning environment. However, in recent years the idea of reducing feedback is deemed most effective in order to benefit long-term performance. Coach feedback is useful, but if given frequently in a session the performer becomes dependent on the information related to performance improvement. Using bandwidth feedback, the amount of coach feedback is gradually delayed and reduced, and is only given when performance falls outside the expected standard, indicating that the performer is struggling with critical aspects of the skill. When performances fall within the bandwidth the coach is empowering the performer to generate solutions for themselves and others. However, it should also be noted that when bandwidth feedback is used as a tool by the coach, some performers will perceive the coach to be neglecting their development and it is vital that a performer understands the importance of decision training.

Questioning

If a coach elects to reduce and delay feedback, then it is of paramount importance that a questioning approach is implemented. The impact of this questioning approach will engage the performer, prompt greater decision making, and also prompt the performer to use kinesthetic awareness to review performance. Questions posed can vary regarding the cognitive demand placed on the respondent, and those high in cognitive demand will prompt analysis and greater application to the task in hand. Divergent or open-ended questions are therefore most effective to promote decision making, and are best described as questions which do not have a 'yes' or 'no' answer. Questions beginning with 'What?' or 'Tell me about?' prompt the respondent to offer an account of a situation or an event, and further encourage the performer to apply their knowledge. The following guide is useful for any individual using a questioning approach, in that questions should:

- focus attention
- invite enquiry
- assess knowledge and understanding
- develop self and peer assessment skills
- be planned in advance and relate to the practice or session focus.

Some common errors in questioning include convergent questions being posed, poor vocabulary and lack of clarity, allowing mass calling out of the answers, focusing on the same performer to respond, not allowing time for an individual to think and answer, ignoring answers, and responding intolerantly to incorrect answers (Bailey, 2001).

Vickers (1996) proposes a staged process for any coach to adhere to when planning a session involving decision training. Initially, the coach should identify the game situation, and be knowledgeable of the decisions a player would need to make to be successful. As an example of this, a basketball team is competing in a forthcoming game against opponents who make fast transitions from defence to attack following a steal or gain in possession. Here the coach must identify the decisions to be made, which would include:

- What method of defence should now be employed on losing possession?
- Where should each player position given the location of the ball carrier?
- Which players should be tracked closely?

The coach would then need to devise the practices where these decisions are best trained in preparation for the forthcoming match. Finally, he should select one or more of the decision-training tools that would ensure the decision can be addressed and worked upon in the practice.

CONCLUSION

In summary, decision training as a coaching method will undoubtedly enhance a performer's desire to take responsibility for their own learning and development. Educating others of the importance of this approach is advocated, particularly since initially performance improvement will be much slower compared to when more traditional methods are used. Traditional methods do not engage the performer in thought processes, and often the performer is engulfed in a mindless and automatic state of performance that is not reflective of a competitive environment. A coach should develop methods to fully engage a performer in the cognitive processes linked to performance in order to promote long-term gains and information retention.

PART 2: APPLYING SPORT SCIENCE PRINCIPLES IN COACHING

10

Planning a Training Programme

by Kelvin Beeching

This chapter examines the components of a training programme and the associated mechanisms a coach must take into consideration when planning a programme in order to achieve physical fitness. The notion of physical fitness is the first to be covered, including an explanation of the components of fitness and the energy systems associated with exercise. This is followed by a description of the principles that govern training, and the impacts these have on performance. Finally, this chapter looks into the cycles involved in planning a training programme, and offers an explanation of the outline of each of the proposed cycles.

Figure 10.1 Achieving physical fitness. (Courtesy of Team Northumbria)

PHYSICAL FITNESS

Physical fitness has been defined in a variety of ways by different authors. Greenberg *et al.* (2004) defines physical fitness as 'the ability to perform everyday tasks'; Martens (2004) states that 'physical fitness is the ability to perform sport at the optimal level of the athlete through meeting the physical demands of the sport'. This differing opinion is due to the varying motives of the individual involved in the fitness plan (Dick, 2007). Howley and Franks (2007) split the concept of fitness into two distinct areas, namely physical fitness and performance fitness, in order to embrace the intentions of all fitness participants. Physical fitness relates to obtaining/maintaining a healthy lifestyle and lowering the risks of disease; performance fitness is the ability to optimise performance in sport through developing the components of sport-specific fitness. For the purposes of this chapter, physical fitness will conform to the performance fitness school of thought.

Performance fitness is made up of many differing components that relate to both the metabolic and muscular readiness of the body to perform exercise. Fitness has been defined as the most controllable and changeable element of performance (Brewer, 2005), and as the most important aspect in achieving high performance (Bompa, 1999). Therefore its significance to coaching is great. By appreciating the difference fitness can have on successful performance, and understanding what each component of fitness is, a coach can have a direct impact upon performance. Accordingly, this text will act as a starting point for coaches by defining the components of fitness and energy systems, and providing a rationale for testing.

The Components of Fitness

Brewer (2005) stated that modern-day athletes are required to be able to exert high levels of speed, agility, power, strength and endurance in order to excel in the sporting domain. Consequently, Brewer proposed that there are five major components of fitness that enable an athlete to achieve optimum performance:

- Power
- Strength
- Speed
- Flexibility
- Muscular endurance.

Power

Power has been described as the most important factor in performance (Kraemar and Gomez in Foran, 2001). This is due to the significance of explosive movements within modern-day sport, and being able to produce these in as short a time as possible is therefore extremely valuable.

Power is the ability to exert high levels of force, via muscular contractions, in the smallest possible time. The longer it takes a muscle to exert maximal force, the lesser the power output. As power is dependent upon strength and speed, increasing these variables will in turn increase power output.

Strength

The strength of a muscle is its ability to generate force against a load. Different athletes require strength in different quantities, and this is defined by the sport they participate in. An athlete's ability to lift, load or move objects depends upon their strength (Greenberg *et al.*, 2004). The production of strength, and thus strength training, is crucial in developing power.

Speed

Speed is the ability of the athlete to move their body quickly (Brewer, 2005). The less time it takes to move the body, the faster the athlete. Its importance depends upon the sport undertaken, but it does give the athlete an advantage in the field. For instance, if a cricketer is able to move between the wickets quickly then he is reducing the risk of being run out. Speed relates to movements that are forwards, backwards and sideways in nature.

Flexibility

Flexibility is essentially the range of motion around a joint: that is, the ability of the athlete to move their joint through its entire range of motion. Levels of flexibility are related to body type, age, gender and physical activity level (Heyward, 2006). Jones and Knapik (1999) found that those with too little and those with too much flexibility are more susceptible to injury. Accordingly, flexibility is an important factor in sport performance as it can decrease the risk of injury and thus aid the athlete in continued performance.

Muscular Endurance

Muscular endurance is the muscle's ability to sustain a contraction or to sustain a number of contractions over an extended time period (Whaley *et al.*, 2006). One's ability to lift an object repeatedly depends upon levels of endurance. Endurance is a vital notion within sport, as athletes are continually asked to execute movements over the course of a performance with the same intensity and quality as the first (for instance, the vertical jump in basketball is a skill that is repeated throughout the entirety of the game).

The Figure 10.2 offers examples of how to train each component of fitness along with associated methods of assessment. Note this is by no means an exhaustive list, merely a starting point for coaches.

Component	Training Method	Test
Speed	Speed Resistance Training Overspeed Training	20 & 40 meter Sprint Tests
Power	Resistance Training Plyometric Exercise	Vertical Jump Test Countermovement Jump
Flexibility	Static Stretching Proprioceptive Neuromuscular Facilitation (PNF)	Sit and Reach Test Back Scratch Test
Strength	Resistance Training	One Repetition Maximum (1RM) Dynamometers
Muscular Endurance	Resistance Training	Push-up Test Curl-up Test

Figure 10.2 Training for fitness.

Energy Systems

Energy is the key to running anything in the modern world. It is required for everyday activities such as heating a house and running a car. The body is no different, and needs energy in order to perform daily tasks (Sherwood, 2008). Energy is provided from the food one eats, and is converted to fuel through metabolism. The food is converted to glucose, which is then converted to adenosine triphosphate (ATP) in the cells of the body. It is ATP that is the fuel for muscular contractions, and is thus used for completing tasks and activities. ATP is produced by three systems within the body: the oxidative, anaerobic glycolysis, and phosphagen systems (Hoffman, 2002). The oxidative system, as its name suggests, is reliant upon oxygen and as such is called aerobic (meaning 'with oxygen'). As both the phosphagen and anaerobic glycolysis systems do not require oxygen, they are called anaerobic.

When there is a requirement for immediate power output, for instance to increase the pace of exercise or to engage in high intensity effort, the anaerobic system provides this energy (Sharkey and Gaskill, 2006). Initially the body uses the ATP stored in the cells to provide fuel; use of this stored energy is called the phosphagen system. However, there is a limited supply of ATP stored in the muscles and so these stores are easily exhausted (as demonstrated in Figure 10.3). Accordingly, the body needs to produce more energy (glucose that can be converted into ATP) in order to maintain this level of activity. To facilitate this, the body uses glycogen stores from the liver and muscles, and the glycogen is then used to produce ATP; this process is known as the anaerobic glycolysis system.

A bi-product of this system is lactic acid, which inhibits performance as it obstructs ATP production, force production of muscles and causes fatigue. The anaerobic glycolysis system is extremely inefficient in terms of its ATP production, and this, coupled with the production of the constricting lactic acid, means the body searches for a more proficient form of energy production. This is found in the form of the oxidative system. The oxidative (or aerobic) system is utilized for exercises of a steady state

Energy System	Energy Source	Duration
Aerobic	Oxidative System	Over 3 minutes
Aerobic and anaerobic	Anaerobic glycolysis and oxidative system	2–3 minutes
Anaerobic	Anaerobic glycolysis	30 seconds to 2 minutes
Anaerobic	Phosphagen and anaerobic glycolysis	6–30 seconds
Anaerobic	Phosphagen	0–6 seconds

Figure 10.3 Energy systems.

nature with less intense, more endurance-based activity. This system utilizes the carbohydrate and fat stores, and combines these with oxygen in order to produce glucose. This glucose is then converted into ATP and used to contract muscles (Martens, 2004). However, the oxygen required for this system cannot be produced instantaneously as it takes the heart, lungs and other systems a few minutes to accumulate the required amounts and deliver it to the cells, hence the need for the inefficient anaerobic glycolysis system.

An understanding of the energy systems is an important attribute for coaches to possess so that training can be prescribed in order to train the appropriate system. Without this knowledge the wrong energy system may be trained, and thus required adaptations will not be made, which will result in negative impacts on performance.

The Need for Continual Assessment of Fitness

Fitness monitoring provides the coach with specific information about an individual's performance, providing the coach with baseline information for designing a training programme (Harman in Beachle and Earle, 2008). Fitness testing demonstrates an individual's training level, strengths, and areas for development. Testing is a useful mechanism for assessing the effectiveness of a particular training schedule, and a coach would use such information to modify the programme if the training were not having the desired effect. It is through this testing procedure that more individualized training programmes can be implemented around the key aspects of strength and conditioning. It is vital that any individual being tested does not participate in any physical activity in the twenty-four hours prior to the testing so as not to skew the results. A coach should make attempts always to test the players at the same time of day, and ensure consistency in the conditions – for example the facility used, the cleanliness of the floor, temperature of the hall, the same warm-up, same ordering of tests. The tests should always be standardized, and the coach should adhere to the documented procedure and guidelines so as to ensure reliability and validity (Beashel and Taylor, 1996).

For players, the tests often serve as a motivational tool and provide the individual with a self-referenced measure of progress. Fitness monitoring should not be used to compare the fitness levels of a group of players, or be used as the single criterion for selection or deselection purposes. An effective training programme will have testing every eight to ten weeks. A coach should schedule the testing and inform players, rather than impose on them without warning. Monitoring is often carried out at the following times: prior to the preparation phase to obtain baseline measures, and at the end of the competition phase to check whether the intensity of training has been appropriate to maintain fitness in this phase.

PRINCIPLES OF TRAINING

The principles of training are the beliefs that govern training and allow for the greatest adaptations following exercise (Dick, 2007). Consequently it can be said that these principles govern adaptation. Therefore it is imperative that a coach understands each principle, and is able to apply them to the prescription of training for their athletes. In applying these principles of training, the coach will ensure that the athlete gets the maximum gains from the time they spend training, and so every programme should be built with these principles in mind (Bompa and Carrera, 2005).

The principles of training may be categorized as follows, and are discussed below:

- Individualization
- Adaptation
- Overload
- Reversibility
- Specificity
- Progression
- Variation
- Recovery.

Individualization

Training programmes must meet the needs of each individual athlete, who will have different requirements for the development of fitness and so there is a need to provide an individually tailored programme for each athlete (Cross in Cross and Lyle, 1999). In addition, each athlete responds to training differently (Whaley *et al.*, 2006), and the prescription of any training programme will need to allow for a number of factors. Factors that should be considered when individualizing training programmes are age, maturity, training age, work capacity, fitness and preparation, and the body type of each athlete concerned (Stone *et al.*, 2007).

Adaptation

A successful training programme will result in physiological advancements, but it is important to note that changes may take place over the

Figure 10.4 A performance gym for training. (Courtesy of Team Northumbria)

training period and the immediate effect may not be visible (Galvin and Ledger, 2003). If adaptations are to transpire, the body needs to be repeatedly placed under stress (Bompa and Carrera, 2005).

The Overcompensation Model

During a training session an athlete will encounter fatigue if they continue to perform a task for a long period of time. This results in a decrease in intensity as the athlete is not able to maintain the current level. It is during the recovery period that the adaptations to the training load take place, and this is referred to as 'overcompensation'. Therefore the recovery time after training is critical, and after this period of rest the body will be able to train at a higher level. This process of overcompensation governs all types of training, whether it is physical, tactical, technical or psychological.

Overload

In order to gain an adaptation effect the training load must be greater than the load the body is normally placed under (Beachle and Earle, 2008): that is, the body must be placed under increased stress, and must do more work than it is used to and indeed is comfortable with. The stress must be greater than that usually required or achieved in either a match situation or training session, and must be out of the comfort zone of the performer. Training loads should be individual to each performer, and are devised through the manipulation of volume and intensity, where volume is determined by the frequency and duration of exercise, and intensity is how close to one's maximum the athlete is working (Galvin and Ledger, 2003). Incorrect prescription of the overload principle has adverse effects on training, as too high a load can lead to injury and too low a load will result in no training adaptation. To aid prescription of a training session or programme, the following FITT principles must be observed:

Frequency – How often will the training sessions occur?

Intensity – How hard should the player train, and how close to their maximum level?

Time – How long should the performer work for (for example, the number of sets or repetitions)?

Type – What is the focus of the training (for example endurance, speed, strength)?

Reversibility

The term 'reversibility' refers to the detraining effect that takes place once training decreases or stops (Wilmore *et al.*, 2008). Any benefits achieved following a training programme will be lost as the process begins to reverse itself. All performers must therefore train regularly, and when a fitness component is not the focal point in a training phase, they must still follow a maintenance programme. In addition, the coach must ensure that a performer is able to recover from the demands of their sport in the off season, but also maintain their fitness in this transition period, although the longer the athlete has trained for, the slower the rate of reversibility (Beashel and Taylor, 1996).

Specificity

The loads and stresses that are placed on the athlete in training will determine the physiological adaptations that are made, thus adaptations are specific to training prescription (McMorris and Hale, 2006). Accordingly, prescription of any training programme needs to fit the requirements of the sport being trained for. The programme must replicate the demands of the game, and should consider sport-specific movements, muscle groups utilized, length of work, and work-to-rest ratios (Ackland *et al.*, 2009). A coach must identify the fitness component which underpins a particular element of performance, and centre a training programme on it; for example, a player wants to improve their speed when sprinting out at a centre pass in netball, so must therefore work at a high intensity and for a short duration.

Progression

As training produces adaptations and improvements to the athlete, the body still needs to be overloaded in order to continue to make any advancement in performance. Accordingly, the training programme must increase in complexity and demand in order to continue this improvement (Whaley *et al.*, 2006; Wilmore *et al.*, 2008). It is vital that an increase in training volume occurs at the right time and at the right level for the performer in order to maximize training benefit. For example, in strength training programmes there would be an increase in the weight lifted, or in an endurance session the rest period would be reduced.

Variation

Most adaptations are completed within the first two weeks of a new training demand (Stone *et al.*, 2007) – that is to say, there is little training benefit associated with repeating practices and tasks. If a training programme is not regularly revised, then the athlete begins to get bored and demotivated. As constant repetition of a practice or training task reduces motivation, the coach must implement a variety of training tasks into practice schedules.

Recovery

The quicker an athlete is able to recover from training and competition, the quicker they are able to return to training (Bompa, 1999); this means that the athlete is able to train more in order to achieve adaptations and excellence in performance. Although training provides the stimulus, adaptations occur during rest following training, which makes recovery an essential element of training (Brewer, 2005). Accordingly, rest and recovery need to be incorporated into the training regime. Rate of recovery is influenced by a number of factors that are both intrinsic and extrinsic: age, experience, gender, environmental factors, flexibility, type of exercise, psychological factors, and efficiency of energy transfer have all been cited as factors influencing recovery (Bompa, 1999).

The effective coach will ensure that all training programmes devised apply these training principles to ensure that a suitable training load is prescribed for the performer. Alongside this, the coach must communicate effectively with the performer to devise, monitor and evaluate all aspects of the training programme.

PLANNING AND PERIODIZATION

Periodization is a widely used concept in designing training programmes. The concept of periodization embraces a purposeful, methodological approach to training which attempts to achieve optimal levels of training and avoid over-training through balancing the training components of volume and intensity (Bompa and Carrera, 2005). If excessive physical demands are avoided then an athlete is able to experience muscular strength and growth, but if they are not, then stress placed upon the body can lead to tissue damage, disease and death (Bompa, 1999: Cross and Lyle, 1999).

In order to achieve this, training programmes are divided into separate training periods, with each encompassing different goals and training methods. Each period is designed to maximize the gains in the various components of performance, and will contain training loads that are calculated with appropriate regeneration/recovery periods. To achieve this systematic, progressive and integrated training programme, the principles governing

Figure 10.5 Getting the most from a training programme. (Courtesy of Team Northumbria)

the process of periodization must be applied. Periodization will ensure that an individual's training is co-ordinated to allow them to achieve a peak performance for the key competitions. Overall, periodization applies the principle of 'overload – recovery – peaking' in order to maximize performance.

The Successful Coach

A successful coach will:

- Plan systematically to ensure organized training and preparation
- Consider the work and study commitments of each athlete
- Consider performances in fitness tests and previous competition
- Integrate all of the performance factors into the training programme
- Divide the training year into a group of fluid and overlapping training periods
- Relate the training periods to the individual's needs, stage of development and timing of key competitions
- Prioritize competitions and ensure that peaking occurs for the major competition(s)

Training should be organized and planned in advance of a competition or performance. It should consider the athlete's potential, physical testing performances, competition results, and the competition calendar. Periodic training divides the training calendar into three types of cycle: microcycle, mesocycle and macrocycle (McMorris and Hale, 2006). The microcycle is usually one week in length; the mesocycle is typically a month, but can be anything between two weeks and a few months; a macrocycle refers to the overall training period, usually represented by a season (one year). There are also longer cycles: Olympic macrocycles invariably cover four or eight years in order to peak for one competition.

The Macrocycle

'Macrocycle' refers to the overall training period, and builds towards peaking for the major goal of the season. Some sports with many fixtures during the competitive season may require multiple peaking (football, rugby and netball, for example), whereas other sports may require just one peak (athletics, boxing and gymnastics). Bompa (1999) suggests that a macrocycle should be broken down into three main training phases: preparation, competition and transition (recovery period).

Preparation Phase
During this initial phase the individual will prepare for the demands of the competition phase. This phase is further divided into the general preparation period (GPP) and the specific preparation period (SPP). In the GPP the focus is on general physical conditioning, and this is also where the foundations are established in all components of performance. The athlete will work at a low intensity in training, but will complete several high volume sessions. A coach should complete a review of the previous season, and from this, identify the needs of the performer in terms of the technical and tactical work to be addressed in this phase. For example, a player in netball may be required to break down and master a particular passing technique or method of getting free.

The player will progress to the SPP, where more sport-specific training is carried out at a greater intensity. This phase represents the transition from general conditioning to more competition-specific training, where the technical and tactical skills are worked on. The SPP is shorter than the GPP, and throughout the preparation period the volume of training will progressively decrease as the intensity of training increases. Here the performer will practise the technical and tactical skills under an increased amount of pressure, and begin to develop their tactical understanding. A coach must ensure that game plans are practised and refined in this phase – for example, defending the centre pass to goal.

Competition Phase
The main objective in this phase is gradually to develop peak performance. As the main competition period approaches training needs to be tapered in order to peak for the main competition. Here the training volume decreases and a coach will engage the performer in simulation activities which replicate the competition conditions. As the competition phase progresses the emphasis is on more sport-specific training. During this phase, the coach should ensure that the focus is on the strengths of a performer and the team

as opposed to reviewing the areas requiring development. In terms of the technical and tactical aspects of performance it is vital in this phase that the players fine tune match strategies in relation to their opposition's strengths and weaknesses.

Transition or Recovery Phase

This phase occurs at the end of the competition period and is a period of active rest. The main focus of this phase is recovery and recuperation following a demanding competition phase. The individual is given the opportunity to recover both mentally and physically from the demands of the competition schedule. Active rest is recommended where the individual will take part in low intensity activity (such as swimming and cycling) to prevent a complete loss of fitness. The length of this phase is dependent upon the duration of the competition phase.

Mesocycle

Mesocycles are sub-divisions of the macrocycles and often span a period of two to six weeks. Several mesocycles make up a training phase, each having their own specified objectives which ensure a progressive programme of training. Each mesocycle differs in content in terms of tasks, structure, forms of training and load (Galvin and Ledger, 2003). A mesocycle may be itemized as follows:

Phase:	Specific preparation period (mesocycle 2a)
Duration:	3 weeks
Sessions per week:	4 (taper in week 3 for adaptation)
Work-to-rest ratio:	1:4
Fitness priorities:	Anaerobic: short-court interval sprints (45–70sec)
	Strength: hypertrophy and general strength
	Speed/agility: short acceleration/reaction to stimulus.

Microcycle

The microcycle is a training period, and in game-based sports spans a seven-day period as this is the amount of time between fixtures and where technical and tactical work can take place (Brewer, 2005). A microcycle outlines in detail information regarding specific training activities, intensity and volume.

In summary, it is vital that the coach has the underpinning scientific knowledge to plan and integrate fitness programmes within the relevant phases of the macrocycle.

11

Sport-Specific Fitness Testing in Squash

by Dr Mick Wilkinson

INTRODUCTION

The challenge for coaches and scientists aiming to improve performance is to identify those factors that determine performance, and to accurately monitor the success of interventions designed to optimize those determinants. Performance determinants can be tactical, technical, psychological and physiological. Fitness assessment is concerned with identifying, monitoring and profiling strengths and weaknesses in physiological factors important for performance.

What Makes a Good Fitness Test?

Specificity, validity, reproducibility and sensitivity are the criteria that fitness tests should satisfy (Winter *et al.*, 2007, Müller *et al.*, 2000, NCF, 1995). Sport-specific procedures should reflect intensities of exercise and their duration, involved muscles, muscle activity, forces and metabolic demands of match play (Winter *et al.*, 2007). The use of non-specific procedures can produce inaccurate physiological profiles and misinterpretations of strengths, weaknesses and adaptations resulting from training.

ASSESSING FITNESS FOR SQUASH

Squash is a multiple-sprint sport, where success depends on physical, technical, tactical and motor skills (Lees, 2003). Match play imposes diverse physiological demands on cardio-pulmonary endurance, muscle endurance, explosive strength, speed and flexibility (Sharp, 1998). The assessment of player capabilities in these physiological factors is a challenge because of the unique and varied movement patterns of the game. However, test specificity is important to ensure validity and sensitivity of procedures, to better enable coaches and scientists to build accurate profiles of player strengths and weaknesses, and for subsequent assessment of the success of interventions (Müller *et al.*, 2000, Winter *et al.*, 2007).

SQUASH-SPECIFIC FITNESS TESTS

Endurance

Although several groups are working in this area, only three previous studies designed to assess the validity of on-court squash-specific protocols for assessment purposes have been published (Steininger and Wodick, 1987; Girard *et al.*, 2005). The procedure of Steininger and Wodick (1987) was devised to mimic the physiological demands and techniques specific to squash movement, but in clearly defined increments to allow the assessment of squash-specific endurance fitness. However, while movement patterns created by the test clearly replicated those of squash play, no account was made for the randomness of true squash movement. The predictable sequence of movements used means the player must only travel *through* the T area *en route* to the next court position.

In contrast, match play is characterized by uncertainty about movement direction. Furthermore, the muscular demands of random movement are likely to be much greater, and different from movement that is predictable. The ability of muscle to accomplish unanticipated changes in direction and speed is a crucial performance characteristic in squash (Behm, 1994), but is likely to go undetected by a test in which movement sequences are predictable.

The squash-specific test described by Girard *et al.* (2005) overcomes the limitations of Steininger and Wodick's test by including uncertainty of movement direction. It does so by means of specialized software on a computer placed at the front centre of the court, a visual stimulus directing players to a particular location on court. However, it should be acknowledged that squash players also make use of auditory stimuli during match play such as the sound of the ball from the wall and an opponent's racket to judge movement direction and speed.

Both studies compared the responses of élite squash players in squash-specific incremental tests and laboratory-based treadmill incremental tests, and showed that higher maximal oxygen uptake was achieved by squash players on the squash-specific tests. Furthermore, both studies also reported strong correlations between player rank and maximum performance (time to exhaustion) on the squash-specific tests, demonstrating the validity of the sport-specific protocols.

Wilkinson *et al.* (2009a and 2009b) described the validation and reproducibility of a squash-specific incremental test using auditory stimuli and random movement patterns. Trained squash players achieved higher maximal oxygen uptake (directly measured via a portable telemetric analyser) on the squash-specific test than on a laboratory treadmill test, while satisfying criteria for the attainment of maximal oxygen uptake to the same extent in both tests. Furthermore, regarding endurance performance (time to exhaustion) the test discriminated between squash players and trained distance runners with similar test-specific maximal oxygen uptake, supporting the specificity of endurance fitness in squash (St Clair Gibson *et al.*, 1998; Girard *et al.*, 2005) and confirming the validity of the squash-specific test. Moreover, endurance performance, maximal oxygen uptake and maximum heart rate were all reproducible, highlighting the sensitivity of the test for monitoring players. Unpublished data collected by the author has also shown that maximal oxygen uptake and endurance performance from the incremental test correlated well with the playing standard in sub-élite squash players. Figure 11.1 shows a squash player performing the incremental fitness test of Wilkinson *et al.* (2009a).

Change-of-Direction Speed

The importance and specificity of aerobic fitness in squash has been discussed and demonstrated above. However, in common with other racket sports, multiple-sprint ability and the ability to change direction at speed are also important determinants of performance in squash (Lees, 2003; Sharp, 1998; Behm, 1992). Squash movements are characterized by rapid accelerations and decelerations over short distances and involve frequent turning, lunging and side-stepping (Eubank and Messenger, 2000; Vučković *et al.*, 2004). A recent match analysis study reported that more than 40 per cent of squash movements occurred within 1m of the court's T-position, and most movements were not in a straight line (Vučković *et al.*, 2004).

Figure 11.1 A participant completing the squash-specific incremental test. (Courtesy of Mick Wilkinson)

The use of on-court sprint drills encompassing multiple-direction changes (ghosting) by élite-standard squash players reflects the recognition that speed training must be undertaken in sport-specific movement patterns (Sharp, 1998). This is supported by findings that straight-line sprint training does not improve sprint performance involving changes of direction (Young *et al.*, 2001). The specific movement patterns of squash provide a unique challenge to physiologists attempting to assess squash-specific explosive capabilities, and suggest that tests should encompass the ability to change direction at speed.

Despite the documented importance of explosive capabilities, a squash-specific test of this aspect of fitness has only recently been developed (Wilkinson *et al.*, 2009c). Figure 11.2 shows the author performing the squash-specific change-of-direction speed test.

Results of the study showed that squash-specific test performance correlated with player rank ($\rho = 0.8$, $P < 0.01$) in a group of trained county-standard squash players. In contrast, there was no correlation ($\rho = 0.43$, $P = 0.21$) between rank and performance of the squash players on the non-specific Illinois Agility Run, a widely used field-based test of change-of-direction speed. Moreover, the squash players outperformed trained footballers of equivalent competitive standard on the squash-specific test, yet the two groups had almost identical performances on the Illinois Agility Run. The difference in squash-specific test performance between the two groups suggests that squash training and the associated skill in squash-specific movements conferred a performance advantage on a test involving repeated changes of direction at speed over short distances, as is required in squash.

Figure 11.2 The author performing the squash-specific change-of-direction speed test. (Courtesy of Mick Wilkinson)

The Illinois Agility Run, where squash players and non-squash players possessed similar capabilities, involves four straight sprints of 10m and weaving around four cones. The squash-specific test in contrast possesses no straight sprints, but instead comprises several lateral movements of short distances requiring rapid and forceful changes of direction. Squash players spend much time training in these movement patterns to improve court coverage and movement speed (Sharp, 1998; Sherman *et al.*, 2004; Todd *et al.*, 1998). The superior performance of the squash players in their habitual movement patterns shown in the study of Wilkinson *et al.* (2009c) provides evidence for the specific nature of change-of-direction speed. The lack of correlation between the performance of the squash players on the Illinois and the squash-specific tests in the study provides further evidence for the specificity of change-of-direction speed.

Multiple-Sprint Ability

Multiple-sprint ability is acknowledged as an important component of squash fitness, along with endurance and the ability to change direction at speed (Lees, 2003; Sharp, 1998; Vučković *et al.*, 2004). The preceding sections have examined the validity and reproducibility of squash-specific tests designed to assess aerobic fitness and change-of-direction speed, and have also demonstrated the specificity of these factors. Physiological profiling requires that all aspects of fitness important for performance are assessed to build a complete picture of player strengths and weaknesses.

Various field-based tests of multiple-sprint ability have been developed (Tumilty *et al.*, 1988; Dawson *et al.*, 1991; Baker *et al.*, 1993; Fitzsimons *et al.*, 1993; Wadley and Le Rossignol, 1998), including procedures specific to soccer (Bangsbo, 1994), basketball (Castagna *et al.*, 2007) and hockey (Boddington *et al.*, 2004). However, with the exception of the 5m MST of Boddington *et al.* (2004), the validity of these multiple-sprint ability tests has been poorly considered. Furthermore, the specificity of change-of-direction speed (Young *et al.*, 2001), an important element in a test of multiple-sprint ability, questions the application of these procedures to sports other than those for which they were designed.

Recently, the author developed and validated a squash-specific test of multiple-sprint ability (unpublished data). The performance of county-standard squash and football players was compared on a squash-specific test and the non-specific Baker's 8 × 40m sprint test. The squash-specific test comprised ten all-out sprints (the duration of which matched the range of average rally lengths) in squash-specific patterns of movement, separated by 20sec recovery (the average rest period from match play analysis). Baker's test comprises 40m straight sprints starting from the middle of a 20m course, with 180-degree direction changes after 10m and 30m. Sprints are separated by 20sec recoveries. In both tests, performance was recorded as the sum of the times for the individual sprints.

Despite similar non-sport-specific multiple-sprint ability assessed on Baker's test, squash players outperformed non-squash players on a test of multiple-sprint ability that used squash-specific movements. Moreover, a positive correlation between squash player rank and performance on the squash-specific test ($\rho = 0.8$, $P = 0.02$) showed that the test discriminated ability in a group of squash players. The absence of correlation between squash-player rank and performance on Baker's test ($\rho = 0.5$, $P = 0.16$) suggests it was an insensitive measure for squash players. The ability of the squash-specific test to discriminate both between groups with similar non sport-specific multiple-sprint ability and in squash players demonstrates the value and validity of the test.

SUMMARY

Sport-specific testing is important for the accurate prescription of training, talent identification and tracking of training-induced adaptations (Müller *et al.*, 2000). Endurance, multiple-sprint capability and the ability to change direction at speed are important determinants of performance in squash (Lees, 2003; Sharp, 1998; Behm, 1992), therefore, valid and reliable squash-specific tests that examine these capabilities are useful additions to existing test batteries for squash players. The results of the studies reviewed in this chapter suggest that squash-specific tests discriminate ability in squash players and between squash and non-squash players better than non-specific tests, and that they are sufficiently reproducible for monitoring changes in fitness.

The specific nature of test performances in squash players suggests that procedures replicating the movements and physiological demands of match play are better for assessing player strengths and weaknesses than non-specific procedures. This is in keeping with the training principle of specificity, and suggests a move away from traditional, non-specific- lab- and field-based fitness tests for optimal profiling, talent identification and monitoring of training intervention success.

12

The Role and Importance of Sport Psychology

by Dr Elizabeth Partington and
Dr Sarah Partington

WHAT IS SPORT PSYCHOLOGY?

There are many definitions regarding what sport psychology is, and what sport psychologists do (Le Unes and Nation, 2002). Definitions of sport psychology range from the study of people's behaviour in sport and exercise settings (Gill, 2000) to the study of the psychology of performance enhancement in sport performance (Andersen, 2000). As Andersen (2000) points out, the definition of sport psychology that one espouses will shape one's answer to the question of what it is that sport psychologists do. Some sport psychologists may focus purely on assisting the coach and athlete to enhance performance via mental skills training programmes, whilst others may take a broader remit, addressing the overall psychological well-being of the coach and athlete.

Coaches and sport psychologists have a long history of collaboration. According to Williams and Straub (2006), coaches were interested in sport psychology before the discipline was even formally recognized – as far back as the 1920s coaches were using pep talks to psych up their athletes. Sport psychology has its origins in the field of physical education, and originally research interest was focused around motor learning. In later years this was extended to include motivation, team cohesion and personality (Williams and Straub, 2006). Coleman Griffith, the 'grandfather' of sport psychology in the USA, was the first to carry out sport psychology research, and in 1925 was hired by the University of Illinois to help coaches improve the athletic performance of their players (Williams and Straub, 2006).

Initially the practice of sport psychology was restricted to the enhancement of sport performance (Gardner and Moore, 2004). In more recent years it has been suggested that performance enhancement is only one area in which sport psychologists could potentially operate, and that they should take a more holistic view of the athlete (Bond, 2001). During his work with the Australian Institute of Sport (AIS), Bond developed a multidimensional programme that was felt to reflect the needs of both athletes and coaches (Bond, 2001). In his paper, Bond argues that in treating only performance issues and delivering only performance enhancement techniques we are operating on a superficial level. We are selling both ourselves and our athletes (and coaches) short.

Bond (2001) suggests a continuum of psychological service delivery, with an increasing requirement for specialized psychological training as you progress through the continuum. The first level of Bond's (2001) continuum is performance enhancement training. This involves service delivery traditionally associated with sport psychology, such as arousal control training, concentration training, imagery and mental preparation. Level two is personal development training, which might include training in communication skills, leadership, conflict resolution and even media skills training. The third level, lifestyle management, involves helping the athlete to develop time management skills, providing educational and career planning and balancing relationships/family with sporting commitments. The fourth level, group and team dynamics, includes team structure and function, team communication and team cohesion. At the fifth level Bond introduces what he terms critical interventions. These are the types of intervention that have traditionally been the domain of the clinical psychologist; examples include interventions for depression, disordered eating, substance abuse, grief and trauma. At the final level, applied research, Bond offers both qualitative and quantitative investigation of relevant issues.

Although the multifaceted continuum described by Bond might be appealing to a coach looking to engage the services of a sport psychologist, a word of caution is necessary. Guidance is required regarding the extent to which a particular sport psychologist has undergone the appropriate training, and whether he/she has sufficient experience to consult within a particular domain or knows when to refer to other specialists (Gardner and Moore, 2004). What this means for sport psychology is that there needs to be careful consideration of the role of the sport psychologist and the competencies required to perform certain tasks. These considerations should be reflected in the professional training pathways of sport psychologists. What this means for the coach is that the qualifications and training of a sport psychologist should be considered carefully before their services are engaged.

Bond (2001) recognizes this concern himself, and suggests that whilst performance enhancement training requires appropriate teaching skills, it does not require the same level of psychological training and competence as would be demanded of a sport psychologist working within the critical interventions category. In fact Bond (2001) argues that the teaching of basic performance enhancement skills does not need to be the exclusive domain of the sport psychologist, and he goes so far as to suggest that this is a role that coaches, with the appropriate training, could fulfil. Whether delivered

Figure 12.1 A Commonwealth Games medallist recognizes the importance of perform-ance enhancement training. (Courtesy of Northumbria University)

by a coach or a sport psychologist, it is clear that the teaching of basic performance enhancement skills has a role to play in producing perform-ance excellence.

CONCEPTUALIZING EXCELLENCE

A review of literature encompassing studies on expert athletic performance suggests that certain factors can play a significant role in its development. These factors are multifaceted and include effective training, effective coaching, parental support, enjoyment, effective recovery, innate ability and psychological skills. Such factors were found to be important in not only the development but also the maintenance of expert performance across all stages of an athletic career (Durrand-Bush and Salmela, 2002).

Greenleaf *et al.* (2001) looking specifically at the Olympics found that factors affecting Olympic performance were also multifaceted. Issues highlighted include departing from normal routine, media distractions, attitude towards the Games, support services and facilitation, mental skills and preparation, and Olympic excitement. In addition, factors such as coaching, injury and over-training and team unity were also found to play a role. What is clear from these studies is that successful élite per-formance is made up of a complex interaction of a variety of factors.

Focusing specifically on psychological/mental skills, Williams and Krane (2001) have produced an extensive review of research. Examination of the studies included in this review highlights that a variety of methodologies have been employed. Some studies include large sample questionnaire-based methods, whilst others have used small group interviews. In terms of who has been studied, again there is a variety, this variety relating to perceptions of what constitutes successful élite performance. Some researchers have studied athletes who have gained Olympic selection (Orlick and Partington, 1988; Vernacchia *et al.*, 2000), while others have limited their sample to athletes who have won Olympic medals (Gould *et al.*, 2002).

In a similar vein, some studies have looked only at successful athletes (Durand-Bush and Salmela, 2002), whilst others have drawn comparisons between Olympic qualifiers and randomly selected athletes (Ungerleider and Golding, 1992), or between Olympians who lived up to expectations in terms of performance achievement and those who did not (Greenleaf *et al.*, 2001). The rationale behind such 'comparison studies' is the identification of key differences between the groups in terms of their psychological skills.

To add to the diversity, some studies have only included athletes in their samples (Vernacchia *et al.*, 2000), whilst others have also sought the views of coaches, parents and significant others (Gould *et al.*, 2002). Athletes from a range of sports have been included – for example, participants from both summer and winter Olympic Games (Orlick and Partington, 1988).

Despite the diversity of samples, the findings of these studies have been consistent. Taken together, the findings indicate that successful athletes are able to cope with and control their levels of anxiety, have high levels of motivation and commitment, can cope with distractions and unexpected events, and have high levels of self-confidence (Gould *et al.*, 2002; Orlick and Partington, 1998; Vernacchia *et al.*, 2000; Williams and Krane, 2001). In addition, these athletes are able to set goals effectively, have well developed plans, and use visualization during their training and preparation (Williams and Krane, 2001). They demonstrate resiliency, competitiveness, a good work ethic, are coachable, optimistic, and demonstrate adaptive perfectionism and sport intelligence (Gould *et al.*, 2002). Finally, it has been suggested that successful athletes are able to focus on the process rather than the outcome of performance (Durand-Bush and Salmela, 2001).

Having identified the psychological skills considered to be important, a key role of the sport psychologist is to help athletes to develop those skills. While there are specific intervention strategies that can be employed (which will be discussed in the next chapter), the start point is to identify the athlete's current psychological strengths and weaknesses. From there, targeted interventions can be applied.

To this end, a variety of psychological profiling tools have been generated to enable athletes and coaches to recognize psychological strengths and weaknesses. Some of these tools are questionnaires, which enable an athlete to score themselves on their mental skills and compare them to norm scores in order to ascertain whether they are scoring high or low. Other tools are more qualitative in nature, incorporating interview or observational methods. A brief review of such tools follows.

PROFILING TOOLS

General Tools

The Psychological Skills Inventory for Sports (PSIS – Mahoney, Gabriel and Perkins, 1987) is a single measure to assess overall psychological skills. Skills assessed include anxiety control, concentration, confidence, mental preparation, motivation and team focus. When administered to élite and non-élite athletes, it was found that the questionnaire could discriminate between these two groups, with the élite athletes exhibiting better psychological skills. Two similar questionnaires are the Sport-Related Psychological Skills Questionnaire (SPSQ – Nelson and Hardy, 1990), and the Athletic Coping Skills Inventory-28 (ACSI-28 – Smith *et al.*, 1995). The latter has also been found to be able to discriminate between groups, with over-achievers exhibiting better psychological skills than normal/under-achievers.

A rather different assessment tool is Butler and Hardy's 'Performance Profile' (Butler and Hardy, 1992). Based on Kelly's 'Personal Construct Theory', the underpinning philosophy of this tool is that coaches and athletes often view performance in different ways, and that each individual has their own unique understanding of their situation. Kelly felt that when understanding behaviour, the therapist (in this case the sport psychologist or coach) would be more useful as a 'skilled mirror' than as an expert – that is, not providing the answers, but acting as a sounding board to enable the athlete to find the answers for themselves. Performance profiling encourages the athlete to generate the psychological constructs that they feel are key, and which they wish to be measured against. The athlete then allocates him/herself a numerical score on each construct (usually out of ten) in order to complete a psychological profile of strengths and weaknesses.

Specific Inventories

Before discussing some of the best known inventories, it is important to recognize that some are trait measures whilst others are state measures. 'Trait' relates to personal or personality characteristics, while 'state' relates to how an individual responds to a particular situation. In essence, trait is how someone 'generally' feels, while state is how someone feels 'right now'.

The ability to control anxiety has been identified as a key element of performance excellence. The Sport Competition Anxiety Test (SCAT – Martens, 1977) measures a construct known as 'competitive trait anxiety', which assesses whether the athlete generally perceives competition as a threat or a challenge. While the SCAT has been a much used anxiety measure, it has recently been superseded by the Sport Anxiety Scale (SAS – Smith, Smoll and Schutz, 1990). The SAS serves the same purpose as the SCAT, but is more sophisticated in that it measures both cognitive (mental) and somatic (physical) symptoms of anxiety.

One of the key measures of state anxiety is the DM-CSAI-2 (Jones and Swain, 1992). This inventory measures cognitive anxiety, somatic anxiety and self-confidence, and in addition to assessing levels of anxiety and self-confidence, it also enables the athlete to assess how happy they are with the levels they are experiencing; thus two athletes may have the same level of somatic anxiety, but one may perceive this level to be facilitative to performance, whilst the other might view it as debilitative. It has been found that élite performers tend to view their anxiety symptoms as being facilitative (Jones and Swain, 1995).

Motivation has also been found to be a key component of performance. The Task and Ego Orientation in Sport Questionnaire (TEOSQ – Duda and Nicholls, 1992) measures whether athletes judge their success based on personal improvement (task orientation), or on how they compare to others (ego orientation). It has been suggested that an athlete who is predominantly ego-oriented may hold the belief that ability is a key determinant of success. This belief system can lead an athlete with low perceived competence to lack motivation and demonstrate maladaptive achievement behaviour (Duda and Treasure, 2006).

A further measure can be taken as to whether the athlete is intrinsically motivated – that is, doing the activity for the activity itself – or extrinsically motivated – performing the activity in order to gain something external (usually monetary rewards or prizes). Whilst external rewards can be motivating in the short term, problems can occur when the reward is taken away. In addition, some athletes find external rewards controlling. The Intrinsic Motivation Inventory (IMI – McAuley *et al.*, 1989) is one way of measuring an athlete's level of intrinsic motivation.

Other questionnaires that can be used to measure aspects of motivation are the Perception of Success Questionnaire (POSQ – Roberts *et al.*, 1998) and the Will to Win (WW – Pezer and Brown, 1980). The POSQ was designed specifically in the context of sport, and recognizes the uniqueness of the sport environment. The competitive orientation subscale is based upon the desire to be superior to other athletes. The task orientation subscale focuses upon the achievement of personal goals (Fogarty *et al.*, 2006). The WW measures the desire to defeat an opponent, so the performance – for example, the score, time or distance achieved – is much less important than winning. Winning is very important to those who score highly on this questionnaire (Fogarty *et al.*, 2006).

Self-confidence measures can be split into those that measure global self-confidence – for example, the Trait Sport Confidence Inventory and the State Sport Confidence Inventory (Vealey, 1986) – and those that measure self-efficacy (task-specific self-confidence), for example, the micro-analytic technique (Bandura, 1977). Whilst self-confidence measures are similar to other inventories, the micro-analytic technique requires the athlete to make a judgement regarding the degree of difficulty of the task that they believe they can perform successfully. A graded list of levels of the task is compiled – for example, if the task is netball shooting, it could be the number of goals scored, ranging from one to twenty. The athlete would then answer 'yes' or 'no' in terms of whether they were capable of reaching each level.

Next for those levels they felt they could reach, the performer is asked to rate how certain they are that they will successfully reach the level. This is usually done on a scale of 1 (very weak) to 100 (very strong), using ten-point values. Because self-efficacy is task specific, a separate measure must be constructed for every skill – for example pass, footwork, movement and so on. However, the generality of self-efficacy can be assessed by counting the number of tasks in which individuals believe they are capable of successful performance.

Concentration can be assessed in a variety of ways, but thought sampling (Boutcher and Rotella, 1987) is considered to be one of the most valid (Moran and Summers, 2004). In essence the athlete is asked to record the thoughts they have during their sporting activity, and a content analysis is then performed to establish attentional focus during performance. To gain a trait measure of concentration, the 'Test of Attentional and Interpersonal Style' (TAIS – Nideffer, 1976) can be employed. The TAIS gives a measure of an individual's preferred attentional style, letting a coach know whether an athlete is most comfortable dealing with small amounts of information at a time, or is able to cope with lots of information at once. In addition, information can be gained as to whether an athlete predominantly adopts an internal focus (focused on his/her own thoughts) or an external focus (focused on the situation around them). The athlete's preferred attentional style can then be compared to the attentional demands of their competitive environment to ascertain under what conditions they are likely to shine or struggle.

Observation and Interview

Systematic observation (De Marco *et al.*, 1996) is a method that provides an objective means of identifying and categorizing athletes' behaviours. Variability in an individual's performance can be identified, and target behaviours monitored and assessed. Behavioural checklists can be used to record single or multiple behaviours, and assessment can be completed by the sport psychologist or by the athlete as a form of self-monitoring (Tkachuk *et al.*, 2003). One advantage of behavioural assessment is that it looks beyond personality characteristics to incorporate the impact of the environment on an athlete's behavior (Tkachuk *et al.*, 2003). Sport-specific behavioural checklists have been developed for twenty-one different sports (*see* Martin *et al.*, 1997). The criteria on these checklists are based on the performance excellence literature discussed earlier in the chapter.

Sport psychology as a discipline is perhaps less formal than clinical or counselling psychology in terms of the type of interviews carried out between psychologist and client (Andersen, 2000). Whilst some consultations with athletes can be carried out in an office/consulting room, much information gathering is done on a more informal basis, for example, a five-minute conversation on the way to a match, or a brief remark made during a training session. From a more formal perspective, Taylor and Schneider's (1992) Sport Clinical Intake Protocol (SCIP) can provide a guide for athlete interviews. Regardless of whether an interview is formal or informal, the key aim of the sport psychologist is to get an athlete to 'open up' by demonstrating empathy, encouragement and interest (Andersen, 2000).

HOW DO PSYCHOLOGICAL SKILLS ISSUES PRESENT?

Having discussed various ways in which a sport psychologist might elicit information from an athlete regarding their psychological skills, we will now look at the way performance enhancement issues may present in real-world settings.

Example Case Study

Luke is a rugby union player for a Division One team. He is one of the senior players and has played as hooker for the team for the last three years. Until recently he was one of the most successful players on the team, and received much acclaim for his skilful and courageous tackling. Six months ago, however, he suffered a quite traumatic neck/shoulder injury while in the scrum, and although physically recovered, his level of play has not returned to his pre-injury achievements. Luke finds that when he is in a scrum his mind wanders back to the occasion he was injured, and he worries about the same thing happening again. He feels that although the doctor has told him that he is fully healed, his shoulder is not as strong as it used to be, and it will not hold up to scrums and tackles. Because of this he feels nervous in contact situations and holds back, and he is finding that because he is not the 'star' he used to be, he is not enjoying his rugby any more and is now thinking about quitting the sport.

What is noticeable in Luke's case is that a range of psychological issues are presenting and interacting. For example, he is lacking motivation and is thinking about quitting the sport, his concentration is not optimal as his mind is wandering, and his anxiety is high as he is fearful of re-injury. Thus at the heart of the issue is a lack of confidence: whilst he used to be renowned for his tackling, he is no longer confident in his physical ability, and taking the issues one by one, it is clear that his lack of confidence is causing him to worry and feel anxious. Worrying thoughts are making him hold back and are affecting his concentration, taking his focus off the game. The end result is that he is not playing as well as he used to, and is therefore becoming disillusioned with the sport and wants to quit.

This case study demonstrates not only that it is important to look for causes as well as looking at symptoms, but also that psychological issues can interact in different and complex ways.

In each of the following two scenarios identify what you think the athlete's issues are. More than one issue may be apparent. Highlight all the issues, and then try to work out which issue is the cause, and which issues are merely symptoms of the underlying problem. What is the interaction between the psychological issues?

Scenario One

Tamsin is a talented netball player who performs extremely well in her national team competitions. She is an extremely committed player who always stays late after training to put in extra practice hours. Her dream is to play for England, just as her mother and older sister have done before her, and she has given up studying for a law degree in order to devote more time to her netball. Her parents are helping her out financially, as they, too, would love her to get her England cap, and her coach is giving her some private coaching sessions to boost her chances.

Tamsin does not want to let down her family, her coach or herself. She had an England trial last year, which did not go as well as she had hoped. She found that when on court she could not stop worrying about performing everything perfectly and not letting herself down. Her muscles felt tense, and she lost her sense of timing and co-ordination, and fumbled some passes. In addition, as she was worrying about her own performance, she missed some important cues and found herself caught out of position a couple of times in the game. She is worried that the same thing might happen at her next trial.

Answer to Scenario One

The issues are high expectations coupled with a poor performance in a previous trial, which have led to worrying thoughts, and these thoughts have led to high levels of muscle tension. Both of these issues have resulted in loss of timing and co-ordination and fumbled passes. In addition, worrying thoughts are affecting Tamsin's ability to concentrate on the game, resulting in her being caught out of position.

- The underlying cause is cognitive anxiety (negative and worrying thoughts due to high performance expectations). These negative thoughts are causing somatic anxiety (muscle tension) and concentration problems.

Answer to Scenario Two

The issues are that Ben drifts off during the early stages of games and then gets caught out of position. Having been caught out of position, he then experiences feelings of panic, and is frantic to redeem himself. Because he is panicking and feels tense, he then makes further mistakes.

- The underlying cause is a concentration problem. Lapses in concentration result in mistakes being made, and these mistakes cause both somatic anxiety (muscle tension) and cognitive anxiety (negative thoughts and panic).

Scenario Two

Ben is a hockey player currently in his fourth year of playing national league. His team this year is very strong, and they tend to take an early lead at the beginning of games, with lots of attacking play. As a defender, Ben finds the early stages of games are fairly easy for him and sometimes he finds himself drifting off and thinking about other things. However, on a couple of occasions the opposing team has made a quick break and Ben has been caught out of position and has ultimately contributed to the opposition scoring a goal. Once this has happened Ben is frantic to redeem himself, but there is never really enough time left in the game. He feels tense, and starts over-hitting or giving away free hits. He wants to sort out his play before he is demoted to the second team.

SUMMARY

Once psychological skills issues have been identified, the athlete, coach and sport psychologist can work together to design and implement a mental skills training programme. In the following chapter we will explore how a sport psychologist could help athletes such as Luke, Tamsin and Ben.

13

Sport Psychology Interventions

by Dr Sarah Partington and Dr Elizabeth Partington

The previous chapter established the importance of training in psychological skills, and demonstrated how to carry out a needs analysis. This chapter will show you how to progress from a needs analysis to designing and implementing an intervention programme.

There are various psychological interventions that can be applied in order to enhance performance (Greenspan and Feltz, 1989). Thelwell *et al.* (2008) point out that although the Test of Performance Strategies (Thomas *et al.*, 1999) questionnaire measures a total of eight psychological strategies, the focus of sport psychologists has tended to be self-talk, relaxation, imagery and goal setting. This chapter will be based upon these four key interventions.

SELF-TALK

Whenever an athlete talks to themselves either overtly or covertly, they are engaging in self-talk (Johnson *et al.*, 2004). Self-talk can aid skill acquisition, enhance motivation, and ensure that attention is focused appropriately, and can also be used to alter mood (Johnson *et al.*, 2004). Although some studies have shown that negative self-talk can be motivational for some individuals (Hardy *et al.*, 2001), sports psychologists generally promote positive self-talk because negative self-talk can be anxiety-provoking and may damage confidence (Dagrou *et al.*, 1992).

It has been suggested that self-talk has two main functions: cognitive and motivational (Hardy *et al.*, 2001). Cognitive self-talk is instructional in nature and can be further broken down into skill development and skill execution. Motivational self-talk can be categorized into mastery (to increase levels of confidence), arousal (to psych up or relax), and drive (to maintain or increase effort and motivation). The type of self-talk used should be matched to task demands (Hardy *et al.*, 2001).

Rogerson and Hrycaiko (2002) suggest that the theoretical mechanisms for the effects of self-talk are grounded in the concepts of attention and information processing. Theodorakis *et al.* (2000) claim that self-talk activates mental processes to influence existing thought patterns. Self-talk is thought to enhance performance, because focusing on the desired thought leads to the desired action (Landin and Herbert, 1999).

It is not enough to eliminate or suppress the unwanted thought: for self-talk to be effective these troublesome thoughts must be replaced with thoughts that are more appropriate. Work by Dugdale and Eklund (2002) suggests that under certain conditions attempting to suppress an unwanted thought can

---

Self-Talk Programme Example

Stage 1: Cognitive awareness

In order to gain control over their thoughts the athlete must first be aware of the thoughts they are experiencing before, during and post performance. This process is called 'gaining cognitive awareness', and is usually achieved by asking the athlete to keep a self-talk diary or thought log (Bunker *et al.*, 1993). In their diary the athlete is asked to record the thoughts they have been experiencing and the situations that have triggered those thoughts. The log can be completed during breaks in performance, or retrospectively.

Stage 2: Analysis of thought content

The athlete needs to identify which thoughts need to be addressed, and the athlete and the sport psychologist should then go through the diary and identify the key thoughts. Knowing which situations trigger the thoughts can help the athlete in later stages when they are producing replacement task-relevant cue words.

Stage 3: Thought suppression (thought stopping)

Once the negative or unproductive thought is identified it should be suppressed. Suppression is usually done by interrupting the thought with a trigger, which can be 'physical' (clicking the fingers, taking and releasing a breath), 'imaginal' (creating the image of a stop sign) or 'verbal' (saying the word 'stop').

Stage 4: Thought replacement (cue words)

Attention should be redirected to task-relevant cues by asking the athlete to generate some task-appropriate replacement cue words. Cues can be 'motivational' (keep going) or 'instructional' (lengthen the stride), and cue words should be brief and phonetically simple – over-verbalization should be avoided (Landin and Herbert, 1999).

create the opposite effect and make that thought more salient. This is known as ironic-processing theory. Dugdale and Eklund (2002) found that these ironic results could be negated if subjects were instructed to focus on a task-relevant cue word in combination with suppressing the negative thought.

Research has informed the way in which psychologists teach athletes to use self-talk, and most self-talk programmes follow a similar structure. An example self-talk programme is described in the sidebar.

PROGRESSIVE MUSCULAR RELAXATION

When teaching an athlete relaxation, the matching hypothesis suggests that the relaxation intervention should be matched to the predominant symptoms (Davidson and Schwartz, 1976). Thus if the athlete suffers mainly from somatic symptoms of anxiety, then a somatic strategy should be used. Conversely if the symptoms are predominantly cognitive, then a cognitive intervention strategy should be used.

It has been suggested that the matching hypothesis model is too rigid as we have evidence of some cross-over effects (Maynard *et al.*, 1995). What this means is that using a somatic strategy will have some effect on cognitive symptoms, and vice versa. In the light of this, multimodal stress management – combined cognitive and somatic interventions – has been suggested to be the most effective way to deal with competitive anxiety (Maynard *et al.*, 1998). Multimodal packages will be discussed at the end of the chapter; in this section we will focus upon progressive muscular relaxation (Jacobson, 1938).

Progressive muscular relaxation (PMR) is a somatic relaxation strategy; it has been used in clinical settings to aid sleep and reduce epileptic seizures (Griffin *et al.*, 1988; Puskarich *et al.*, 1992). It is thought that the underpinning mechanism for these effects is reduced muscular tension. As athletes often suffer from inappropriate levels of muscular tension during competitive situations, it is not surprising that PMR has been applied in sport – although little research has been conducted on PMR in a sport setting. Research that has been done has tended to look at PMR as part of a multimodal mental skills package (for example, Patrick and Hrycaiko, 1998). This makes it difficult to claim a direct effect of PMR on sports performance.

Despite the lack of substantiated sport research, PMR is a popular sport psychology intervention. The idea is that through repeated pairings of tension and relaxation, relaxation becomes the conditioned (automatic) response to any feelings of tension. PMR training involves the systematic focus of attention on the gross muscle groups in the body. The athlete learns to identify inappropriate levels of tension in those muscles, and to relax them to an appropriate level.

Like a physical skill, PMR is usually learnt over a series of stages, which can be completed separately for different purposes, or they can be combined to create a comprehensive training programme. Applied relaxation programmes using PMR tend to move from deep to momentary relaxation, and use a combination of the PMR stages. Ost's (1988) programme is one example; a further example can be seen in the sidebar.

PMR Programme Example

Stage 1: Active PMR (deep relaxation)

Active PMR is a form of deep relaxation that takes athletes to total relaxation; it should never be completed immediately prior to performance. It is known as 'active' because the athlete is asked to actively (artificially) create tension in the muscles by completing full-out muscle contraction. Full-out contraction is followed by complete relaxation, the aim being to make it as easy as possible for athletes to understand the difference between tension and relaxation.

Stage 2: Differential active PMR

This stage begins to move the athlete towards a more realistic experience of muscular tension. In this stage the athlete reduces the level of muscular contraction so that instead of a full-out contraction being completed, contraction is adjusted to 75 per cent, then 50 per cent, and so on.

Stage 3: Differential relaxation

Instead of performing a full-out relaxation of the muscles following contraction, the athlete begins to reduce the amount by which they release. This is done to progress the athlete towards conditions that more closely resemble the situation they would be in, in their sport. When playing sport, a certain level of muscular relaxation is required, but not all muscles would need to be completely relaxed.

Stage 4: Passive PMR (momentary relaxation)

In passive PMR the athlete is asked to scan the body for inappropriate levels of muscular tension; he/she should then address those muscles where levels of tension are inappropriate with the conditioned relaxation response, relaxing them to the correct level required for effective performance. Ultimately this process can be performed extremely quickly and efficiently. This is known as momentary relaxation because the athlete remains alert and able to perform effectively.

IMAGERY

Imagery is defined as a quasi-sensory/quasi-perceptual experience (Richardson, 1969). It involves using all the senses to create or recreate an experience in the mind (Vealey and Walter, 1993), and is frequently included in psychological skills training packages for improving both skill acquisition and performance (Beauchamp et al., 1996).

Imagery has been found to improve motor skills more than no practice at all (Feltz and Landers, 1983). It has also been found to improve self-confidence (Winters, 1999) and to enhance motivation (Martin and Hall, 1995); however, Greenspan and Feltz (1989) caution that the effects of imagery on performance may be overestimated. It has been argued that much of the early imagery research relies on study designs that do not isolate the pro-gramme elements to identify their relative impact (Wollman, 1986).

In response to early criticisms, Martin *et al.* (1999) developed a model to reduce the numerous imagery-related variables that have been studied in the sport context into the smallest possible set of theoretically meaningful fac-tors. From a comprehensive literature review they identified four key con-structs: imagery type, imagery outcome, sport situation and imagery ability.

Imagery Type

When selecting the type of imagery to use, the goal of the intervention (for example confidence, motivation) should be considered (Pavio, 1985; Suinn, 1996). Initially imagery was described as either positive or negative (Woolfolk *et al.*, 1985), but more recently other types of imagery have been identified (Martin *et al.*, 1999).

Martin *et al.* (1999): Taxonomy of Imagery in Sport

This taxonomy is based upon Paivio's (1985), which was verified by Hall *et al.* (1998):

- Motivation specific imagery (MS): Represents imagery of a spe-cific goal, for example imagining winning a medal
- Motivational general mastery (MG-M): Represents imagery of coping with a challenge, for example imagining being confident during a difficult performance event
- Motivation general arousal (MG-A): Represents imagery relating to feelings of relaxation, arousal and anxiety.
- Cognitive specific (CS): Represents imagery of completion of a specific skill, for example, imagining taking a penalty shot.
- Cognitive general (CG): Represents imagery of strategies linked to an event, for example, imagining set plays.

Imagery Outcome

When assessing imagery outcome, research has concentrated on the effects of imagery on skill and strategy learning/performance, modifying cogni-tions and regulating arousal/competitive anxiety.

In terms of skill and strategy learning/performance, cognitive specific imagery has been found to be superior to the other types (Burhans *et al.*, 1988). Some case studies have shown the effectiveness of cognitive general mastery imagery, but there are few controlled studies on this (Martin *et al.*, 1999). In contrast, in terms of changing an athlete's thoughts and beliefs, motivational general mastery imagery has been found to be the most effective for enhancing self-confidence (Callow *et al.*, 2001), while motivation specific imagery has been found to be most effective for enhancing motivation (Martin and Hall, 1995). To date no reliable association has been found between cognitive specific imagery and self-efficacy.

When it comes to regulating arousal, athletes have reported using imagery to help them relax; however, this has not been tested empirically (Vadocz, 1997). The use of cognitive specific or motivational general mastery imagery did not reduce pre-competitive state anxiety (Terry *et al.*, 1995). In general it has been suggested that when it comes to relaxation, imagery is most effective when combined with other strategies (Martin *et al.*, 1999).

The Sport Situation

The sport situation has also been found to affect the type of imagery used. Novices tend to use imagery for its cognitive functions because they are focused on learning skills and strategies, and analysing and correcting performance errors. In contrast, experts have acquired the appropriate skills and use imagery to help them produce skills under competitive conditions (Martin *et al.*, 1999).

Athletes who use imagery as a pre-competitive strategy have been found to perform better than a control group (Cogan and Petrie, 1995; Kerr and Leith, 1993). Research has also suggested that motivational imagery is more prevalent and more effective than cognitive imagery immediately prior to performance (Martin *et al.*, 1999). Unfortunately, few studies have examined imagery use in actual competition.

A final situation in which imagery is likely to be used by athletes is during injury. Motivational imagery has been used to facilitate adherence to rehabilitation programmes, to manage anxiety and stay positive (Murphy and Jowdy, 1992). Cognitive specific imagery has been used to replace physical practice (Martin *et al.*, 1999), and healing imagery has been used to cope with pain (Murphy and Jowdy, 1992) and to speed up rehabilitation (Gordon *et al.*, 1998). More research is required to identify the effects of different types of imagery with injured athletes.

Imagery Ability

While everyone has the ability to generate and use imagery, not everyone can do this to the same degree (Paivio, 1986). High imagery ability has shown greater performance improvements than low imagery ability following a cognitive specific imagery intervention (Goss *et al.*, 1986). However, Gregg *et al.* (2005) suggested that imagery ability did not moderate the imagery-performance relationship. They highlighted the fact that it is difficult to detect performance improvements in élite athletes, and suggested that a more detailed and specific outcome measure is required to truly test the relationship.

Imagery Perspective

Cumming and Ste-Marie (2001) examined the influence of imagery perspective (internal versus external) on the cognitive and motivational functions of imagery. They hypothesized that the most appropriate perspective is determined by the characteristics of the skill: for example, if looking at technical form, external imagery would be better, whereas if looking at perceptual, awareness-based skills internal imagery would be most appropriate. Their findings revealed that external imagery was not more effective for technical skills. However, it was suggested that this lack of difference may have been due to the fact that their participants were very familiar with the task, whereas an external perspective may be most useful for new, unfamiliar tasks.

Imagery Training Programmes

Examples of imagery training programmes are available in the literature (for example Cumming and Ste-Marie, 2001). In addition, Weinberg and

---

Example of Imagery Training Programme

Stage 1: Evaluate imagery ability

Prior to beginning training, imagery ability can be evaluated using measures such as the Sport Imagery Questionnaire (SIQ) (Hall *et al.*, 1998).

Stage 2: Basic imagery training

Basic imagery training should focus on teaching athletes to gain self-awareness, controllability and vividness. Using a video tape or actually performing skills prior to imaging can be helpful. It is important that the athlete uses all the senses to make the image as vivid and realistic as possible. Athletes must be able to manipulate their images to ensure they are imaging what they want to image. Vealey and Walter (1993) suggest some vividness and controllability exercises that can be incorporated into a training programme.

Stage 3: Advanced imagery training

Once the athlete has mastered the basics they can move on to advanced imagery. This includes more complex images and sequences of images. Athletes should use the different types of image from the imagery taxonomy, and should think about matching the type of imagery to the function and outcome. Imagery perspective can be incorporated and matched to the task. The creation of imagery scripts, to allow for guided imagery, can be helpful when dealing with extended sequences.

Gould (2007) suggest key factors to consider when designing a pro-gramme: these include an appropriate setting, evaluating imagery ability, teaching athletes to create vivid and controllable images, maintaining a positive focus when imaging, making use of video and audio tapes to support image creation, imaging a skill and an outcome, and imaging in real time. Similarly Holmes and Collins (2001) have developed a model (PETTLEP) of effective imagery practice. They suggest considering the physical state of the athlete, the environment, the nature of the task, maintaining the timing of the skill, changing the content of the skill as learning takes place, including an emotional element in the image, and considering imagery perspective.

GOAL SETTING

Goal setting is one of the most researched strategies for enhancing performance and productivity in industrial, sport and educational settings (Weinberg *et al.*, 2001). Locke and Latham (1990) reviewed over 201 studies with over 40,000 participants and showed a 91 per cent success rate.

In sport, goal setting has been found to have powerful effects, although the findings are not as robust as those from industrial settings (Weinberg *et al.*, 2001). Kyllo and Landers (1995) completed the first meta analysis (thirty-six studies), and results indicated that it can be a successful technique for enhancing performance. Wanlin *et al.* (1997) reported that goal setting led to improved 500m times in a group of ice skaters, with the biggest improvements being found in lap frequency. However, Weinberg *et al.* (2001) point out that many competitive goal setting studies have been conducted in laboratory settings and have used non-athletes or recreational sport populations. We still have no real understanding of how, when and why athletes set goals, what barriers impede goal attainment in athletes, and which kinds of goal are most important to them.

Despite these criticisms, it has been suggested that goal setting can direct attention, mobilize effort, stimulate persistence, offset boredom, and aid the development of new and effective strategies (Locke and Latham, 1985). Burton's (1983) cognitive theory suggests that goal setting works because of the effect that it has upon psychological factors such as anxiety, motivation and confidence.

Goal Difficulty, Specificity and Proximity

Performance has been found to improve linearly, with increasing goal difficulty until the task becomes too difficult; at this point performance begins to decrease (Locke and Latham, 1985). More specifically, Bar-Eli *et al.* (1997) found that different levels of difficulty had different effects upon a sit-up performance task over time. The groups that were set difficult but realistic goals (20 per cent improvement in performance) showed the greatest improvement gains.

Figure 13.1 Each team member will have specific and individualized goals. (Courtesy of David Griffiths)

Specific goals have been found to be more effective than vague goals (Bandura, 1997; Locke and Latham, 1985). Bar-Eli *et al.* (1997) found that all groups given specific performance goals (for example, 10 per cent improvement, 20 per cent improvement, 40 per cent improvement) outperformed the group given a 'do your best' goal.

In terms of goal proximity, short-term goals have been found to be more effective than long-term goals because evaluation is more frequent (Bandura, 1986). Tenebaum *et al.* (1999) found that participants with long-term goals of eight weeks were not motivated to seek performance gains over four or six weeks, and those with more distal goals (eight weeks) were found to progress more slowly than those with proximal goals (four or six weeks). Tenebaum *et al.* (1999) suggested that if goals are too far removed in time, then athletes believe that there is time to work towards them later. In addition, more distal goals offer less frequent mastery experiences and so progress is more gradual.

Outcome, Performance and Process Goals

When left to their own devices, most athletes set outcome goals (for example, 'win this race'); however, a sole focus on outcome goals may result in unrealistic expectations and disappointment (Weinberg and Gould, 2007). Such a focus without the potential buffering effects of self-confidence can lead to a decrease in confidence, effort and performance (Weinberg and Gould, 2007).

To offset negative effects, athletes should set a combination of performance, process and outcome goals (Filby *et al.*, 1999). Performance goals (for example, achieving a certain time) and process goals (technique related, such as drive with the arms) are under the athlete's control and are thought to produce realistic expectations, increase confidence, effort and perform-ance and decrease anxiety (Weinberg and Gould, 2007). However, it has been suggested that performance goals may also have negative effects in that they may become internally controlling (Decci and Ryan, 1985). These findings indicate that we need to set goals carefully and attain an appropri-ate balance.

Example of a Goal-Setting Programme

Stage 1

The athlete should be introduced to goal proximity, difficulty and specificity. He/she should be encouraged to set difficult but achievable goals, to make goals specific, and to include long-term, medium-term and short-term goals.

Stage 2

The athlete should be introduced to process, performance and outcome goals, and should be encouraged to include all three types of goal in their programme.

Stage 3

The process, performance and outcome goals could be mapped to time frames. Set a distal outcome goal and some short- and medium-term performance and process goals. The goals should link together so that the process goals will facilitate the performance goals, and the performance goals facilitate the outcome goals.

Stage 4

Once goals have been set, the athlete should be encouraged to write down their goals and to evaluate them regularly. In addition they need to think about how they will achieve their goals – what behaviours will they engage in to ensure their goals will be met successfully? For example, staying behind for 15 minutes after every practice session to practise shooting.

MULTIMODAL PACKAGES

So far we have considered mental skills interventions in isolation; how-ever, studies have shown that training packages can have a positive impact on performance (Patrick and Hrycaiko, 1998). Patrick and Hrycaiko (1998) created a skills package designed for two triathletes and a runner containing relaxation, imagery, self-talk and goal setting. The package was effective in improving the running performance of the participants, who reported that combining the interventions enhanced each individual intervention. This effect has been reported before, where imagery and relaxation combined were found to be more effective than imagery alone (Weinberg *et al.*, 1981). The use of multimodal packages has proved popular, but sport psychologists must think about how interventions are combined and implemented so as to avoid overloading the athlete, and the constraints of the situation may dictate how much can be done in the programme (Weinberg and Gould, 2007).

IMPLEMENTING INTERVENTIONS

There are no hard and fast rules as to how to implement interventions; it is up to the sport psychologist to use their knowledge, skills and expertise to work with the athlete to find a programme that is both appropriate and suitable. We will now go back to our three athletes from the previous chapter to see how a sport psychologist might proceed. Have a look at the example in the sidebar, and then design the other two programmes.

Example Case Study

Rugby player Luke was suffering from a lack of confidence in his physical ability following an injury. To enhance his confidence the sport psychologist could introduce Luke to an imagery training programme focusing on cognitive specific and motivational general mastery imagery. As Luke still has some doubts about whether he has fully recovered from his injury, healing imagery could also be introduced. Self-talk, particularly motivational mastery, could also be applicable to help Luke deal with his worrying thoughts.

Case Studies: Tamsin and Ben

How would you help the following two athletes? Tamsin the talented netball player who is suffering from cognitive anxiety due to high performance expectations, and Ben the hockey player who has concentration issues that result in cognitive and somatic anxiety.

For Tamsin, it would be useful to start with self-talk to target her cognitive anxiety. Motivational mastery self-talk would be implemented to change her thoughts and beliefs. This could be combined with motivation general mastery imagery (enhances confidence) or motivation general arousal imagery (aids relaxation). PMR could be used to target the somatic symptoms.

For Ben, goal setting could be applied to focus his attention and create a new challenge for him. To increase his effort and motivation on the field, motivational drive self-talk could be applied. Finally PMR could be applied to the somatic symptoms.

14

Case Study Examples from Sport Psychology Interventions

by Jane Lomax

The preceding two chapters have given an insight into the variety of approaches, theories and mental skills available to sport psychologists. This chapter aims to highlight the application of these ideas to two specific case studies. As sport psychologists, we are encouraged to recognize our own philosophy in the methods and theoretical approaches we adopt to support the performers in dealing with the issues they face (Poczwardowski, Sherman and Ravizza, 2004; Hill, 2001). The case studies discussed here utilize a cognitive behavioural approach, as many other sport psychologists do (Hemmings and Holder, 2009). Whatever theoretical standpoint underpins the work, though, the effectiveness of support work is determined by the quality of the relationship and rapport built with the performer. Dialogue with the performer is central to the work and often involves exploring their thoughts, emotions and behaviours to support the development of a positive outlook on events (Hemmings and Holder, 2009).

CASE STUDY 1: BREAKING INTO ÉLITE LEVEL SPORT

Many youngsters dream of representing their nation on the World or Olympic stage, but breaking into top level sport is a highly competitive journey, often fraught with setbacks and frustrations. This case study draws on work with one performer, Olivia, as she moves from a sixteen-year-old, nervously entering national representation, through to her arrival on the senior international stage. The work was part of a governing body organized, multi-disciplinary support programme provided to the England Netball squad over a number of years. At no stage was any of the psychology support work part of the selection process.

Assessment of Needs

A variety of approaches was used to assess Olivia's needs, and to monitor the changes in those needs over time. The performance profile (Butler and Hardy, 1992; Butler, Smith and Irwin, 1993) identified Olivia's perceptions of the qualities of an élite player, and where she currently saw herself (*see* Figure 14.1). The subsequent discussions enabled the bringing together of coach and athlete perceptions, and co-ordinated, individualized support from the coach, the physiologist and myself (Jones, 1993; Dale and Wrisberg, 1996).

Other pencil and paper tests were used to investigate further aspects of performance and support observations, coach comments and discussions. The Psychological Skills Questionnaire (UCNW – Bull, Albinson and Shambrook, 1996) gave an indication of natural tendencies towards the performer's use of different mental skills. We monitored the development of emotional issues through the use of the Profile of Mood States (POMS, McNair, Lorr, and Droppleman, 1971) and the Competitive State Anxiety Inventory (CSAI-2). The latter explored not just the intensity of emotions experienced, but also how helpful (or not) Olivia found the levels of anxiety and confidence she experienced across different matchplay scenarios (Jones and Swain, 1992).

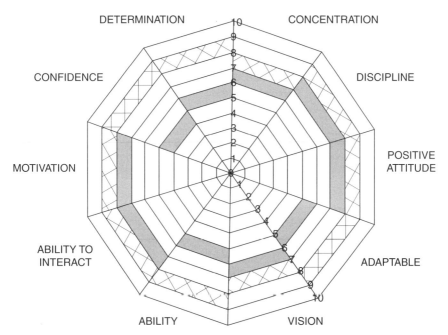

Figure 14.1 An initial performance profile: the shaded areas indicate the performer's perceptions of performance at the start of the Under 18 age group. Note the relatively low self-confidence score for mental aspects of performance.

The grid score lines represent the performer's perceptions as she progresses to the Under 21 age group, enabling the monitoring of developments in perceptions of mental skills, particularly self-confidence.

Interpretation of the CSAI-2 scores suggested Olivia found lower levels of cognitive anxiety and higher levels of self-confidence facilitative. Mid-levels of somatic anxiety were most frequently reported, and were found to be quite facilitative. The POMS results (*see* Figures 14.2–14.5) gave an indication of the emotions being experienced by our performer. The first diagram indicates the classic iceberg profile thought to indicate a desirable emotional state, and was experienced by Olivia in club and county matches.

The other examples evidenced mood state changes in different situations. Raised tension and confusion rates in her first England cap were quite understandable, but at Under 21 level these reflected an increased awareness of the expectations on her in the preparation for the World Youth Championships. The skewed profile in favour of fatigue identified issues relating to managing the demands of tours, and the increased anger at inter-counties highlighted frustrations with niggling injuries. The pencil

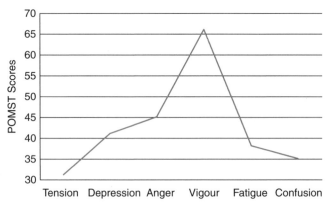

Figure 14.2 POMS Iceberg Profile 1: Profile of Mood State scores at club and county level of matches. Note the peak of vigour above the population average of 50, and other construct scores below average. This mirrors the classic Iceberg Profile generally associated with successful performers (Morgan, 1987, in Weinberg and Gould, 2003).

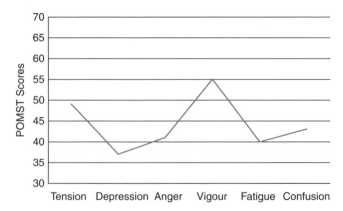

Figure 14.3 POMS Iceberg Profile 2: Profile of Mood States scores in the early stages of Under 21 play. Note here the raised tension and confusion levels.

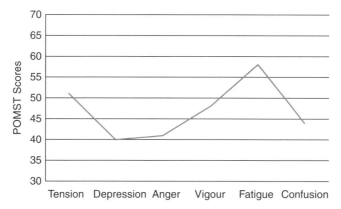

Figure 14.4   POMS Iceberg Profile 3: Profile of Mood State scores during a tour. Note the skewed profile in comparison to the ideal, particularly the peak in fatigue rather than vigour and the increased tension levels.

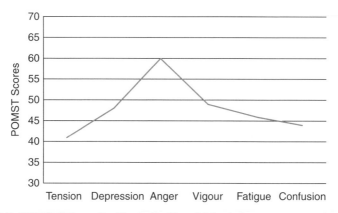

Figure 14.5 POMS Iceberg Profile 4: Profile of Mood States scores at inter-county championships. Note the increased anger scores and loss of vigour.

and paper tests informed multidisciplinary support enabling adjustments to the training programme to be made as necessary, but were only possible due to the frequency and longevity of contact – such tests can easily become overbearing.

Developing a Solid Basis of Mental Skills

Mental skills were introduced through group sessions, with follow-up exercises and then one-to-one sessions to support practising the skills and individualizing their use in training and competition (Kirschenbaum, 1984; Bull, 1995). We also recognized the value of integrating the mental skills with the learning process throughout (Sinclair and Sinclair, 1994). The mental skills training included goal setting, concentration, arousal and anxiety management, confidence building and imagery (Weinberg and Gould, 2003).

As the profile indicates, self-confidence was a particular need and we often returned to different aspects of its development as Olivia progressed through the age groups. Process goals were used from an early stage to underpin the performance and outcome goals (Filby, Maynard and Graydon, 1999) and to achieve a number of aims – motivation with training, building confidence and adjusting the goals set to accommodate recovery from injuries. Best performance imagery and mental rehearsal supported this development, and helped cope with injury and reduced physical training loads (Bandura, 1997; Munroe, Giacobbi, Hall and Weinberg, 2000). Relaxation skills were developed to regulate tension levels via breath control and progressive muscular relaxation with audio tapes to develop the skill of deep relaxation as well as quick-fire techniques (Hardy and Fazey, 1986, 1990; Bull, 1996).

Climbing Through the Ranks

With increasing age, the demands on Olivia's life changed, and short-term process goals helped to relieve pressure, and helped her juggle training and life issues more effectively. In a combined approach with the physiologist her training programme was adapted to suit her changing lifestyle demands. Once the profile scores indicated the development of mental skills (*see* Under 21 scores on the profile), later work could integrate the skills more directly with court play work and physical training.

Movement into the Under 21 squadsaw a fierce fight for places, as it was a World Youth Championship year. Olivia had a shaky transition with illness at trials, and was surprised to be selected. She was left feeling she had 'cheated a bit', and the resulting emotions endangered the growth in self-confidence achieved over the previous two years. Cognitive restructuring techniques were employed to help Olivia view the situation more positively by 'demonstrating the potential to be selected despite the performance on the day', and to view this as a compliment (Mace, 1994; Jones and Hardy, 1993; Bunker, Williams and Zinsser, in Williams, 1993). Team-building activities helped Olivia to settle within the new combinations and to move from strength to strength, though we continued to monitor her self-confidence levels as the pressure to perform increased.

Preparation for the World Youth Championships

Our aim now was to develop Olivia's level of sophistication in her application of mental skills. For example, the vividness and controllability of mental rehearsal techniques was increased by greater use of visual and kinesthetic aspects of the image (Blair, Hall and Leyshon, 1993; Vealey and Walter in Williams, 1993). This was coupled with a short period of relaxation prior to the start of the practice sessions, to ensure that a successful and technically correct image was practised.

Integrating Mental Skills with Physical Training

This aspect of training involved power and speed work. An interdisciplinary approach was adopted to apply the mental skills to support physical training aspects delivered by the physiologist. Mental rehearsal skills were used to cue in to kinesthetic feedback and help learn new training routines. Key words and positive self-talk supported the quality execution of exercises (such as 'push', 'slow', 'drive'), and we explored the use of iconics – the use of animal images to simulate movements (Hemmings, 1995, pers. comm.). Thus an image of a springbok simulated the short, light touches needed for the plyometric jumping exercises; and the 'stalking' and preying behaviour in a large cat was helpful for 'off the ball' movement within attack or defence. The 'stalking' represented the player movement when seeking out weaknesses in the opposition, followed by explosive movements to drive on to the ball or to exploit the interception.

Integrating Concentration Skills into Matchplay

Olivia had already practised controlling her use of different attentional focus dimensions, and switching between them in training and matchplay (Nideffer, 1985; Nideffer in Williams, 1993; Weinberg and Gould, 1995). We now applied those skills to court work delivered by the coach, developing a zone defensive strategy that required good teamwork and communication skills. Different approaches to cue selection and problem solving were developed whilst in play. Training practices were adapted, and the concept of the 'Three Rs' was developed:

Recognise: recognize the relevant cue (Butler, 1996)

Respond: execute the response efficiently between you and other players

Return: return as quickly as possible to the task at hand.

The Three Rs approach was later extended to support attacking strategies too, particularly the development of shooter rotation. A productive off-shoot of this work was player discussions in relation to their cue identification and focus of attention at different times. This heightened awareness, and encouraged players to help each other react and recover more effectively, which increased task cohesion and group productivity.

Coping with Injury

Ongoing niggling injuries required monitoring by the physiotherapists, training adaptations with the physiologist, and sensitive amounts of court time from the coaches. This further challenged Olivia's self-confidence, and Bandura's (1997) model of self-efficacy was used to develop each element of confidence (Gould, Hodge, Paterson and Gianni, 1989). Goal setting was adapted to support Olivia's ability to cope and adhere to changes in training, and best performance imagery to maintain confidence. Imagery skills provided mental practice to help compensate for loss in physical practice, and positive self-statements helped with verbal persuasion skills.

Impression Management – Exuding Confidence

As the World Youth Championships drew nearer, we examined the use of non-verbal communication skills to create more confidence both on and off court (James and Collins, 1995; Leary, 1992, 1995). Videos of team march-ons and player reactions to different events during the games were analysed to identify individual and team responses to stressful events within matches. We worked on exuding a more confident aura and exhibiting emotionally controlled responses to a range of match situations (Gallmeier, 1987). Individualized mini routines helped with composure at key moments within matches, for example immediately prior to stepping into the centre circle to take the centre pass.

The 'Three Rs' approach used within the concentration work was adapted to a 'Three Cs' approach to produce the mindset of the image to portray, namely 'Cool, Calculating and Confident'. Key words (for example, 'walk tall') were utilized, and the players developed strategies for different elements of the game, similar to Bull's (1995) work with the England women's cricket team. This benefited team cohesion and productivity, too.

Selection to the Full National Squad

Olivia and the Under 21 squad returned with a bronze medal ready to challenge for her dream of a position in the Senior England squad. The transition from a youth national squad through to the full senior squad is a competitive journey often with setbacks along the way, including the likelihood of increased bench time. Although Olivia gained immediate selection to the full England squad, her confidence and motivation were again challenged as her first choice position was already occupied by the current England captain.

Coping with Recurring Injury

The coaches and medics pulled Olivia from the Test Series she had been selected for, due to recurrent shin splints. This was devastating news for Olivia, whose concern was missing out on her big break and the realization of a lifetime's dream. Although she had experienced injury before and the loss of confidence that often follows that, this time she experienced a more severe emotional reaction over a number of weeks.

Support work focused on raising her awareness of the likely responses to injury (Kubel-Ross model, 1969, cited by Henschen in Williams, 1993), and also reflected on the previous season to identify the stages she experienced during its course when she did not stop, and when she had been stopped by others. A number of cognitive strategies were employed to support Olivia's recovery, and to keep her thinking more positive:

Reframing (Bunker, Williams and Zinsser in Williams, 1993): this strategy helped Olivia to consider the current situation in a more positive light – as an opportunity to sort out the injury properly, to recover completely from the Youth Championships, to make the most of her break when it came, and to take the support given by coaches as a compliment.

Thought stopping (Nideffer, 1985): ideas were highlighted to stop negative thoughts when they appeared. Relaxation, best performance imagery and positive self-talk were revisited to support the reframing once the negative thoughts had been stopped.

Return to goal setting: We encouraged a long-term perspective and recognition of Olivia's potential lifespan in the sport. It was important to focus on mid-term targets to be ready for other selection opportunities – tours to the southern hemisphere and the Commonwealth Games. Adapted goals were agreed in order to focus on the process of rehabilitation, with reference to physiotherapists and physiologists, reinforcing the value of process goals to underpin product ones (Korn, 1983, in Green, 1992), and using multiple goal-setting strategies (Hardy, Jones and Gould, 1996; and Filby, Maynard and Graydon, 1999).

Coping with feelings of isolation: Olivia reported feelings of isolation, and demonstrated signs of being 'on the periphery' during training. We agreed she would observe the following parameters:

- Ensure she involved herself more in any training sessions where she was present, for example, help with drinks, feed balls in practices
- Use mental rehearsal strategies to provide some replacement for lack of physical practice and assist motivation
- Consult the physiotherapist and physiologist for a permitted exercise plan to help deal with frustrations
- Watch the Test matches to learn about playing at that level. Then mentally practise seeing herself on court for the England Seniors
- Short-term focus – use the above to help move through the stages of response to injury, and work towards acceptance and developing a positive, hopeful and realistic return to competition.

Returning to Full Fitness

Mental toughness to realize the dream! Olivia's adherence to the adapted training programme reaped its benefits. The coaches gradually increased Olivia's court time and the physiotherapists were hopeful of a full recovery. Despite the enforced rest, Olivia's improvement in play was still very evident and she did, indeed, gain her desire of selection to full international status and a Test Series tour to South Africa.

Now the issue Olivia faced was again a return to confidence building, as self-doubt crept back with the recognition of possibly completing all the training just to spend time on the bench. Confidence development in her second choice position was crucial here, to turn it into another first choice position. An important progression was to identify factors within Olivia's control, and those that were not. We kept Olivia's perception of the current situation in a longer term context, to help her maintain a positive outlook. Mental toughness work included the addition of performance reviews (Bull *et al.*, 1996) to encourage Olivia to recognize strengths and to keep a more positive interpretation of any mistakes. The idea of 'parking' thoughts about previous perceptions of southern hemisphere teams was encouraged, to open her mind to more positive beliefs about England's ability to perform against the world's best teams; and 'PRIDE' – 'Personal Responsibility for Delivering Excellence' – was introduced, to help contextualize individual goals.

Figure 14.6 Our performer, Olivia Murphy, pictured here playing for the Loughborough Lightning Superleague team after enjoying a very successful international career including a number of years as England Captain. (Courtesy Fotoccompli/David Griffiths)

Arousal management techniques were explored, based on the Zone of Optimal Functioning Theory (Krane, 1993), to raise awareness of desirable arousal levels and then take control of managing them to suit Olivia's needs. At times this meant 'psyching up' if under-aroused, at other times it meant 'psyching down' if too aroused or experiencing anxiety (Bull *et al.*, 1996).

Conclusion

Olivia successfully completed the tour to South Africa, without as much bench warming as she had worried about. From then on her game moved from strength to strength, culminating in a distinguished international career as England captain.

CASE STUDY 2: REDISCOVERING LOST FORM

Once the struggle to reach the top in sport has been overcome, athletes then need to maintain form to stay there. The client in this case study, Jo, was a hammer thrower who had already achieved a gold medal perform-ance at the previous Deaf Olympics. When we met, Jo was experiencing a loss of form since that gold medal performance and she was keen to explore the opportunity to address the feelings she was now experiencing of 'I need a new head!' Within the forthcoming three-year period there were two particularly important competitions to Jo: the first Deaf World Championships in Turkey, and the Deaf Olympics in Taipei.

As a deaf athlete Jo had no funding support, which restricted the number and frequency of sessions she could have. We aimed to make the sessions as self-sufficient as possible, and agreed to use emails and texts to support contact between sessions. The methods adopted with Jo were more flexible than within the previous case study, with less face-to-face contact and observation.

Assessment of Needs

We worked on the assumption that Jo still had the appropriate motor pro-gramme for the movements available, but that 'other factors' were causing the disruption of their execution (Collins, Morriss and Trower, 1999). This loss of form seemed likely to relate to some level of inhibition (Collins *et al.*, 1999). Possible sources were identified as residual concern over inju-ries, loss of fitness during illness, or perhaps Jo herself was disrupting her optimal motor programme by attempting too much conscious control in order to make the desired changes in her movement pattern. Jo was also aware of the appearance of younger throwers on the international circuit who had the capability to out-throw her, making a successful defence of her Olympic title particularly challenging.

The assessment of needs was conducted through dialogue and did not include any collection of quantitative information or even the completion of a profile, in the sense that the previous case study had. The working relationship here tended to be reactive to the athlete's needs as she saw it in that instance of time. It became quickly apparent that work would be largely from a cognitive-behavioural approach again (Hill, 2001) as Jo was experiencing many negative cognitions.

Monitoring and evaluation of work relied on performance measures, observations, comments from the client and my own reflections (Cropley, Miles, Hanton and Niven, 2007). Later on in the work this would also include comments from Jo's coach. A continuous point of reflection was the effectiveness of the communications process. Using email and text loses the 50–75 per cent of communication skills that is normally trans-ferred through the tone of voice used and non-verbal body language (Weinberg and Gould, 1995). Given this potential loss of information, it was important to reflect on my articulation of ideas, and whether the ath-lete's level of understanding was indeed that expected. Also because Jo is a deaf athlete it was important to recognize and pick up on any informa-tion losses in the course of face-to-face meetings.

Changing Thought Processes – Adopting the Inner Game Approach

In order to address the issue of too much conscious control over move-ments we introduced the 'Inner Game' (Gallwey, 1997) approach to learning

as a basis to work from. This concept is appealing in its simplicity: it identifies 'Self 1' as the chattering part of the mind and 'Self 2' as the natural
performance mode of the performer. As long as Self 1 is quiet or involved
in thought processes that support the body's natural execution of movement patterns, performance tends to run smoothly. However, once Self 1
starts to 'chatter', performance starts to suffer, either through Self 1 voicing doubts about the athlete's capabilities, or indeed trying to over-ride
the movement execution by 'trying too hard' or focusing on thoughts that
interfere generally with the movement.

We raised awareness of when Self 1 was detracting from performance,
and developed skills that would either keep Self 1 quiet or occupy Self 1
with more productive thoughts. We examined strategies that would help
Jo cope with the stresses she was currently experiencing in her life, and the
emotions that she was experiencing as a result. Frustration and anxiety
were playing a major role. During the eighteen months that this case study
focuses on, in the build-up to the first of the two competitions important
to Jo, she experienced a roller coaster of emotions. The first season was cut
short abruptly with a serious illness resulting in significant loss of fitness.
At this stage, work focused on supporting Jo back to fitness, a road which
was to include a number of further set-backs along the way.

Prior to the enforced break due to illness we had explored Jo's use of
relaxation to help control tension levels, particularly in the forehead and
stomach areas which Jo had reported as undesirable. An adaptation of the
'Progressive Muscular Relaxation' technique similar to Bull *et al.*'s (1996)
ten-step relaxation approach was developed to match the somatic symptoms experienced (Davidson and Schwartz, 1976; Maynard, MacDonald
and Warwick-Evans, 1997), and this gave Jo more control over tension
levels while performing. When used in the evening, this had the added
benefit of relieving the difficulty she at times experienced sleeping.

The Power of Positive Thought

When Jo was starting to recover from her illness she expressed a desire to
rebuild her self-confidence and self-belief. Some reading material based on
Bull *et al.* (1996)'s ideas provided a start. Then we developed Jo's control of
thought processes to help Self 1 be more productive and reduce the cognitive element of anxiety. Dealing with frustrations was important to move
Jo away from 'I am so disappointed yet so powerful, I know I can do it if
only I can be more positive and relaxed'. Reframing this kind of mindset to
focus on Jo's strengths and capabilities was important, and greatly helped
by realigning Jo's use of goal setting to be more realistic to her stage in
recovery. This presented a continuous challenge to Jo, as it conflicted with
her desired goals when considering competition preparation.

Performance reviews encouraged Jo to report back on positive elements
of performance, and then to view things that had gone wrong as opportunities for development – a powerful thought change when trying to maintain
positivity. When Jo experienced a number of 'no throws' and started to self-
talk with 'Don't throw into the cage', we needed to explore the connection

between what we think and what we do: thus if someone says to you 'Don't think of an orange', what do we tend to think of immediately? Normally, an orange! So if we are thinking 'Don't throw into the cage' we have just increased our chances of doing exactly what we are trying to avoid.

Thought-stopping techniques, followed by some process goals and positive self-statements, were needed to help Jo replace these thoughts with what she needed to do to successfully deliver the hammer and land a legal throw.

Pre-Throw Routines

Managing anxieties and distractions at competition was explored. Observations at training and a video of competition suggested that the pre-throw routine, once within the throwing circle, was fairly consistent and gave Jo confidence.

We focused on the time immediately before entering the circle, where a number of distractions were evident – for example, officials holding up your throw whilst one of the sprint races is starting. Jo also identified the need to work on her thought processes anything up to two hours before the competition. Adopting the philosophy that mastery over threats and stressors is vital to athletic functioning (Bandura, 1997; Feltz, Short and Sullivan, 2008), we identified what was within Jo's control and how to stay in the 'here and now'. Concentration skills were also used to cut out distractions, rather than picking up on others who may be watching.

Figure 14.7 Our performer, Jo Davison, utilizing her mental preparation skills in competition. (Courtesy of Joanne Davison)

We continued to develop the use of key words and short self-talk statements to support technical aspects of performance. Self-affirmation statements helped build confidence, and concentration skills encouraged a more direct link of process goals to performance; these helped appropriate focusing immediately prior to entering the cage to prepare to throw.

Preparing for the World Championships – Managing Further Setbacks

In the final approach to the competition Jo was hit with another bout of illness, and she needed to refocus and recognize the tiredness of her body. She needed to maintain enjoyment of her work, focus on keeping timing 'nice and smooth', attack the circle with increased speed, and think 'hip ahead of hammer'. Mental rehearsal, best performance imagery and relaxation were returned to in the final stages of preparation, as far as was possible – breath control was particularly helpful in assisting Jo to be aware of what she could do and how far to go.

This was not an ideal preparation for a major competition. Despite this, Jo threw a personal best, achieved her performance goal of throwing over 50 metres that had meant so much to her, and came back with a bronze medal. This was a real triumph over adversity, and Jo reported that this medal meant more to her than the gold one from three years before, due to the number of obstacles that she had overcome.

Figure 14.8 Jo Davison enjoying her well deserved medal-winning performance. (Courtesy of Joanne Davison)

EVALUATION METHODS

Sport psychologists are always encouraged to be good reflective practitioners and seek to evaluate and reflect on work covered. A range of strategies are available to do this, some more objective than others. The first case study included more formal evaluation methods and annual reports from players utilizing the Consultant Evaluation Form (Partington and Orlick, 1987). This gave feedback on individual sessions, as well as an overview so others' perceptions of our work could be included in the self-reflection process. An annual report for the programme organizer and governing body encouraged another level of reflective practice over and above that normally conducted on a regular basis throughout the consultancy work. Individual reflection was enhanced with quantitative measures from pencil and paper tests, though as time progressed pencil and paper tests were used less, and qualitative measures and personal reflections became the main sources of evaluation.

Evaluations within the second case study relied on performance accomplishments of outcome and performance goals, my own reflections, feedback from the performer and more latterly feedback from the coach. Reflections often focused on the quality of communication, and have certainly raised awareness of such issues (Cropley *et al.*, 2007) and generated improvements in my clarity of communications.

Working with Sport Psychology: Some Thoughts for You

Sport psychology support work has raised a number of issues worthy of highlighting here, not just for the practitioner but also for the coach who may want to utilize the services of a sport psychologist. Most coach education training nowadays includes skill acquisition issues, some social psychology issues and the use of mental skills, so more experienced coaches could quite easily be utilizing some mental skills whilst coaching. Indeed, much of my consultancy work has involved supporting coaches to develop their understanding and use of sport psychology concepts within the coaching process. Here are some thoughts for your consideration.

Working as a Sport Psychologist – Friend or Foe?
When a performer talks with a sport psychologist, are they perceived by the coach and their peers as being 'well rounded individuals attending to all aspects of their training', or are they perceived as 'having a problem'? The first interpretation leads to a far more productive working environment than the second, and in order for the sport psychologist to work effectively with coaches the implications of this are as follows:

- Agree and be prepared to 'manage' the dynamics between sport scientist and coach
- Introduce yourself as a sport psychologist in a non-threatening manner
- Ensure that the issue of 'confidentiality' is fully explained, and the boundaries clearly identified and agreed with all parties

- Support the coach with overcoming any concerns they may have should they find your work threatening
- Decide whether you want to be part of the selection process, and ensure this is clearly communicated
- Agree your role with the coach and other support workers, and be prepared to review these working relationships on a regular basis to maintain effective communication channels
- Understand and communicate clearly the limits of your expertise and underpinning training, and know where and when to make referrals to support your work effectively
- Remember you need an outlet for your work and the issues you deal with too, so regular contact with a 'supervisor' or experienced colleague as an outlet can assist the management of your own emotions.

One of the most valuable parts of the training to become an accredited sport psychologist has been the need to obtain a qualification in counselling skills. A sport psychologist needs to be ready to deal with the unexpected – a seemingly straightforward presenting problem always has the potential to 'open a can of worms'. The resultant support may be very different from that expected in the first instance!

15

Nutritional Guidelines for the Athlete

by Dr Emma Stevenson

The routine training load experienced by sportsmen and women increases daily energy, carbohydrate and protein requirements. It is important that these needs are met so that optimal training can continue from day to day. A good diet is therefore essential to help support consistent intensive training without the athlete succumbing to excessive fatigue, illness or injury. Good food choices can also promote adaptations to the training stimulus, enhance recovery between workouts, and speed recovery from minor injuries (Hawley *et al.*, 2006). It is important that all athletes are well educated about the importance of nutrition to their daily training and competition, and that they are aware of their nutritional goals and how to achieve them. This chapter aims to provide guidelines for the best nutritional practices; however, coaches should remember that every athlete is different, and there is no single diet that meets the needs of all athletes at all times.

THE TRAINING DIET

The primary goal of the training diet is to provide sufficient energy and nutrients to the athlete to allow optimal training and to maximize recovery between workouts. The energy requirements of athletes are influenced by a number of factors, including body size, growth and the energy cost of their training load (intensity, duration and frequency of training). The pursuit of weight loss or weight gain must also be considered.

Energy Balance

Daily energy balance is an important concept to understand in order to maintain body mass. Little fluctuation occurs in body mass as long as an equilibrium exists in which energy input (calories in food) exactly balances energy output (calories expended in daily physical activities). A surplus of as little as 100kcal a day equals a yearly gain of approximately 4.7kg (10.4lb) of body fat! Some athletes are faced with the challenge of having to maintain a very high energy intake to support extremely high training loads or to maintain a high fat-free mass; others have to restrict energy intake in order to maintain a low body mass or low body fat levels. It is therefore important for athletes to plan their nutrition and carefully monitor their caloric intake to prevent excess body fat accumulation.

Results from dietary surveys reveal that male athletes typically report daily energy intakes of approximately 4,000–5,000kcal (Burke *et al.*, 2001). Due to a smaller body size, the expected energy requirement of female athletes should be about 20 to 30 per cent lower than her male counterpart.

Diet Composition

Exercising muscles rely on carbohydrates and fat as the main sources of fuel. Carbohydrate is stored in the muscle as glycogen, however, stores are limited and will be depleted by approximately 90 minutes of exercise. Small amounts of glycogen are also present in the liver. Fats provide the largest nutrient store in the body and can fuel 100–200 hours of exertion. Protein is also an essential nutrient for athletes, and although they contribute very little to energy metabolism, proteins are essential for the repair of damaged body tissue and the building of new proteins in the body in response to training. As a general guideline for athletes, it is recommended that carbohydrates make up at least 60–70 per cent of total energy intake, protein 12 per cent, with the remainder coming from fat. The diet also needs to satisfy vitamin, mineral, fibre and fluid requirements.

Carbohydrates

In athletic events of high or long intensity, performance is generally limited by carbohydrate availability. Carbohydrates are therefore the key nutrient for athletes, and the athlete's daily eating plan needs to provide enough CHO to fuel his/her training programme, and to optimize the recovery of muscle and liver glycogen stores between training sessions. Low carbohydrate stores result in fatigue and impairment in performance, and have a negative impact on the immune system (Gleeson *et al.*, 2004).

Carbohydrate requirements depend on training loads and demands of competition; however, general targets are provided for carbohydrate intake based on an athlete's body mass (BM).

It is important to remember that not all athletes need a high carbohydrate intake every day. Thus on high activity days carbohydrate intake may need to be increased, whereas on rest or low activity days, carbohydrate intake may need to be reduced. The needs of individual athletes should be finely tuned to match their training regime.

Minimal physical activity	2–3g carbohydrate per kg body mass
Light physical activity (3–5hrs per week)	4–5g carbohydrate per kg body mass
Medium physical activity (10hrs per week)	6–7g carbohydrate per kg body mass
Elite athletes (20+ hrs per week)	7+ g carbohydrate per kg body mass

Figure 15.1   Carbohydrate intake goals. (Burke et al., 2010)

Protein

Protein is required in the daily diet for the development, maintenance and repair of muscle as well as for the development of skin and bones. Most athletes consume sufficient protein in their diet to meet their daily needs, however additional protein may be needed in some circumstances. Endurance athletes undergoing a heavy training programme may require additional protein to cover a proportion of the energy cost of their training or to repair damaged muscles during recovery. Strength-trained athletes may also have an additional need to increase muscle size and strength following resistance training.

There is some evidence to suggest that athletes require a slightly higher protein intake during the early stages of a new exercise programme when intensity, volume and/or duration are increased. However, once the body adapts to the increased stress, protein requirements return to normal levels.

Other Nutrients

Athletes should follow general recommendations for a healthy diet by reducing intake of high fat foods, particularly those high in saturated fats, increasing the intake of fibre-rich foods, and consuming at least five portions of fruit and vegetables a day. Alcohol intake should also be limited.

Sedentary	0.8g protein per kg body mass
General training programme	1.0g protein per kg body mass
Endurance athlete undertaking a heavy training programme	1.2–1.6g protein per kg body mass
Strength athlete undertaking a heavy training programme	1.2–1.7g protein per kg body mass

Figure 15.2   Guidelines for maximum protein requirements for different athletes. (Burke et al., 2010)

Vitamins and minerals: do not provide energy, but are an essential part of any diet. Vitamins play an important role in the formation of red blood cells, and trigger or control many metabolic processes within the body. Vitamins must be present in the daily diet because they cannot be synthesized by the body at a sufficient rate to satisfy its needs. The best way to ensure a sufficient supply of vitamins in the body is to include five portions of fruit or vegetables in the diet. Minerals are used by the body in complex ways, and interrelate with each other to perform different functions. They are vital even though they are only needed in tiny amounts. Two of the most important minerals are calcium and iron.

Calcium intake is important for the formation and maintenance of bones and teeth. Milk is the best source of calcium, and low fat milks contain just as much calcium as full fat milk. Female athletes consuming a low energy intake are at high risk of a low calcium intake. If athletes are not meeting their calcium needs through dietary sources, then a calcium supplement may be warranted. To avoid interactions with other foods, calcium supplements are best taken between meals or last thing at night. The absorption of calcium is most effective when the supplement is taken in doses of 500mg or less.

Iron is needed for the formation of haemoglobin in the blood. This carries oxygen around the body. A deficiency of circulating haemoglobin is referred to as anaemia, and symptoms include fatigue, weakness, breathlessness and impaired aerobic capacity. Those involved in high intensity training are more susceptible to anaemia and therefore must ensure that their diet provides a sufficient source of iron. Female athletes also have higher iron requirements than males because of menstrual blood losses. Good sources of iron include red meats, fortified breakfast cereals and green leafy vegetables. Some foods inhibit iron absorption such as tea, coffee and excessive intakes of bran. Consuming iron-rich foods with vitamin C-rich foods will enhance iron absorption substantially.

By consuming a varied, balanced diet, athletes should be able to achieve their nutrition goals and enjoy the food that they consume.

PREPARATION FOR COMPETITION

Every athlete's goal is to perform to their optimum during competition. Several factors that can impair performance are related to nutrition, and therefore it is essential that the athlete's nutritional preparation is carefully considered. Nutritional factors that can cause fatigue or a decline in performance include depletion of muscle glycogen stores, hypoglycaemia (low blood sugar levels), dehydration and gastrointestinal upsets.

Some athletes may not need to change their nutritional strategies in the run-up to competition, however in some sports it is necessary to alter energy or macronutrient intake to make weight or to 'carbohydrate load' for the event. In either case, athletes should have an eating strategy for competition day that has been tried and tested during training.

Figure 15.3 Nutritional preparation is essential for competition success. (Courtesy of Team Northumbria)

Carbohydrate Loading for Endurance Events

During prolonged endurance events, glycogen concentrations can reach critically low levels and therefore it is essential to maximize stores before the start of the competition. Carbohydrate loading usually increases muscle glycogen stores 50–100 per cent above normal concentrations. Carbohydrate loading strategies have been studied for a number of years, and it is generally accepted that a taper in training and a high carbohydrate intake (8–12g CHO per kg BM) for 36 to 72 hours before competition will maximize muscle glycogen storage.

The Pre-Competition Meal

Although many athletes do not like to consume meals before competition, the food and drinks consumed in the hours before exercise have a role in fine-tuning competition preparation. Although the main goals of a pre-competition meal are to ensure that muscle and liver glycogen stores are topped up and the athlete is well hydrated, this meal will also help prevent feelings of hunger, and may be eaten as part of a psychological preparation for competition.

The timing of a pre-competition meal is dependent on individual tolerance to food and the competition schedule. Ideally, a meal should be consumed three to four hours before the start of competition to allow full digestion of the food. However, early morning events sometimes mean that this time scale is not possible. Research suggests that if 200–300g (7–10.6oz) of carbohydrate is consumed 2 to 4 hours before exercise, endurance performance is significantly improved (Wright *et al.*, 1991).

The pre-competition meal should be rich in carbohydrates and generally low in fat and in fibre, and have a moderate protein content. This should help to avoid gastrointestinal discomfort in the postprandial period. Consuming carbohydrate foods with a low glycaemic index (GI) is often advised. The GI compares the characteristics of different carbohydrates, and refers to the degree to which the concentration of glucose in the blood rises after consumption of the food. Foods with a low GI are digested and absorbed more slowly, resulting in a slower increase in blood glucose than foods with a high GI (which tend to be rapidly digested and absorbed). Low GI foods, therefore, result in a gradual release of glucose into the bloodstream, preventing a sudden drop of glucose during the early stages of exercise, and also provide a supply of glucose throughout exercise. Some studies have also shown that a pre-exercise LGI meal can help prevent feelings of hunger and also increase the rate of fat oxidation during exercise (Wee *et al.*, 1999; Wu *et al.*, 2003; Stevenson *et al.*, 2006).

Ideally athletes should choose foods that suit their personal preference and avoid gastrointestinal discomfort. Different pre-competition nutritional strategies should be experimented with during training. Some ideas for pre-competition food intake are provided in Figure 15.4.

Pre-Exercise Hydration

Fluid intake is very important in both training and competition. Large amounts of fluid are lost from the body through sweat during exercise, even in a cold environment, and if the fluid is not replaced the athlete will become dehydrated. Dehydration not only limits muscular endurance, but it can also affect mental functioning: dehydration by as little as

- Muesli with semi-skimmed milk and fruit

- Beans on wholegrain toast + fruit juice

- Pasta with tomato based sauce

- Tortilla wrap filled with lean chicken or ham and salad

- Fruit salad and yoghurt

- Wholemeal pitta bread with filling

- Oatcakes with low fat cottage cheese

- Crumpets or English muffins with honey or jam

Figure 15.4   Pre-competition food ideas.

2 per cent of body weight can severely limit exercise capacity and therefore needs to be avoided.

To try to avoid dehydration during exercise, it is essential to commence exercise in a fully hydrated stated. Generally, ingesting excess fluid before exercise is ineffective as the kidneys excrete any excess body water. Studies have investigated the effect of consuming salt or glycerol solutions to minimize the usual diuresis when a euhydrated individual ingests excess fluid (Shirreffs *et al.*, 2004). However, palatability issues and gastrointestinal discomforts mean that hyperhydration techniques are rarely used. If euhydration is maintained during exercise, then the general consensus is that hyperhydration has no meaningful advantage.

NUTRITION FOR RECOVERY

Good nutrition between training sessions is essential for rapid and effective recovery. The recovery diet needs to replenish muscle glycogen stores, body water and electrolytes. Good nutrition during recovery is also essential to repair and regenerate muscle tissue following the damage caused by exercise.

Carbohydrate Intake Post Exercise

Athletes should aim to consume sufficient carbohydrate to meet their fuel requirements for training and to optimize muscle glycogen resynthesis during the recovery period. General recommendations can be provided, however individual differences in training load and energy requirements should always be considered.

> - Immediate recovery after exercise (0–4hr): 1– 1.2g carbohydrate per kg per hr consumed at frequent intervals
>
> - Daily recovery: moderate duration/ low intensity training: 5–7g carbohydrate per kg per day
>
> - Daily recovery: moderate to heavy endurance training: 5–7–12g carbohydrate per kg per day
>
> - Daily recovery: extreme exercise programme (4–6hr + per day): 10–12g carbohydrate per kg per day

Figure 15.5   General recommendations for carbohydrate intake during recovery from exercise.

> ■ 2 cereal bars
>
> ■ 3 slices of toast
>
> ■ 4 Weetabix
>
> ■ 3 crumpets
>
> ■ 2 milky ways
>
> ■ 2 bananas
>
> ■ 850ml Lucozade
>
> ■ 4 fig rolls
>
> ■ 2 wholemeal pitta bread

Figure 15.6   Recovery snack options that provide approximately 50g of carbohydrate.

The recovery strategy adopted by an athlete depends on the time between exercise sessions. It takes approximately 24 hours to fully restore muscle glycogen, therefore, if the recovery time is shorter – with athletes training twice a day, or late evening and early morning – adaptations to the recovery strategy need to be made. When the period between exercise sessions is less than 8 hours, carbohydrate intake should begin as soon after exercise as is possible. The first 30 minutes after exercise is known as 'the window of opportunity', because this is when the enzymes that promote muscle glycogen resynthesis are at their highest concentration. Athletes should aim to consume 50–100g (1.76–3.5oz) of high GI carbohydrates within the first 15 to 30 minutes after exercise. High GI carbohydrates are recommended, as they provide a rapid source of glucose into the bloodstream for glycogen resynthesis. If foods cannot be tolerated post exercise, sports drinks are a good option.

The co-ingestion of protein with carbohydrate during recovery has also been shown to be beneficial to the enhancement of post-exercise protein synthesis, and may also augment muscle glycogen resynthesis if carbohydrate intake is not optimal (Ivy *et al.*, 2002). Although further research is required in this area, substantial enhancement of post-exercise protein synthesis can be achieved by consuming 3–6g (0.1–0.2oz) amino acids. This equates to approximately 10–20g (0.3–0.7oz) protein.

Rehydration

The replacement of water and salts lost in sweat is an essential part of the recovery process. Athletes should aim to drink about 1.2–1.5 litres (2.6–3 pints) of fluid for each kg (2.2lb) of BM lost during the exercise session (Shirreffs *et al.*, 2004). Plain water is not the ideal post-exercise rehydration drink when rapid and complete restoration of fluid balance is necessary. Drinks should contain sodium (the main electrolyte lost in sweat) if no food is eaten during the initial recovery period. Most sports drinks contain electrolytes as well as carbohydrates, making them an ideal recovery product. When fluid losses are high – greater than 2 litres (3.5 pints) – higher sodium intakes may be required (50–80mmol/L). This can be achieved by consuming salty foods as recovery snacks, or adding salt to meals. Oral rehydration solutions will also contain higher sodium concentrations.

Cooled and flavoured drinks are more palatable and therefore will increase voluntary consumption. Caffeinated drinks and alcohol should be avoided during recovery, as they will increase urine loss.

CONCLUSION

The importance of diet and good nutritional practices in the daily training schedule, competition preparation and recovery of athletes cannot be underestimated. While general guidelines can be provided, nutrition requires a very personalized approach, and each coach and athlete should take on the responsibility of being aware of their nutritional needs and set nutritional goals. Any athlete's needs will change throughout the year, therefore their diet should be monitored and reassessed at regular intervals. Achieving the right dietary intake and eating patterns will help athletes to perform to their optimal ability both in training and competition.

Table 1 Carbohydrate intake goals

Minimal physical activity	2–3g carbohydrate per kg body mass
Light physical activity (3–5hr per week)	4–5g carbohydrate per kg body mass
Medium physical activity (10hr per week)	6–7g carbohydrate per kg body mass
Élite athletes (20+ hr per week)	7+ g carbohydrate per kg body mass

Table 2 Guidelines for maximum protein requirements for different athletes

Sedentary	0.8g protein per kg body mass
General training programme	1.0g protein per kg body mass
Endurance athlete undertaking a heavy training programme	1.2–1.6g protein per kg body mass
Strength athlete undertaking a heavy training programme	1.2–1.7g protein per kg body mass

16

Athlete Recovery

by Emma Cockburn

Athletes train and compete throughout cycles (pre-season, Olympic cycle) with the aim of preparing and performing successfully in a specific event. To achieve this aim, athletes place a lot of importance on promoting physiological adaptations to enhance performance – for example, muscle hypertrophy for increased force production. However, the importance of recovery for achieving these aims can be overlooked. This chapter aims to allow coaches to understand why athletes need to recover, and the modalities that can be used.

WHAT IS RECOVERY, AND WHY DO ATHLETES NEED IT?

Following training and/or competition an athlete's performance may be impaired, which could last from minutes or hours, up to several days. Performance can be impaired by damage to the muscles and surrounding tissues, depletion of energy stores, fatigue of the brain and muscles, and psychological fatigue. Recovery should be incorporated into training cycles to limit performance, physiological and psychological impairments to allow the athlete to train at the levels necessary for successful training and competition. If an athlete does not recover fully then they may be predisposed to injury (Barnett, 2006). Finally, recovery should be incorporated into a training programme so that the body has time to adapt physiologically.

Recovery encompasses a number of situations. Athletes should ensure that over the long term, fatigue does not build up by incorporating recovery methods into their yearly/seasonal/competition programmes. An athlete should focus on the basics before delving into more complicated and expensive strategies (*see* Figure 16.1). Rest is of primary importance for recovery, and coaches should ensure that athletes have enough rest by incorporating recovery days or weeks into training schedules, and altering the intensity, load and frequency of training programmes. Sleep is also very important, as sleep deprivation can have negative impacts on mood, motivation and completing training sessions competently (Reilly and Edwards, 2007). Finally, ensuring that an athlete's diet and hydration is

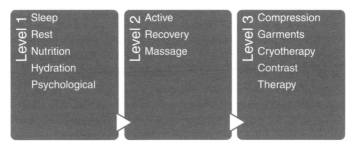

Figure 16.1 Levels of recovery.

optimal for health, immune function and fuelling performance is important to limit fatigue. These aspects are discussed in greater detail in Chapter 17 'Fatigue Management' and Chapter 15 'Nutritional Guidelines for the Athlete', and this author would refer you to those chapters.

This chapter will focus on acute methods of recovery between training sessions, and how they affect physiological recovery (repair of damaged muscles and tissues, replenishment of energy stores and ensuring the brain and muscles are no longer fatigued), perceptions of recovery and subsequent performance.

RECOVERY METHODS

This section outlines a number of recovery methods that are commonly used in performance sport. There are other methods used, but this section is limited to those that are most popular among athletes at this time.

Nutrition

Chapter 15, 'Nutritional Guidelines for the Athlete', discusses the intake of carbohydrate and protein for replenishing energy stores and repairing muscle tissue, therefore for more information this author would refer you to that chapter. This section will focus on the use of milk or milk-based products as a recovery method. These products are readily available and can be a cheap method of recovery. The consumption of milk has been found to limit the decreases in force production observed following muscle-damaging exercise (eccentric muscle actions, for example, the downward phase of a squat), but it did not attenuate the increases in perceived muscle soreness (Cockburn *et al.*, 2008). Milk has also been shown to be a useful post-exercise hydration strategy (Shirreffs *et al.*, 2007) and beneficial as a recovery drink for endurance performance (Thomas *et al.*, 2009). This demonstrates that the use of milk may limit damage to the muscle tissues, improve hydration status and benefit performance, which would allow subsequent training and/or competition to take place at closer to optimal levels.

Active Recovery

Active recovery involves athletes completing light aerobic exercise immediately post training or competition. The benefit of active recovery is primarily based on the increase in blood lactate removal following exercise
(Coffey *et al.*, 2004). The use of an active strategy for recovering from
muscle-damaging exercise has also been investigated, and there are equivocal findings. Suziki *et al.* (2004) found that in comparison to a passive recovery, active recovery did not affect muscle tissue damage measured via
neutrophil function, whereas Gill *et al.* (2006) found that the clearance of
creatine kinase (CK) was enhanced with active recovery. CK is an extremely
variable marker of damage to the muscles, and therefore these findings
must be interpreted with caution.

Although this demonstrates that active recovery can be beneficial for
aspects of physiological recovery, coaches need to know if this translates
into performance improvements. From the research it would appear that
there is very little evidence to suggest that active recovery is beneficial for
subsequent performance (Tessitore *et al.*, 2007; Coffey *et al.*, 2004; Spencer
et al., 2008). However, there may be a psychological benefit. It has been
found that following a period of active recovery, perceived muscle pain
(Tessitore *et al.*, 2007) and POMS tension score (Suzuki *et al.*, 2004) are
lower in comparison to what they would be after a period of passive recovery. The ability to alter an athlete's psychological state via active
recovery can be crucial, as an athlete's working attitude may be changed
(Tessitore *et al.*, 2007).

Coaches must, however, be aware of the potential downfalls of a recovery intervention. Active recovery could possibly decrease the rate of glycogen synthesis post exercise in comparison to passive recovery (Fairchild
et al., 2003), which could be crucial for subsequent performance. An athlete's post-exercise CHO consumption may also be affected by recovering
actively (Barnett, 2006), in that as athletes are performing light exercise
they do not consume CHO (or enough CHO) within the optimal timeframe for beneficial recovery.

Stretching

Stretching is commonly used by athletes both before, during and post exercise. The main role of stretching is to increase the range of movement
around the joints. There are very few studies investigating the effects of
stretching for recovery benefits, and the studies that have been conducted
have focused on muscle soreness. It appears that the effects of stretching on
reducing muscle soreness are minimal, so currently there is no apparent
benefit of using stretching for recovery. Further to this, pre-exercise stretching has been shown to be detrimental to sprinting (Nelson *et al.*, 2005) and
does not improve running economy (Jones, 2002). Therefore if stretching
can be detrimental to performance, then it is probably not advisable as a
recovery intervention.

Figure 16.2 Active recovery can be beneficial for physiological recovery. (Courtesy of Northumbria University)

Massage

Massage is widely used by athletes for recovery following intense exercise since it is considered to have a number of physiological and psychological benefits. It is mainly thought that massage reduces pain, oedema and DOMS and enhances blood lactate removal (Weerapong *et al.*, 2005) through increased muscle blood flow (Barnett, 2006), and that this is how recovery is improved. However, this explanation no longer stands due to studies using new techniques demonstrating no changes in muscle blood flow with massage (Shoemaker *et al.*, 1997). Therefore, there is a lack of evidence for physiological recovery.

There is very little scientific evidence that massage improves muscle function (strength and ROM) or subsequent performance in the days post exercise. This is an important point for coaches to note. However, many athletes use massage as they are convinced by its potential to reduce muscle soreness (Howatson and van Someren, 2008); there is sci-entific evidence to suggest that massage does reduce perceptions of muscle soreness (Zainuddin *et al.*, 2005).

It would appear that massage may aid recovery through changes in perceived muscle soreness, but there is very little evidence of any other recovery benefits. Barnett (2006) states that if muscle soreness is reduced without any physiological or performance benefits, then an athlete may perceive they are capable of higher training loads than their actual capacity. This may lead to more stress and fatigue than would be appropriate, and potential injury risk (Barnett, 2006). However, changes in soreness do not necessarily relate to changes in muscle function (strength), therefore this may not be a high risk; however, coaches must be aware of this factor.

Compression Garments

The use of compression garments for recovery is becoming more popular among the athletic population, and in the sporting world there seems to be an acceptance that they are beneficial for recovery. However, there have been very few scientific studies conducted in this area, and of those conducted there are equivocal findings.

It is possible that the use of compression garments may increase lactate removal. However, studies have found both decreased blood lactate concentration (Chatard *et al.*, 2004) and no difference (Duffield *et al.*, 2008) when wearing compression garments compared to control groups. There are also equivocal findings regarding the use of compression garments for recovery from muscle damage. Kraemer *et al.*, (2001) found that changes in CK, ROM, soreness and swelling were attenuated, and recovery of force was enhanced with compression garments. However, compression was applied for five days, and this may not be applicable for athletes who train and compete on consecutive days. In support of compression garments benefiting recovery, Gill *et al.*, (2006) found an enhanced rate of recovery, measured by CK, when wearing compression garments compared to passive recovery following a rugby match. However, a number of other studies have not found improved rates of recovery from muscle damage with compression (Montgomery *et al.*, 2008; Duffield *et al.*, 2008; French *et al.*, 2008).

Very few studies have investigated performance improvements. One study found improved maximal work in a 5min exercise bout with compression garments worn during an 80min recovery period (Chatard *et al.*, 2004).

Figure 16.3 The use of compression garments for recovery is becoming popular. (Courtesy of Team Northumbria)

However, other studies have found no beneficial effects on performance (French *et al.*, 2008; Duffield *et al.*, 2008).

There are many different commercial compression garments on the market, and athletes will purchase these to aid recovery from exercise. However, there is little evidence to suggest they are beneficial. Furthermore, commercial compression garments apply approximately 18mmHg of pressure, which may not be sufficient to impact on recovery (Montgomery *et al.*, 2008).

Water Immersion

A number of different recovery methods involve an athlete being immersed in water. This section will cover cryotherapy and contrast therapy, as these are two of the most popular strategies used in recovery. Two other water immersion techniques that will not be discussed are thermotherapy, which involves immersion in hot water (> 36°C) and water immersion per se which is immersion in water between 16 and 35°C (Wilcock, Cronin and Hing, 2006).

Cryotherapy

Cryotherapy is the application of cold. This can involve, but is not limited to, immersion in cold water of less than 15°C. In the field, this method is more commonly referred to as ice baths, and consists of putting bags of ice in containers filled with water. The time immersed in water varies from 5–15min. This now appears to be a popular method of recovery used in high performance sports. Cryotherapy is thought to be of benefit to recovery, especially from muscle-damaging exercise, by reducing inflammation, swelling, oedema and pain (Swenson, Sward and Karlsson, 1996).

There are equivocal findings with regard to the benefits of cryotherapy on recovery following muscle-damaging exercise. Measures used to demonstrate recovery have been indirect markers of muscle damage, such as CK and myoglobin, muscle soreness and muscle function or performance. For coaches it is important to understand the effect of cryotherapy on perceptions of recovery (soreness) and performance. Roswell *et al.* (2009) found no beneficial effect of cold water immersion on recovery in physical performance tests related to football over a four-day tournament. However, there was less general fatigue and leg soreness in those receiving this recovery intervention.

In contrast to this, it has been found that following a simulated football match (LIST), cryotherapy limited perceptions, of soreness and muscle function for up to forty-eight hours (Bailey *et al.*, 2007). This is similar to Vaile *et al.*, (2008), who found benefits of cold water immersion on muscle function and performance. However, other studies have found no benefit of cryotherapy on muscle soreness or muscle function (Howatson, Goodall and van Someren, 2009; Sellwood *et al.*, 2007).

There appears to be evidence that demonstrates a lack of effect of cryotherapy. However, this may be due to the lack of empirically based guidelines on how to use it (Howatson *et al.*, 2009). As with any recovery intervention, coaches must be aware of any potential limitations. From a practical standpoint, this form of recovery may be impractical for team sports due to the time required to treat all athletes (Wilcock *et al.*, 2006). In addition, although this intervention is about enhancing recovery for optimal subsequent training, there is a worry that training adaptations may be hindered due to alteration of the inflammatory process. Again, coaches must be aware of the potential limitations of certain interventions.

Contrast Therapy

Contrast therapy involves the athlete immersing their body (or parts) in alternating temperatures of water. This consists of cold water (< 15°C) immersion followed by hot water (> 36°C) immersion, repeated in cycles of approximately 30–300sec (Wilcock *et al.*, 2006). The benefit of contrast therapy is said to be due to increased venous return, and increased removal rate of metabolic waste products (Cochrane, 2004). In this regard it has been found that contrast therapy decreases blood lactate concentration following high intensity running (Coffey *et al.*, 2004), and decreases CK following a rugby match (Gill *et al.*, 2006).

In terms of performance, however, the results are equivocal. Vaile *et al.*, (2008) found contrast therapy to be beneficial to performance; other studies have found no benefits of contrast therapy on subsequent performance or muscle function (Coffey *et al.*, 2004; French *et al.*, 2008). In terms of perceptions of recovery, Coffey *et al.*, (2004) found that with contrast therapy, athletes reported lower perceptions of fatigue, discomfort and stress during recovery.

Strategy	Physiological	Perceptions	Performance
Nutrition (milk)	✓	?	✓
Active Recovery	✓	✓	X
Stretching	?	X	X
Massage	?	✓	X
Compression Garments	?	?	?
Cryotherapy	?	✓	?
Contrast Therapy	✓	✓	?

✓ - Likely benefit
? - Equivocal results/not enough research to draw conclusion
X - Limited benefit

Figure 16.4   Benefits of recovery strategies.

There has been little research conducted in this area in terms of recovery; of what exist, implies there may be a physiological and psychological benefit, but without a benefit to performance. Therefore, there is potential for contrast therapy to be used as a recovery intervention, although for some coaches their use of this strategy may be limited due to practical reasons.

CONCLUSION

It is clear that for most recovery interventions there are findings that show them to be beneficial, and research demonstrating the opposite; some are beneficial for perceptions of recovery, whereas others have benefits for physiological recovery (*see* Figure 16.4). The key for coaches is ensuring that recovery is included in training programmes, the basics are done to a high standard, and the recovery intervention chosen is suitable for the individual. For example, an individual may like a particular recovery intervention as it makes them 'feel' better, even though there are no studies to justify this and no physiological or performance benefits.

'Individual' is a key word, and it is not only important that the athlete supports the use of the chosen recovery method, but also that recovery is individualized. Thus different athletes may benefit from different recovery interventions. Other factors that coaches should account for when implementing recovery interventions is that a combination of strategies may be most beneficial, and to ensure continued benefits, variety is employed. To reiterate, throughout all of this it is important that level 1 of recovery is implemented. The uses of these techniques are cheap, require no specialists to come in to apply the recovery intervention, and can be done by the athlete themselves.

Finally, as a coach it is your role to educate your athletes in recovery, to ensure they are implementing the basics correctly, and to inform them of the pros and cons of recovery interventions.

- Level 1 of recovery must be implemented

- The 'individual' is key

- Employ variety

- Use a combination of recovery techniques

- Be aware of the pro's and con's of each recovery technique

- Keep up-to-date with advances in old and new recovery techniques

- Educate and inform your athletes

Figure 16.5 Tips for coaches.

17

Fatigue Management in the Preparation of Athletes

Dr Paula Robson-Ansley
and Dr Les Ansley

The main goal for all athletes is to improve their performance, and this is achieved by increasing the frequency, volume and intensity of their training. Increasing training load is often successful and results in an improved athletic performance. However, all athletes will inevitably experience fatigue following training and competition, ranging from short-term 'normal' fatigue when recovery is achieved within hours or days, to longer-lasting 'abnormal' fatigue where recovery is prolonged (a week or two in the case of overreaching, and months or even years in the case of overtraining or unexplained underperformance syndrome, otherwise known as 'UUPS'). Since performance and training will be compromised during periods of fatigue, the management of fatigue is an essential part of athletic training. Athletes and coaches need to be able to monitor and effectively manage fatigue in order to optimize recovery and performance.

The aim of this chapter is to explore a range of practical and contemporary methods of fatigue monitoring and general fatigue management for athletes. More specific fatigue management strategies, including short-term recovery methods, nutrition and hydration strategies for athletes, will be covered in other chapters.

TOOLS FOR MONITORING FATIGUE

Not every athlete will have regular access to an exercise testing facility or laboratory, so it is not possible to use objective measures to assess an athlete's condition on a daily basis. Therefore asking an athlete to personally assess their level of fatigue using psychological 'pen and paper' questionnaires provides a more practical method of monitoring fatigue and recovery

Figure 17.1 Monitoring fatigue in the laboratory.
(Courtesy of Northumbria University)

in athletes. Indeed, research suggests that a self-assessment questionnaire completed by the athlete on training load, perceived stress and mood state may give a more reliable indication of how the athlete is coping with training, as well as provide a more practical and reliable method of assessment than costly laboratory-based tests.

Assessing Training Load

High training loads are often associated with high levels of fatigue as well as signs of under-recovery and overreaching, which may lead to the development of the long-term debilitating syndrome, UUPS. Therefore, it is essential that during periods of high training loads, athletes and coaches devote sufficient time to ensure optimum recovery from the previous training session. An estimation of training load can be calculated by three main methods.

The first is the observational method, which involves observing and recording real-time measurements such as type and duration of a training session with split times or workloads to assess intensity, or recording the session on a video camera for time/motion analysis. Real-time measurements can provide accurate training load information and show evidence of an athlete's compliance to prescribed training, but this method is time-consuming and it is potentially costly for the recorder to be present at each training session as well as to analyse the data.

The second is a physiological method involving the monitoring of key physiological variables such as heart rate, blood lactate concentration and oxygen consumption during training sessions: these provide information on the intensity of steady-state exercise. The measurement of lactate can provide an indication of training load, however, daily variations in muscle glycogen stores and diet can affect lactate concentration and may lead to inaccurate results if not rigorously controlled or standardized prior to each training session. Oxygen consumption would give an accurate indication of exercise intensity, but this requires costly equipment and technical expertise at each training session, which would outweigh its usefulness for measuring load during routine training.

Finally, a useful yet simple method of assessing training load developed by Dr Carl Foster (1998) is to ask athletes to give a subjective estimate of their perceived level of exertion during a training session. Athletes decide upon a score from the rating of a perceived exertion scale (Borg 1982), which reflects their perceived exertion during the training session known as sRPE (session rating of perceived exertion). The daily exercise load is calculated by multiplying each day's exercise rating of perceived exertion used by the total exercise duration (in minutes); the result represents in a single number the magnitude of exercise load. A score for training monotony (standard deviation of the weekly load) and training strain (load x monotony) can also be calculated from the total weekly load and noted in a diary, which would give further insight into the athlete's adaptation to training.

This method has been used to indicate to coaches the athletes who are not coping well with training and who are at risk of developing long-term fatigue problems and/or UUPS. Athletes should give their sRPE score at least 30 minutes post exercise to ensure that the score is reflective of the entire session, rather than just a score based on the final part of the session. The recommended threshold for weekly training load is 4,000–5,000 units; if an athlete is reporting greater loads, then they may be at risk of UUPS.

Day	Duration	sRPE score	Total daily load
Mon 15th April	60 mins	8	480
Tues 16th April	75 mins	6	450
Wed 17th April	180 mins	6	1080
Fri 19th April	75 mins	8	600
Sat 20th April	65 mins	7	455
Total for week			**3520**

Calculation of scores:

a) Weekly load   **3520**
b) Daily average load   704
c) Daily standard deviation of load   268
d) Monotony (b/c)   2.6
e) Strain (a x d)   9152

Figure 17.2   Training load diary and calculation of load scores (Foster 1998).

Questionnaires

Profile of Mood State Questionnaire (POMS)

The mood state of an athlete is often indicative of the physical or psychological stress they are experiencing. Mood state has been shown to be related to training load: thus a worsening of global mood disturbance has been positively associated with an increase in training load, whereas an improved mood state has been shown to be indicative of an athlete recovering from UUPS, which also paralleled improvements in athletic performance.

A questionnaire commonly used by athletes to assess mood state is the Profile of Mood State questionnaire (POMS) developed by Morgan and colleagues (1987). The original POMS questionnaire is fairly lengthy, and as a consequence a shortened POMS questionnaire has also been developed by Grove and Prappavessis (1992), which may be more practical and less time-consuming. Changes in total mood disturbance (TMD) can be calculated by an athlete or coach by adding together the five negative scores (fatigue, anger, depression, confusion, tension), then adding 100 and subtracting the one positive mood score, vigour. If the questionnaire were completed on a regular basis during training and the TMD logged in a diary, then a baseline could be established. Any elevations above the TMD baseline could be highlighted by the athlete and discussed with the coach/ sport scientist to ensure the athlete is adapting well to training load.

Daily Analyses of Life Demands for Athletes Questionnaire (DALDA)

The Daily Analyses of Life Demands for Athletes (DALDA) questionnaire was developed by a Canadian swimming coach, Brent Rushall (1990), to assess the athlete during training but also during the time they are not training. Often athletes are under psychological stress unrelated to their chosen sport – family bereavement, divorce, work-related stress – and this may have a significant impact on their athletic performance and adaptation to training.

The DALDA questionnaire is divided into two key sections: Part A represents the 'sources of life' stress – such as personal relationships, home life – and Part B represents the 'symptoms of stress' – for example, generalized fatigue, a sore throat. The DALDA questionnaire is normally completed by the athlete daily or on alternate days, and the athlete or coach can graphically plot the day-to-day responses to the questionnaire. The athlete is asked to indicate the scale of their stress on the questionnaire in response to each question: a) worse than normal, b) normal, c) better than normal.

A significant rise in the sum of the 'worse-than-normal' responses above baseline, and which remains elevated for several days, may indicate an athlete who is not coping with training and/or has some life event which may impact on performance and could possibly result in UUPS. The DALDA appears to be a sensitive indicator that is responsive to changes in training load. One study reported a significant increase in the 'symptoms of stress' inventory (Part B) before a fall in innate immune function was detected during a two-week period of intensified training

Part A

1.	a	b	c	Diet
2.	a	b	c	Home-life
3.	a	b	c	School/college/work
4.	a	b	c	Friends
5.	a	b	c	Sport training
6.	a	b	c	Climate
7.	a	b	c	Sleep
8.	a	b	c	Recreation
9.	a	b	c	Health

1.	a	b	c	Muscle pains
2.	a	b	c	Techniques
3.	a	b	c	Tiredness
4.	a	b	c	Need for a rest
5.	a	b	c	Supplementary work
6.	a	b	c	Boredom
7.	a	b	c	Recovery time
8.	a	b	c	Irritability
9.	a	b	c	Weight
10.	a	b	c	Throat
11.	a	b	c	Internal
12.	a	b	c	Unexplained aches
13.	a	b	c	Technique strength
14.	a	b	c	Enough sleep
15.	a	b	c	Between sessions recovery
16.	a	b	c	General weakness
17.	a	b	c	Interest
18.	a	b	c	Arguments
19.	a	b	c	Skin rashes
20.	a	b	c	Congestion
21.	a	b	c	Training effort
22.	a	b	c	Temper
23.	a	b	c	Swellings
24.	a	b	c	Likability
25.	a	b	c	Running nose

Part B

a = worse than normal   b = normal   c = better than normal

Date:	Part A	Part B
Total 'a' response		
Total 'b' response		
Total 'c' response		

Figure 17.3   Daily Analyses of Life Demands in Athletes (DALDA) questionnaire score sheet (Rushall, 1990).

(Robson-Ansley *et al.*, 2007). When training resumed normal levels, the worse-than-normal scores in the symptoms of stress inventory returned to baseline. The DALDA may also be a useful daily self-monitoring tool for athletes to develop a sense of self-awareness of sources and symptoms of physical and psychological stressors from both the sporting and non-sporting environment, which could impact on their performance and well-being.

Performance Tests

In general, under-recovered and fatigued athletes are unable to sustain normal training and have a diminished sports-specific performance capacity. Although they are usually able to start a normal training sequence or a race at their normal training pace, they are not able to complete the training load they are given, or to race as usual. Therefore, a performance test is considered to be essential for confirming normal recovery following periods of high training load, but can act both as an early warning system for the onset of UUPS, or may indeed confirm that an athlete has recovered from prolonged UUPS.

Debate exists as to which type of performance test should be used for evaluating an athlete who may be under-recovered and at risk of UUPS. In general, time-to-fatigue tests – exercise at a fixed intensity until the athlete is unable to maintain the prescribed work rate – will most likely show greater changes in exercise capacity than incremental exercise tests. In order to detect subtle performance decrements it is advisable to employ a sport-specific performance test.

Blood and Saliva Screening

Many studies have attempted to identify a biochemical, haematological or immunological biomarker that could be used to distinguish between well trained healthy athletes, overreached athletes, and athletes with UUPS, but no single, reliable diagnostic marker has yet been found. Increased levels of creatine kinase (CK) and/or urea measured in the blood under standardized, resting conditions may provide information concerning elevated muscular and/or metabolic strain, but they are not suitable to indicate overreaching or the presence of UUPS. Similarly, although the saliva concentration of specific antibodies – for example, immunoglobulin A – may fall during intensive training (Tharp *et al.* 1990), these measures are not reliable markers of overreaching, partly due to large day-to-day fluctuations in an individual, which may provide misleading information.

Other measures of the immune system are generally too time-consuming and expensive to be of practical use. While blood parameters (for example, blood cell counts and haemoglobin concentration, serum C-reactive protein, creatinine, liver enzymes, glucose, ferritin, sodium, potassium and so on) cannot detect under-recovered or overreached athletes, or those with UUPS per se, they are helpful in providing information on the actual health status of the athlete.

GENERAL FATIGUE MANAGEMENT STRATEGIES

Rest

One of the most obvious methods for managing fatigue and enhancing recovery is adequate passive rest and obtaining sufficient sleep. Athletes and coaches should aim for at least one passive rest day each week, and possibly more in times of competition and high training load. Research has highlighted that the absence of a recovery day, especially during intensive training periods, leads to athletes becoming overreached and under-recovered.

A passive rest day can also act as a 'time-out' period for athletes, preventing them becoming totally preoccupied with their sport, and possibly encouraging them to pursue a different (passive) interest. Such distractions

Fatigue monitoring tools	
Self-scored questionnaires	Easy to administer and effective for monitoring athletes and developing self-awareness. Questionnaires include POMS, DALDA.
Training load assessment	Questionnaire based training load assessment provides a simple but effective method. Observational and physiological methods are time consuming and costly.
Performance tests	Need to be sport specific. Time to fatigue tests currently favoured.
Blood/saliva screening	Expensive and time consuming. No reliable diagnostic marker for UUPS. Useful for providing information on athlete health status.
General fatigue management*	
Rest	Minimum recommendation is one day passive rest per week. Essential for ensuring recovery and avoid UUPS. Alleviates training boredom and reduces stress perception.
Sleep	Essential part of fatigue management. Sleep deprivation impacts on cognitive performance and fine motor skills. One full night sleep can compensate for previous poor sleep.

*(guidelines for nutrition and hydration see Chapters 15 and 16)

Figure 17.4   Summary of methods for monitoring and managing fatigue in athletes.

from the daily routine of training may alleviate boredom and reduce stress perception. Common sense must prevail when prescribing rest; for example, if an athlete has undergone excessive training or is exhibiting abnormal levels of fatigue, longer periods of passive recovery may be required.

Sleep

Sleep is an essential part of fatigue management, as persistent sleep loss can negatively impact on the quality of a training session and the athlete's general well-being. Poor sleep can impair cognitive functions, and in particular the ability to concentrate. Mood state can be affected by sleep loss, and can reduce an athlete's motivation to exercise and complete training sessions competently (Reilly and Edwards, 2007). Research suggests that athletes are able to overcome the effects of sleep deprivation and perform supra-maximal exercise, but they become less motivated to maintain a high level of performance in sustained exercise, or in the repeated exercise bouts that commonly occur in training (Reilly and Piercy, 1994). Sleep deprivation studies have shown that three nights of partial sleep deprivation can impair the performance of fine motor skills, whereas gross motor functions can remain unaffected.

Individuals have different requirements for sleep, and to prescribe the dose of sleep that a highly trained athlete requires would be misleading. The general advice is to sleep for the amount of time that is required to feel wakeful during the day, which may vary considerably between individuals. Poor sleep may be compensated for by short post-lunchtime naps. Napping for 30 minutes with a 30-minute post-nap recovery period has been shown to improve sprint performance and reaction time following a night of reduced sleep (Waterhouse, Atkinson, Edwards, Reilly, 2007).

The ability to nap for short periods during the day may be a useful skill for athletes to develop, because for many individuals a disturbed night's sleep prior to an important competition is probably not uncommon. However, caution should be taken, as longer daytime naps will result in longer post-sleep inertial periods, and resumption of optimal performance may take longer. In the case of disturbed night sleep from noise, the use of earplugs should be recommended. There are also practical implications for travelling: for example, when selecting accommodation, it is sensible to request a quiet room away from a busy street and not close to entrances, stairs, lifts or bars and restaurants.

A full night of undisturbed sleep can result in full recovery from a period of poor sleep.

Nutrition and Hydration

The key point in relation to nutrition for an athlete is that diet affects both health and performance: the foods and drinks that are consumed in training and competition will affect how well an individual can train and compete (*see* Chapter 15).

OVERVIEW

As athletes strive to improve their performance they will inevitably experience varying levels of fatigue, which will require effective management and monitoring by both the athlete and coach. Self-reports by means of questionnaires such as the POMS and DALDA questionnaires appear to be practical and effective methods of indicating changes in training-related stress and overreached athletes, whereas immune measures may prove expensive and potentially misleading.

With an effective strategy for the monitoring and management of fatigue, athletes should be able to optimize training sessions and realize their true potential in the competitive arena.

18

Performance Analysis and the Role of Biomechanics

by Dr Su Stewart, Kelvin Beeching and Melanie Tuckwell

Performance analysis is the recording of a specific sporting movement, performance or game, in order to obtain quantitative data (Bartlett *et al.*, 2006). The term 'performance analysis' encompasses all facets of the process, from the gathering of the data to its analysis and communication to coaches and athletes (Robertson, 2002).

Sport has always included some forms of analysis, whether it is by the performer undertaking self-analysis, the spectators or the coaches. Over the last few decades, however, sport has developed many different notational systems. Coaching is about enhancing the performance of an individual, a unit or a team, and importantly this is done using feedback. A coach needs to gather this information through both observation and memory; however, researchers have consistently shown that human observation and memory, impressive though they are, are not reliable enough to provide the detailed information necessary to secure desired behavioural changes (Franks and Miller, 1986).

Performance analysis enables objective data to be gathered on events (Hughes and Franks, 2004). This data is reliable (Borrie *et al.* 2002), and avoids the potential for bias that coaches, managers or broadcasters may incur (Reilly and Williams, 2003; Hughes and Franks, 2004). Franks and Miller (1986, 1991) demonstrated that coaches are only correct 30–50 per cent of the time in their post match analysis of events, which highlights the need for objective, reliable analysis. Therefore many coaches now employ more objective measuring tools – for example, hand notation and video analysis.

The key task for a coach is to analyse and gather data about an individual and/or team performance, and then use this information to provide players with the necessary feedback for skill development and performance enhancement. Information on performance is obtained through the use of notational analysis, which is a technique for producing a permanent record of events being analysed (James, 2006). In order for a coach to give feedback with a clear, objective, statistical account of the match, a notational analysis system can be devised that categorizes what key actions have occurred within a match. Figure 18.1 highlights the importance of analysing play, as the coaching process generally comprises a number of steps or cycles (adapted from Franks *et al.*, 1983).

The coach initially observes and analyses the play, then interpretation of the information obtained on match performance is necessary before feedback can be given to the players. The coach utilizing this information will plan subsequent practices/strategies, and then their delivery to the athletes. Performance analysis enables the coach and the performer to compare their performance with models of optimal skill built up from observations of élite performers in the field, combined with theoretical models of what could optimally be achieved (McMorris and Hale, 2006). Good coaches have a mental picture of what they are looking for in terms of optimal skill, and compare and match the observed skills of a performer with their model of optimal performance (Bartlett *et al.*, 2006).

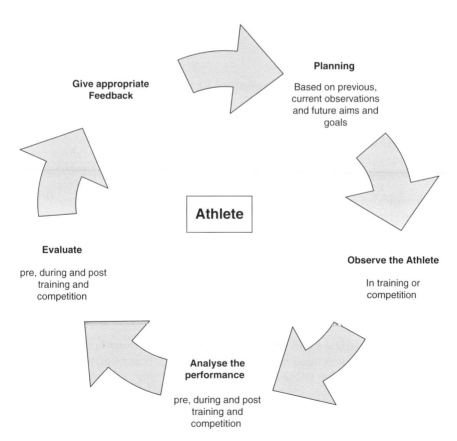

Figure 18.1   The Coaching Process Model.

NOTATIONAL ANALYSIS SYSTEMS

Notational analysis stems back many years to the Egyptians, who used hieroglyphs to read dance, and the Romans who exercised a primitive method of notation for recording salutory gestures. The major 'starting base' for the development of a general movement notation system came through the medium of dance. The greatest development in dance notation was the system referred to as 'Labanotation', named after the inventor, Ruldoph Laban. The next step in development came in 1947 in the form of another dance notation, known as 'choreology'. After this period, movement notation systems developed in the field of expressive movement, eventually turning into notational analysis in sport.

The earliest recordings of findings of hand notational systems were by Fullerton in 1912 (Hughes and Franks, 2004), who analysed the probability of success by baseball players in batting, pitching and fielding. However, in 1939 the first team notation system was devised by Messersmith and Bucher, who studied the distance covered by specific basketball players in a match. Since these early days notational systems have been developed to fit several purposes; for example:

- To identify patterns of play of successful and unsuccessful teams
- To analyse the outcomes of different patterns of players/strategies
- To identify physiological parameters that characterize different team sports.

The match analysis process (computer or manual) is based on four key observed factors:

- The performer involved
- The action itself
- The location (position) of the action
- The time at which the action took place (Robertson, 2002).

Information regarding the player is simply their name/position. Where the actions took place – the location – can be recorded according to the half of pitch (defending half), for example, or in more detail (the opponent's goal area). The field of play can also be broken down into segments or zones. Action time can be recorded as the exact time the action occurred, or in segments every two minutes. The action type can also be very often recorded at different levels, from one-to-one contest to more complex total figures – for example, the number of passes/kicks/runs/ tackles made.

When designing a hand notation system there are four key stages, and importantly coaches need to understand what is being collected and the relevance of the data. These are:

- Deciding the quantity and type of information
- Designing the hand-based system
- Checking on the accuracy of the data
- Collating and presenting the findings.

The basic parts of a hand-based match-analysis system comprise the player, the action and the position; more complex systems would include the time and sequence of events. A simple notation system may use a tally system to record match actions, as seen in Figure 18.2 below. A more complex system that looks at positional data can be notated by breaking down the pitch into segments, as highlighted in the diagram.

When using notational analysis the coach must consider which methods to use (hand notation or computer package), and also the skills needed, and then filter this on to the paper/computer. The speed with which data can be entered, and the length of time it takes to collate the findings at the end, must also be considered. Therefore, coaches need to be cautious about the method to use, and the relevance of the data being collected. Simple notation systems that focus on a small number of actions and which can give quick results pitch side, are of greater value than those that produce a larger amount of data.

	Successful Actions	Unsuccessful Actions
Pass	✔ ✔ ✔ ✔ ✔	✔ ✔ ✔
Shoot	✔ ✔	
Intercept	✔ ✔	✔ ✔ ✔
Dribble	✔ ✔ ✔	✔ ✔
Tackle	✔ ✔ ✔ ✔ ✔	✔ ✔
Total	17	10

Figure 18.2   A simple tally sheet to record frequency counts of successful and unsuccessful actions.

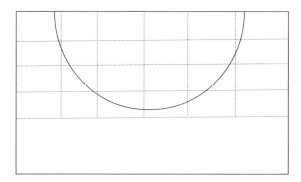

Figure 18.3   A schematic sheet that could be used to determine the frequency of shots on goal within the shooting circle in hockey.

Developing a Notational System

When devising a notation system there are many ways of collecting the data. First of all, discussions should take place between the coach and the analyst as to why the analysis is being undertaken. A simple flow chart can help to create the type of analysis needed. Franks and Goodman (1984) devised the game of hockey in two models: either Team A has possession of the ball, or the opposing Team B does – this would be at the top of what they term the hierarchy. The next level in the hierarchy is to question:

- Where on the field did Team A or Team B gain and/or lose possession?
- Can these be identified on the pitch (for example, by dividing the field into a number of areas)?
- Which player on the team gained or lost possession?
- How was the possession won or lost (for example, was it a tackle, ball off the pitch, missed shot)?

These questions can be included in a structure as indicated in Figure 18.4.

Due to the complex nature of sport and the many factors that affect a player or team, it is important that no matter what data the coach requires, whether it is to include physiological or psychological factors, it is advisable to start simple and gradually add other actions and their outcomes. Franks and Goodman (1984) suggest three steps or tasks to be undertaken in their evaluation of performance. These are:

Task 1: Describe the sport from the general to the specific
Task 2: Prioritize key factors of performance (see Figure 18.4)
Task 3: Devise a recording method that is efficient and easy to learn.

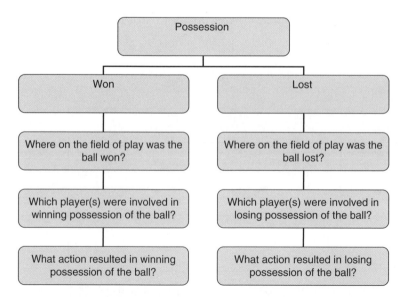

Figure 18.4   Developing a simple notational analysis system for invasion games.

Detailed actions and outcomes – such as where and how possession was won and/or lost – can then be included in the model for events that take place.

Coaches often decide what information is useful according to their personal philosophy, previously defined objectives, and the previous performances of the team (Franks *et al.*, 1983). Many coaches will work with key performance indicators (KPI's): for example, in netball, the KPI may be to score 80 per cent of their team's own centre pass. Primary analysis may look at the number of centre passes that are scored or not. Secondary analysis breaks this information down and will look at where on court the possession is being lost, by whom, and the subsequent outcome.

The main barrier to adopting these manual methods of performance analysis are the perceived complexity and the significant investment of time needed to code, analyse and interpret the data (James, 2006). Many coaches now utilize both a hand notation system combined with a video recording of the match. This causes problems, however, as it can become very time-consuming and tedious with the constant rewinding and fast forwarding of play.

VIDEO ANALYSIS

In the multi-billion pound sports industry the need to log events accurately, reliably and objectively is imperative. Due to the pace of modern games, video and software analysis is increasingly used to provide comprehensive, accurate analyses at both a team and individual level.

Analysis at Team Level

Models of performance can be developed at team level. These take into account the analysis of overall performance factors such as match tactics, team strategies and cohesion. Whole sport analysis at a macro level is now a common practice for team sports, with a number of easily learned software packages available for simple, real-time analysis. An excellent example of this type of system analysis has been developed by Dartfish Professional. This enables a coach to watch a match while simultaneously entering (tagging) details such as time on the ball, number of passes, type of stroke, number of tackles and so on.

More detailed analyses can also be made after the match, when the contribution of individual players throughout the match can be quantified from the analysis of video. An example of one type of possible analysis can be seen using Prozone software (http://www.prozonesports.com). This shows the activity levels and positioning of an individual player within the team tracked during the first half of a match.

This process of analysis can be time-consuming; however, developments in global positioning satellite (GPS) motion tracking systems has enabled software to be developed to track individuals in real time during practice games. Data on individual players within a team can be gathered and compared, and this can be utilized by the coaches to develop and

Figure 18.5   Dartfish Professional software being used to 'tag' a rugby union match. (Reproduced with the permission of Dartfish)

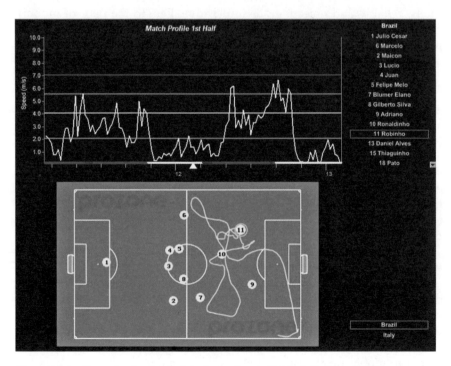

Figure 18.6   Example of a detailed analysis of an individual during a match using Prozone software. (Courtesy of Prozone)

monitor training programmes and performances. It can also be used in talent identification and scouting systems (Bartlett, 2001).

Analysis at Individual Level

In individual sports performance, analysis can enable a coach to develop a profile of a player's strengths and weaknesses, and to build a database of the strengths and weaknesses of potential opponents. The prior knowledge of an opponent's profile of strengths and weaknesses gives a competitor, or a team, a massive advantage. Knowing an opponent's preferred tactics, what skills they possess, and how they are likely to react to different situations, can provide information from which a game plan or strategy can be devised, and can also inform team selection (Bartlett, 2001). For example, it is very useful to know areas where an opponent is likely to be technically weak but tactically naïve – in other words, areas where they are willing to engage, but do not have the necessary expertise, exposing a potential area of weakness that can be exploited.

One way of profiling opponents is to rank them on a number of different continua. For example, a player can be placed on the continuum from 'warrior' to 'finesser', described by Czajcowski (2004) as follows:

Warrior: a bold, assertive player, limited in their range of effective moves, does not plan ahead, is able to react quickly and think on their feet; an opportunist, who can beat technically better players through bullying tactics.

Finesser: an intelligent player who thinks and plans their way ahead, cautious in terms of capitalizing on errors, prefers to set up attacks two or three moves ahead, and plays the percentages; unwilling to take risks.

Players all fall somewhere on this continuum between the two extremes. They have an effective operating range on the continuum where they can compete effectively against different types of opponent, and under different conditions of fatigue and competition stress and anxiety. They also have a preferred range where they are most skilful, and feel most comfortable: their 'comfort zone'. They may also have an extended range 'under development', where they are being coached in new techniques. This continuum can be represented as shown in Figure 18.7.

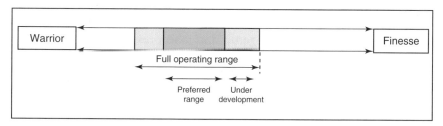

Figure 18.7 The 'warrior–finesse' continuum.

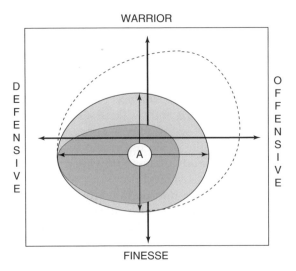

Figure 18.8   Bi-axial continuum.

Players can also be considered as being either predominantly offensive or defensive, and again there is a continuum between the extremes. Players are likely to have an effective working range within which they can comfortably adapt their strategy to changing circumstances within a competition. A player's effective operating range can therefore be represented on a bi-axial continuum plot.

In Figure 18.8 the pale green zone represents the usual effective range of the skills of a player, 'A', who has well developed skills, but who likes to play in a defensive style. He is more of a 'finesser' than a 'warrior', however if pushed, he can attack effectively. The pale green area represents the area where he can operate effectively and win points successfully; his comfort zone, the darker area, is significantly smaller, and this is where he retreats when under pressure. The area within the dotted line, the training zone, is where he can expand to when playing a much weaker opponent who presents little risk, and where he can try out skills under development.

This can be used by the coach to plan what areas to develop. For example, in Figure 18.9, 'A' is a player who is predominantly an offensive warrior with a somewhat limited repertoire. If her coach were planning to increase her ability to use some more moves involving finesse and effective forward planning within a game, and to improve her defensive skills, this could be represented by the training zone. Interestingly, if her coach were to try and introduce a defensive skill requiring great finesse (as represented by 'B'), this would probably be unsuccessful, since she has not yet learned sufficient skills to be able to effectively link the new skill to her repertoire.

The ultimate problem facing the analyst is how best to transform the ocean of data into something meaningful (Hughes and Franks, 2004). Collecting the data, then collating and presenting it in a simple manner, can become a

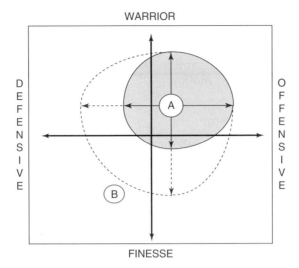

Figure 18.9   Individual athlete profile.

very time-consuming process, so the introduction of computerized notation with customized keyboards means that less time need be spent learning. In addition, the use of real-time analysis or post-event analysis in conjunction with video allows an immediate and easy access to data. As a result, Hughes and Frank (2004) have developed four major categories of computerized notation, defined as:

- Analysis of movement
- Tactical evaluation
- Technical evaluation
- Statistical compilation.

Computerized notational systems store a large amount of information in large databases, allowing coaches to access the bit of data or footage that they need. This has led to the development of match analysis systems using digital video footage and computers – for example, Dartfish, Plozone, Silicon Coach. For more information on how to present data from match analysis, refer to Carling *et al.* (2005).

SPORTS BIOMECHANICS

The individual skills of performers can be examined in detail at the micro level, and the skill can then be compared with a model of the most efficient means of achieving the desired outcome. This is determined again through observation of the performer and comparison with the skills of élite performers, a consideration of the underpinning mechanical principles, and an appreciation of what is anatomically and physically possible for a specific individual.

   Sports biomechanics is the process by which a performer is modelled as a mechanical structure consisting of a system of levers (bones) and actuators (muscles). In order to develop mechanical models of the human body it is necessary to have an in-depth knowledge of human musculo-skeletal anatomy – indeed, it is essential to know how bones and joints articulate, their optimal alignment, their ranges of possible motion, and the factors that limit their motion.

Methods of Observation

Coaching specific technical skills at the individual level is based on observation. Close observation and analysis is required in order to compare an observed skill with a model of optimal performance. Good coaches develop the skill of observation to a very high level; however, the coaching process can be greatly enhanced by the use of video, which has the following advantages:

- It enables the coach to record performances to give feedback to the performer, enabling them to see their own performance
- It replaces the coach's memory
- It provides a record of progress
- It provides information on the opposition and on élite players
- It enables the recording of information when the coach is not present.

One of the greatest opportunities afforded by video is the opportunity for slow-motion playback, and the capability of freezing the motion at moments of interest.

The use of affordable software packages such as Dartfish (http://www.ambra-solutions.co.uk/Dartfish) makes two-dimensional kinematic analysis a lot simpler for coaches in the field. These allow the coach to display and compare multiple video images, and to manipulate images by adding text, drawing lines, and measuring angles and displacements. It is also possible to compare video data with records of earlier performances, or of performances by élite performers. Figure 18.10 shows a weight-lifter with overlaid information, including the path of the end of the bar with the displacement and velocity values calculated.

Some software packages have been specifically developed to evaluate specific sports. One excellent example of this is the Gasp system (http://www.gaspsystems.com), which has been developed as a coaching aid to analyse the golf swing. Modern video cameras record directly to computer memory or to DVD, which allows direct transfer to computer software for analysis.

Comparative analysis of mechanical aspects of specific skills is made a lot simpler if the skill is broken down into key positions and key phases. Video data allows the coach and athlete to compare the athlete's key positions and phases with earlier performances in order to evaluate improvement, or those of an élite performer, or against a model of optimum performance, in order to evaluate where further improvements can be made. For example, for the football throw-in, the key positions are starting position, initiation of transition, end of take-back, release, and end of follow-through. The key phases are the movement between the key positions: take-back, transition, throw and follow-through.

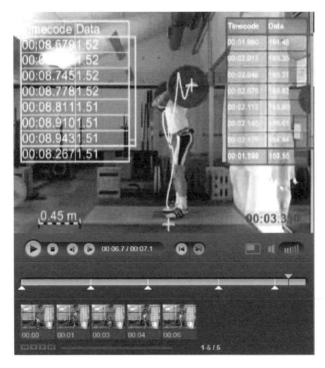

Figure 18.10   Dartfish software being used to look at simple kinematic data during a squat. (Reproduced with the permission of Dartfish)

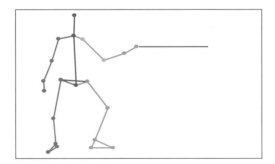

Figure 18.11   Spatial model of a fencer in the 'on guard' position.

Normal domestic video cameras sample motion at a frame rate of twenty-five frames per second (25Hz). For some sporting activities 25Hz is not fast enough to capture the fine detail of the action – for example, the string release (or loose) in archery, the golf swing, racket sports, martial arts or fencing. In order to conduct detailed analyses of these skills it may be necessary to employ high speed video. High speed cameras are available with frame rates in excess of 2000Hz, but there are problems associated with high frame rates related to the rate of storage of information needed to accommodate the speed of capture. High speed cameras require a high capacity dedicated computer memory to store the data in real time.

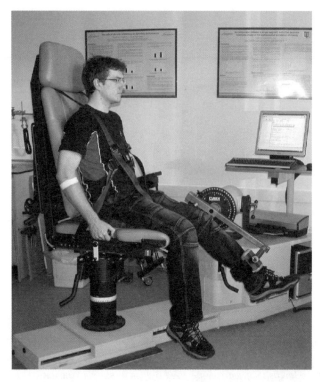

Figure 18.12   Isokinetic dynamometry in action. (Courtesy of Su Stewart)

High speed cameras also need very fast shutter speeds. In mechanical cameras the shutter speed refers to the length of time the iris behind the lens is open to emit light. The faster the shutter speed, the shorter the length of time the light is let in and the data captured, and therefore the more light that is needed to illuminate the subject. Shutter speeds are recorded in fractions of a second. Fast movements need a very fast shutter speed in order to freeze the action; an insufficient shutter speed causes the action to appear blurred. At least 1/1000sec is needed to capture a golf swing, whereas 1/125sec is adequate to capture a weightlifting action.

Fast shutter speeds therefore need very bright lighting conditions to illuminate the subject, as the iris is open for a very short time. Bright sunlight is usually sufficient, but indoors additional spotlights can be needed.

In order to compare a performer's skill against a model in any analytical depth, a sound understanding of the scientific principles of kinematic and kinetic analysis is required.

Kinematic Analysis

Software based on one video camera allows quick feedback to athletes, and can be used in the field. It is, however, limited to the analysis of activities that are largely two-dimensional, that mostly take place in a plane at right angles to the camera. More complex activities generally require three-dimensional analyses to be examined in any depth.

For the finer tuning of specific skills of élite performers, and for complex skills around more than one plane or axis, it may be necessary to use multiple cameras and more sophisticated software packages. These have often been developed for medical or clinical applications – for example, gait analysis, such as looking at the walking mechanics of children with cerebral palsy – or the military market, looking at the ergonomics of military hardware. They frequently require a period of familiarization before they can be used by coaches. They are also usually very expensive and laboratory based. They can give immediate feedback, but require a certain amount of data manipulation before feedback can be given. The main reason for this is because the subject is not represented as a video image, but as a spatial model within the software. Spatial models represent the athlete as a structure of points and linkages, and can be as simple or as complex as is needed to derive the required information. A common simple spatial model is the fourteen segment, twenty-one point model as shown in Figure 18.11.

These spatial models are superimposed on to the video image by a process of digitizing. Here the coach identifies each point of the model in the video and informs the software, which can then automatically recognize each point and track it in 3D space. To use these systems requires the subject to be 'marked up' with light reflective markers on key anatomical bony landmarks. The markers are usually small spheres covered with light reflective tape, usually between 2mm and 10mm (0.1 and 0.4in) in diameter, and these are attached with double-sided adhesive tape to key surface anatomical landmarks such as an ankle bone or a patella.

The subject then performs their skill in front of an array of cameras. The bright points of reflected light are identified in the software as specific markers, and the computer then calculates the position of each marker, for each frame in terms of X, Y and Z co-ordinates, into a large spreadsheet. This data can then be smoothed and manipulated to create visual representations and graphs of linear and angular displacement, velocity and acceleration.

Kinetic Analysis

Kinetic analysis is the study of motion in terms of the underpinning forces needed to cause motion. Forces can be either a push or a pull in terms of the effect they have on something, causing either a movement or a deformation (Hamil and Knutzen, 2008). A coach should understand the principles of how force is generated in the human body, and how this is transmitted to external objects, and how external forces are absorbed. He/she should also know the optimal alignment of bones and joints in order to transmit or absorb forces, in terms of both mechanical efficiency of the skill, and injury prevention.

Forces can be assessed by observation, or through the use of simple measuring devices such as scales, load cells or strain gauges. These are readily available to coaches and relatively inexpensive. More complex and expensive systems based on devices such as pressure plates, force plates and isokinetic dynamometers may only be available in specialist centres.

The isometric dynamometer is a useful tool with which to screen players for potential weaknesses, and to monitor players returning from injury. It is also an excellent rehabilitation tool.

The measurement of forces can be combined with video-based analysis to calculate 'turning moments', or torques, through the process of inverse dynamics. A turning moment is a force causing rotation, such as forces applied to bones by muscles causing movement at a joint – for example, forces applied by the biceps muscle causing flexion at the elbow joint. These are automatically calculated by the isokinetic dynamometer software, but can also be calculated by kinematic software such as the Vicon system to analyse the forces within joints of the body.

PART 3: IDENTIFYING AND DEVELOPING TALENT

19

Modelling Long-Term Athlete Development Pathways in Sport

by Dr David Morley and Professor Richard Bailey

This chapter highlights the process of development for athletes should they pursue a pathway from participation towards high-level performance within sport. Its foci are some of the main dimensions of participant and talent development pathways; in particular, it explores the following areas:

- Traditional understandings of participant development
- UK and international perspectives on talent development in sport
- Academic participant development models.

A BRIEF DISCUSSION OF TERMS

We have chosen to use the term 'athlete' as a generic term for the child, young person or adult involved in the pathway. The decision to use this term was not one taken lightly; indeed, the language of sports development is highly problematic, and littered with issues relating to the representation of an individual involved in physical activity and sport. Through debating and defining key terms used within talent development, we can begin to understand the central features of processes and systems that delineate and influence an athlete's progression along a pathway.

Alternative terms to 'athlete' are used by others, such as 'sports player', but this obviously refers to someone involved in sport, which in the UK is usually understood in terms of a certain type of formalized game, which does not capture the more general understanding of an individual who participates in physical activity or 'any bodily movement produced by skeletal muscle that results in caloric expenditure' (Bouchard, Shephard and Stephens, 1993).

The term 'participant' is used widely by various organizations (such as Sportscoach UK) and is an alternative, but in this context it seems useful to distinguish between different processes of development: participation and performance. In this sense, participation simply means an athlete's involvement in certain activities, irrespective of any aspiration of the participant or the facilitator (coach, teacher, parent, carer) for achieving higher levels of competence associated with performance. The differentiating factor that allows for a separation of the two terms is that performance asks us to quantify the level of competence within participation in order that the athlete can access further performance-based pathways.

The phrase 'long-term development' is used to express the longitudinal processes involved from an athlete's early experiences of casual and more structured types of physical activity through to recreational and/or élite level participation in sport. What is implied here, as an underlying principle, is that a range of factors outside of sport affects participation in sport. Therefore, those responsible for the processes and systems employed to recruit and retain talented athletes within sport must be cognisant of peripheral influences on athletes as they progress along a pathway. Indeed, this could lead to opportunities to synchronize developmental approaches for talented athletes offered by a range of agencies (e.g. NGBs) that allow certain athletes to maximize their potential. However, successful inter-agency approaches are rare, since the potential for such relationships is often neglected because approaches to pathway development become compartmentalized (e.g. within a sport), and fail to understand the athlete's development at the centre of the process.

STRENGTHENING THE BASE OF PYRAMIDAL PATHWAYS

Successful talent development pathways will ultimately be reliant upon the development of a motivated and well equipped base of athletes who possess a wide enough set of skills to respond to the changing needs and demands of sport over time. The need to attract athletes into physical activity and sport in the early stages of their lives, coupled with the subsequent establishment of a rewarding, enjoyable and meaningful environment, is therefore crucial. We might call this the 'Sweetenham rule', since it is based on the philosophy of the well known Australian swimming coach Bill Sweetenham: 'The best form of talent identification is mass participation' (*cf.* Green, 2007).

However, traditionally the focus on appropriate participation programmes for young athletes has been minimal in comparison to the development of performance programmes for élite and would-be élite athletes. The interdependency of these two aspects of talent development has been most often represented as a pyramid, which describes the role of participation at the base of the pyramid. It is often claimed that it is at the start of a talent development pathway that the greatest scope for improvement within coaching and sport development exists.

Kirk and Gorely (2000) state that the 'pyramid model of sport development is now well entrenched and is known to many people ... as the sport development continuum' (p. 121). Simply put, this model is as follows: a broad base of foundation skills participation, with increasingly higher levels of performance, engaged in by fewer and fewer people (*see* the diagram below). Houlihan (2000) has suggested that versions of the pyramid characterize many UK sports development policy statements, and Kirk, Brettschneider and Auld (2005) argue that its influence can be seen in numerous international sports participation models, and that 'the assumptions underpinning the pyramid model continue to have a powerful residual influence on thinking about junior sport participation and sport development in sport policy' (p. 2). Moreover, the language of a recent UK government-supported research report into élite dance development is interesting in part because of explicitness: 'Constructing a pyramid of progression for talent in dance' (Schmidt, 2006).

Figure 19.1 demonstrates the typical relationships found within a pyramid.

The Role of Physical Education in Strengthening the Base

Historically, the curricular area of physical education (PE) has been used to represent the mass participation required at the base of the pyramid to widen the pool of talent at the most appropriate time in which identification

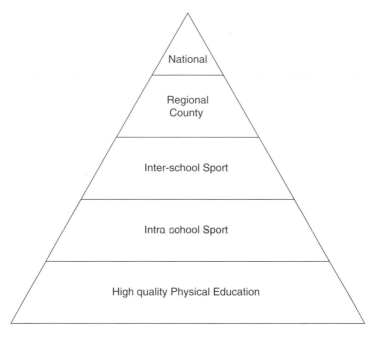

Figure 19.1   A pyramidal model representing the relationship between PE and sporting excellence (based on Kirk and Gorely, 2000).

would naturally occur. The debates around what constitutes an appropriate base layer of a pyramid are rife, and revolve primarily around an
understanding of the relationship between school-based PE and sporting
excellence (Kirk and Gorely, 2000; Penney, 2000). In general terms, the
'process' orientation of PE (learning, enjoyment, engagement) is seen by
some to clash with the 'outcome' orientation of sport (winning). This has
led to the belief that such conflicting orientations have caused a quandary
concerning the development of talented athletes in a school environment
using 'outcomes' of performance in sport without compromising educational principles of offering the 'process' of PE to all (Lee, 2004).

The conflict between PE and sport has also been discussed in a way that
suggests politicians and policymakers often use élite sport to frame discussions about PE. In what has been referred to as the 'commonsense
consensus', concerns have been raised about the factual accuracy and
ethical integrity of an approach that suggests that PE is able to, and indeed
should, act as the foundation for élite sport development (Kirk, 2004).
Furthermore there are other, more fundamental potential difficulties with
a traditional sports development model based on a pyramidal approach.
Kirk and Gorely (2000) offered some points by way of warning:

- If children are taught poorly at the base, we will be left with a large
  number of poor performers
- Built into the pyramid's design is the systematic exclusion of young
  people, no matter how good they are, as fewer and fewer players can
  play at each level.

Some suggest that there are four components that would enhance the relationship between participation, primarily within PE, and performance in
a more inclusive and productive way (Kirk and Gorely, 2000). These essential components are:

- Clearly articulated pathways
- The widespread use of modified games and sports
- Teacher and coach education
- Intelligent policy development.

The mapping of these components comes as a result of the perceived need,
suggested by the authors, to view entrance points to healthy active lifestyles and talent development pathways simultaneously. However, there
is a danger that a focus on the convergence of such parallel pathways
could detract from the task of understanding the specific focus of the relationship between PE, sport for all, and sporting excellence. Indeed, Kirk
(2005) has continued to critique the role of PE in establishing practices that
are supportive of a child's lifelong participation in sport. He documented
the importance of early learning experiences, suggesting that current
interventions are failing in this area.

Other research has also highlighted athletes' perceptions of PE as part
of their talent development pathway. A number of athletes identified as
talented in PE by their teachers suggest that they often experience frustration, anxiety and a lack of challenge within PE lessons, with the main

focus of their development being focused upon extra-curricular activity (Morley, Cobley and Bailey, 2005). From this evidence, it seems that the role of PE in acting as the base of any developmental pathway responsible for nurturing talented athletes is flawed at a number of levels.

Similarly in America, through an interpretation of the ways in which athletes become socialized into sport, Siedentop (2002) attempted to comprehend the relationships between the various facets of sport. He suggested that the primary goals of junior sport are the public health goal, the educative goal, and the élite-development goal, with a less apparent goal of enhancing, preserving and protecting sport practices. Siedentop recognized the significant three-dimensional conflicts that exist in junior sport, and it was the critical tensions that exist between the 'educative', 'élite' and 'public health' goals that were at the forefront of his concerns when he stated:

> One can legitimately question the degree to which élite-development goals of a junior sport system can be served as part of a comprehensive system and still direct sufficient resources to achieve the educative and public health goals that are more fundamental to the system as a whole (p. 396).

Siedentop suggests that educative and élitist notions of youth sport compete against each other and therefore cannot coexist. In Siedentop's model, educative goals are those that perpetuate inclusivity, diversity and adaptability; élitist goals, on the other hand, facilitate the most talented athlete's pursuit of excellence and the realization of their potential. It is clear that there are differences between English and American schools, and it could be suggested that Siedentop's reflections are more a portrayal of the Varsity culture of American schools, in which sport plays such a pivotal role in the school curriculum.

Furthermore, it could also be argued that this would result in the notion of élitism becoming more readily accepted as an integral element of schooling through the perpetuation of cultural and traditional influences. That said, the point being made here is more to do with an understanding that there are competing notions of development that will influence the ways in which an athlete progresses along a pathway, and such notions must be acknowledged by coaches in order to support successful athlete progression.

One way of counteracting the exclusivity related to some athlete development pathways is to adopt coaching systems and practices that respond to the needs of a wide range of athletes. The mantra required to ensure a semblance of co-existence of élitist and educative notions of development is related to how we establish practices that conform to both philosophical notions. To do this, we must configure coaching practices in a way that develops those athletes who are demonstrating higher potential than their peers, whilst also using practices that offer opportunities for optimal development of all athletes. Figure 19.2 demonstrates the dual delivery dimensions of such an approach.

Talent development	Developing talent
Maximises potential in all	Develops individual potential
Equates with the principle of equity	Concerned with principles of excellence
Relies on breadth of existing pedagogical practices	Relies on norm-referenced assessment of children in specific domains
Assessment based on individual performance and improvement	Predominantly concerned with current performance

Figure 19.2   Dual delivery support of athlete development pathways.

While it is an oversimplification to suggest that recreational levels of participation in physical activity, sport or PE are responsible for talent development, and sport for developing talent, it is reasonable to suggest that certain environments may be more conducive to certain types of practices than others. Moreover it is interesting to note that the agent of delivery is, to some, the key defining feature, as Sue Campbell, the English government's adviser on PE and sport explains: 'The coach will be looking to increase performance whilst having a concern for the individual. The teacher is looking to achieve wider educational objectives through a physical medium' (Kay, 2003, p. 8).

So it seems that provision within participation at the base of the pyramid as part of an educational context remains, in the main, as part of a sporting network of practices that contributes to, rather than determines, the pathway of athlete development. Participant development in sport and physical activity is dynamic and non-linear, and there are multiple pathways that individuals may take as they progress in their activity (Abbott, Button, Pepping and Collins, 2005). This non-linearity, coupled with the importance of 'key events and transitions' in the developmental pathway (Ollis, Collins and McPherson, 2006), suggests the vital importance of support systems that offer flexibility, individual development and 'return routes' as features of any formal 'pathway to excellence'.

Traditionally, excellence in sport has been conceptualized in terms of outcome measures in the form of medals, records and victories (Penney, 2000). More recently however, and reflecting growing interest in life-long participation in physical activity, there has been a call to expand this definition to include excellence in terms of personal participation and improvement (Miller and Kerr, 2002). The former conception of excellence is clearly concerned with performance excellence in high level sport such as national and international competition. Conversely, the latter conception frames excellence as the achievement of challenges across the length of one's lifespan, as well as the acquisition of those personal qualities which contribute to lifelong health and well-being (Cimons, 1999). As such, accomplishments such as completing a marathon, making a personal best, or participating in recreational activity, can be considered as the pursuit of 'excellence' when, from the performer's perspective, they are measured in terms of personal achievement (Weiss and Chaumenton, 1992).

Actual resources	c.%	Required resources	c.%
Psychological	3	Psychological	60
Fundamental motor skills	7	Fundamental motor skills	30
Anthropometrical	90	Anthropometrical	10

Figure 19.3   Abbott et al.'s (2002) findings on 'actual and required resources in talent identification'.

A UNITED KINGDOM PERSPECTIVE ON TALENT DEVELOPMENT IN SPORT

In England, the development of young athletes identified as talented in sport to date has been mainly directed by Sport England, UK Sport and the Youth Sports Trust. Sport England's (2004) current presentation of the relationship between learning, participation and excellence clearly reflects the traditional pyramidal model outlined above. According to this approach, the main role of schools (and especially PE) is to act as the foundation of young people's sports participation by developing basic knowledge, skills and understanding in a range of activities.

Scotland's lead agency for sport, Sport Scotland, operated a pilot Talent Identification and Development Programme in partnership with three local authorities, which used a series of physical tasks and an interactive CD-Rom to determine the suitability of sports for young people (Abbott *et al.*, 2002). The subsequent academic review was highly critical of the use of physiological and anthropometrical testing, suggesting that 'these [characteristics] are unstable during adolescence, they vary with age, and recent studies have proved inconclusive' (Abbott *et al.*, 2002, p. 2). According to the report, such tests may eliminate prematurely those with potential and favour early maturers, although even these children will be disadvantaged as they may not be technically developed as the emphasis would tend to be on their strength and size. Abbott and her colleagues also suggested that there was a dichotomy in terms of required and actual resources in talent identification. These are highlighted in the accompanying table.

Abbott *et al.*, suggested that some of the factors influencing this dichotomy were the 'lack of visibility of innate characteristics in early childhood'; 'the environmental impact on the development of the individual'; and the realization that 'the determinants of potential are largely psychological' (p. 7). Whilst the study was limited in terms of the scale of the research undertaken and the lack of detail provided regarding the methods used, the report was revolutionary in nature in that it challenged some of the historically fundamental frameworks of talent identification used throughout the UK and internationally. In particular, the perception that there was an existing over-reliance on anthropometrical measurements,

Figure 19.4   (Courtesy of David Griffiths).

allied with the dearth of psychological aspects involved in talent identification, raised questions as to the most appropriate methods of identifying talent in sport at the time.

Sport England (2002) has previously used an interactive, school-based CD-Rom system, entitled 'Sport search', which 'empowers young people to make informed choices about sport' (p. 1). The system was designed to 'support secondary teachers with the delivery of PE' (Sport England, 2002, p. 1), and it worked by matching physical, physiological skill profiles and preferences with sports that the students might enjoy with a number of physical tasks undertaken during PE. 'Sport search' did not claim to be a talent identification programme, rather a sports encouragement programme; although it is suggested that teachers may identify some young people from the results who are potentially talented, and refer them to other development programmes.

The Youth Sport Trust (2008) continues to refine a junior athlete education programme, which was implemented through the specialist sports college network, school sports partnerships and selected national governing bodies of sport. The programme was based on three levels of support:

- Workshops for talented young athletes
- A workshop for their parents
- Mentor support from teachers and/or coaches.

The whole system was based around the concept of 'Team You', focusing on the individual athlete while recognizing the critical role of parents/carers and teachers in the process of talent development; this concept is highlighted in the accompanying diagram.

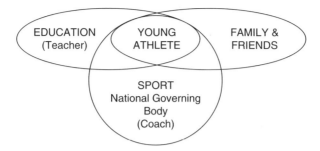

Figure 19.5   Youth Sport Trust (2008) Junior Athlete Education 'Team You' concept.

The programme emphasized the need for quality support for the young athlete, and this entailed the training of teachers and parents to enable them to effectively support the talented performer. This structure raises issues regarding the commitment of all individuals who are expected to be involved in the mentoring process, particularly from outside the formalized existing structure of PE. It could be argued that additional commitment is an integral part of any talent development programme, but although the crucial role of the parents is acknowledged, there is concern over the reliance of the programme on commitment from parents to devote their time to attend the required workshops and training events.

When considering the evidence presented in this section so far, the main perceived flaw of the junior athlete education programme is not so much in its system of provision, but more in its method of identification, which relies solely on the use of county level representative honours, utilizing current performance as the single criterion for nomination. This defies previously mentioned research that suggests that potential and non-sport specific ability should be an integral component of any talent identification system (Abbott *et al.*, 2002). There is also potential for conflict in the way that the programme is administered within an educational environment that fails to acknowledge the worth of pupils succeeding in areas of PE other than sports performance.

One of the first significant studies conducted specifically to explore talent development for younger people in England was Rowley's (1992) Training of Young Athletes (TOYA) study, which was commissioned by the Sports Council following growing concern about the negative effects of intensive training on children. A total of 282 parents of children involved in football, gymnastics, swimming and tennis were interviewed. Although the study is now fairly dated, it did provide some interesting data about the reasons why children become involved in sport, and the factors affecting their progression into intensive training. Rowley included physical, psychological, familial, educational and general social background amongst important factors in performance potential, and adds 'the lack of any systematic screening in school means that for a child to be identified they must first be participating in some level, in sport' (p. 4). This obviously discounts the role of the school and – whether intentionally or not – PE in effective talent development, and may have tainted the overall outcomes of the project.

The results of the research suggested that parents played a major role in introducing children to sport (swimming 62 per cent, gymnastics 33 per cent, football 36 per cent, and tennis 45 per cent), with variations on the influence of either or both parents. The reasons why children start intensive training are generally shared between identification by a regional or club coach and the children themselves through self-motivation. In contradiction of this, Csikszentmihalyi *et al.* (1993) suggested that only a minority of youngsters who show early indications of promise respond to the need to increase effort and commitment to develop their talent.

In summarizing the report, Rowley (1992) suggested that 'talent identification in this country is not carried out in any systematic way, and depends almost exclusively on the motivation of parents and their children' (p. 9). He concluded by highlighting the ineffectiveness of coaches in the talent identification procedure if children have not been initially encouraged to participate in sport by parents. The implications of the findings of this study suggested that more should be done to acknowledge the important role that parents play in the process of talent development, and links with parents should be forged at the earliest opportunity.

The English Sports Council (1997) – the earlier manifestation of Sport England – conducted research using a variety of methodological instruments, ranging from interviews with twenty-three officers from national governing bodies to a postal questionnaire sent out to 1,434 élite and pre-élite performers. A variety of factors affecting 'pathways to excellence' for élite performers were explored, such as ethnicity, social class, educational qualifications, coaching, medical services and opportunities to compete. Although this study offered a retrospective insight into the development of talent, it is interesting to note that 'In order to reach the performance level [necessary for selection], competitors generally had to achieve a consistent level of performance (61%) or they took part in trials (60%)' (p. 12).

The use of competition as an effective means of talent identification in its own right has been documented before (Peltola, 1992). However, it is the athletes who do not succeed in the particular sport that they have chosen whose potential may be wasted as a result of lack of opportunities 'to identify potential performers from outside a sport's participant base' (English Sports Council, 1997, p. 12).

INTERNATIONAL MODELS OF TALENT DEVELOPMENT IN SPORT

It is difficult to discuss international developments in the same detail as those in the UK, as similar levels of investment are not always as apparent. Many countries have developed national talent search programmes in a quest to unearth and nurture previously wasted potential across a range of sporting activities.

For example, the Australian Institute of Sport has developed a programme that prepares talented athletes (aged eleven to twenty years) for participation in domestic, national and eventually international competition, utilizing information across all disciplines of sports sciences to identify young athletes with characteristics associated with élite perform-ance (Kirk, Brettschneider and Auld, 2007). Athletes are then directed into a specialist sport chosen from a list of over twenty nationally recognized activities. The recognition that club systems alone do not provide a suffi-cient pathway for élite level performance has prompted the design of the programme to use schools as its focal area of testing (Hoare, 1995). The programme sought to measure the following attributes:

- Psychological
- Physiological
- Physical
- Skill/decision making
- Kinesthetic
- Sociological.

With the high-profile success of recent Australian teams it would seem that the Australian Talent Search programme has proved extremely successful. However, the use of physiological, psychological and kinanthropometrical testing within a school environment raises questions as to the role of PE, the use of battery tests for children in PE, and the possible negative effects of employing such a system for all children (Abbott *et al.*, 2002).

Germany developed a different approach, and many schools contribute to its talent development scheme. For example, talent identification and selection takes place in schools, and sports groups work with teachers to analyse performance in sports competitions and physical ability tests. Also, as in England, Germany has seen the development of specialist sports schools ('Sportschule'), although these have a different character and intent. German sports schools were designed specifically to support the education and sporting development of talented young people through opportunities to board at the school, as well as flexible timeta-bling of lessons and formal tests, to make it as easy as possible for these young athletes to succeed both within school and in their chosen sports. Distinctive elements within the German specialist school model were:

- Lessons were organized to allow sports training twice a day
- School examinations were co-ordinated with the training schedule and competition calendar
- Remedial school lessons were available following sports training courses
- Admission to university could be delayed
- Specialist teachers were available at the boarding schools, to support the young sports people (Kirk, Brettschneider and Auld, 2003).

With a smaller population than the majority of its international counter-parts, New Zealand does not have the benefit of large groups of players to form a substantial foundation for subsequent élite participation. Therefore the system here emphasized the close collaboration between sports clubs and schools and explicitly based talent development on general participation and recreation. The following illustration represents the ways in which schools worked alongside other areas of sports participa-tion, to help nurture and develop talent in New Zealand.

ACADEMIC PARTICIPANT MODELS

Istvan Balyi's Long-Term Athlete Development

Long-Term Athlete Development (LTAD), associated with the ideas and theories of Istvan Balyi, has probably been the most influential model of participant development in the UK in recent years. All the main national governing bodies for sport have been required to adopt and adapt a version of LTAD, and to promote it among their members. Stafford (2005) acknowledges that the model's primary aim is to produce greater numbers of performers who are capable of achieving at the highest level, but also claims that it provides a platform for coaches and participants at every level 'to fulfil their potential and remain involved in sport' (p. 1).

Balyi (2001), like almost everyone who writes about developing excellence, quotes Herbert Simon as a way of introducing and justifying his model: 'It takes ten years of extensive training to excel in anything.' Long-term development, he argues, is the basis for realizing and optimizing potential. This development is conceptualized in terms of a series of stages through which players pass; the precise timing and nature of these stages is determined by the type of sport in question. Balyi distinguishes between 'early' and 'late' specialization sports. Early specialization sports include gymnastics, diving, figure skating and table tennis; in other words, those sports that conventionally require their players to begin to specialize and seriously train from a relatively early age. Late specialization sports, which are made up of almost all other sports, and Balyi's model prescribe a more generalized approach, including an emphasis in the early stages on fundamental movement skills. The accompanying illustration outlines LTAD's stages and progressions for early and late specialization sports.

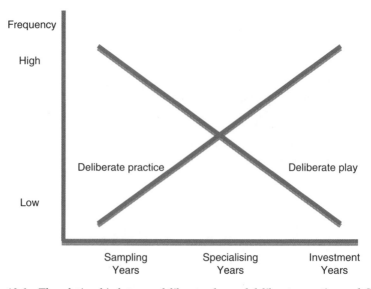

Figure 19.6   The relationship between deliberate play and deliberate practice, and Côté's three levels of sport participation (Côté and Hay, 2002).

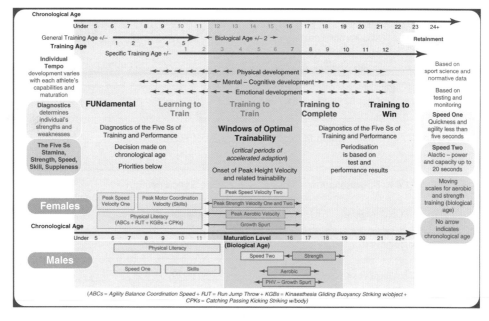

Figure 19.7   Adaptation to training and optimal training (Balyi and Way, 2002).

Balyi's work has been primarily addressed to coaches and coach educators, and he has not published his work in mainstream academic, peer-reviewed journals. This does not, in itself, raise doubts about the veracity of his claims, nor their relevance to practical coaching; but it does mean that LTAD has not undergone the usual quality assurance procedures associated with scholarly work. Moreover, many of the sources he quotes

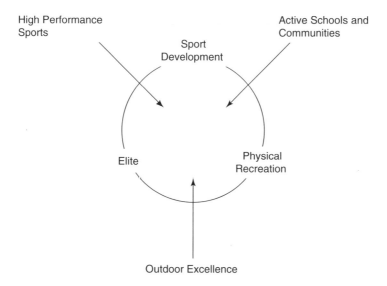

Figure 19.8   The New Zealand model (based on Kirk, Brettschnieder and Auld, 2003).

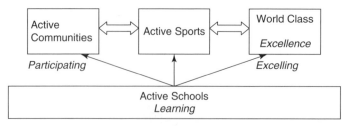

Figure 19.9   Sport England's model of junior sport participation.

Early Specialisation	Late Specialisation
FUNdamental	FUNdamental
Training to Train	Learning to Train
Training to Compete	Training to Train
Training to Win	Training to Compete
Retaining	Training to Win
	Retaining

Figure 19.10   LTAD stages (Stafford, 2005).

as offering support for LTAD's central claims are either difficult to access or read, as many originate from the former Soviet Union.

The type of sources Balyi cites suggests that LTAD has its origins in the biological or physiological tradition. Overall, LTAD can reasonably be described as a physiologically orientated development model, as is evidenced by the figure reproduced in Stafford (2005), which outlines relevant factors related to adaptation to training and optimal training. While the figure refers to mental-cognitive and emotional development, all the structural and constraining variables come from biology theories, such as peak height velocity, critical periods of accelerated adaptation, and growth spurts. LTAD can be interpreted as Balyi's interpretation of biological ideas like this, and the result is a framework of guidance that integrates ages, stages and training principles.

Côté's Developmental Model of Sport Participation (DMSP)

If Balyi's LTAD model can be described as a biologically or physiologically orientated framework, then Jean Côté's DMSP model is a psychological one. Côté and colleagues (Abernathy, Côté and Baker, 1999; Beamer, Côté and Ericsson, 1999; Côté, 1999; Côté and Fraser-Thomas, 2007) extended Bloom's earlier work with talented individuals through qualitative

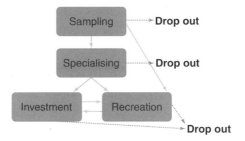

Figure 19.11   The Developmental Model of Sport Participation (adapted from Baker and Côté, 2006).

interviews with élite Canadian and Australian gymnasts, basketball players, netball players, hockey players, rowers and tennis players. Similar to Bloom, Côté identifies three stages of development:

The sampling phase (six to twelve years): children are given the opportunity to sample a range of sports, develop a foundation of fundamental movement skills, and experience sport as a source of fun and excitement.

The specializing phase (thirteen to fifteen years): the child begins to focus on a smaller number of sports, and while fun and enjoyment are still vital, sport-specific commitment emerges as an important characteristic of sport engagement.

The investment phase (sixteen-plus years): the child becomes committed to achieving a high level of performance in a specific sport, and the strategic, competitive and skill development elements of sport emerge as the most important.

Progression from the sampling phase can take one of three forms: children can become more seriously involved in one or two sports in the specializing phase; they can choose to stay involved in sport as a recreational activity; or they can drop out of sport. Likewise at the specializing phase, players have three options available to them: recreation; drop out; or progress to the investment phase, when they aspire to a high level of performance in one sport. Those players who have reached the investment years can subsequently either progress to recreational sport, or simply drop out.

The DMSP contains another important distinction, between 'deliberate play' and 'deliberate practice'. Ericsson, Krampe and Tesch-Römer (1993) concluded their comprehensive review of the literature-into-skill acquisition and expert performance with the finding that the most effective learning occurs through participation in what they called 'deliberate practice'. This form of practice requires effort, is not inherently enjoyable, and is specifically designed to improve performance. Ericsson and his colleagues demonstrated that expert performance was the result of extensive deliberate practice (at least ten years). Subsequently, sports researchers have corroborated aspects of Ericsson's conclusions (Deakin and Cobley, 2003; Helsen, Starkes and Hodges, 1998; Hodges and Deakin, 1996). Côté (1999) introduced the term 'deliberate play' to describe sporting activities that are intrinsically motivating, and involve a modified version of standard rules. 'Deliberate play' requires minimal equipment, flexible contexts and challenges, and allows children the freedom to experiment with different movements and tactics.

The Figure 19.12 represents the relationship between deliberate practice and deliberate play at different stages of participant development.

Stage	Approximate Age Range (Years)	Key Points
FUNdamental	6–8 (girls)/ 6–9 (boys)	• Need to sample a wide range of movement activities in fun, playful and creative environments • No sport-specific specialisation – a multi-skills approach to be adopted • Emphasis on development of basic movement skills, not formal competitive events • Parents involved and supportive, encouraging participation in as many different activities as possible • Speed, power and endurance developed using fun games and challenges • Opportunity for optimum development of speed • No periodisation and lots of FUN!
Learning to Train	8–11 (girls)/ 9–12 (boys)	• Begin to introduce basic skills and fitness to preferred activities • Start to reduce number of sports/activities but recommended at least three • Focus on mastery of basic sport skills through regular practice in fun-based environments, using discovery learning • Emphasis on learning to train and practice, not on performance outcome, but element of appropriate competition introduced (eg 25% of training programme).
Training to Train	11–15 (girls)/ 12–16 (boys)	• Individualised programmes based on individual development • Progressive development of technical, tactical and mental capacities • Squads split into groups of early, average and late maturers for physical conditioning and fitness work • Girls and boys may or may not train together depending on nature of activity • Regular height checks to identity key periods for appropriate training and optimum benefit • Regular, but appropriate and sensitive, medical monitoring and musculo-skeletal screening **(care must be taken here as bodies are changing and young people may be very sensitive)** • Excessive, repetitive weight-bearing aerobic activities should be avoided.

(continued)

Training to Complete*	15–17 (girls)/ 16–18 (boys)	• Focus on diagnosing individual strength and weakness for selected event/position and devising programme accordingly • All-year-round training that is high in intensity and specificity • Structure of learning activities should simulate realistic variety of competitive event conditions • Key support structures, such as those relating to fitness, psychology and nutrition, are individualised and integrated • Performers strive to win at carefully selected competitive events, but emphasis on learning from those experiences, rather than only on winning.
Training to Win*	17+ (girls)/ 18+ (boys)	• Assumes all relevant capacities have been developed • Focus of training on optimising performance or peaking at specially selected competitive events • Importance of planned rest breaks to avoid burnout and injury • General training decreased but significant increase in sport-specific training loads • Multi-periodisation approach developed.
Retaining	Varies depending on the individual and the sport	• Performers take up alternative activities after withdrawing from competitive sport (eg coaching, administration, mentoring, other sports/hobbies, competition at masters level) • Performers should consider *training down* if used to competing at a high level.

Figure 19.12   LTAD ages, stages and training principles (Stafford, 2005).

CONCLUSION

We have suggested that the process of participant and/or talent development can be usefully structured around the inter-dependent aspects of participation and performance. It would be remiss of any such conversation to exclude a discussion that stressed the virtue of considering this interdependency as the two are so inextricably linked, both in terms of shared concepts and in practice. It is important that any athletes entering a talent development pathway have had quality experiences of participation in physical activity and generic dimensions of sport, and that these diverse experiences provide a strong base that is important for recruitment and retention within high-level sport.

It is crucial within these early interventions that teachers and coaches recognize the need to consider a dual delivery approach to talent development that meets the needs of both current high-level performers and other athletes, some of whom may yet move on to become élite performers. These experiences strengthen the foundation of any talent development system, and as such deserve at least as much attention and resources as those afforded to athletes further along in their sports careers.

The role that school PE can play as part of the base of a pathway is contentious and problematic in a number of ways. While schools can provide routes into talent development pathways, their ability to provide high quality physical activities commensurate with the needs of early stages of talent development pathways is questionable.

Various theorists and agencies within the UK have conducted research and developed initiatives around talented athletes in sport, with some highlighting ways of supporting athletes as they progress along a pathway. Internationally, talent development programmes in sport seem more explicit, particularly in the ways in which identification of talent occurs, and the relationships between physical education and sporting excellence. Academic models of participation have evolved dramatically in recent years, with the majority of modelling reflecting a need to consider talent development as a long-term process. There is a greater understanding of the developmental phases of an athlete's progression along a pathway, and the critical processes involved within each phase to maximize potential.

What still remains to be discussed are the contexts in which such systems can be readily employed, and indeed, which agencies are most appropriately placed to deliver such theoretical constructs. The application of these theories will form the core of future chapters as we begin to consider the nature of high quality physical activity experiences at the beginning of a talent development pathway, and provide examples of communities of practice that can support such environments.

Multi-Skills Contexts and Constraints

by Dr David Morley

The recent proliferation of multi-skills opportunities for children and young people in England predominantly of primary school age, has led rapidly to the establishment of an infrastructure that facilitates the child's development of a range of fundamental movement skills (FMS), occasionally as part of a talent development pathway. 'Multi-skills' (MS), as a concept, seems to have evolved from the need to harness the development of FMS as an integral aspect of the enhancement of an *athlete's* general physical competence; as such, the prominence of MS is perhaps attributable to one of the most successful branding exercises in PE and sport, in recent times. The term *'athlete'* is used here as a generic term for the child or young person involved in recreational or performance sport, or physical activity.

Examples of MS programmes designed so far through existing multi-skills clubs and academies centre around FMS or 'observable, goal-directed movement patterns' (Burton and Miller, 1998, p. 5) for athletes aged seven to twelve years old. At its core, MS relates to the development of movement skills such as balance, co-ordination, reaction and timing – the building blocks of sport and most forms of recreational physical activity.

The use of MS in connection with activities in support of talent development programmes seems to have emerged naturally because an MS environment embraces the use of movement skills in a non-sports-specific manner, and this forms the bedrock of physical literacy required for high levels of performance across a range of sports. Using this type of environment at the correct stage of an athlete's development can contribute to the overall pathway of the athlete as they progress through certain developmental stages in relation to their capabilities.

One way of considering these developmental stages is within the context of Balyi's Long-Term Athlete Development (LTAD) programme (Balyi and Hamilton, 2000). To recap, LTAD suggests that until about the age of twelve years old (for late specialization sports) the athlete should concentrate on acquiring a range of 'FUNdamentals', and not be concerned with acquiring sport-specific skills. Furthermore, in order to achieve balance in overall development and improve retention in sport, LTAD guidance recommends 'that there should be no specialization before the age of ten years' (Stafford, 2005, p.10), albeit with an addendum that suggests these recommendations are age-typical and not age-dependent. Within the LTAD model it is suggested that if MS are emphasized and developed in a systematic manner, participants should be 'better equipped and more confident, more willing to try a range of sports... able to find at least one sport that captures their interest and more motivated to make sport a continuing part of their lives' (Stafford, 2005, p.9).

Likewise, Côté and Hay (2002) speak in broadly similar terms when they write of the importance of an early 'sampling' phase, during which young players participate in a range of sports that are designed to emphasize motor development and fun (Strachan, Côté and Deakin, 2009). In both cases, the use of a MS environment at such a formative time of the athlete's development is often presented as a way of counteracting the potential for 'burnout' – best described as an athlete's withdrawal from a sport due to a reduction in their enjoyment or an increase in stress associated with participation in the sport (Smith, 1986). Although there is an acceptance that early specialization and associated increases in time spent on deliberate practice can be key constituents of a successful pathway to élite performance, the related costs to the athlete – such as lower levels of enjoyment and reduced levels of physical health – have also been documented (Law, Côté and Ericsson, 2007).

The UK government's Department for Culture, Media and Sport (DCMS) and the Department for Education and Skills (DfES) (now the Department for Children, Schools and Families, DCSF) both endorsed a MS approach under the original auspices of the Physical Education, School Sport and Club Links strategy (PESSCL) (DfES, 2003) and the recently introduced superseding PESSYP (... and Young People) strategy, through the establishment of multi-skills clubs and multi-skills academies, respectively. Talent development pathways are also considered within the rationale for the establishment of multi-skills, in that they are included in the 'building foundations for élite sport' plans for ensuring sporting success (DCMS, 2005a, p.32).

For the sake of brevity, as the MS environment embraces opportunities for children both within and beyond school, it is important to clearly define the use of the terms 'PE' and 'sport'. 'PE' is defined here as a school-based curricular subject area delivered under the guidance of the National Curriculum for PE (DfEE, 1999; DCSF, 2008), and is concerned with knowledge, skills and understanding. 'Sport' is defined as 'all forms of physical activity which, through casual or organized participation, aim at expressing or improving physical fitness and mental well-being, forming relationships or obtaining results in competitions at all levels' (Council of Europe's European Sports Charter, 2001). Within these environments, this Chapter outlines some of the contexts in which multi-skills have emerged, and the constraints associated with developing and delivering such an approach for children and young people in English schools and sports communities.

MULTI-SKILLS CONTEXTS

Contexts embrace the use of fundamental movement skills (FMS) in a multi-skills (MS) environment.

Multi-Skills Clubs

Multi-skills clubs were launched in February 2005, and form the foundation of the multi-skills pathway through the facilitation of wide-scale access on to an activity programme (Youth Sport Trust, 2009). The clubs are intended for children aged seven to eleven years old, and involve the delivery of non-sports specific activities with a central focus on the 'ABC' of agility, balance and co-ordination, which are normally delivered outside school hours by a community coach or qualified teacher. There is a strong emphasis on links between the School Sport Partnership and the County Sports Partnership in the design and delivery of multi-skills clubs.

The clubs are funded by DCMS, and it is suggested that there are approximately 650 clubs nationally (DCMS, 2005b). MS clubs may provide the first club experience for a young person, and as such are intended to bridge the school-to-community gap and create the first step from school sport to club sport. As such they have been established to act as 'holding tanks' which can feed sports clubs with physically literate children; they also form part of the player pathway for children who have been identified as gifted and talented.

As well as attention to the actual performance of the movement skills, the MS club resource cards, designed for practitioners to use at the clubs, require a consideration of the cognitive processes involved in performing the various movements through a delivery strategy involving the use of a second mnemonic to add to the ABC, of 'FABB' – feet, arms, body and brain.

Multi-Skills Academies

Multi-skills academies (MSAs) were launched in 2003 and are funded through the DfES, again under the umbrella of the PESSYP strategy. MSAs aim to develop talented pupils in PE and sport through the creation of a programme of activities which are delivered normally in school holidays or as an after-school activity. There are approximately 450 MSAs across the country, equivalent to one being hosted by every specialist sports college within a SSP and delivered by PE teachers and/or coaches, where appropriate. The academies are designed to offer a range of activities that develop pupils' ability to perform and understand fundamental movement skills, develop game-playing abilities, and also 'identify potentially talented young people for National Governing Body programmes' (Youth Sport Trust, 2009b).

Figure 20.1 Developing game-playing abilities is a feature of the academies. (Courtesy of Team Northumbria)

Selection for attendance on the camp is conducted within primary schools attached to the SSP, and is exemplified in an Information and Guidance Pack (Youth Sport Trust, 2009b), which offers an identification template similar to the National Curriculum level descriptors for Key Stage 2 (Department for Education and Employment (DfEE), 1999). Although guidance is not entirely prescriptive for MSAs, what seems to be the consensus across all case study examples of programme content is the international lack of sport-specific practice within the academies, and the sentiment that fundamental generalized movement skills form the core of activities (Youth Sport Trust, 2009). Specifically trained multi-skills coaches or teachers run the academy and focus on developing the pupils' physical and thinking abilities, whilst challenging their creative, personal and social abilities as part of the multi-abilities framework (Morley and Bailey, 2006).

Although MSAs are portrayed as an extension of curricular PE, what is not so apparent is the interdependency between National Curriculum for PE objectives and multi-skills programmes. As selection for a MSA is conducted at primary school level and therefore without specialist PE teachers, the suggested use of a multi-ability talent identification tool is likely to prove difficult to some teachers, the majority of whom have very limited dedicated PE training during their initial teacher training programmes. Coupled with problems surrounding the initial identification process is the issue of standardization and moderation across the SSP, and the measures taken to promote a consensus of agreement.

Other studies of talent development have suggested a great deal of uncertainty in the identification of talent in PE, with physical prowess demonstrated in one specific sport often dominating the process (Bailey *et al.* 2009). There is a legitimate concern that problems like this could be replicated within the identification of talent for selection on to a MSA, and could detract from the more holistic, multi-ability, multi-skills approach proffered in the guidance.

To summarize, Figure 20.2 represents the intended place of multi-skills in the performance pathways of young people.

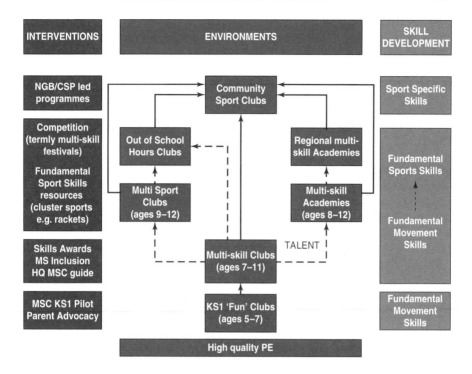

Figure 20.2   Youth Sport Trust performance pathways for young people. (Courtesy of the Youth Sport Trust)

Regional Multi-Skills Academies

Following the establishment of pilots within a select number of higher education institutions (HEIs) to consider the need for an additional tier to the MS environment, regional multi-skills academies (RMSAs) have now been established to bring together the most successful athletes from the MSAs at a centralized venue (Morley, Tremere and Bailey, 2005). Each RMSA is a one-day event split into two strands:

- A multi-skills day for young people designed and led by the HEI staff with an emphasis on MS and multi-ability development. Assessment and athlete profiling form a key constituent of the athlete's experiences.
- A Continuing Professional Development (CPD) element for MSA practitioners that aims to improve the standard and consistency of MSA delivery across the country, and to share new thinking.

The stated outcomes for the talented athletes are:

- To provide an advanced and innovative experience for young people using the multi-ability concept, with a particular focus on physical and cognitive/thinking abilities.
- To reward and encourage young people, helping them to understand the multi-ability concept and how this relates to becoming a better sportsperson.

- To provide assessment and feedback/profiling to young people in an innovative way.
- To share good practice and innovation with other hosts and throughout the network.

(Adapted from Youth Sport Trust, 2009)

The Place of Multi-Skills in Assessing Movement Competency

On examination, MS objectives and content (Youth Sport Trust, 2009) relate closely to theoretical principles describing the development of a child's FMS (Burton and Miller, 1998: Vereijken and Bongaardt, 1999). Indeed, there is a direct correlation between guidance for the use of specific multi-skills activities, and the use of activities to assess FMS in relation to physical activity (Youth Sport Trust, 2004; Okely *et al.*, 2001). Although research involving the use of a MS environment is limited, there is empirical and conceptual literature that relates to the development and assessment of FMS. Indeed, the range and amount of literature relating to FMS, motor skill acquisition and related fields is quite substantial (*see*, for example, Burton and Miller, 1992; Gallahue and Ozmun, 2006).

When considering the literature related to FMS, the use of assessment and observation of participants in order to inform teaching, coaching and learning seems instrumental in the pedagogical understanding of how participants effectively acquire and develop new skills. Moreover, the adoption of one type of assessment platform over another will influence the shape and design of the planned activity. Hands (2002) discusses the *qualitative* nature of assessing FMS, with assessment being viewed as fit for purpose, with some of those purposes most salient to this context being to provide feedback to the performer or to predict performance in the future (Burton and Miller, 1998). On the other hand, *quantitative* measures of movement skill proficiency, through the employment of screening tests, allow for the testing of large groups with minimal understanding on the part of the tester in terms of movement competencies.

Tests most readily employed by schools to assess athletes within the PE curriculum are generally quantitatively framed and include agility and speed runs, a variety of muscular and cardiovascular endurance tests, as well as power and balance assessments (Cale, 2000). Furthermore, this type of assessment protocol is used more specifically as a key element of talent identification (Bailey, Morley and Dismore, 2009; Morley, Tremere and Bailey, 2005), with the ensuing results commonly being used for baseline assessment of students, particularly in the early years of secondary schooling (eleven to thirteen years of age).

While the assessor's intent may be to assess the current levels of proficiency of an athlete and how this proficiency changes over time, the reality of the situation is that this assessment protocol may simply be assessing and tracking maturation. Ulterior motives of this type of testing, associated with perceived positive benefits in terms of health and physical activity, have also been questioned; many tests currently employed within schools have been designed for élite adult populations, with minimal consideration for the differences in children's physiological and psychological responses to exercise (Cale and Harris, 2009). Moreover, it is difficult to understand the place of such an assessment regime in relation to the developmental phases already purported by theories proposed in the area of long-term athlete development within sport (Balyi and Hamilton, 2000; Côté and Hay, 2002).

Although these forms of test minimize standardization problems between testers and perhaps ensure a high level of reliability in terms of tracking and profiling, the quality of the movement is not assessed. Furthermore, factors inherent in a high or low level performance are not observed, and the development of future programmes may not be influenced by this type of feedback.

Qualitative assessment – looking at *how* the skill is performed – seems to have dominated pedagogically focused research recently, with the use of observation sheets and criteria checklists designed to inform the most appropriate subsequent intervention to enhance performance (Gallahue and Ozmun, 2006). Once assessment of a qualitative nature has been conducted, there is greater opportunity to facilitate the athlete's progression through the developmental stages of motor learning (Jess and Collins, 2003). In one particular approach to understanding and observing skill acquisition, dynamic systems theory, an emphasis is made upon the 'importance of exploration' and the requirement for children not to repeat through repetition but by looking to refine movements for a better outcome (Vereijken and Bongaardt, 1999). This approach bears resonance with MS guidelines that recommend MS sessions utilize a range of activities and exercises which are not always directly relevant to a particular movement within a recognized sport (Youth Sport Trust, 2004). There is also a theoretical underpinning to the documented motives of the recently established MS environments, in their efforts to lead children on to further development of FMS by suggesting links to other clubs, as it has been suggested that improved performance of FMS has a positive relationship with participation in organized sport (Okely *et al.*, 2001).

It is clear that children become less active the older they grow (Armstrong and Macmanus, 1994), and although the reasons for this are not as clearly established as the actual statistics, it is plausible that if children are not afforded the experiences in which they can develop a vocabulary of skills, their subsequent participation in sport and physical activity in general will be limited. Furthermore, there are wider social implications for a child that has not been supported effectively in developing their movement competencies, as children who have not developed adequate motor skills are likely to be relegated to a life of exclusion from physical activity and sport experiences, often as a result of their frustrations in early movement behaviour (Seefeldt *et al.*, 1979).

The contexts in which MS can be found across PE and sport are influenced by a wide range of factors. The following section discusses factors affecting the successful delivery of MS through an examination of constraints that could hinder its implementation.

MULTI-SKILLS CONSTRAINTS

Existing Research

The only research that has explored a structured MS environment as endorsed by DCMS and DfES, and provided in the main by the Youth Sport Trust, sought to understand the impact of an MSA through focus group interviews with participants (Morley and Bailey, 2006; Morley, Tremere and Bailey, 2006). The findings of this research suggest that in many cases children reported a sense of uncertainty about the relevance of the MSA to their development, citing a lack of understanding of how multi-skills activities related to their development in their preferred sport(s). Participating children generally expected more sport-specific approaches, and were often bemused when asked to diversify their knowledge, skills and understanding to generic activities that were not directly associated to a specific single sport.

These findings offered the first indications that, although sports and teaching administrators and policymakers clearly recognized the need for a generic movement-based approach for children involved in sport, children were seemingly more resistant to the approach. Moreover, as well as children and young people finding it difficult to comprehend the meaning of multi-skills for their development, teachers have also reported anxiety and concern over the use of MS within PE and extra-curricular practices (Mckenna, 2008).

In a report outlining the effectiveness of a multi-skills initiative as part of the newly introduced National Curriculum at Key Stage 3 (QCA, 2007), Mckenna (2008) highlighted some major strengths of the approach, with an increase in pro-social behaviours, particularly for girls, and a greater involvement in certain types of physical activity. However, the adoption of the approach was met with mixed feelings from some teachers who believed that the efficacy of such a developmental approach was limited to lower ability students, was more suitable for primary school-aged children, and required a closer relationship to traditional sport to have more meaning for more secondary school-aged students.

The Five Cs

The research findings suggest uncertainty in terms of the potential for success in implementing a generic movement-based approach through the auspices of MS provision. Elements of a constraints model developed to explain motor-skills acquisition in relation to the individual, task and environment (Newell, 1986) will now be used to assist in our understanding of where the uncertainty in MS provision lies. Newell suggests a constraint is any task, environmental or individual-related factor that shapes or influences the outcome of movement that is observed. Whilst Newell's model is configured around the specific moment of movement development and has been used by others to explore these dimensions (Hamilton *et al.*, 2002), the constraints discussed here also explore wider mitigating factors that will shape the structure and developmental pathways that athletes may experience within a MS context.

In more general terms, through personal experiences of working with a multitude of practitioners across a range of MS environments, it is clear that colleagues are meeting resistance or experiencing constraints in their efforts to introduce multi-skills to children and young people in a range of teaching and coaching environments throughout the stages of a child's movement development. While other theorists have used a 'Five Cs' framework to hypothesize a way of explaining positive youth development – Competence, Confidence, Connection, Character and Caring – (Lerner *et al.*, 2000), the use of the Five Cs here relates to the constraints experienced within the establishment of a task, the engagement of an individual, or the influences of the environment, related to MS, as follows:

- Culture
- Confidence and Competence
- Clarity
- Consistency.

Culture

Culture constraints illustrate the sport-specific traditions of children's development in PE and sport. Contained within the subtexts of culture are notions of historical and traditional influences. If we consider the historical developments of curricular approaches to PE and traditions surrounding participation in the related area of sport, it becomes more apparent as to why the constraint of sport-specific approaches to both curricular and extra-curricular delivery limits the likelihood of success for a MS approach. Here, the term 'sport-specific' is used to represent an environment that concentrates on the development of technical, relatively narrow sets of core skills found within a single sport. This approach is clearly at odds with a MS approach that uses a delivery approach reliant upon non-repetitive, non sport-specific approaches, particularly during the acquisition of FMS during the earlier stages of movement development.

In order to understand the reasons why sport-specific approaches are apparent in PE, it is important to look back in time to gather evidence relating to how PE has been shaped over the past decades of school and curriculum development. Whilst accepting the complex and multi-faceted history of PE, in essence the PE curriculum we have today is a natural end-product of a series of evolutionary developments that have affected the values and purpose of PE over the last century. One of the earliest official syllabi, the first 1909 Syllabus of Physical Exercises produced by the Board of Education (1909), outlined two main effects of physical training: the physical and the educational.

Although the development of posture and a robust physique continued to dominate the PE landscape up to and including the next major syllabus of 1933, the importance of games and general physical fitness became a mainstay of PE design and delivery (Kirk, 1992). The use of invasion games in particular was deemed as significantly important in terms of the moral and character-building benefits associated with the militaristic preparation of young people for war, and it was also viewed as an anti-dote to anti-social behaviour amongst the working classes.

Young (1998) suggests that the current curricular dilemma involving the ongoing domination of sport-specific approaches as the main delivery vehicle for PE is primarily a left-over of past traditions, which have come to be seen as the only way of organizing knowledge. There have been sug-gestions that the dominant conceptualizations of competence and perform-ance in the context of PE revolve around the individual realization of characteristics associated with high levels of performance within sports (Bailey *et al.*, 2005; Penney, 2000; Whitson and Mackintosh, 1990). Moreover, notions of excellence in sport are reinforced by the integral use of the organizational framework of 'areas of activity' such as 'games' and 'athletic activities' (Penney, 1998, 1999, 2000; Penney and Evans, 1999).

Although the latest modifications to the National Curriculum for PE (NCPE) suggest the more subtle use of 'areas of activity' in the way that the range and content of a PE curriculum is shaped, examples of where this con-tent could be delivered, such as 'outwitting opponents, for example games' are still given (QCA, 2007). This gives rise to serious implications for the ways in which teachers continue to develop the culture of PE using sport-specific areas of activity to support a child's development. This culture ultimately constrains the delivery of MS that demands a non-sport specific, varied and non-repetitive environment where transferability of skills in a free-flowing and expressive environment is crucial in establishing positive, meaningful and developmentally appropriate movement experiences for children.

The changing ways in which children are afforded opportunities for the unstructured development of MS presents another cultural constraint in terms of the diminishing environment for children to play in the outdoors. The risk-averse society that has evolved as a result of overly cautious plan-ning and delivery regimes used to determine the extent of children's free-dom, particularly in outdoor domains, may have limited the mindset of children when they select their play activities. This situation, combined with parents' perceived risks associated with their children playing out-doors, will invariably restrict the number of opportunities children have to be physically active, with the resulting constraints on the appropriate MS development for children (Bailey *et al.*, 2005).

Another potentially controversial cultural constraint when considering the introduction and ongoing use of a multi-skills environment is the place of competition. As illustrated in Chapter 19, in one of the first extensive studies of talent in sport undertaken in the UK, Rowley (1992), comment-ing about the use of competition, trials and other aspects of the talent identification process, reported that 'talent identification in this country is not carried out in any systematic way' (p. 9). The English Sports Council (1998) built upon Rowley's research and found a variety of factors affect-ing 'pathways to excellence' for élite performers, such as ethnicity, social class, educational qualifications, coaching, medical services and opportu-nities to compete. It is clear within the report that competition plays an integral and influential part in the talent identification process, as evidenced by the statement: 'In order to reach the performance level [necessary for selection], competitors generally had to achieve a consistent level of performance (61%) or they took part in trials (60%)' (p.12).

The use of competition in sport as an effective means of talent identification in its own right has been documented and challenged before (Peltola, 1992). To understand the place of competition and some of the potential barriers that the use of competition presents to the establishment of a multi-skills environment, it is helpful to consider the impact of competition on the experiences of participants. There is a body of research that suggests that adults have a tendency to exaggerate the abilities of others who are better than themselves during competition in what they view as prestigious activities. Alicke *et al.* (1997) call this the 'genius effect', where social comparison involves a reduction in the positive reporting on other people outperforming them in order to maintain their own self-esteem. By elevating the performance of more able individuals, the less able performer 'can maintain their sense of competence while magnanimously acknowledging the superior attributes of the outperformer' (Alicke *et al.*, 1997, p. 781).

Although Alicke *et al.*'s study is limited due to its focus on the adult population, Horn and Weiss (1991) report a general agreement across several studies that social comparison was used by children under the age of ten years old and its frequency increased with age. Social comparison is one way in which children form their own self-concept, and Marsh (1993) suggests this is affected by what he terms the 'big-fish-little-pond effect' (BFLPE). BFLPE occurs when children of equal ability have a low self-concept when they compare themselves to more able children, and a higher self-concept when they compare themselves with less able students.

Chanal *et al.* (2005) allow for an interpretation of BFLPE in their study of its application into a physical setting using gymnastic skills as a focus. They found that BFLPE was just as apparent in a physical setting as had been proved in academic settings, and this had implications for a range of established physical activities. Consequently, they recommend the avoidance of highly competitive environments that encourage social comparison processes and the development of assessment procedures that emphasize individual, self-paced goal setting. Issues surrounding the widespread negative effects of social comparison within competitive environments have been documented elsewhere. A Sports Council for Wales (1995) report suggests that most children who do not currently play for a team would like to do so and with children of their own standard where they would not feel as intimidated.

In a study aimed at understanding the 'pupil's voice', children identified as talented within PE provided a glimpse of some of the benefits they experienced through competition (Morley *et al.*, 2006). The following conversation reveals interaction between focus group members identified as talented discussing the importance of resilience and fair play:

'If you lose, just keep on a high and carry on going' (initial comment).

'And if you lose, you are not being a sore loser' (response from another member of the group).

'Well done to the other team. Now you've got to pick yourself up and go!' (additional response from another member).

Within the same study, extra-curricular activities were considered by some pupils as offering the optimal period of development for challenging pupils identified as talented in PE. Research suggests that extra-curricular activities are dominated by competition, games and the ability of participants to demonstrate physical competency (Penney and Harris, 1997; Sports Council for Wales, 1995). It is likely that pupils suggest that this is the optimal environment for the development of their talents because of the discrete exposure to their preferred sport, the opportunity to participate with like-minded athletes, and also perhaps because some PE teachers provide more effective and targeted instruction here than in PE lessons (Williams, 2009).

While the signs within both PE and sport clearly seem to point towards a reduction in competitive environments, particularly for younger populations, questions have been raised in terms of the nation's ability to adopt a less competitive culture to nurturing children within sport. One example of this is from England's national sport of football, where Arsene Wenger, a French Premier League team manager suggested:

> In my experience of going around the world, England loves football more than anybody. But at the pre-club academy stage and schoolwise it is behind everybody! There is no uniformity, no consistency over the whole country. Every age is important – if you miss that stage you will never get it back. It is one reason why the quality of young English players has suffered for so long. The English culture and mentality to 'win at all costs' is proving detrimental to developing our youngsters (Dickens, 2008).

Furthermore, it is the athletes who do not succeed in the particular sport they have chosen whose potential may be wasted as a result of lack of opportunities 'to identify potential performers from outside a sport's participant base' due to the over-reliance on outcomes evidenced within single sport-specific competition (English Sports Council, 1998, p.12). Sportspeople themselves have recently been surveyed on a range of aspects related to their development, and considering that 66 per cent of respondents were former professional sports players, the findings are very enlightening in relation to their perspectives on the use of competition. The manner in which the press reported the summary of findings offers an interesting insight into what would capture the public's imagination, with the suggestion that 'There was an overwhelming response that an obsession with winning (at too early an age) was an obstacle to the learning and acquisition of excellent technique/technical skills and athlete development' (Barnes, 2009).

Some final thoughts on competitive culture perhaps encapsulate the enormity of the task of changing the existing environment to one more receptive to the use of multi-skills. Thus Raedeke and Smith (2004) call for the social organization of sport to create a better fit between the athlete and their competitive environment, while others suggest that the role of coaches and peers is crucial in enabling positive experiences for all participants within this reorganization (Strachan *et al.*, 2009).

Competence and Confidence

The interrelated constraints of competence and confidence have been twinned as a reflection of the interdependency of these traits and their combined impact on the successful implementation and sustainability of a MS environment. As previously reported, athletes involved in talent development pathways have a relatively low perception of the place of MS in their athletic development. Moreover, teachers themselves find difficulties in understanding the true potential of a MS environment for athletes in their care.

One way of cascading information as to the nature and potential usefulness of a particular strategy is through the implementation of policy. Teachers and coaches are faced with a constant, and at times what must seem like a relentless stream of messages regarding the most appropriate ways to develop the abilities of the children and young people in their care. Although some practitioners may say that they are adopting certain policy-driven approaches or strategies in their practices, in reality they may be doing something very different in practice, in that the state of the original policy or intent becomes fragmented, and in doing so they could resort to using what is termed as 'strategic rhetoric' (Bowe *et al.*, 1992).

It is understandable, given the deluge of policies that teachers and, to a lesser extent, coaches must come to terms with, that they may arrive at a situation which demands the adoption of certain practices they believe will have a positive impact on their students, and at the same time ignore or resist the aspects of a policy they think will not. This is termed 'policy slippage', and occurs during the filtration process between policymakers and policy implementers (Sparkes, 1988). In this sense, any policy related to a MS approach must be clearly articulated and relate to the PE and sport professions in ways that are familiar to practitioners in their respective environments. This should enhance levels of teacher and coach confidence in believing that a MS approach is developmentally appropriate for athletes in their care, and in doing so will ensure a reduction in policy slippage. An athlete-centred policy would provide the appropriate mechanism to remove this constraint, and provide consistent messages for both PE and sport environments.

Confidence will also be developed as a result of increased knowledge and understanding about athletes operating within the varying contexts in which MS can be delivered. This suggests that continuing professional development is paramount to practitioners operating within MS environments, and this provision should be presented within a 'fit for purpose' framework of understanding developmentally appropriate practices for athletes. In sport, the emerging UK Coaching Framework (Sports Coach

UK, 2008, 2009) is forging structural platforms for a coach development model that establishes a specialist workforce in four key areas:

- Children's coaching
- Participation coaching
- Performance development coaching
- High performance coaching.

With a concurrent emphasis on a participant needs-led environment, this emerging coaching landscape certainly seems well placed to influence the confidence and competence of coaches in understanding the key differences within these environments. What remains to be seen is whether the integrity of the initial aspirations of the framework are upheld during the filtration of information down to coaching practices that directly influence the athlete's experiences. A demonstration of the way in which one particular national governing body has embraced a 'fit for purpose' approach within the context of the UK framework is presented in a later chapter. What is worth noting within this section are the high levels of willingness expressed by a range of coaches across a national governing body in terms of their realization of the need for change in their coaching practices, and their reported confidence in bringing about this change (Morley and Webb, 2009).

Clarity

Although the use of the term 'multi-skills' has been highly effective in raising awareness of an approach that can be used to counteract problems associated with early specialization and overly technical approaches to the development of children's movement competencies, the current level of information relating to what multi-skills actually are is restricted, and this threatens to limit its successful implementation. Guidelines produced to date regularly explain multi-skills as being 'fundamental movement skills' entailing the development of agility, balance and co-ordination ('ABCs'), and explicitly target this delivery for athletes at Key Stages 1 and 2 (children aged five to eleven) of their schooling through MS clubs and academies (Youth Sport Trust, 2009).

However, using FMS alone to describe what multi-skills are is a constraint to a real understanding of how movement development occurs, and could consequently hinder the full range of developmental processes needed to ensure all athletes achieve their full potential. When considering movement from a lifelong perspective it is clear that children do not suddenly begin movement development at the age of five; they have progressed through a series of movement phases related primarily to instincts concerned with survival in the way that they initially reach, grasp and suckle, through to the development of the types of movements that we take for granted, such as walking and the manipulation of certain objects such as holding a racket or hockey stick. Although it could be argued that MS could still be developed effectively without this knowledge, it would be remiss of any movement development programme to fail to consider the prior and next stages of development for children.

Fundamental Movement Skills (FMS)

Stability	Object Control	Locomotor
Turning	Throwing	Walking
Twisting	Kicking	Running
Freezing	Catching	Jumping
Stretching	Dribbling	Skipping
Curling	Bouncing	Galloping
Landing	Striking	Bounding
Pivoting	Collecting	Hopping

Figure 20.3   Fundamental movement skills. (Courtesy of Education and Special Projects)

The development of FMS is a widely accepted stage of movement development (Burton and Miller, 1992; Gallahue and Ozmun, 2006), but what the current level of understanding around MS has not recognized is that this is followed by two further critical areas of development that are particularly relevant to children and young people typically between the ages of eight and thirteen years of age. The development of movement skills is age-typical, not age-dependent, with factors such as previous experience and opportunities to practise through structured and free play, and exposure to quality instruction and encouragement, all having the potential to influence the rate at which children progress through the different stages of movement skill development.

FMS are therefore seen as the building blocks of all sports and/or physical activity. They include basic movements under three main categories, namely stability, object control and locomotion (SOL). The table above outlines some of the movements associated with SOL. Noticeable within this table is a different use of terms from the terminology used within existing MS programmes. The table uses 'SOL' as the key configuration related to the development of FMS, and not 'ABCs' that are currently recommended within existing guidelines. Granted, ABCs are easier to remember, and as such it is not surprising that this is used to ensure that the message is well received, and more importantly, used to make a difference to children's movement experiences. However, when considering the extensive range of movement that children need to develop at this stage of their development, the terms are limited.

For example, from personal experiences of working with primary school teachers, 'balance' is often associated with static notions of movement in terms of perhaps the ability to stand on one leg, and so conveying a wider, deeper understanding of the dynamism involved with, for instance, moving into and out of 'balance', is often difficult. Within the same environment, 'co-ordination' is also often limited in the way that 'hand-eye' is often mentioned as the overriding construct within the range of movements; the use of subdivisions of manipulating or controlling objects such as kicking, gripping and the general use of implements is often considered as an afterthought. 'Agility' is also problematic as a term to orientate practitioners' understanding of the range of children's movement competencies, as it is

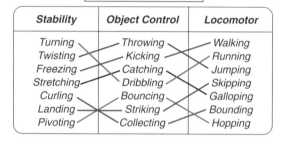

Figure 20.4   Specialized and functional movement skills. Adapted from the 'Multi-skills Training Award' Level 3, Education and Special Projects, 2009. (Courtesy of ESP)

often construed as zigzagging movement rather than the more appropriate multitude of locomotion possibilities related to movement from point A to point B.

SOL offers a more extensive, rigorous and theoretically framed foundation for movement development that leads naturally to the next stages of movement development (Gallahue and Ozmun, 2006). Once FMS have been developed successfully by children so they can demonstrate quality in terms of their precision, control and fluency in movement, they are ready to progress to the development of specialized movement skills (SMS).

SMS are fundamental movement skills that have been refined and combined to create movement skills or phrases of movement that could be used in specific sports or physical activities. For example, as demonstrated in the figure below, when learning to evade an opponent in an invasion game such as hockey, football or rugby, athletes need to be able to combine the fundamental skills of running, turning and dribbling. These specialized movement skills are carried through to the final 'functional phase' when they are selected and applied during the actual sport or physical activity. For example, during an invasion game, athletes are able to select and apply the specialized skill of running, turning and dribbling to evade and outwit an opponent.

Every specialized and functional movement skill involves the combination and application of a number of the fundamental movement skills.

Although the use of this 'ages and stages' approach covers the whole continuum of movement beyond the currently adopted sole use of FMS, there is a danger that introducing athletes to specialized and functional movement skills prior to developing a wide variety of fundamental movement skills will result in frustration, failure, feelings of incompetence, and a significant decline in motivation. This in turn could lead to withdrawal from sport, and in some cases withdrawal from physical activity in general, for life. Therefore it is incumbent upon the facilitator of the learning environment that every opportunity is given to children to develop appropriate and high quality movement patterns in a range of contexts before progressing them to more complex and sport-orientated (functional) situational tasks that utilize such movements.

Consistency

Consistency is desirable in all agencies following a common form of delivery across all environments. One of the key messages that can be drawn up to this point in the discussion is how many different environments and practitioners can potentially be involved within the MS community. In order to maximize the potential impact of MS for athletes as they progress along their chosen pathway, it is important that all stakeholders recognize the instrumental part that they play in ensuring a common and coherent delivery platform for developmentally appropriate practices for athletes. A useful way of viewing what this environment looks like is through an understanding of what constitutes a 'community of practice' (CoP), and through this what needs to happen to create a 'community of action'.

A CoP is generally defined as groups of people who share a concern or a passion for something they do, and who learn how to do it better as they interact regularly (Wenger, 2007). Wenger suggests that a CoP has three core characteristics: domain, community and practice. Within the *domain*, the group's identity is defined by their shared interest, with a MS CoP sharing the ultimate goal of providing developmentally appropriate practices for athletes within both participation and performance domains.

Groups of people operating within the *community* are in effect 'agents of change', and it is the ideologies, beliefs and practices of these agents of change that will shape the CoP. In a MS context, agents of change are parents, siblings, peers, coaches and teachers, and it is imperative that the whole range of agents is informed and educated effectively in supporting the athlete's aspirations and developmental needs as they progress along a pathway.

In terms of *practice*, a CoP harnesses a number of activities that enable agents of change to operate effectively within a MS environment; these can be classified as opportunities for 'creating', 'collaborating' and 'coordinating'.

Creating: Problem Solving

What are developmentally appropriate activities for the different age ranges that we are currently working with? How do we develop these skills from fundamental to specialized? How do we know when athletes are ready to progress through the phases?

Collaborating: Requests for Information/Seeking Experience/Cascading Knowledge

What/who is the conduit for information – is this through an existing network of people, electronic virtual interface (for example 'Facebook') or a dedicated website? How do I access information relating to how the different agents of change can contribute to the CoP?

Strategically, it may be fruitful to identify the key aspects of a MS environment that each agent of change is comfortable with when making a contribution. This division of responsibilities will ultimately lead to more effective and streamlined ways of working, with a greater level of accomplishment for the athlete in terms of their fluid journey along the talent development pathway.

It is argued that this type of collaboration with a shared focus and ethos brings people together effectively within CoP, and as such has the ulterior benefit of offering opportunities for developing relationships with like-minded agents of change (Wenger *et al.*, 2002).

Co-ordinating: Instilling Synergy/Reusing Assets

Can we combine our resources? Resources include agents of change such as coaches and teachers, and whether their expertise can be used across the CoP, with tangible resources such as session plans and activity cards offering tools for the delivery of a cohesive programme of activities under the umbrella of MS, but perhaps using multiple vehicles for delivery (for example, a multi-skills club, a gymnastics club, a community sports club, a summer camp).

Figure 20.5 summarizes the key constituents of a MS CoP.

SUMMARY

This chapter aimed to outline the contexts and constraints associated to MS environments within schools and sports communities, concerned in particular with the individual, task and environment, drawing upon Newell's

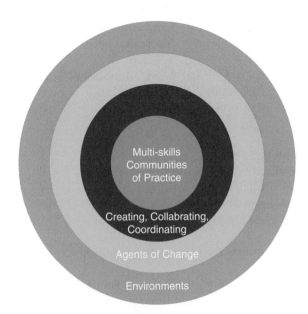

Figure 20.5   Key constituents of a multi-skills community of practice.

(1986) constraints model as a way of structuring the examination. It is clear that there is a growing number of opportunities for athletes to participate within designated MS activities, and the emerging structures presented by key agencies in PE and youth sport development seem to be harnessing this approach as part of their core offer to athletes.

What is less clear is how such agencies are coming to terms with some of the underlying constraints that exist in this type of provision being effectively realized. The consideration of constraints such as culture, confidence and competence, clarity and consistency, reveals a complex and contested notion of the efficacy of proposed MS interventions. On a more optimistic note, the delivery of positive developmentally appropriate activities through MS environments is not insurmountable. Indeed, the presentation of a suggested framework around MS 'communities of practice', with an ensuing understanding of clearly defined needs, roles and responsibilities within such a community, suggests that MS environments are not only achievable but could ultimately lead to the delivery of a wider range of goals and objectives for participating partners.

In evidence throughout this discussion is a realization that the shift required in terms of alleviating the social and cultural constraints articulated is considerable. In certain circumstances there will be a need to unfreeze, change and refreeze (Lewin, 1947) the ideologies of some of the agents of change, and as always changing attitudes when working with a diverse range of key stakeholders will be time-consuming and strategically demanding. The level of systemic cultural change necessary here bears resonance with organizational reform in education, and the literature of organizational restructuring suggests that the chances of successful implementation of change are greatly improved with the involvement of all stakeholders, including those who will be delivering the changes and those who will be affected by these changes (Bloom, Bullion, and Caldwell, 1998; Hargreaves, 1995; Lazerson, 1997; Mills, 2003; Stringer, 2004).

These sentiments suggest, once again, that clear, effective communication needs to be paramount within the CoP, with all agents of change and athletes fully aware of the direction in which they are travelling and the changes that need to be made to existing practices in order to follow this new direction.

Morrison (1998) suggests that the nature of change is affected by a range of underlying characteristics inherent within the environment that is being affected. Some of these characteristics relate to the extent to which the change is different from the core patterns and norms of the stakeholders, as well as the number of groups that may be affected by the change. Other characteristics of change include the compatibility of the proposed innovation, in this case developmentally appropriate activities through multi-skills, as well as the visibility of change to all parties involved. In terms of visibility, there is a need to articulate MS approaches in clear, transparent and rigorous ways that ensure that all interested parties are fully aware of the rationale and importance of developmentally appropriate activities endorsed within MS environments.

The modelling of long-term athlete participation (Balyi and Hamilton, 2000, Côté and Hay, 2002) and athlete capabilities (Morley and Bailey, 2006) provides the structural platform for this to occur, but a further process of localized, strategic and collegiate implementation across the CoP needs to be implemented so that inherent constraints typically found within these environments can be considered and counteracted. Given the extent of constraints that have been articulated here, it is likely that the amount of change needed in certain quarters to ensure the effective implementation of MS environments will be considerable. Others involved in organizational change have realized that 'with change comes a certain amount of chaos that must be tolerated' (Maulding and Styron, 2005, p.10), and that cultural change requires paying attention to all the consequential and parts of group dynamics at once.

It is inconceivable to believe that 'agents of change', whether they be coaches, teachers or parents, can operate effectively as separate individuals in their bid to provide developmentally appropriate practices and pathways for athletes in their care. Whilst the micro contexts of coaching, teaching and parental support can clearly have a positive influence on the athlete's development, it is only when the macro context of the CoP is fully considered and operationalized, through effective, clear and consistent communication and practice, that the potential for all athletes to progress along their chosen pathway will be fully realized.

A 'Fit for Purpose' Approach Within the Rugby Football League

by Dr David Morley, Bob Muir, Dr Gareth Morgan, Andy Abraham and Vinny Webb

This chapter strengthens and contextualizes lessons learned from the previous chapters on talent and multi-skills development through an understanding of how a national governing body has interpreted national and international influences in these areas. It is hoped that what is becoming obvious to the reader is that talent development is not solely concerned with simply plucking out those visibly currently achieving in their given sport and putting them on to a scholarship programme. Talent development entails an understanding of key episodes in an athlete's development, and the systematic use of tools and strategies to maximize their potential and reduce any barriers that they may face.

One of the key strategies that is often under-used within talent development is the use of approaches within athlete 'participation' routes that seek to effectively support, nurture and encourage children to develop appropriately and enter performance pathways adequately equipped for success. The interdependency of participation and performance has already been established across a range of contexts in previous chapters, and this chapter further emphasizes the relationship between the two as it endeavours to articulate how the Rugby Football League (RFL) made sense of a 'fit for purpose' (FfP) approach to their sport.

This chapter is a reflection on the process of understanding what FfP actually means within the RFL, and how best to realize the most appropriate mechanisms for supporting coaching practice that will facilitate this approach. Indeed, to affect any potential change this chapter unearths a range of debates concerning participant's needs, the use of core skills, coach education, and the demands of the sport itself. Moreover, this chapter presents the multifaceted aspects of RFL delivery that affect a 'fit for purpose' approach to coaching young athletes as a method of understanding how high quality practices used within practices for all can improve the routes to successful performance.

In the first instance, the background to the project will be presented detailing the use of developmentally appropriate practices in participant development, and exploring some of the current notions of participation and performance for this age range. This will be reiterating a great deal of what has been expressed in previous chapters, but it is important to understand here what was central to the RFL's thinking as we moved through the project. This will be followed by an understanding of the receptivity of coaches to the notion of delivering developmentally appropriate practices for athletes in their care.

Using a mosaic method of data capture, this section will use the RE-AIM framework as a useful way of understanding the 'Reach, Aim, Effectiveness, Implementation and Maintenance' of the proposed shift in the coaching environment as a way of interpreting the data to assess the likelihood of success of an intervention aimed at affecting the approaches to coaching young athletes within the RFL.

Through the integration of motor development (Gallahue and Ozmun, 2006) and coach decision-making models (Abrahams and Collins, in press), findings will be considered and recommendations will be made in relation to suggested changes to the RFL's future provision in terms of the task, the individual and the environment:

Task: understanding the sport – developmentally appropriate technical and tactical sport principles

Individual: how children learn – biological, psychological and social development

Environment: establishing the learning climate – coach education, coaching practices, participant and parental support.

To smooth the journey, this chapter is split into the following sections:

- Background and RFL specific considerations
- RFL skills matrix analysis
- Coaches' perceptions
- Recommendations for future practice.

BACKGROUND AND RFL
SPECIFIC CONSIDERATIONS

This section will present an overview of the current structural elements offered for coaches involved in coaching young athletes, firstly focusing upon the nature of developmentally appropriate practices, primarily drawing upon the current overarching concept of 'multi-skills'. The modelling of participant development within environments that are designed to cater for both participation and performance participant pathways will follow, to offer an understanding of the perceived pathways of children's involvement in sport. Finally, as coach education and coaching practices greatly influence the environment that is established for any participating child, an understanding of current thinking on coaching practices will be presented in order to understand the context in which this project is located.

The Nature of Developmentally Appropriate Practices

As identified in the previous chapter, currently in the UK, and within national youth sport development programmes, multi-skills (MS) opportunities for children seem to be the flagship method of delivering developmentally appropriate practices. At its core, MS relates to the development of movement skills such as balance, co-ordination, reaction and timing – the building blocks of sport and most forms of recreational physical activity. The use of MS in connection with activities in support of talent development programmes has also been highlighted, as a MS environment embraces the use of movement skills in a non-sports-specific manner, which in turn forms the bedrock of physical literacy required for high levels of performance across a range of sports.

Using this type of environment at the correct stage of a young athlete's development can contribute to the overall pathway of the athlete as they progress through certain developmental stages in relation to their capabilities. However, there are constraints to using this approach in terms of culture, confidence and competence, clarity and consistency, and these constraints became apparent during the development of an understanding of a FfP approach with the RFL.

Modelling Developmental Participation

This section provides a summary of the principles of participant development, and in doing so re-establishes an awareness of how these principles affect decisions made when establishing and facilitating the coaching environment. As various models have already been discussed in detail in the previous chapter, the following text will highlight the areas that were often mentioned in discussions during the project in a way that interrogates key principles of the approach and offers guidance for suggested recommendations, and the next steps. This will ultimately allow for an introspective consideration of the various models more effectively as a collective, rather than having to revisit each model in detail.

There has been an upsurge in the ways in which the most desirable progression for young athletes in sport has been modelled by a range of theorists drawing upon personal insights and a range of research environments. This modelling allows the coaching community to reflect upon the holistic and longitudinal aspects of its participants' development, and to understand the consequences this potentially has for coaching practice. Recent attempts at modelling participants' development in sport range from long-term cumulative models that map a child's development through critical phases as they build experience and expertise (Balyi and Hamilton, 2004; Côté and Hay, 2002), to models that refer to the characteristics or traits of athletes in a bid to represent their multi-faceted dispositions and highlight the required sophistication of the coaching environment needed to support them (Morley and Bailey 2006; Jelicic *et al.*, 2007).

Long-Term Participant Development Models

Balyi's notion of Long-Term Athlete Development (LTAD) has probably been the most influential model of participant development in the UK in recent years. The RFL undertook their own modelling process around LTAD, and have a strategy that underpins both theory and practice. This development is conceptualized in terms of a series of stages through which athletes pass, the precise timing and nature of these stages being determined by the type of sport in question.

Balyi distinguishes between 'early' and 'late' specialization sports, and his framework is generally grounded within biological and physiological domains, whilst Jean Côté's developmental model of sport participation (DMSP) model leans more towards a psychosocial premise. Côté and colleagues (Côté, Baker and Abernethy, 2003; Côté, 1999; Côté and Fraser-Thomas, 2007) identified three stages of development concerned with an athlete's socialization into sport: the sampling phase (six to twelve years); the specializing phase (thirteen to fifteen years); and the investment phase (sixteen-plus years).

Another long-term development model, less referred to in participant development literature, is Gallahue and Ozmun's (2006) Lifespan Motor Development (LMD) model that presents a sequential understanding of the phases of motor development through which children progress as they acquire sports skills. This has been added to the discussion here to exemplify typical movement patterns associated with children as they develop fundamental movement skills, combine these to exhibit transitional complex or specialized movement skills, and then finally apply these skills into sports-type situational tasks, or modified scenarios related to a game or activity. This addition is crucial in understanding the relationship between the use of developmentally appropriate practices and long-term participant development models, and as such formed the mainstay of developments within the RFL in their FfP approach.

Participant Characteristics-Based Models

Morley and Bailey (2006) have developed a model that presents the typical traits of children in their attempt to model talent development in school-based physical education. Their construct also included more global considerations of developmental pathways for children in terms of personal and environmental characteristics necessary for success, as well as detailing a range of aspirational intended outcomes. They suggested that a talented child demonstrates potential over and above that of their peers in one or more of physical, creative, personal, social and/or cognitive traits, and these traits have since been integrated into support strategies for young talented athletes, as demonstrated in Figure 21.1.

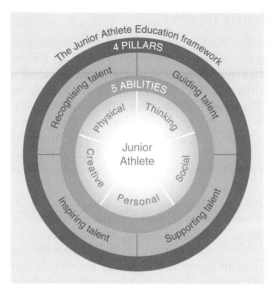

Figure 21.1   The Junior Athlete Education Framework (Youth Sport Trust, 2009). (Courtesy of the Youth Sport Trust)

More recently, other theorists (Jelicic *et al.*, 2007; Côté *et al.*, 2009) have drawn on the Positive Youth Development (PYD) literature to propose a framework of the Four Cs (Competence, Confidence, Connection, Character/ Caring) as appropriate outcomes that should emerge from the interactions of coaches and children in a sporting environment (Côté *et al.*, 2009), building upon the original notion that these characteristics were readily used to describe a 'thriving youth' (Lerner, 2005). Côté's Four Cs perspective on child development offers a useful framework from a psycho-social perspective, with key messages for coaches relating to:

- **Competence:** individualize competence information that is positive, but that is also realistic in relation to what participants can observe through peer comparison
- **Confidence:** enable competence to be evaluated by participants according to self-referenced improvement and effort
- **Connection:** promote positive participant, peer, parent, and coach interaction, and the demonstration of pro-social behaviours by encouraging cooperation and recognition of the needs and abilities of others
- **Character/caring:** promote moral reasoning and provide opportunities to demonstrate character and caring – important for coaches attempting to understand their athletes.

The theory around PYD offers an interesting insight into developmental processes during adolescence at a time when most of a person's biological, cognitive, psychological and social characteristics are changing in an interrelated manner from what is considered childlike to what is considered adult-like.

Participant Models Together

Whilst some of the models explicitly refer to talent development, it is likely that all of the models, if successful, will have the end result of harnessing and enhancing the capabilities of children, whether that is within performance or participation environments. In order to summarize these models effectively, those that have been presented by various theorists as having longitudinal dimensions (in that they stipulate and encapsulate an 'ages and stages' approach), such as LTAD, DMSP and LMD, will form the core of the landscape; those that suggest typical traits of a developing child within sport will wrap around the core pathways, as demonstrated in Figure 21.2.

Ultimately, any participant development model is simply a 'rough guide', and the most important consideration for coaches of children is that of 'individualization': coaches must pay attention to the bio-psycho-social development needs of each child in order to provide a platform for its future engagement in sport and physical activity. Importantly, coaches must look beyond 'here and now' markers of physical skill and maturation, and must consider factors that 'distinguish between potential and the ability to translate that potential into performance' (Bailey *et al.*, 2009, p. 57).

What is recognizable from the interwoven representation of developmental and characteristics-based models is that there is a consensus of agreement that a fundamental base is necessary as a precursor to more specific application within narrowing environments. This fundamental phase is termed as 'early diversification' and is typified by generic, varied and non-specialized activity, and as such is included within all long-term participant models as providing a fundamental base to subsequent positive engagement.

This is in contrast to 'early specialization', where a single sport is pursued predominantly without structured engagement in other sports. The remaining dilemma for coaches is whether it is most beneficial for a young athlete

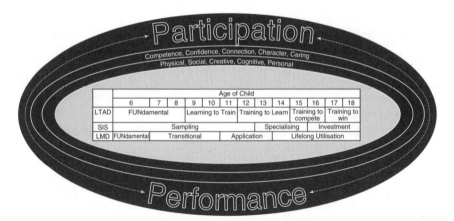

Figure 21.2   Long-term and characteristics-based participant models.

to experience a range of activities and sports in which they acquire a diverse skill-set across a number of contexts (early diversification), or whether they should concentrate their efforts and acquisition of skills, knowledge and understanding primarily within one sport (early specialization).

Early Diversification/Specialization

Despite significant research attention in this area, the strengths and weaknesses associated with early or late specialization in child development are still not clear. Indeed, a recent review by Baker, Cobley and Fraser-Thomas (2009) argued that inadequate evidence exists to resolve the issue in favour of either approach. The concept of early specialization has been associated with the development of sport expertise through deliberate practice (Ericsson *et al.*, 1993; Balyi and Hamilton, 2004).

In one of the few sport-specific explorations of early specialization, the findings suggested that successful soccer players spend more time in deliberate practice and play in their primary sport, and engage in minimal sporting diversity in other sports (Ford *et al.*, 2009). As a result of the findings, researchers advocated an appropriate balance between domain-specific deliberate practice (for example, team practice) and participation in domain-specific play (fun activities that are likely to foster motivation and independent decision-making skills) in order to develop expert performers in soccer.

However, it is also evident that early specialization can lead to negative outcomes, both physical (overtraining, staleness, failure to develop transferable skills), psychological (decreased enjoyment, sense of failure, burn-out) and social (limited social opportunities) (Côté and Hay, 2002). In contrast, an early diversification approach can afford the opportunity for children to develop the physical, cognitive and social skills needed to be successful across a range of sport settings during adolescence and adulthood (Bailey *et al.*, 2009).

Such distinctions in the developmental level and personal goals of children, in the sporting context and culture, reveal much about the construction and complexity within coaching practice (Cushion, 2007). How, then, do high-performing coaches of children plan and deliver their practice to meet the needs of their participants within the social, cultural and contextual constraints?

Coach Education

Coaching is a complex, multidimensional process that is influenced and guided by a plethora of contextual factors such as the child's experience, stage of development and goals, the ability and expertise of the coach, and the sporting context, level of competition, rules, regulations and culture. In addition to these contextual factors, the impinging structure, strategies, techniques, accepted practices and performance culture within each sport significantly impact upon coaches' practice. It is suggested that these contextual and traditional perspectives are often made manifest through overly sport-specific practices, delivered by coaches who promote structure and rules as they strive to deliver progressive, tidy and regulated practices full of demonstrations, drills and corrective feedback (Muir *et al.*, in press).

Recent literature shows the extensive number of ways in which coaches acquire and develop their coaching knowledge in order to function effectively within their environment. These include structured coaching programmes, personal experience, internet sources, books, videos and DVDs, formal mentoring, discussion with other coaches, and coaching seminars (Côté, 2006; Wright, Trudel and Culver, 2007).

Some authors (Potrac *et al.*, 2000; Jones, Armour and Potrac, 2002) believe the social world in which coaches interact needs to be considered when trying to understand the ways in which they learn. This is because sports coaches do not work in structured classroom settings; rather, they have to deal with continually changing micro and macro social situations throughout their coaching career, putting their knowledge and expertise into practice. Youth sport coaches in particular learn from previous experiences as players or assistant coaches (Lemyre, Trudel and Durand-Bush, 2007).

One thing that is rarely mentioned in research exploring coach effectiveness is, what qualities characterize a good coach? In other words, 'What makes an effective coach?' Recent attempts have been made to rectify this problem, however, with the end product of producing a coach decision-making model based on understanding children, understanding the sport and understanding pedagogy (Muir *et al.*, in press).

A coach's philosophy is defined by their actions and beliefs (Thibert, 2008), and developing a formal coaching philosophy can potentially increase their effectiveness (Nash, Sproule and Horton, 2008; Thibert, 2008). A coaching philosophy that focuses on developing the life skills of athletes, facilitating success in other areas, rather than a 'win at all costs' ethos, is more likely to be successful in the long term (Vallee and Bloom, 2005; Collins *et al.*, 2009). Together with a coach's experiences and social situation, their philosophy can have a significant impact on how successful their athlete or team is (Jones, Armour and Potrac, 2002; Cushion, 2007).

Coaching philosophy is examined throughout the various coaching programmes in the UK; these incorporate different levels, allowing coaches to specialize at a particular level (Lemyre, Trudel and Durand-Bush, 2007). In RFL there are three levels:

Level one: is aimed at those who are inexperienced or new to coaching; for example parents, students or volunteers who primarily coach children who are learning the game, but have no coaching experience

Level two: is aimed at those with some experience of playing or coaching rugby league, and who have an aspiration to perhaps coach at club level

Level three: is aimed at those with greater experience of the game, and who wish to coach élite or thirteen-a-side teams (RFL, 2006).

A great deal of coaching knowledge derives from experience, but those intending to become expert coaches at their chosen level need to undertake formal training in order to understand and explain the processes they oversee (Nash and Collins, 2006). Evidently, coaches have a positive view on the need for coaching education and the requirements of coaching certificates (Vargas-Tonsing, 2007). Consulting present/potential coaches about the content of the RFL coaching programmes should give an insight into their confidence and competence in delivering recommended changes to the course curriculum, and the views of these coaches will be explored later in this chapter.

Although all of these sources of learning should be considered when recommending improvements to coach development, it is beyond the capacity of this project to consider so many. Instead, the present study will address the content and structure of RFL coaching programmes, recommending improvements for the programmes, particularly in relation to developmentally appropriate practice for young athletes.

RFL SKILLS MATRIX ANALYSIS

So far we have revisited the nature of developmentally appropriate practices, examined long-term participant development models that are commonly used within RFL strategy, and explored current thinking on coach education. By doing this we now have an appropriate background to build upon, and this will hopefully allow for an understanding of why the FfP strategy was shaped in certain ways. What remains to be covered to complete this landscape is an understanding of what I, as project consultant, was trying to achieve when supporting the RFL. These considerations were highlighted and shared with the RFL at the start of the project, and it is important for the reader to understand how these considerations may have influenced the subsequent decision-making process:

1. **Core skills:** The RFL uses a set of 'core skills' within coaching practices, and these are clearly articulated in a range of resources used for coach and athlete education. Whilst an understanding of these core skills might be important, they are only useful as a way of understanding how players respond to the needs of today's game. It is incumbent upon the analysis of a FfP approach to reflect the holistic development of the athlete, irrespective of present-day demands of the game. It is hoped that this participant-centred, impartial and holistic approach will facilitate the development of an athlete who has the core skills necessary to be responsive to the changing needs of the game, and as such will allow them to become more proficient in any given sports situation.

2. **Effective participation:** The ability of any child to be able to participate effectively and experience success during the early years of motor development is paramount to their levels of participation and ultimately to their future engagement. The focus on the establishment of core movement skills, occasionally irrespective of their significance in terms of Rugby League, is vital to the athlete's subsequent inclusion in any form of physical activity.

3. **Fun and fundamentals:** In terms of the early stages of a talent development pathway, the approach adopted here, which uses a skills matrix analysis, draws upon the concept that these early stages for any

élite performer are characterized by a focus on fun and fundamentals that leads to a stage of further skills development and more specialized coaching. The typical age (albeit not chronologically age-dependent) for progression from the early stage to middle stage is often represented anywhere between nine and twelve years of age. In this sense, the matrix will concentrate on the introduction of specialized skills in a way that configures to the overall sequence of motor development and skill acquisition, offering typical ages merely for general guidance.

4. **Constraints:** The progression of children and young people through the different phases of motor development is affected by the task (in terms of how it is presented), the individual (how the task is received) and the environment (the influence of conditions, such as the surface, size and shapes of objects used).

5. **The RFL approach:** The current use of an RFL developmental approach to the introduction of certain skills within practices will be observed, and this involves four phases:

- Introduce
- Develop
- Optimize
- Maximize

The 'introduce', 'develop' and 'optimize' phases are particularly relevant to this analysis.

RFL Skills and Lifespan Motor Development Matrix Analysis

A cursory analysis of RFL coaching practices, through observation of existing (RFL) coaching programmes and an examination of associated resources, revealed that the RFL predominantly focused on ways in which *the same* rugby skills are delivered and developed with players across the full spectrum of participation (six years to élite). It is fair to say that the RFL were already aware of this discrepancy, and were consequently interested in understanding the developmental appropriateness of their approach, particularly in relation to young players in the target group of six to fourteen years of age.

It was important to provide evidence of how developmentally appropriate existing development was, and the most appropriate starting point for this was agreed as being an examination of the RFL's core skills. In order to assess the appropriateness of the RFL's skills development approach, Gallahue and Ozmun's (2006) Lifespan Motor Development model was used to compare and contrast.

Process
The actual process of the analysis is articulated here in order to provide an insight into the mechanics of conducting a comparative analysis of a theoretical and practically applied framework, and hopefully to spur on others to assess their own practices in the same way (*see* Figure 21.3).

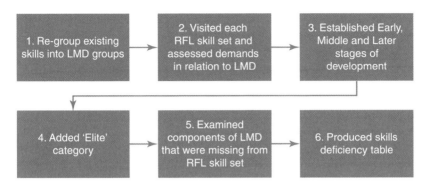

Figure 21.3   The process of a skills analysis matrix.

Areas of skill	Current skill demands	Early (4–7 years)	Middle (8–12 years)	Later (13 years +)	Elite (existing skill sets)
Throwing Ability to impart force to an object in the general direction of intent	● Static ○ Weighting ○ Timing ○ Accuracy ● Moving ○ Weighting ○ Timing ○ Accuracy	Thumbs point inwards Difficulty in judging Action from elbows Resembles a push Follow-through forwards and downwards Little rotary action Limited weight transfer Feet remain stationery	Thumbs point upwards Ball is recoiled before release Ball does not pass centre or side of body line in preparation Trunk and shoulders rotate towards throwing side Sideward and forwards shift of body weight Opposite leg strikes ground to throwing side	Ball passes centre or side line of body offering full recoil in preparation Trunk, shoulders and hips fully rotate Able to demonstrate proficiency on both sides Opposite leg to throwing side acts as block to produce force Arms extend fully in direction of throw	**6 o'clock** Over the front foot Ball pointed down Shoulders rotated Wrist hands **Dummy half-pass** Approach Move into sit position (step to ball) Scans sit

Figure 21.4   A 'throwing' example of RFL skills and lifespan motor development model (Gallahue and Ozmun, 2006) matrix analysis.

- Through an examination of resources detailing the RFL's core skills, regroup these skills into generic motor development groups to allow for comparative and longitudinal analysis. For example, regroup 'passing' as 'throwing', and group 'tackling' under 'axial movements'
- Examine the components of each existing skill set within the resource (for example, kicking), and assess demands in relation to the stages of development contained within the LMD model
- Establish early, middle and later patterns of development, associated to existing skills being delivered, and attempt to encapsulate existing technical aspects into the new LMD three-stage approach. These were couched as potential developmental difficulties, with the recognition that coaches could use these developmental traits to plan future interventions for supporting young athletes
- As it was deemed essential to retain the existing core skills in some shape or form, add an 'élite' category to contain those core skills evidenced within existing resources
- On conclusion of this initial process, re-examine the LMD model, and investige which motor skills were not being developed within the RFL's existing skills development programme
- Produce a new 'skills deficiency matrix', to demonstrate skills that are critical to the participant's needs, but were not currently delivered within the existing RFL skills programme.

Reflections on RFL Skills Matrix Analysis

This analysis demonstrated that a range of developmentally inappropriate practices were being used to develop certain skill sets with youngsters in the target group. For example, 'rotated shoulders' is required in the RFL's existing skill sets, but the LMD framework suggests that a child aged between four and seven years old would have 'limited rotary action' and 'limited weight transfer' to enable this required movement. Moreover, certain skills that were deemed developmentally appropriate for certain age groups within the motor development framework, and viewed in many ways as prerequisite in the future development of more complex or specialized skills, were not featured within the RFL's published skill sets.

The RFL was keen to understand more about strategies and interventions that could be used to bring about a shift in skill delivery more akin to developmentally appropriate practices for athletes within the target group. This initial phase of the 'fit for purpose' strategy clearly demonstrated that the documented core skills promulgated to coaches within the RFL were considerably inappropriate as an approach to coaching younger athletes in particular. Moreover, the absence of crucial fundamental movement skills and differentiated opportunities within the existing core skills beckoned a 'call to action' that considered more developmentally appropriate approaches within coaching practices.

To respond to this call to action the following strategy objectives, in terms of the *process* and likely areas for *recommendations*, were determined, and these form the following sections of this report.

Areas of skill	Skill demands	Early (4–7 years)	Middle (8–12 years)	Later (13 years +)
Running Brief period of no contact with the supporting surface	• Efficient and refined run (arms and legs) • Increased speed of run • Increased stride length • Greater extension of support leg at take off • Increased arm swing • Observable flight phase	Short, limited leg swing Stiff, uneven stride No observable flight phase Incomplete extension of support leg Stiff short swing of arms with limited bend at elbow Arms swing outwards horizontally Swinging leg swings outwards from hip Swinging foot toes outwards Wide base of support	Increase in length of stride, arm swing and speed Limited but observable flight phase More complete extension of support leg at takeoff Swinging foot crosses midline at height of recovery to rear	Stride length and speed at max Definite flight phase Complete extension of support leg Recovery thigh parallel to ground Arms swing vertically in opposition to legs Arms bent at right angles Minimum rotary action of recovery leg and foot

Figure 21.5   A 'running' example of a deficiency analysis following RFL and LMD matrix analysis.

Process

- To conduct an examination of the existing coaching climate across a range of delivery environments:
  - Coach education (Levels 1, 2 and 3)
  - RFL coaching 'retreats'
  - Club coaching.

Likely areas for recommendations:

- From an analysis of the examination:
  - Suggest refinements to existing coaching practices that reflect developmentally appropriate practices, acknowledging the need to retain certain technical and qualifying elements of the courses whilst simultaneously identifying opportunities for integrating a 'fit for purpose' approach to delivery
  - Offer clear suggestions for the integration of multi-skills type activities with existing skill sets
  - Consider the potential receptivity of any suggested refinements from the position of the variety of coaches involved, demonstrating an understanding of the range of existing competencies related to understanding developmentally appropriate practices
  - Recommend refinements to existing modified games to highlight the link between appropriate motor development practices and the use of modified games

○ Recommend any necessary changes required to the delivery of coach development sessions in line with the adoption of developmentally appropriate theory and practice. These recommendations to be modelled around *explicit* (change the existing) and *implicit* (adjust the existing) modifications to delivery, as well as the necessity to make *additions* to the content (deficiencies from the skill-set analysis, multi-skills type activities, and amendments to modified games).

COACHES' PERCEPTIONS

Process

In order to effectively audit coaching environments, some useful tools and models were used to guide the investigation. The first model to be used was the RE-AIM framework, which is a comprehensive, systematic approach to evaluating the impact of interventions, previously used to assess the impact of the health interventions (Glasgow, Vogt and Boles, 1999; Jilcott, Ammerman and Sommers, 2007).

The interesting feature of the framework for use within this strategy is the way in which information can be sought in an organized and targeted manner to assess the likely efficacy of a proposed intervention (a 'fit for purpose' approach), and, more importantly, effectively inform future direction and courses of action while maximizing the likelihood of success. The framework consists of five dimensions that should be assessed to establish the likely overall impact of an intervention. Figure 21.6 presents an explanation of each dimension, and the table on page 252 outlines the specific focus of investigation.

Interviews
Semi-structured focus group interviews were conducted with coaches participating in coaching awards at Levels 1, 2 and 3, and RFL coaches involved in a training day. These interviews lasted between 45 and 90 minutes, and were centred on a stimulus card that asked coaches to initially work through the following task:

- Drawing on your experience of coaching qualifications and your own coaching practices, consider aspects of coaching that you feel:
  ○ are appropriate and you would like to: KEEP
  ○ require some changes/modification: ADAPT
  ○ are inappropriate and you would like to get rid of: BIN
  ○ are needed and not currently included within your coaching practices and/or on coaching courses
- Probe: How do you think your responses relate to Coaching Levels 1, 2 and/or 3?

Coaches were asked to write down their responses on Post-its and place them on to the stimulus card, as demonstrated in Figure 2.17.

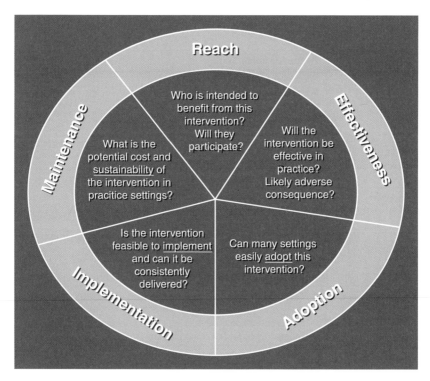

Figure 21.6   The RE-AIM framework.

Figure 21.7   Example of a stimulus card used during semi-structured focus group inter-views with coaches.

Focus of investigation using RE-AIM

Dimension	Focus for investigation
Reach	Eligible population prioritized: • Coach development tutors • Coaches • Players • Parents
Efficacy/ Effectiveness	• Early specialization/ diversification debate • Reduced emphasis on core sport-specific skills • Use within participation and/or performance pathways
Adoption	• Current behaviour • Likely constraints to affecting behaviour • Acceptance of newly proposed behaviours • Willingness, confidence and competence of course tutors and coaches adopting the recommended changes • Differences between regions and clubs • Player and parental attitudes towards new practices
Implementation	• Re-alignment of coaching courses and associated resources; • ability of course tutors, coaches and parents to facilitate the recommendations • Receptivity of participating players
Maintenance	Coaching courses and associated resource design; mentoring and quality assurance

---

After this initial discussion, the following questions were used as a guideline for a wider discussion around generic principles of approaches to coaching children:

- What do you feel is an appropriate environment for coaching children?
- What do you believe an expert in coaching children and participation looks like, or does?
- Picture this: you are directed to use developmentally appropriate practices when coaching children within certain participation and performance environments. In effect, this could mean, for instance, *less emphasis* on:

  ○ sport specific core skills
  ○ competition against others
  ○ strength, speed, endurance
  ○ repetitive activities

And *more emphasis*, for instance, on:

  ○ generic movement skills (non sport-specific)
  ○ personal achievement
  ○ quality of movement
  ○ variety of activities

- What are your thoughts on this?
- What barriers exist to the use of this approach?

- What support, if any, would you require to make this approach work?
- What effect would this approach have on participants
  - that you already work with?
  - entering the environment?

Observations

Observations were conducted at club academy, representative and club training sessions, as well as the filming of the new RFL awards scheme for children. These observations entailed an understanding of movement capability in terms of the categories of movement skills, namely stability, object control and locomotion.

The observations also involved speaking to coaches, parents and players about their experiences within rugby league, and whether they would be receptive to change using the semi-structured guidelines used when interviewing coaches as detailed above. The observation process afforded an opportunity to assess the filtration of information from formal coaching qualifications and policy guidelines into applied experiences in a range of coaching communities.

Findings

Reach

Who is intended to benefit from this intervention? Will they participate?

The hypothesis here is that the FfP strategy's primary beneficiaries are likely to be children as they will experience a wide range of skills that will allow for a more versatile and flexible player further on in their development, sufficient to meet the demands of the changing game. Moreover, because of the link between the task, individual and environment, it is highly likely that coaches and parents will also benefit from understanding more about the developmental needs of children in their care.

Findings within this study suggested that there is general support for the notion of developmentally appropriate practices under the auspices of fundamental movement skills-type provision. Many coaches suggested that this type of approach was already in use, as they were following guidelines already promulgated within the RFL's adoption of the LTAD initiative. Some of the more junior coaches contested the purpose of multi-skills, with their perceived usage of this type of intervention generally being split into multi-skills leading to one of two outcomes: the more holistic development of athletes; or better rugby players because they had enhanced generic movement skills. For example:

> If I went around my area and did FMS they'd have some fantastic rugby players. (Junior coach)
>
> It will be good for children who don't like rugby and prefer football, as they won't realize that they are learning fundamental rugby skills as well. Can't pass or catch so don't play rugby, this approach addresses that … participation would go up, definitely. (Senior coach)

It is clear that coaches are voicing benefits for both participation and performance elements of their approaches to coaching children. Some coaches suggested that the reach of the intervention could be more significant in certain areas than in others:

> It [multi-skills type delivery] would be good for areas where there's no particular rugby league at all ... we can get them into little skills and games where they don't think they are playing rugby, particularly those that don't want to play rugby, and teach them skills that can then be transferred if they ever do play rugby. (Junior coach)
>
> It will be good as it will rule out a lot of the kids who just stand there and don't get involved; I think if they've been involved with those kind of games [multi-skills type development] at a really young age we'll have less of them and less kids that have got no coordination. (Junior coach)

In many ways coaches commented upon how the demographic of the children coming to sessions would expand if multi-skills practices were used, and this would be advantageous on broadening the base of participation necessary for performance pathways to be established more effectively. There were some negative aspects concerned with the reach of the proposed intervention, the main issue centring on the impact of the current quandary regarding the amount and nature of competition for children. When reflecting upon what he would like to adapt in coaching practices and qualifications, one coach suggested:

> We need less competition, less sport-specific training and approaches, but as long as leagues have competitions there will always be sport-specific training. (Senior coach)
>
> Very much depends on the area; there are big differences in the approaches used and competitions. (Junior coach)

Effectiveness
Will the intervention be effective in practice? Is there likely to be an adverse consequence?

This was the area of RE-AIM in which participants in the research were most vocal in the way they expressed their opinions about how effective a FfP strategy would be. It was often necessary to explicitly portray what a developmentally appropriate environment could look like to elicit these thoughts effectively, as there seemed to be confusion as to what an effective approach to coaching younger athletes should actually look like. Hence the scenario that was developed and used within the focus group interviews became a crucial factor in establishing coaches' understanding of the effectiveness of the proposed intervention.

The general feeling was that the intervention would be effective in practice, but these sentiments carried with them certain disclaimers. Some coaches questioned the adverse consequence that might occur, in that there would probably be a reduction in the delivery of core skills. These consequences were manifest in a number of ways:

If we're moving away from core skills, the children will say 'We're going to play football!'

It's OK incorporating developments from ABCs, but we need the core skills.

I'm concerned about moving away from the core skills, but if we are told that there is compelling evidence that multi-skills delivery is beneficial for children we are coaching and is the right way to go, then I will do it.

(Level 3 delegates)

If you do core skills, rugby skills, they understand what they are going to be playing; if you just did FMS they can't relate it to rugby. It's a catch twenty-two: FMS would theoretically make them better players, but would it affect participation? – I'm not entirely sure. (Junior coach)

Adoption
Can many settings easily adopt this intervention?
It was noticeable from the stimulus task that, in the main, coaches felt that there was a need to overhaul the existing coaching qualifications, and this meant that they were receptive to ideas introducing new concepts related to coaching younger athletes. Delivery of content related to physiology and psychology came in for the largest amount of criticism, for example:

If we take out physiology and brought in this multi-skills effectively it wouldn't take much, but it would make a massive difference.

The problem with physiology is that you do need to know some physiology for open age or performance level, but in general you don't.

(Level 3 delegates)

One of the critical factors associated with the potential success of the FfP strategy was regarded as being the actual nature of the coaching environment established during the completion of coaching qualifications. It was felt by many coaches that the environment was overly regimented, and focused upon the concept of coaching rather than providing opportunities to reflect upon the contexts in which delegates were involved in their own applied settings. Senior coaches, in particular, felt a need for more experiential learning and guided discovery within their own courses as a way of understanding how to use these approaches when coaching younger athletes. For example:

It's all about ticking boxes; it's a very unnatural and sterile environment.

There is a need to know how to coach, but the courses need to be less rigid.

(Senior coaches)

There was a perceived need for a pre-course evaluation to be conducted in order to assess the different needs of delegates prior to them attending a

A coach should integrate developmentally appropriate practices. (Courtesy of David Griffiths)

course. Respondents made more of this point when considering their competencies in relation to coaching younger athletes, and suggested that a differentiated, almost personalized approach to their own professional development would be needed if younger athletes were to be coached in a more structured and specialized way.

RECOMMENDATIONS FOR FUTURE PRACTICE

Recommendations will be made in the light of the initial analysis of existing skill sets and their delivery, and research findings presented here. For the purpose of clarity in terms of the application of suggested recommendations, these will be presented under the sections of task, individual and environment.

Task

Finding
Coaches recognize the need to upskill their understanding of coaching children, and generally accept the notion of multi-skills development as an aid to achieving this. The REA of this is affected by a perception among coaches that rugby-specific core skills need to remain in some shape or form.

Recommendation 1: Developmentally appropriate practices are integrated with the skill-set analysis matrix, clearly demonstrating the linkage between fundamental, transitional and application skills across the stages of development. This could entail the implementation of some of the following areas of content that are designed to provide a greater understanding of core principles necessary as a prerequisite to developmentally appropriate sport-specific skills:

- A fundamental basis to the development of both performance excellence and lifelong participation requires the incorporation of a wide variety of motor skills into the development programmes of all children
- Children up to six years of age require informal learning opportunities in the home and pre-school environments, aimed at developing rudimentary movement skills and a love/enjoyment of physical activity
- From approximately five/six to eight/nine years of age, children benefit from a broad range of fundamental skills in a playful context, with these contributing to participation in sport and developing more advanced skills in later years
- Then from eight to twelve years, appropriate opportunities should be provided for participants to learn to play and practise a wide range of different sports, activities and skills, with a focus on sampling a range of sports and developing basic sports skills
- As athletes progress in training age and skill, fundamental skills should assume proportionately less of the practice time, with sport-specific and decision-making skills emphasized to underpin the development of future successful performance and involvement in more specialized activities.

Individual

Finding

Through interrogating the resources used for the delivery of Levels 1, 2 and 3, it is clear that there is some content regarding child-specific considerations for coaches within the resources for the different coaching certificates. However, these are generally aimed at safeguarding and child protection, and lack sufficient detail with regard to differentiating practices for children. Some sections, for example skill acquisition, refer to fundamental movement patterns, but there is minimal guidance on sequential, developmental progression, and how children's needs can be addressed throughout this time. Assessment criteria does mention the requirement for the coach to identify, describe and establish goals, and plan for the different needs of a range of participants, so the REA of a child-specific component is high due to the existing, albeit vague, nature of matching delivery with participant needs.

Recommendation 2: Opportunities are highlighted to extract specific syllabus content and re-design to offer information related explicitly to approaches to coaching children. Example sessions need to be provided to demonstrate typical coaching environments for children. A greater understanding of a child would come from developing a sound knowledge of the following principles:

- Children are characterized by a number of core traits (Morley and Bailey's multi-abilities, Côté's Four Cs)
- All human development is facilitated and constrained by an interactive dynamic of biological, psychological and sociological factors that change as children grow chronologically

- Children have been found to possess a variety of reasons for participating in sport, but these essentially comprise a mixture of desiring skill development, physical development and social interaction
- These motives, however, will likely change over time, with younger children seeking excitement and pleasure, while older children strive for achievement and satisfaction
- Children's skeletal, muscular and nervous systems develop at different rates throughout childhood, with the variance associated with this having significant implications for each individual child's physical development and, consequently, their sporting performance and improvement. Each child's perceptions of 'getting better' will therefore have associated psychological implications
- Further, this biological development will have most obvious connotations for children's psycho-motor development. That is, each child's capacity to demonstrate the movement skills fundamental to sports participation (for example, balancing, travelling, controlling objects) will vary according to the maturity of their physical make-up. Hence, as developing these psycho-motor behaviours is critical to all children, whether they progress to elite-level sport or life-long participation, coaches should be considerate of each child's individual needs.

Environment

Finding
This report concludes that coaches generally felt that the environment established within coaching qualifications is not meeting their needs in that it does not facilitate their involvement, is overly concept-based, and fails to draw upon examples from their own environments. As a result of this, the opportunities to probe ideas and examples of coaching children in particular are limited.

Recommendation 3: The delivery style of coaching qualifications becomes more heuristic and discovery-based, particularly when delivering elements pertaining to approaches to coaching children. Coaches are offered opportunities to draw upon their own contexts and experiences.

Finding
There is a vast cross-section of expertise on coaching qualifications, particularly at Level 2. Due to the perceived lack of differentiated delivery, this results in an environment where some coaches become frustrated through lack of challenge as they believe they already have some of the skills being delivered, and others become anxious as they lack the knowledge to be able to contribute fully within theoretical or practical activities.

Recommendation 4a: Delegate's needs are assessed prior to their attendance on the coaching qualification; this would also offer an opportunity for the delegate to reflect upon their personal and professional needs prior to attending the course. This assessment is then used by course tutors as a way of determining which elements of the core delivery are most appropriate for the needs of the delegates.

Recommendation 4b: Either existing coaching qualifications should be redesigned to modular (with Level 2 a priority), rather than a sustained course of intense delivery, or there should be a dedicated 'children's coach' route, leading to a dedicated 'advanced children's coach' qualification. If modular, it is recommended that 'approaches to coaching children' becomes a discrete module that delegates opt into, but then certain elements of required information are also permeated through other aspects of the course. Content regarding the environment, which would lead to a greater understanding of teaching and learning, would come from developing a sound knowledge of the following principles (with the obvious overlap between environment and individual here):

- Irrespective of a coach's style or philosophy, careful planning is required if learning is to be strategically facilitated across the long-term (for example seasonally) to short-term (individual session) continuum. To achieve this, bio-psycho-social and sport-specific targets must be established and worked towards through consideration of the overall management of sessions (as in the use of space, time and equipment), selection of learning tasks and cues, and identification of learning assessment methods
- Certain coaching behaviours, when used appropriately, can greatly facilitate children's learning, and others can be detrimental
- For instance, demonstrations can be very effective for learning (especially with new skills; Weiss and Williams, 2004), but not so effective at other times (for example, refining already learned, or introducing complex, skills; Weiss and Williams, 2004), and on certain occasions can even be ineffective or harmful (in situations where one specific technique is not necessarily required to achieve an outcome; Wulf, 2007). Hence, coaches need to think about how they use this behaviour with their children
- Coaches should also consider what type of feedback they should be providing, when, and how often, with descriptive feedback that is delayed and provided infrequently most beneficial for learning (Wulf and Shea, 2004)
- Further, the questions coaches ask can encourage children to take responsibility for their own learning and develop their understanding of techniques/tactics (when these are relevant, challenging, and provoke learners' curiosity); alternatively they can create anxiety and defensiveness within children (when the learner feels they are being tested; Morgan, 2006). Thus once again coaches may feel they need to attend to their use of questioning
- The type of practice tasks coaches devise for their children can impact on children's learning. This can also be linked to the overall structure of the learning programme within which children participate
- In terms of the practice type, blocked and constant practice of a skill leads to improved short-term performance, whereas random and variable

practice is associated with better learning in the medium to long term (*see* Ford and Williams, 2009, for a review). Hence coaches need to consider the associated trade-off between short-term feelings of competence and longer-term retention within their coaching when selecting practice tasks for their children

- The larger-scale programme structure within which children participate and through which they progress can be adapted to most effectively promote long-term participant development towards excellence and/or life-long physical activity

- During the early stages (sampling years) of participation, with an emphasis on playful activities (deliberate play), the coach's role is mainly to act as a 'resource person' (MacDonald, Côté and Kirk, 2005) who can modify the environment or supply basic instructions to enable efficient use of practice time

- As children grow (specializing years), coaches should shift the emphasis of their practices slightly in order to retain the sense of (deliberate) play that perhaps made initial participation so appealing, but should now also introduce a more intensive direction towards learning and improvement (deliberate practice)

- With a further maturing of age, children will either become more intensely involved in development (investment years) or they will seek to participate for other reasons (recreational years). Within the latter, coaches should carry on the role they performed during the specializing years. To assist participants' ongoing development, however, the coaches' technical and tactical instruction should become more focused, with an increasingly 'serious' (MacDonald, Cote and Kirk, 2005) approach to athletes' practice involvement.

SUMMARY

This chapter offered an understanding of a context in which talent development, the interdependency of participation and performance, and the use of developmentally appropriate practices became real-life issues for a national governing body of sport. The strategy that encapsulated this context became known as the 'fit for purpose' approach, as it questioned the effectiveness and suitability of coaching practices and environments that were designed to support athletes as they participated in Rugby League. The strategy entailed a comparative analysis of existing skills sets used within Rugby League with a Lifespan Motor Development model (Gailahue & Ozmun, 2006) as well as interviews with, and observations of, coaches, parents and players in a range of settings.

What became evident at an early stage in the exploration of whether the RFL had a FfP approach was the vacuum that existed between what was being delivered, and what was reported as being developmentally appropriate practice within a motor development continuum. The most encouraging and crucial aspect of this investigation has been the receptiveness of the RFL to recognize the deficiency, and the fact that they have the vision and courage to do something about it. At least now the RFL are aware of the deficiencies that exist and can put actions and measures in place to ensure that future development in this area progresses in an appropriate direction.

It is hoped that should the recommendations be considered, a number of benefactors will emerge from an effective investigation of this nature. First, coaches will become more acquainted with the principles of children's development, and will see the needs of the participants, and not the sport, as paramount. Second, and most importantly, children will be offered a diet of activity that actually meets their needs and is based at an appropriate level so that the challenge matches their ability.

Appendix 1

RFL skills and Lifespan Motor Development model (Gallahue and Ozmun, 2006) matrix analysis

Areas of skill	Current skill demands	Early (4–7 years)	Middle (8–12 years)	Later (13 years +)	Elite (existing skill sets)

Throwing
 	
Ability to impart force to an object in the general direction of intent
	● Static
	  ○ Weighting
	  ○ Timing
	  ○ Accuracy
	● Moving
	  ○ Weighting
	  ○ Timing
	  ○ Accuracy
		Thumbs point inwards
		
		Difficulty in judging
		
		Action from elbows
		
		Resembles a push
		
		Follow-through forwards and downwards
		
		Little rotary action
		
		Limited weight transfer
		
		Feet remain stationery
			Thumbs point upwards
			
			Ball is recoiled before release
			
			Ball does not pass centre or side of body line in preparation
			
			Trunk and shoulders rotate towards throwing side
			
			Sideward and forwards shift of body weight
			
			Opposite leg strikes ground to throwing side
				Ball passes centre or side line of body offering full recoil in preparation
				
				Trunk, shoulders and hips fully rotate
				
				Able to demonstrate proficiency on both sides
				
				Opposite leg to throwing side acts as block to produce force
				
				Arms extend fully in direction of throw
					6 o'clock
					
					Over the front foot
					
					Ball pointed down
					
					Shoulders rotated
					
					Wrist hands
					
					Dummy half-pass
					
					Approach
					
					Move into sit position (step to ball)
					
					Scans sit
					
					Head and upper body towards target
					
					Nearest foot in front of the ball pointing at receiver
					
					Contact
					
					Pass from the ground in one movement (heel to toe)
					
					Follow through with fingers

					Alive – next action
					Spin pass
					Upper body turns so that shoulders are square and face the receiver
					Arms are taken further back
					Follow through and flick of the wrists is more pronounced
					Rear hand becomes dominant and propels the ball by moving forward and over the ball
Catching Receiving force from an object	• Catching ○ Early ○ Timing	Arms extended and held in front of body	Elbows held at side	Eyes follow ball into hands	**From sender**
		Body movement limited until contact	Avoidance reaction (close eyes)	No avoidance reaction	Target hands up
		Avoidance reaction (turn of head)	Arms trap the ball	Arms relaxed at side, forearms extended forwards	Shoulders rotated
		Scooping action	Thumbs upwards, hands held in opposition to each other	Arms adjust to flight of ball and give on contact	**High ball from opponent**
		Other body parts used to 'trap' ball	Squeeze is attempted on contact and is poorly timed	Thumbs in opposition to each other	Keep eyes on the flight of the ball and move quickly into position
		Palms held upwards	Able to track ball moving in an arc	Hands grasp in well-timed manner simultaneously	Arms held out and upwards in a searching manner with fingers spread
		Fingers extended and tense		Fingers grasp more effectively	Allow the ball to land in the cradle formed by the hands, forearms and chest
					Trap the ball as high as possible on the chest with the hand and forearm
					At the point of catching the ball:

(Continued)

Appendix 1 (continued)

RFL skills and Lifespan Motor Development model (Gallahue and Ozmun, 1996) matrix analysis

Areas of skill	Current skill de-mands	Early (4–7 years)	Middle (8–12 years)	Later (13 years +)	Elite (existing skill sets)
		Hands rarely used in catching action	Increase speed of pass and introduce movement of players	Visual perception is fully mature – able to track, anticipate and respond to moving objects in relation to themselves	Elbows close together
		Able to track ball in a horizontal plane			Bend knees
		Use different ball sizes, colours and textures			Turn sideways on to opposition
		(Boys more developed than girls at all ages)			
Kicking Imparting force to an object with the foot	• Place kick ○ Goal kicking ○ Restarts	Stands next to the ball to engage contact	One or more deliberate steps taken toward the ball	Approach to the ball is either a run or a leap	
		Limited range of leg movement – backswing and follow through	Preparatory backswing is centred around the knee	Arms swing in opposition to each other during kick	
		Upper body remains erect	Kicking leg stays bent throughout kick	Trunk bends at waist during follow-through	

	Arms are used to maintain balance Pushing of the ball is more noticeable than a strike	Follow through limited to forward movement of the knee	Force from kicking leg is generated from the hip Support leg bends slightly on contact Follow through is high. Standing foot rises to toes	**Landing position** *Elbows and knees* Sweep – leg round Touch – play the ball *Belly* Snap – knees to chest Sweep – leg round Touch – play the ball *Back/side* Roll to ball Snap – knees to chest Sweep – leg round Touch – play the ball
Playing the ball	○ Foot action ○ Sweep ○ Touch ○ Snap ○ Roll ○ With control ○ With speed	*From ball rolling* Straddle stance	Stride stance	Stride stance

(Continued)

Appendix 1 (continued)

RFL skills and Lifespan Motor Development model (Gallahue and Ozmun, 1996) matrix analysis

Areas of skill	Current skill demands	Early (4–7 years)	Middle (8–12 years)	Later (13 years +)	Elite (existing skill sets)
Collecting	• Stationery ball • Moving ball				Move quickly to the ball Eye on the ball. On approach adjust feet to position **correctly** (?) Run at the side of the ball to enable a straddle so that inner leg is at back of ball Lean the body down close to the ground if the ball is lengthways across Scoop ball with rear hand going underneath the ball and the other at the front (preventing a knock on) If the ball is lying with the point facing the player they should scoop up the ball by placing the hands at each side of the ball
Grip and carry	• One-handed grip • Two-handed grip				Thumbs spread greater than right angle Arched palm Centre of ball Elbows out Carry with two hands and at centre of body

Being tackled	Fluency of recovery actions	*Dynamic balance*	*Axial movements*		
Dynamic balance	Controlled systematic use of body parts	Walks along line, alternating feet	Combined with emerging object control skills such as throwing, catching and kicking		
Maintaining equilibrium as the centre of gravity shifts	Positioning of body following roll	Performs basic and then mature forward roll			
Static balance	• falling	*Static balance*			
Maintaining equilibrium as the centre of gravity remains static	• rolling • tumbling • standing	Balances on one foot for three to five seconds			
Axial movements		Supports body in basic 3-point inverted positions			
Static postures that involve bending, stretching, twisting, turning		*Axial movements Developed in isolation*			
Tackling	• position of body	Exaggerated base of support	Good balance	Smooth, rhythmical flow	**Low**
Axial movements	○ shoulder ○ arms ○ feet ○ head	Momentary loss of balance	Appropriate base of support	Sequences several movements with ease	Thighs for front passive-side and rear
			Requires visual model		Under the ball for the drive tackle

(Continued)

Appendix 1 (continued)

RFL skills and Lifespan Motor Development model (Gallahue and Ozmun, 1996) matrix analysis

Areas of skill	Current skill demands	Early (4–7 years)	Middle (8–12 years)	Later (13 years +)	Elite (existing skill sets)
Static postures that involve bending, stretching, twisting, turning	• approach • contact • finish	Visual monitoring of body and model when possible Combined movements appear jerky and segmented Lack of fluid transition from one level or plane to another Only one to two actions possible at a time	Does not have to monitor own body Good coordination of similar movements Poor transition in dissimilar movements Can combine two to three actions into one fluid movement	Vision unimportant Appears totally in control Can combine four or more movements into one fluid movement	**Head positioning** *Side of the ball carrier* Front passive Drive Rear *Behind the ball carrier* Side **Target areas** Above the waist The ball for the smother tackle **Head positioning** Side of ball carrier **Approach** Arc-positioning player Prepare to step in short steps Hands up Head up **Contact** Disarm (fend) Step in Hit (shoulder contact)

				Grip (handle) **Finish** On top Unload at front Alive (ready for next action) **Other considerations** Right shoulder-right foot Left shoulder-left foot Sit position Head up
Evasion	Fluency of coordinated movements Use of deception Use of both sides of movement plane Control led lateral movement Body parts used in fake Crossing of feet • sidestep • swerve • fend • hit and spin • bump off	Segmented movements Body appears stiff Minimal knee bend Weight is on one foot Feet generally cross No deception	Movements coordinated but with little deception Performs better to one side than the other Too much vertical lift Feet occasionally cross Little spring in movement Sometimes outsmarts self and becomes confused	Knees bent Slight trunk lean forward (ready position) Fluid directional changes Performs equally well in all directions Head and shoulder fake Good lateral movement

(Continued)

Appendix 2

Deficiency analysis following RFL & LMD matrix analysis

Areas of skill	Skill demands	Early (4–7 years)	Middle (8–12 years)	Later (13 years +)
Running Brief period of no contact with the supporting surface	• Efficient and refined run (arms and legs) • Increased speed of run • Increased stride length • Greater extension of support leg at take off • Increased arm swing • Observable flight phase	Short, limited leg swing Stiff, uneven stride No observable flight phase Incomplete extension of support leg Stiff short swing of arms with limited bend at elbow Arms swing outwards horizontally Swinging leg swings outwards from hip Swinging foot toes outwards Wide base of support	Increase in length of stride, arm swing and speed Limited but observable flight phase More complete extension of support leg at takeoff Swinging foot crosses midline at height of recovery to rear	Stride length and speed at max Definite flight phase Complete extension of support leg Recovery thigh parallel to ground Arms swing vertically in opposition to legs Arms bent at right angles Minimum rotary action of recovery leg and foot
Jumping	• Efficient combined use of arms and legs	Inconsistent preparatory crouch	Knee flexion exceeds right angle on preparatory crouch	Preparatory crouch with knee flexion from 60 to 90 degrees

(vertical) Involves a one-or two-foot takeoff landing on two feet	• Use of flexion in preparation phase • Increased extension during flight phase • Alternate thrust of reaching and non-reaching hands • Two-foot takeoff • Increased distances • Increased heights	Difficulty in taking off with both feet Poor body extension on take off Little or no head lift Arms not coordinated with the trunk and leg action Little height achieved	Exaggerated forward lean during crouch Two-foot takeoff Entire body does not fully extend during flight phase Arms attempt to aid in flight (but often unequally) and balance Noticeable horizontal displacement on landing	Forceful extension at hips, knees and ankles Simultaneous coordinated upward arm lift Upward head tilt with eyes focussed on target Full body extension Shoulder girdle tilt elevates reaching arm combined with downward thrust of non-reaching arm Controlled landing very close to point of landing
Jumping (horizontal) Involves a one-or two-foot takeoff landing on two feet	• Arms in front of body in preparation • Elbows out to maintain balance during flight • Deep preparatory crouch • Knee and hip extension	Limited swing; arms do not initiate jumping action During flight, arms move sideward-downward or rearward-upward to maintain balance Trunk moves in vertical direction; little emphasis on length of jump	Arms initiate jumping action Arms remain toward front of body during preparatory crouch Arms move out to side to maintain balance during flight	Arms move high and rear during preparatory crouch During takeoff, arms swing forward with force and reach high Arms held high throughout jumping action Trunk propelled at approximately 45 degree angle Major emphasis on horizontal distance

(Continued)

Appendix 2 (continued)

Deficiency analysis following RFL and LMD matrix analysis

Areas of skill	Skill demands	Early (4–7 years)	Middle (8–12 years)	Later (13 years +)
	• Hips and thighs flexed and parallel to ground in flight	Preparatory crouch inconsistent in leg flexion Difficulty in using both feet Limited extension of the ankles, knees and hips at takeoff Body weight falls backwards on landing	Preparatory crouch deeper and more consistent Knee and hip extension more complete at takeoff Hips flexed during flight; thighs held in flexed position	Preparatory crouch deep and consistent Complete extension of ankles, knees and hips at takeoff Thighs held parallel to ground during flight; lower leg hangs vertically Body weight forward at landing
Hopping One-foot takeoff landing on the same foot	• Increased distances, rhythmical and skilful action • Non-supporting leg flexion • Forward lean • Rhythmical arm action	Non-supporting leg flexed 90 degrees or less Non-supporting thigh roughly parallel to contact surface Body upright Arms flexed at elbows and slightly to side	Non-supporting leg flexed Non-supporting thigh at 45 degree angle to contact surface Slight forward lean, with trunk flexed at hip	Non-supporting leg flexed at 90 degrees or less Non-supporting thigh lifts with vertical thrust of supporting foot Greater body lean Rhythmical action of non-supporting leg (pendulum swing aiding in force production)

	Little height or distance generated in single hop Balance lost easily Limited to one or two hops	Non-supporting thigh flexed and extended at hip to produce greater force Force absorbed on landing by flexing at hip to produce greater force Arms move up and down vigorously and bilaterally Balance poorly controlled Generally limited in number of consecutive hops that can be performed	Arms move together in rhythmical lifting as the supporting foot leaves the contact surface Arms not needed for balance but used for greater force production
Galloping Combines a walk and a leap with same foot leading throughout	Arrythmical at fast pace Trailing leg often fails to remain behind 45-degree flexion of trailing leg during flight phase Contact in heel toe combination Arms of little use in balance or force production	Moderate tempo Appears choppy and stiff Trailing leg may lead during flight but lands adjacent to or behind lead leg Exaggerated vertical lift Feet contact in a heel-toe, or toe-toe combination Arms slightly out to side to aid balance	Moderate tempo Smooth, rhythmical action Trailing leg lands adjacent to or behind lead leg Both legs flexed at 45-degree angle during flight Low flight pattern Heel-toe contact combination Arms not needed for balance; may be used for other purposes

(Continued)

Appendix 2 (continued)
Deficiency analysis following RFL and LMD matrix analysis

Areas of skill	Skill demands	Early (4–7 years)	Middle (8–12 years)	Later (13 years +)
Skipping Combines a step and a hop in rhythmic action	• Skilful skipping • Step and hop • Weight transfer • High to low • Fluency of combined movements	One footed skip Deliberate step-hop action Double hop or step sometimes occurs Exaggerated stepping action Arms of little use Action appears segmented	Step and hop coordinated effectively Rhythmical use of arms to aid momentum Exaggerated vertical lift on hop Flat-footed landing	Rhythmical weight transfer throughout Rhythmical use of arms (reduced during time of weight transfer) Low vertical lift on hop Toe-first landing

Figure 21.8   RFL skills and Lifespan Motor Development model (Gallahue and Ozmun, 1996) matrix analysis.

ACKNOWLEDGEMENTS

I would like to thank all the participants and staff from the RFL, particularly Vinny Webb, Haydn Walker, Tony Smith and Fiona Allen.

Establishing a Talent Development Pathway

by Dr David Morley

The last three chapters have covered the areas of talent development, multi-skills, and the RFL's perspective on adopting a 'fit for purpose' strategy as part of their participation and performance pathways. The chapters have contained a number of key concepts that span the area of talent development, such as multi-skills, the interdependency of participation and performance, coaches' perceptions and practices, developmentally appropriate practice, and the importance of athlete-centred approaches to developing talent.

This next chapter moves from concept to context in that it explores the opportunities that exist in a range of environments where some of the conceptual frameworks previously articulated are transferred into a range of contexts. These opportunities will be presented as a case study in which athlete-centred, developmentally appropriate practices are paramount in coaches' planning and delivery. The case study is that of local authorities, and is situated largely in school-based physical education, although what will become very apparent is the multi-agency approach that is used to achieve the aims. The examination of this case study will offer an insight into the establishment of structured environments that facilitate an athlete's participation, with the subsequent linkage to performance.

The case study highlights the structural considerations related to the development of a talent development strategy related to a number of local authorities aiming to raise the profile of talented athletes by the establishment of a performance pathway across a whole county. The following section is also written in a way that will demonstrate the method behind some of the decisions made about the establishment of the pathway, and the thought processes that were involved. This process of establishing a pathway is particularly useful to those coaches either wanting to understand where their delivery fits into wider dimensions of talent development, or those who have been tasked to develop a strategy to support athlete development themselves.

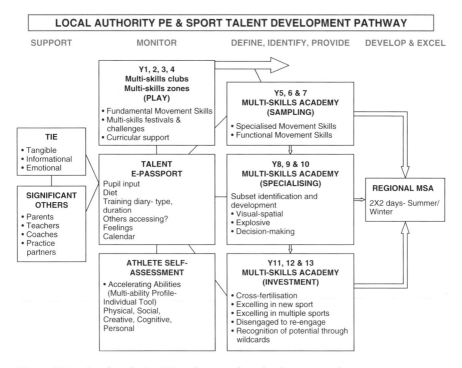

Figure 22.1   Local authority PE and sport talent development pathway.

ESTABLISHING THE PATHWAY

When considering any pathway it is crucial to understand the longitudinal dimensions of an athlete's progression. It is impractical and short-sighted to attempt to view the athlete in isolation, either within a given, singular sport, or at a particular stage of their development. Both approaches are destined to fail, because without an understanding of the long-term patterns, structures and critical moments of athlete development, the athlete will be compartmentalized and will never truly fulfil their potential.

The pathway presented in Figure 22.1 shows a long-term pathway development strategy that was employed across a number of local authorities, as they aimed to increase the effectiveness of talent support in their areas. The intended outcomes of the talent development pathway were as follows:

- To provide an infrastructure of talent development support services for children and young people aged five to nineteen years

- To accurately identify a talent development cohort across the region, and in doing so allow appropriately skilled athletes to enter the talent development pathway

- To standardize talent development practices to ensure consistent and inclusive approaches to developing talented children and young people across the authority
- To establish a community of practice to enable inter-agency approaches to talent development in PE and sport.

The pathway is moulded around four key talent development themes, namely:

- Support
- Monitor
- Define, identify and provide (DIP)
- Develop and excel.

These mechanisms encapsulate the full breadth and depth of a dynamic and supportive talent development pathway that is sufficiently rigorous to cope with the demands of athletes from a range of environments. What the pathway does not include are all the concurrent and parallel pathways that exist, such as those demonstrated in the previous chapter. This is deliberate, because the pathway presented here is situated in predominantly educational settings, so it is crucial that all athletes can access the scheme, irrespective of the availability of a wider range of opportunities elsewhere. That is not to say that other pathways are not as meaningful to the athlete's development. On the contrary, the formation of any new pathway must be cognizant of parallel pathways, but not reliant on their effectiveness on achieving the fundamental aims of a holistic talent development pathway.

Once the pathway was fully articulated, the next phase would be to determine which elements of the pathway were of a higher priority than others. The crux of the pathway was originally formed around opportunities within multi-skills academies, and the ways in which PE teachers and coaches working within schools were able to 'define, identify and provide' (DIP) for talented athletes more effectively. Once these priorities were determined, a series of training and resource requirements was listed in order to achieve the necessary outcomes. Therefore some of the following sections ('support and monitor') were viewed as second phase priorities, whereas others ('define, identify and provide', and 'develop and excel') were deemed as first phase priorities. As such, the themes of 'support' and 'monitor' will simply be discussed to give an outline of their importance on a pathway, with the areas of DIP, and 'develop and excel' being covered in more detail as these themes were actually delivered from the outset.

Support

Tangible, Informational and Emotional

This column of the pathway relates to the range of athlete support structures that can be provided to effectively maximize the chances of an athlete as they progress along the pathway. Talented athletes require support in a number of ways, and these facets of support can by typified as 'tangible, informational and emotional' (Holt and Morley, 2004). *Tangible* support is often noticeable, for example, as the provision of transport to and from training and competition venues, as well as the purchase of appropriate equipment to train and compete. *Informational* support is required for the athlete to progress in terms of their knowledge and understanding of their sport, particularly as they progress to the demands of the performance environments of the sports they are pursuing. Other forms of informational support could also include training plans, nutrition, preparation for performance and coping strategies.

Emotional support is also necessary to help provide the appropriate learning climate for success, and to strike a balance between home, friends and education. Athletes will be required to make certain sacrifices along their talent pathway, as well as being faced with important decisions that could ultimately affect their whole lives, so it is important that they are fully supported through these fairly turbulent times. It was noted that although families play an important role in providing emotional and financial support, their influence tends to diminish as the performer matures, and the coach then becomes more significant in the athlete's development (Bloom, 1985; Côté, 1999; Csikszentmihalyi *et al.*, 1993; Glaser, 1996; Rowley, 1993).

During the regional multi-skills academy (RMSA) that became the centrepiece of the first phase of the pathway, workshops were delivered to parents, coaches and teachers on the following themes:

- Supporting the athlete using the multi-abilities framework, with a particular focus on creativity
- Observing movement within a multi-skills environment
- Education/socializing/sport balance
- Coping with success.

An example of the resource cards used when focusing on creativity is highlighted in Figure 22.2. This card is one of a series of tasks used within a sequence of activities that explores 'off the ball movement using hands' in a game-like situation. Parents were asked to consider creativity in terms of their child's range of ideas, tactics and solutions to the problems set when performing in these types of environment.

In subsequent RMSAs, as well as having access to a 'talented athlete' forum, resources will be developed and delivered through workshops offering advice to parents on supporting their child in other areas, such as:

- Signposting to, and applying for, financial assistance
- Developmentally appropriate 'ages and stages' training plans
- Nutrition.

Significant Others

The role of 'significant others' cannot be underestimated in any talent development pathway. The positive involvement of peers, family, teachers, coaches and practice partners within an athlete's development can make the difference between failure and success. While most coaches

Creativity in Physical Education	**Phase 1: Activity 1** **Off-the-ball movement and support using hands**

Warm Up

Organisation
20 x 20 metre area
12–15 players per game

Task
Two 'Taggers' HOLD bibs.

Another two players hold a ball each.

The remaining players are spread about the area.

'Taggers' pass the bib over to the pupils they Tag.

If a pupil moves out of the area, they change places with one of the 'catchers'.

Players in possession of a ball are safe and cannot be tagged.

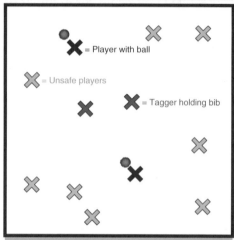

Teaching Points
"Call for the ball if you are in danger"
"If you have the ball, look for people in danger"
"Keep your eyes on the balls and taggers"

Creativity in Physical Education	**Phase 1: Activity 2** **Off-the-ball movement and support using hands**

Situational Task

Organisation
1 v 2 Situation

Task
One player is asked to stand on a specific spot (use a throw down spot); this player is not allowed to move with the ball.

The other two pupils choose to be either an attacker of defender.

The defending pupil guards/marks the attacking pupil.

The defending pupil is conditioned to start IN FRONT of the attacking pupil as shown in the diagram.

The attacking player attempts to receive the ball from the Player on the spot.

Teaching Points
"Changing direction quickly"
"Shout when you want the ball"
"Point where you want the ball"

Creativity in Physical Education	**Phase 1: Activity 3** **Off-the-ball movement and support using hands**

Game Related Task

Organisation
15 x 15 metre area
6 players per game

X = Attacker

Task
The game starts in the central square with an attacking player in possession.

Attacking players try to pass the ball among themselves without defending players intercepting the ball.

Players must combine to pass the ball between them five times to score one point.

The defending pupil guards/marks the attacking pupil.

X = Defender

On scoring a point, they give possession in the central square back to the opposing team as shown in the diagram.

Teaching Points
"Changing direction quickly"
"Shout when you want the ball"
"Point where you want the ball"

© DM Morley Consultancy Ltd 2008

Creativity in Physical Education	**Phase 1: Assessment Template**

Ability to think of a range of ideas, tactics and solutions to the tasks		
Bronze	Silver	Gold
Finds it difficult to think of different ideas and tactics	Thinks of some ideas and tactics	Demonstrates a range of ideas and tactics
Finds it difficult to independently recognise solutions	Independently recognises some solutions to the tasks	Independently recognises a range of solutions to the tasks
Shows little confidence and relies on others for ideas and guidance	Shows some confidence working independently from others but requires some guidance	Shows lots of confidence to work independently and requires minimal guidance from others

© DM Morley Consultancy Ltd 2008

Figure 22.2   Example of a creativity task.

would perhaps recognize the influence of a range of individuals within an athlete's development, the crucial role of practice partners is often neglected, yet these are the very people who allow the talented athlete the opportunities to practise and hone their skills in order to reach higher levels of capability within a sport, or range of sports.

Once again, in the second phase the intention is to provide workshops for parents to fully understand the importance of 'significant others', with practical ideas for the ways in which support can be offered.

Monitor

Although there is an obvious link between the ways we support and subsequently monitor an athlete as they progress along the talent pathway, it is essential that the methods of monitoring employed provide effective feedback that will enable the coach, teacher, parent and, most importantly, the athlete to determine three major aspects of their developmental journey:

1. Where are they now?
2. Where would they like to go?
3. How are they are going to get there?

Self-regulation, or what can be seen as the 'personal' aspect of the multi-ability framework, is central to monitoring, as attempts are made to shift the onus of responsibility away from significant others and more towards the athlete themselves. The emphasis on this particular aspect of an athlete's development is in keeping with recent developments in education, in which schools are being asked to consider more carefully their use of self-assessment procedures to monitor the educational success of students. Therefore, the athlete should be increasingly familiar with this method of monitoring, and the coach can use this familiarity to their advantage in structuring appropriate monitoring strategies within their own practices.

For the purposes of this talent development pathway, the dilemma of asking athletes to monitor and map their own development heralded the creation of a new set of resources designed to accelerate the abilities of athletes. As one of the main intended outcomes for the RMSA was the effective support of the athlete in terms of their 'multi-ability' development, any resource developed would have to align closely to this delivery framework. Consequently, an 'Accelerating Abilities' wheel (AA wheel) (Create

Figure 22.3 Monitoring an athlete's progress is critical in the Talent Development Pathway. (Courtesy of David Griffiths)

Development, 2009) has been designed to allow the athlete the opportunity to complete a self-profiling tool, online with the support of their parents, that can be accessed by the coach, teacher and athlete themselves. 'Health' has been added to offer support around nutrition, rest and lifestyle balance, and 'physical' has become particularly focused on acquiring and developing skills. An example of the AA wheel is illustrated in Figure 21.4.

This AA wheel will be used to effectively support and monitor talented athletes at subsequent RMSAs, and the talent cohort will also be tracked to detect commonalities of the group in terms of needs and any impact of established environments. It is anticipated that the AA wheel will form part of a wider strategy related to an e-passport specifically designed to profile talented athletes more effectively. (For further information on the AA wheel visit www.createdevelopment.co.uk.)

Define, Identify, Provide, Develop and Excel

Overarching Principles
When trying to understand the overarching principles involved in a longitudinal talent development pathway, it is crucial that key phases of athlete development are integrated. In order to promulgate the key phases

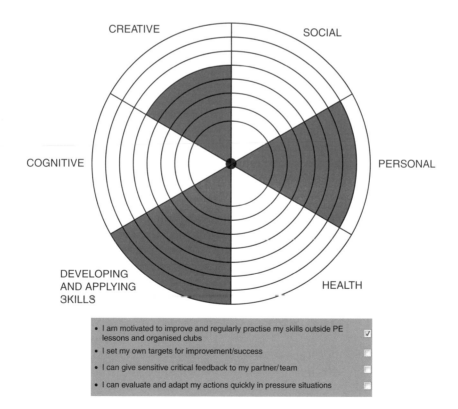

Figure 22.4   Accelerating abilities wheel. (Courtesy of Create Development)

to all involved, Côté's Developmental Model for Sports Participation (DMSP) (Côté, 1999; Côté and Fraser-Thomas, 2007), as outlined in previous chapters, was used. Figure 22.1 demonstrates how the pathway was separated into three transitional phases, as Côté suggests: sampling, specializing and investment. As a reminder of this concept, Côté found that in his research, élite athletes generally experienced three key phases within their athletic development:

The sampling phase: (six to twelve years) children were given the opportunity to sample a range of sports, develop a foundation of fundamental movement skills, and experience sport as a source of fun and excitement.

The specializing phase: (thirteen to fifteen years) the child began to focus on a smaller number of sports, and while fun and enjoyment were still vital, sport-specific emerged as an important characteristic of sport engagement.

The investment phase: (sixteen-plus years) the child became committed to achieving a high level of performance in a specific sport, and the strategic, competitive and skill development elements of sport emerge as the most important.

As the pathway in some local authorities needed to consider the whole learning journey, a 'play' phase was added, and this also served to inform users of the model of the importance of these early learning experiences in the subsequent development of movement competency. Multi-skills academies were used as the medium for athletes to enter the pathway, and each of these MSAs had a distinct role to play in supporting the athlete as they progressed along it.

The focus of the early phase of strategic pathway development was centred on MSAs and RMSAs, with athletes in the 'sampling' phase of their development being given priority. This prioritization occurred for a number of reasons, such as logistics (the time of year the project started) and finance (only being able to fund one age range for MSAs and RMSAs in the early stages), although the theoretical rationale came from an understanding that athletes in this age range were subject to the following constraints:

- They were about to change schools and therefore needed a measure of talent to take with them to ensure this transitional period was as smooth as possible, and that they didn't risk slipping through the net
- They were at risk of specializing too early in sport so would be given the opportunity to sample a range of sports environments
- They required consistent and informed messages about their future.

MSAs AND THE RMSA

Whilst certain supporting and monitoring structures can be established to guide the athlete effectively along the pathway, the key priority from the outset was to define and identify talented athletes effectively. This was a critical part of shaping the pathway when considering if athletes not identified accurately enough would have provision that was geared toward a particular type of athlete. This would be rendered ineffective and would certainly fail to meet the needs of those athletes attending the RMSAs. In terms of 'develop' and 'excel', as the RMSA was recognized as the pinnacle of the pathway for talented athletes as they were about to enter their secondary school education (aged eleven to twelve years), it was deemed highly important to address the ways in which talent was being defined, and the identification procedures that were being used to nominate athletes for the academies.

Definition

Historically, across all authorities that participated in the formation of a talent development pathway, athletes were identified for the RMSA using predominantly physical capability as a primary indicator of talent, and this was manifest in current achievement in sport. Simply put, identification was based on an athlete's ability to perform in a sport, and the higher their representative achievements, the more chance they had of being nominated for the RMSA. As outlined in previous chapters, the reliance on current achievement in sports domains, coupled with an over-reliance on peak performance indicators of physical prowess, is flawed as a unitary measure of talent.

It was important to define two related, but distinctly separate elements of an athlete as fitting him to be an ideal candidate for selection to the RMSA. First, the *physical* capabilities of an athlete needed to be assessed, but in ways that were largely unaffected by previous participation in sport, that could in turn be affected or at least influenced by socio-economic and cultural factors related to access and opportunity. This was achieved through the use of a fundamental movement assessment protocol suitable for this age range, and built upon assessments used across a range of environments, both nationally and internationally. Second, multi-abilities that are equally important for the holistic development of the athlete, as defined by the multi-ability framework, would be used to profile the athlete as they came on to the RMSA. Therefore, the following definition could be used:

> A talented athlete demonstrates (or has the potential to demonstrate) physical ability within a multi-skills environment over and above that of their peers, and is highly capable across all of the multi-abilities (creative, personal, cognitive and creative).

IDENTIFICATION

Physical Ability

The cornerstone of the RMSA is clearly multi-skills, and it was incumbent for any talent identification protocol to rely on multi-skills as part of its identification procedure. As previously suggested, it seems foolish to use an identification strategy that does not relate to either the definition or the types of provision being used within the pathway. The use of qualitative assessment is a reliable indicator of movement competency at an early age, particularly in the light of issues surrounding early maturation, relative age effect, and the frequency of early specialization. An assessment tool used on previous RMSAs was therefore utilized as the identification tool to select athletes for entrance to the academy. The qualitative assessment framework consists of a series of seven complex movement skills that reflect elements of stability, object control and locomotion:

- Kick
- Send and receive on one leg
- Send and receive
- Zigzag run
- Travel and bounce
- Overhand throw
- Side gallop.

The assessment was conducted in all schools to maximize the involvement of all athletes, and entailed the use of teacher and pupil resource cards containing a description of the movement and criteria for assessment. An example of one of the cards can be seen in Figure 22.5.

This form of assessment can be viewed as 'summative', in that it summarizes the athlete's ability to perform a task. The other type of assessment commonly used by coaches and teachers is known as 'formative assessment', and involves the coach building up a picture of an athlete's capabilities over a period of time as they progress along their learning journey. Training was provided for practitioners involved in facilitating the assessment protocol for the RMSA, and one of the areas developed during this training was the ability of coaches and teachers to accurately observe a collection of video footage of athletes demonstrating the seven movement skills. The effective observation of movement was paramount in order to ensure athletes had an equitable opportunity to access the RMSA, therefore simple guidance was given as to how observation within the assessment should be conducted. The coaches and teachers were asked to observe the same movement three times, with the following guidance in their minds.

Observation One
On first observation coaches and teachers were asked to take a global perspective of the movement by asking themselves the question 'Does it look right?'. To further support this notion, if practitioners needed more structure to their first observation, the acronym FABB (feet, arms, body and brain), used to structure activities on the Youth Sport Trust Multi-skill Club resource, was used to guide the observation. It was also important at this stage to emphasize the link between observation, teaching and learning, and how accurate assessment of movement can lead to more meaningful subsequent interventions.

For example, in order to accentuate the importance of breaking down the movement, look at Figure 22.6. When working with John, I asked him to try to put his *feet* on the spot, with his toes facing forwards at his teaching assistant (TA). I asked the TA to move more slowly and make her steps

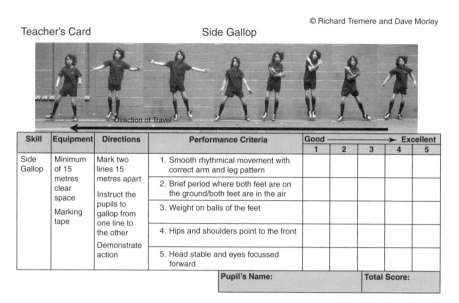

Teacher's Card   Side Gallop

Direction of Travel

Skill	Equipment	Directions	Performance Criteria	Good				Excellent
				1	2	3	4	5
Side Gallop	Minimum of 15 metres clear space Marking tape	Mark two lines 15 metres apart Instruct the pupils to gallop from one line to the other Demonstrate action	1. Smooth rhythmical movement with correct arm and leg pattern					
			2. Brief period where both feet are on the ground/both feet are in the air					
			3. Weight on balls of the feet					
			4. Hips and shoulders point to the front					
			5. Head stable and eyes focussed forward					
			Pupil's Name:			Total Score:		

Figure 22.5   Example of a multi-skills assessment framework: side gallop.

Figure 22.6   An example of an athlete developing walking skills.
(Courtesy of David Morley)

more pronounced, as John was actually mirroring her movements as she walked backwards and he moved forwards – notice where his eyes are looking. Mirroring the TA's feet is what John was thinking about during the movement, and this was obviously how his *brain* was working in response to the task. John's *body* was originally too upright and he was unstable, which is why we asked him to lean further forwards and accept the support of his TA; the next progression for John is to find equilibrium and gain independence in walking. Once he is familiar with this position he can then engage his *arms* more, and improve his stability by holding his arms out at either side.

Observation Two

Having read the criteria, coaches and teachers were asked to observe the movement again from a different angle, and suggest where the athlete fitted into the marking bands. On this observation terms such as 'precision', 'control' and 'fluency' are used as overarching principles of what the movement should contain, and ultimately guide the observer in making banding decisions. A score should be proposed after this observation and a note made as to levels of uncertainty that remain about any particular criteria.

Observation Three

This observation is concerned with ratifying previous thoughts about a score for the performance of the movement. If the observer is unsure about performance related to certain criteria from the previous observation, these should be revisited here, and decisions made as to a final score for the performance. Again, if possible, viewing the movement from another angle is advantageous during this observation.

Multi-Abilities

Once the athletes had been observed, the talented athletes, at least in terms of their physical ability, with the highest scores were profiled across the other abilities. This profiling, or MOT (measure of talent), provided another differentiating opportunity to make final decisions on who would be nominated for the RMSA. The MOT also became a crucial part of personalizing each individual athlete's experiences during the RMSA, and enabled the athletes to be developed holistically using the multi-ability framework. Figure 22.7 shows the profiling tool used for each athlete selected for the RMSA.

It is anticipated that talented cohorts within coaching and school settings will also be using the AA wheel as outlined previously, and this will further aid an understanding of multi-ability recognition throughout the pathway.

PROVISION

As has already been stated, the fluency of any talent development pathway relies upon an understanding of the interdependency of its constituent elements. In terms of talent development, the major constituents are how we define talent, how we select it, and then what we do with athletes once they have been identified – in other words, how we define, identify and provide. From experience, while as a community of practitioners we

Please respond: 5=Excellent 4=Very good 3=Good 2=Satisfactory 1=Poor		Rating
Age of Performer:	Level of Player:	
Physical		
Explores and develops skills demonstrating control, fluency and quality in a range of activities		
Demonstrates a range of skills in different compositional and tactical situations		
Demonstrates good peripheral vision and use this in a range of situations across activities		
Shows precision when executing movement skills with high levels of co-ordination and balance		
	Sub-total	
Social		
Demonstrates the ability to take the lead when working with others		
Communicates clearly to others when describing their performances showing an understanding of tactics/strategies and compositional ideas		
Demonstrates the ability to make good decisions when working collaboratively		
Enables and empowers other pupils in participating effectively in activities		
	Sub-total	
Personal		
Shows motivation, commitment and focus when working		
Demonstrates the ability to self-regulate learning in independent learning environments		
Demonstrates the ability to evaluate their own performance effectively		
Handles feedback in a constructive way and uses this to develop levels of performance		
	Sub-total	
Cognitive		
Demonstrates the ability to transfer skills effectively across a range of activities		
Demonstrates the ability to plan and utilise a range of strategies in a number of activities		
Identify strengths and weaknesses, offering suggestions for improvement, across a range of performances		
Uses a broad analysis vocabulary when describing performances		
	Sub-total	
Creative		
Consolidates and develops skills in a creative, inventive and innovative way		
Responds to stimulus in an innovative way		
Offers a range of productive and viable solutions to a problem		
Is confident in experimenting with acquired skills and ideas through application (e.g. within a gymnastic sequence, dance composition or game)		
	Total	

Figure 22.7   Multi-ability profile. (produced by David Morley and Richard Tremere)

may be sceptical and feel inexperienced when asked to define and identify talent, particularly when asked to consider younger athletes in non-sports-specific environments, the art of coaching and teaching, or pedagogy, is something that we are generally more comfortable with.

Although the pathway has a culminating event in the guise of a RMSA, there are a number of other features of the pathway that require consideration in relation to how we provide for athletes at certain stages of their development. The area of parental support and the role of significant others has already been discussed earlier in this chapter, but the up-skilling of teachers and coaches is another feature of the pathway that was instrumental in providing coherent and consistent messages about talented athletes. Primary link teachers responsible for coordinating PE in primary schools, and coaches involved in school-based activity programmes, attended training to support their understanding of multi-skills and multi-ability development.

'Raising the Bar' (Create Development, 2009) resources were used to practically demonstrate how multi-skills and multi-ability development can be delivered concurrently, maximizing opportunities for development in areas of fusion warm-ups, games and observation, and plan and review. 'Raising the Bar' is a cutting-edge, personalized multi-skill and multi-ability programme and resource for achieving outstanding learning in physical education and sport, built around the belief that high quality teaching and learning should focus on the development of the whole child, player or athlete. It helps deliverers in their planning, and encourages a more open, exciting and creative approach to learning, teaching and coaching.

'Raising the Bar' is completely flexible, and can be used in several environments and to achieve several objectives, including:

- Developing outstanding learning, teaching and coaching
- Accelerating learning
- Establishing innovative and effective schemes for multi-skill clubs, academies and RMSAs
- Personalization in learning
- Assessment for learning for all athletes
- Developing the whole child
- Extending talented athletes
- Enhancing and enriching the coaching environment
- Performance improvement at all stages of development
- Enabling the athlete to 'own' their own learning journey.

Some examples of the resources used are given in Figure 22.8.

Some authorities adopted a more global view of provision across their authorities, and sought ways of influencing multi-skill development over and beyond curricular and/or sports club provision. The key stakeholders in some authorities were aware of the potential of certain under-used environments as havens of activity, and one such context was the playground. Local authorities commissioned the organization ESP (Education and Special Projects) to deliver across every school in their care, with their whole programme of playground-based multi-skills revolving around

Figure 22.8   Raising the bar resources. (Courtesy of Create Development)

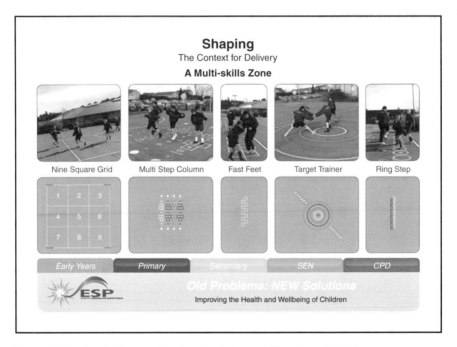

Figure 22.9   ESP's 'Famous Five' multi-skills zone. (Courtesy of ESP)

their multi-skills zones. (For more information on ESP's multi-skills approach, please visit www.esppplay.co.uk.) These zones have proved extremely successful in raising activity levels and improving the movement competencies of athletes, for the following reasons:

• The zones are a permanent fixture in a playground, therefore they are always accessible to athletes

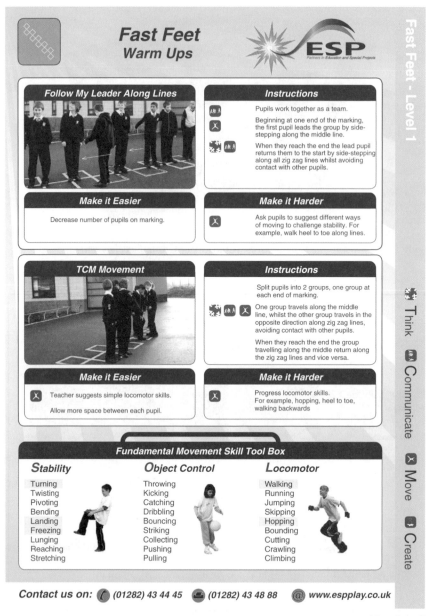

(Continued)

- There are certain constraints around the successful implementation of a multi-skills environment, one of which is the heavy burden of traditional sports delivery within our culture. The multi-skills zones offer a neutral space where athletes can express themselves without perhaps experiencing discomfort when faced with participation in a specific sport
- ESP offers a suite of modules that up-skill and empower coaches, teachers, parents and young leaders, as well as working with professional sports clubs and national governing bodies of sport. This encapsulates

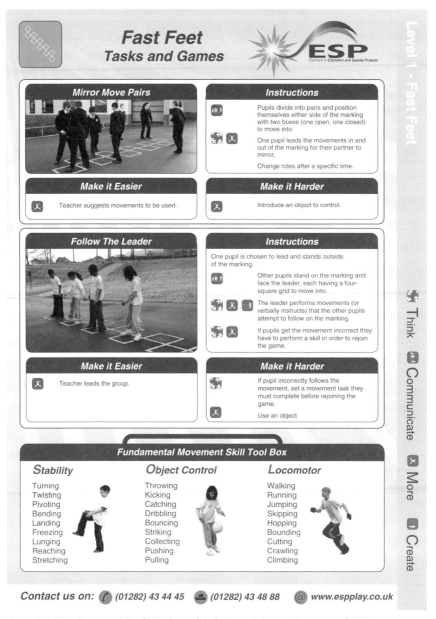

Figure 22.10   An example of ESP's multi-skills activities. (Courtesy of ESP)

the 'communities of practice' approach, and ensures that those consistent messages regarding developmentally appropriate practices are delivered effectively to a number of 'agents of change'

An example of a multi-skills zone is demonstrated in Figure 22.9, the second is an example of an activity used within the CPD awards (*see* Figure 22.10), and the third demonstrates the use of a toolbox to inform practitioners of the variety of movement that an athlete is capable of (*see* Figure 22.11).

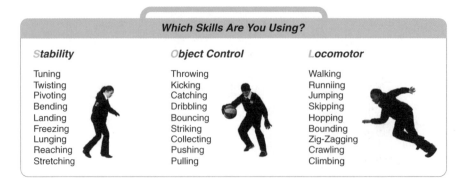

Which Skills Are You Using?

Stability	Object Control	Locomotor
Tuning	Throwing	Walking
Twisting	Kicking	Runniing
Pivoting	Catching	Jumping
Bending	Dribbling	Skipping
Landing	Bouncing	Hopping
Freezing	Striking	Bounding
Lunging	Collecting	Zig-Zagging
Reaching	Pushing	Crawling
Stretching	Pulling	Climbing

Figure 22.11   ESP's multi-skills toolbox. (Courtesy of ESP)

SUMMARY

This chapter has outlined the key features of a talent development pathway as employed by a range of local authorities over recent years. What is perhaps underplayed in this chapter is the crucial aspect of ensuring that everyone involved in the pathway is completely convinced that the approach is appropriate and will enhance the ability of the athletes involved. A strategy on paper is worthless unless there is a belief that some of these new and exciting approaches to developing talent actually have a place in an athlete's long-term development.

There is obviously a great deal of work to be done in order to realize the full effect of a pathway for athletes across the age range, but the initial success has been down to clear and consistent messages delivered in fair, transparent and rigorous ways. This, aligned with a multi-agency approach, has meant that athletes are better supported, are identified more effectively, are provided for in developmentally appropriate ways, and ultimately have a better chance of fulfilling their potential in their preferred activity domain.

PART 4: ATHLETE SUPPORT AND MANAGEMENT SYSTEMS

23

The Delivery Structure of High Performance Sport in the UK

by Claire Bruce and John Porteous

OVERVIEW OF SPORT POLICY

Sport in the UK (at all levels) is very much driven by sport policy, including élite, community and school-based sport. The decision to award the Olympic Games to London in 2012 has been followed by a wealth of new sport policy in order to achieve élite sport targets and leave a lasting legacy for sport and its development in the UK. This has resulted in some realignment of current strategies alongside the reallocation of resources for the next funding cycle.

Green and Houlihan (2005) have written extensively about the issues and implications on sport policy of government involvement, the impact on 'sport for all' as a result of élite sport investment, and the funding implications for sports and national governing bodies (NGBs). It is essential for those people working in sport coaching and development to have an understanding of sport policy in order for them to put into context the environment in which they are operating.

Early public sports policy was influenced by the Wolfenden report (1960), which established the 'context within which public involvement in sport was to be considered for the next generation' (Houlihan and White, 2002, p.18) and helped to establish the boundaries of dominant discourses within sport development. In many ways, the Wolfenden report highlighted the 'gap' that existed in British sport, and, together with 'sport for all', provided a unifying banner for those interested in grass-roots sport, élite sport, and the sports role in wider welfare issues (Henry, 2001; Houlihan and White, 2002; Bramham, 2008).

Over the last thirty years the emphasis of sport policy has changed, depending on the government's strategy for sport. Sometimes the focus has been the development of people through sport (for example, social inclusion and physical activity) and at other times it has been the development of sport (sport for sport's sake). These changes have reflected the country's performance (or non-performance) at major sporting events, the perceived inactivity of the general population, or the decline in school sport. One additional major contributory factor in aiding sport development has been the national lottery and resultant funding for élite and community sport (for example the Lottery Fund strategy 1999–2009).

While there have been many significant policy directives for sport over the last few years, it is worth mentioning one or two that have played, and are still playing, a significant role. These policies are particularly significant when considering the delivery structure of high performance sport in the UK. For example, Sport: Raising the Game (1995) focused on the development of élite athletes and the establishment of an élite training centre; the Élite Sports Funding Review (2001) rationalized the funding for the World Class Programmes; and Game Plan (2002), which recommended prioritizing funding to NGBs (Green and Houlihan, 2005).

More recently, in 2008, the Department of Culture, Media and Sport (DCMS) in their policy document entitled 'Playing to Win: A New Era for Sport' emphasized the need to 'create a world-leading sporting nation' (DCMS, 2008, p. 8) in an effort to be successful at London 2012 and beyond. Figure 23.1 summarizes a historical as well as a visionary perspective. Naturally, to achieve this vision a complimentary and seamless delivery system is needed.

SPORT DELIVERY SYSTEM

As is evident in Figure 23.1, three key organizations are accountable for delivering sport at the élite, community and school levels. Before considering élite sport delivery in more detail (*see* UK Sport, next section), it is worth highlighting some key issues surrounding the other two areas, because of their role in ensuring a seamless pathway. One key aim for the DCMS is to produce a 'seamless ladder of talent development from school to élite level' (DCMS, 2008, p. 8). To achieve this they need key delivery organizations working in partnership.

The Youth Sport Trust is the key organization in supporting the delivery of school sport. They adhere to the PE and Sport Strategy for Young People (PESSYP), and work with Sport England and the DCMS to increase school sport both in and out of curriculum time. This is referred to as the 'five hour sport offer', and will involve key partnerships with local authorities and County Sport partnerships to ensure its success. They also ensure that support mechanisms are in place for gifted and talented sport athletes to balance their educational, sporting and lifestyle commitments.

It appears that Sport England have also aligned their strategy (2008–11) to assist the DCMS in achieving their aim of being a 'world leading sport

1997		2007	Vision for 2017
PE and School **Sport**	• No centrally co-ordinated school sport system • Poor school – club links • In 2002 an estimated 25% of 5–16s were doing 2 hours of PE and sport each week • Negligible targeted investment	• 86% of 5–16s doing 2 hours of PE and sport each week • 3000 Community Sports Coaches • 450 school sport partnerships • 90 competition managers • Over 3,200 Secondary Co-ordinators and over 18,000 primary link teachers • Over £1.5 billion invested over last 5 years	• A world-leading system for PE and sport • All 5–16 year olds offered 5 hours of PE and sport each week • All 16–19 year olds offered 3 hours of sport each week • Competition and coaching at the heart of the school sport system
Community	• £32 million annual funding to Sport England • Crumbling sports facilities	• Over £125 million annual exchequer funding to Sport England • 4000 facilities built or renovated • Over £1 billion of investment in facilities since 2001	• A world-leading community sport system, continuing to increase participation year on year • Significantly reduced drop off at 16 years • High quality clubs encouraging talent development • World leading coaching infrastructure
Elite	• 36th in 1996 Olympics medal table, 4th in Paralympic • Funding of £70.7 million	• 10th in 2004 Olympics medal table, 2nd in Paralympic • Funding of £216.4 million	• Ultimate goal for 4th in 2012 Olympics and 2nd in Paralympics medal table and sustaining that to 2016 • Over £400 million available for London 2012 Olympic cycle • A legacy of a world leading elite sport infrastructure including high quality coaching

Figure 23.1   Where are we now? – the sporting landscape. (DCMS, 2008)

nation'. Sport England's main focus is community sport, and after years of bureaucracy and a lack of clarity over sport or physical activity there is now an emphasis on 'sport for sport's sake' (Sport England, 2008, p. 1). In order to achieve their targets they have entrusted the NGBs with the key role in delivery. This means that the NGBs will have greater autonomy and responsibility, but will have to deliver against the out-comes they specify in their whole sport plans.

The Labour government's policy of partnership working runs through-out the sport delivery system. As stated earlier, the Youth Sport Trust is responsible for school sport, alongside other partners, which include Sport England who are keen to ensure a quality experience beyond the 'school gate'. In addition, the NGBs provide a clear link to the club network to aid the transition from school to club. The NGBs also look after the talent sys-tem, by acting as a conduit for talented athletes to progress to the World Class Programme. This is where a clear link is needed between the NGBs and UK Sport, who are the ultimate deliverers of élite sport in the UK.

UK SPORT

UK Sport became fully operational in 1997, with a remit of 'developing and supporting a system capable of producing a constant flow of world class performers' (UK Sport, 2009). Therefore, élite sport is strategically organized by UK Sport, who are responsible for co-ordinating policy, sup-porting élite athletes, enforcing anti-doping and organizing major sport-ing events. Their strategy is one of a 'no compromise' approach to funding and support. This means that they reinforce the best, support those devel-oping, and look to change those under-performing.

Figure 23.2 Elite sport is strategically organized by UK Sport. (Courtesy of David Griffiths)

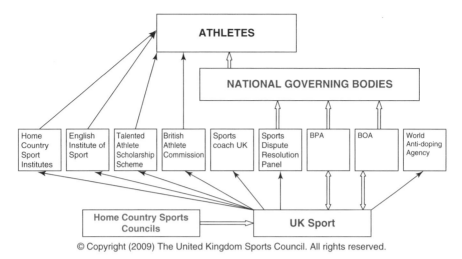

Figure 23.3   UK Sport and partner organizations. (Courtesy of UK Sport)

Their mission is to 'work in partnership to lead sport in the UK to world class success' (UK Sport, 2009). As before, partnership working is essential, and the accompanying diagram [Figure 23.2] illustrates the links UK Sport has in achieving podium success for UK athletes: it clearly shows that at élite level, there are a number of key organizations working in close conjunction. Thus UK Sport has to work with not only the NGBs and the Sports Councils, but also a number of partner bodies. These include the Home Country Sport Institutes, the British Olympic Association, and the British Paralympic Association to support training, preparing and selecting British and home country teams competing in international sporting events.

UK Sport support the vision and targets for 2012 and beyond (*see* Figure 23.1) through their 'World Class Programme' for both athletes and coaches. The World Class Performance Programme supports Olympic and Paralympic athletes likely to be in the next Team GB. It consists of three levels, namely podium, development and talent, which reflect athlete world standings, past performances, and the level of personal award they receive. This means UK Sport provides strategic investment and support to NGBs for their athletes and coaches (World Class Coaching Programme), as well as through the following means:

- Talent identification programmes (for example, Girls 4 Gold)
- Research and innovation (for example, cycling technology)
- Performance lifestyle (support to athletes to manage their sport and other life; this is covered in more detail in Chapter 24)
- Sports medicine and science via the Home Country Institutes.

(Adapted from DCMS, 2008, p. 16)

HOME COUNTRY SPORT INSTITUTES (HCSI)

The HCSI (England, Scotland, Wales and Northern Ireland) came to frui-
tion as a result of the initial policy 'Sport: Raising the Game' (1995). The
initial intention was to have one central site, like Australia; however, based
on UK athlete needs, current infrastructure, resources and logistics, a more
regional and localized operation resulted. The over-arching responsibility
for strategic leadership and co-ordination is in the hands of UK Sport, but
naturally, a close working relationship between UK Sport and the HCSI is
essential for athlete success. A more detailed insight into the English
Institute of Sport is available in the next chapter.

The key function of the HCSI is to provide services to athletes who are
identified by their NGB to be on the World Class Performance Programme
and financially supported by UK Sport. These services include sport science, sport medicine, physiotherapy, nutrition, strength and conditioning,
performance lifestyle, psychology, performance analysis and biomechanics. To provide a quality and holistic support service for the athletes these
services (where appropriate) are integrated, which means the service
providers will work in consultation with each other to identify the best
solution for the athlete to maximize their performance.

Another advantage of the HCSI and integrated working is that when athletes have to relocate, for either sporting or personal reasons, there is a recipro-
cal agreement between institutes to support the athlete. This means that when
an athlete relocates from Edinburgh to Sheffield, for example, service practitioners from the Scottish and English Institutes of Sport will liaise closely to
ensure a smooth transition. This integrated network maximizes athlete support across the UK, and in return maximizes athlete performance.

*Figure 23.4 An integrated network
of HCSI supports an athlete who
relocates. (Courtesy of Northumbria
University)*

MULTI-AGENCY WORKING WITHIN SPORT

Partnership working within sport regardless of the delivery focus (élite, community or school sport) is a further vital step towards realizing successful delivery of sport policy and strategic direction. Eady (1993) observes:

> The best and most sophisticated (sport) programmes involve numerous agencies ... in a comprehensive and cohesive delivery network.

Simmonds (1994) supports this point further, with references to the continually changing political climate and sport's move from a solely local authority (LA) delivery provision towards increasing private sector investment and voluntary sector engagement. The introduction of compulsory competitive tendering (CCT – 1980s), best value (1999) and public private partnerships (PPP – 2003) within the realms of public sector finance highlighted a clear partnership approach to the need for linked delivery across public sector service provision. This approach has also transcended 'non-statutory' service delivery, which includes sport, and it is this partnership approach across sectors and organizations that best represents where we currently sit in relation to how the sports industry within the UK at present operates. It is through this adoption of such partnership/linked delivery approaches that multi agency (MA) working within sport has dictated, and continues to significantly dictate, the future direction of sport delivery (Torkildsen, 2005).

Sport is a complex industry (Parkhouse, 2001), with multiple user groups participating at varying levels for a broad spectrum of reasons, presenting sport managers and coaches with numerous challenges. It has been claimed that 'The plethora of organizations running British sport is damaging both élite and grassroots levels (of sport)' (BBC, 2009).

This was highlighted in detail through the independent sports review undertaken in 2005 by two former sports ministers who sought to 'embrace the principle of constructiveness' (*The Independent Sports Review*, 2005, page 2) through its evaluation of the delivery agencies within the structure of sport in the UK. One of the most visual recommendations proposed was the complete overhaul and restructuring of sport within the UK, which pared down the key delivery agencies to just two principal driving organizations responsible for the landscape of sport delivery in its entirety (community, élite and school).

At the time the report was delivered, the then Minister for Sport Richard Caborn described the proposed new delivery structure as being '... too London-centric' (BBC) – therefore the overall concept of rationalizing delivering agencies within sport was apparently dismissed. However, we now have a current situation within the UK sport delivery system that has seemingly adopted some of these 'rationalization' principles by nominating UK Sport, Sport England and the Youth Sports Trust as the principal deliverers of sports policy and strategy. Today we can see the most obvious example of multiple agencies working together when we look at the three delivery systems and the partners they engage with to realize the required strategic delivery goals.

There are many agencies that feature across each of the three identified delivery systems, highlighting the linked approach that sport organizations are adopting across all levels of sport participation and delivery (élite, community and school). Sports Coach UK is a clear example of an organization that fulfils a role not only within high performance sport (élite), but as Figure 23.5 illustrates, also supports developments across the community and school sport systems. Lyle (2002) observes that:

> The continuing commercialisation of top-level sport, increases in public and private funding, and increased rewards for performers, have resulted in greater levels of commitment to preparation for sport and more full-time athletes and coaches. (Lyle, 2002, p. 23)

It is by defining the top levels of sport delivery as a 'commercial business' entity that the drive to develop a coherent linked approach across high performance sport delivery has arisen. Within the context of Sports Coach UK, this is apparent through their approach in developing a '... world-leading (coaching system) by 2016' (Sports Coach UK, 2009), which will only be realized through a multi-agency approach using/working with the home country sports councils (Sport England, Sport Northern Ireland, Sport Scotland and the Sports Council for Wales) and national governing bodies of sport.

High performance sport is clearly only one element of a much broader landscape of delivery within sport. The current primary priority of sport delivery in the UK is focused on attracting and sustaining participation within and across sport/s (DCMS, 2002). This mission is certainly not one that should be lightly accepted as being easily attainable in the short term, reflecting on the challenging roles UK Sport, Sport England and the Youth

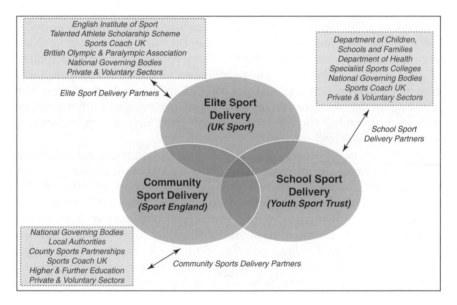

Figure 23.5   UK Sport system: multi-agency delivery.

Sports Trust are tasked with as the facilitators of the delivery strategy. Operating within an environment where success is distinctly determined by the need to engage multiple agencies to 'buy into' a coherent direction forward demands robust management systems, a dynamic approach to delivery, and the ability to operate within a continually chaotic macro environment. De Bosscher, de Knop, van Bottenburg and Shibli (2006, p.1) observe that:

> .... literature reveals that more than 50 per cent of the determinants of success are at macro level variables that are beyond the control of politicians.

The challenges of MA working within sport are heightened due to the non-controllable macro factors that fuel continual changes in political, economic and social contexts. Within sports coaching the numerous national governing bodies of sport that Sports Coach UK currently engage with presents this organization with an ever-increasing agenda of non-controllable macro impacts that must be managed in order to fulfil the aim of establishing a cohesive coaching system across the UK. By acknowledging the existence of this additional layer of macro environmental complexity within the industry of sport, a clearer understanding of why priority is placed on linked delivery throughout the sport systems can be understood. It is difficult to visualize a viable sports industry within the UK that can realize sustainable success without the integration of MA-linked delivery/working.

In essence, it is to be accepted that the sports industry is a challenging, complex environment in which to operate, where multiple stakeholders set out linked strategies in order to deliver success within their specific areas of sport (Eady, 1993). It has also previously been acknowledged by central government that the administration structures tasked with delivering sport are complex and '... have evolved, ad hoc, over a long period of time' (DCMS, 2002, p. 38). With the message that sport is good for us clearly understood today, particularly among younger people (Burrows and Wright, 2004), the demands placed on the public sector to fulfil its social and cultural responsibilities have never been more apparent with the importance of sport in society today being greater than it has ever been (Watt, 2003). The sport delivery systems as they have been developed today rely wholly on links across the élite, community and school sport systems supported by a multiple agency partnership approach in order to attain sustainable implementation of current strategic sport policy.

24

The Role of the English Institute of Sport

by John Porteous

HISTORY AND BACKGROUND

In 2005, the decision of the International Olympic Committee (IOC) to award the Olympic and Paralympic Games to London in 2012 was greeted with national euphoria. The opportunities now available to sport in the UK are immense, not only for current and future élite athletes but also for developing and sustaining the sporting infrastructure. In particular, the need to maintain and enhance world class support services to élite performers will be paramount if the 'ultimate goal' of achieving fourth in the Olympic and first in the Paralympic medal tables is to be realized (UK Sport, 2006).

The IOC decision was closely followed in the UK by the government announcement in the 2006 budget to provide additional 2012 performance funding. The Chancellor announced an additional £200 million of public money for high performance sport through to 2012, to be added to the £60 million a year already invested in Olympic and Paralympic success (UK Sport, 2006). While underpinning performance through to 2012 (that is, including Beijing 2008), this additional funding will allow UK Sport, the government agency responsible for the funding and support of Olympic and Paralympic sport, to aim for the 'ultimate goal' in 2012. It will also allow UK Sport to scale up their activity and ensure that a world class system is in place to support potential medal winners.

One of the key partnerships to ensure the world class support system is in place for élite athletes is between UK Sport and the English Institute of Sport (EIS). Under the streamlining of performance sport in the UK in 2006, the EIS became funded as an independent body by UK Sport. This means that they will work closely together to ensure support for élite athletes over the coming years. As Campbell (2006, p. 4) stated:

> The decision to streamline the performance pathway was a truly momentous moment for everyone involved in high performance sport. Our élite athletes exist in a different world to the vast majority – almost a parallel universe. So it is absolutely right that the support they are offered, in terms of coaching, finance and, crucially, through the services provided by the EIS, is structured in a way that maximizes impact and minimizes duplication of effort and resources.

In 2008, a new UK Sport funding model for sport science and medicine provision was agreed for the Olympic funding cycle 2009–2013. It provides the EIS with funding specifically targeted toward the development of service providers and the EIS core infrastructure (management, administration, facility leasing costs, ICT, equipment and consumables), while directly funding national governing bodies of sports (NGBs) to invest in science and medicine service providers. These changes are designed to ensure the EIS can develop its service providers towards the perhaps immeasurable goal of becoming world class service providers. It also tries to ensure that the NGB is accountable for every aspect of its world class programme, as it gives the NGB the choice either to invest in the EIS, or to employ its own service providers or find alternative arrangements (independent service providers, commercial enterprises, university services).

The EIS will be continually challenged to provide world leading service providers and to maximize their integration within sports. The NGB will be involved in the service providers' recruitment, work programme, appraisal and development. It is anticipated that this will ensure that all NGBs have the level of support services required to help achieve the medal tally set for 2012. In addition it is envisaged that NGBs investing in the EIS will feel a true sense of 'buy in' with regard to the service providers that are employed.

The English Institute of Sport (EIS) originated in 2002, and the 'quiet revolution' (as identified by the EIS management team at its inception) has gradually been gathering pace to provide world class support services to élite athletes. The challenge of working with NGBs and UK Sport is helping to set new standards of support to élite athletes. This is happening through the expertise, innovation and commitment of EIS service providers.

The original mission statement of the EIS clearly reflects what they want to achieve:

> Sustained international success in sport for England through the delivery of world class, integrated and innovative services.
>
> Cram (2004, p.2)

This reflects a desire to provide a nationwide network of world class support services which will foster the talents of our élite athletes and coaches. Therefore, the aim of the EIS is to provide world class athletes with the best high performance training environment in the world. This has been achieved through Sport England/Lottery investment of £120 million in developing eighty world class facilities at the universities of Bath and Loughborough, as well as bases in Manchester, Sheffield, Gateshead, Lilleshall, Bisham Abbey, Holmepierpont and London (this is in addition to some satellite sites).

Figure 24.1   EIS at Sheffield. (Courtesy of John Porteous)

Figure 24.2   EIS at Lee Valley. (Courtesy of John Porteous)

It is also being achieved through the recruitment, selection, training and development of key service providers across England to 'make the best better' (the EIS motto developed at its first national conference). However, as Calvin (2006, p. 11) reminds us: 'The EIS is more than bricks and mortar, it is about winning hearts and minds' of athletes and coaches – which clearly emphasizes the importance of their staff.

Figure 24.3   EIS at Gateshead. (Courtesy of John Porteous)

Figure 24.4   The EIS motto is to 'make the best bester'. (Courtesy of David Griffiths)

The EIS prides itself on its holistic multi-disciplinary approach to delivering services. No individual works in isolation, and there is a strong emphasis on partnerships with athletes, coaches and sports. Consistent high quality delivery of support is the hallmark of the EIS, and this, combined with an innovative approach, is impacting on élite sport in England. The values of excellence, commitment, innovation and integrity are at the heart of élite service providers in the EIS in order to ensure that élite athletes receive the best service.

STRUCTURE AND OPERATION

In the 1990s, the Conservative government under John Major envisaged a UK Sports Institute based in Sheffield along similar lines to the Australian model. However, after much debate it was felt that one centralized location for all NGBs, coaches, athletes and service providers would not meet the needs of élite sport in the UK. Hence, as highlighted in Chapter 23, UK Sport decided it was best to work nationally with the home country sports institutes and NGBs to provide services to athletes through regional multi-sport hub sites and an evolving network of satellite centres. These regional hub sites were developed in a three-tiered structure that reflects the requirements of the EIS customers, namely local high performance athletes, their coaches and the NGBs.

There are those in high performance sport who will argue that the NGBs can fulfil the role currently undertaken by the EIS. However, despite the possible controversial and complex process of setting up the UK Sports Institute (Theodoraki, 1999), it is now well established and flourishing. As Caborn (2006, p. 4) pointed out:

> We have listened to sport, to the athletes, coaches and performance directors, and given them what they want – a flexible, simple framework that allows innovation to flourish and partnerships to be developed.

National EIS Structure

Before considering the regional structure, it is important to understand that there is a national EIS management team that provides strategic direction and support to the regional offices. The national management team works with the EIS national board and includes the National Director, Head of Communications, Head of Business/Finance, Director of Sport Science, Director of Sports Medicine, Director of Human Resources and Head of Information Technology. The role of this national team is to establish and develop the service strategy and framework, and to develop and maintain the business and information structure.

In addition, the national management team is supported by a number of national service leads in biomechanics, nutrition, performance lifestyle, performance analysis, physiotherapy, psychology, physiology, psychology and strength and conditioning. The national lead service providers are based across the EIS network, and they develop the national service strategy for their respective discipline and provide hands-on delivery as appropriate. A major focus of their role is the continual professional development of that discipline.

Regional EIS Structure

The regional offices implement the national programme at the local level. They align national and regional requirements, with the specific aim of having a positive impact on the performance of the NGB, athletes and coaches. The regional manager who hosts a national sport programme is the lead manager for that sport, and it is his/her responsibility to ensure that EIS services:

- should impact on performance outcomes
- must be of a consistently high quality across the network
- are provided to UK Sport and Sport England priority-funded athletes (as identified by the NGB) without cost.

Services are offered from nine regional multi-sport hub sites and an evolving network of satellite centres. The nine EIS sites are developed around a three-tiered regional structure to reflect the needs of athletes and the demands of NGBs.

Tier One

Tier one includes London, East Midlands and the South East, and features the largest number of NGB identified athletes with a significant number at the podium level. Due to the NGB structure and set-up – coaches, facilities and so on – there is also an athlete migration to these regions, with a major focus as key delivery centres for the primary services supplied by the EIS. For example, Loughborough University and Holmpierpont are the EIS hub sites for the East Midlands region, offering multi-disciplinary support to the national programmes for swimming, triathlon, BPA (British Paralympic sports), canoeing and cricket. Support for these programmes is co-ordinated nationally from Loughborough; they also offer services to athletes on a regional basis for athletics, badminton, netball and hockey.

Tier Two

Tier two includes the North West, South West and West Midlands regions. These regions feature a number of key medal prospects, with a significant number of NGB-identified development athletes. There are some significant national sports programmes within the regions, together with key delivery for EIS primary services. For example, the regional hub site, Sport City in Manchester, oversees the nationally co-ordinated services to cycling, squash and disability swimming. Squash benefits from performance analysis, the service for which the North West is the national lead. In addition the region services swimming, netball, taekwondo, athletics, disability athletics, boxing and gymnastics.

Tier Three

Finally, tier three includes the East, Yorkshire and North East regions. These regions feature smaller numbers of podium athletes, and so there is a major emphasis of high quality delivery to development athletes. The regions are also characterized by athletes migrating from them to tier one or two, and as a result there is more work being carried out with talent identification and development in specified sports to increase the talent pool. For example, the Yorkshire region, based at EIS in Sheffield, is emerging as a significant site for national training camps for a number of sports (such as boxing, netball and diving). EIS staff who operate in this region play a key role in supporting medal-winning performances in boxing and diving.

Staying Ahead of the Competition

Whatever region or whatever EIS service is being provided, there is always a challenge to meet or exceed the needs of the athletes and the sports in question. Nationally and regionally this is one of the things that 'keeps the EIS awake at night' in trying to provide an integrated approach by managing its service providers efficiently and effectively for sport in England so that it can stay ahead of the competition.

MANAGING SERVICE PROVIDERS IN THE EIS – AN INTEGRATED APPROACH

Before considering the processes and issues of managing service providers in the EIS, the system in operation to effect service delivery to the athletes needs to be highlighted. EIS only supports those athletes identified by their NGB and on the World Class Programme (that is, either talent, development or podium). The service to be provided to the NGB athletes is agreed between the EIS lead manager for that sport and communicated to all staff in a service level agreement. Service providers will then work with the athletes at training camps or regional sites either in a group or on an individual basis. To ensure an integrated approach between service providers, EIS hold frequent case conferences for individual athletes to review service provision, thus maximizing athlete performance.

As previously stated, the EIS is based at nine major regional sites with additional hub sites in various geographical locations in order to meet athlete and sport needs (EIS, 2008). It currently employs in excess of 250 people, with the greatest concentration of service providers in regions of higher élite athlete numbers. Therefore, regional disparity means that some are highly specialized (service providers work with one sport – they are fully integrated), some are high profile due to the sports they support (for example, in the North West – cycling), and some have to be more innovative and creative in their plans and solutions for the athletes. Other regions with fewer athletes provide a more multi-sport approach in their support, and have developed partnerships with professional sport to aid sustainability. For example, the North East EIS region employs a biomechanist/performance analyst, a post that is part funded by Durham County Cricket Club and the University of Teesside, providing the person with a larger athlete population to support as well as an applied research focus.

All regions present managers at the EIS with their own set of challenges. In Olympic year, for example, everything is pulled into sharp focus. Athletes, coaches and performance directors know that they will ultimately be judged on what happens during two weeks in August. The same is true for élite service providers and their managers, because in the end performance really does matter. However, one must also consider the four-year Olympic cycle, because it is so important to ensure continuity of support, to build trust and develop relationships between service providers and their élite athletes. This is also true for other major sporting championships, including World Cups and World Championships.

Ideally, managers would like élite service providers to spend all their time in direct contact with their athletes. However, there is also a need for service providers to be developed in order to retain the most talented through professional development and to deliver world class support, which requires research and innovation. In addition, there is an element of administration required to satisfy performance management requirements. EIS also needs to capture scientific and medical data across regions and sports, as knowledge transfer has been the major weakness of previous science and medical support programmes employed directly by sports (that is, isolation of service provider experience and learning). Balancing workload priorities, accounting for the peaks and troughs of international competitions and camps, avoiding service provider burnout, and ensuring employees have a work/life balance, are some of the challenges facing EIS regional managers as they strive to deliver the service level agreement for the sports.

In high performance sport a great deal of responsibility falls on élite service providers to ensure that the interactions between athletes and the organization are positive. This principle of 'front line contact' – direct contact with the customer, which in the case of EIS is athletes and coaches – is reinforced by Stamper and Van Dyne (2003). Further literature (Pennington, 2003 and Hoots, 2005) suggests that motivation of employees is crucial if exceptional customer service is to ensue. Therefore, management teams need to play an active role in developing an appropriate culture within the organization (Smith, 2003).

Townsend (2004) examined the issues of culture and motivation in various sports organizations. While not specifically focusing on élite sports organizations, he concluded that formal and bureaucratic structures contributed to the development of a culture of resistance. EIS does not have a totally informal structure and so the greater staff morale, commitment and job satisfaction may be due to other factors, such as 'national identity' (Karkatsoulis and Michalopoulos, 2005) and team cohesion around a common goal – winning medals.

Working in high performance sport may indeed foster the social phenomenon of 'national identity'. This may be particularly true of élite service providers in the EIS who take great personal pride and joy in the achievements of Olympic and other élite athletes. This pride strongly motivates people to work, despite all the time and anti-social hours involved in servicing élite athletes.

This latter point is crucial for managers within the EIS, as there have been a number of European employment directives that have placed constraints on human resource management (HRM) practices. MacVicar and Ogden (2001) examined the challenges inherent in managing employees within this environment. The adoption of greater flexible working practices was one key strategy used to ensure that employee work/life balance needs were being met. The need for greater flexibility in working practices is a strategy the EIS are pursuing to meet both the needs of élite athletes and employees.

Pettinger (1998) and Stredwick and Ellis (1998) both highlight the need and the push for more flexible employment strategies. In all sectors it is now seen as a key competitive strategy, and it may include numerical, functional, locational or financial flexibility. This is further explained in Figure 24.4 with some specific EIS principles and examples.

The introduction of European legislation in the UK has meant that high performance sports organizations have had to evaluate their employment practices in terms of the quality of working life and the relationship between work and home life in the light of servicing élite athletes. The Employment Relations Act (HMSO, 1999) emphasizes the government's fairness at work and family friendly policies. Similarly, the UK Working Time Regulation 1998 and 2003 amendment (HSE, 2008) will also affect management strategies to employment. Finally, the Employment Protection (Part-time Employees) Regulation 1998 (GEE, 2000) means that part-time employees cannot now be excluded from full-timers' contractual rights. As EIS employ full-time, part-time and contractual staff, they need to be aware of all these regulations.

The basic rights and protections (BERR, 2008) that the regulations provide are as follows:

- A limit of an average of forty-eight hours a week, which a worker can be required to work (though workers can choose to work more if they want to)
- A limit of an average of eight hours work in twenty-four, which night workers can be required to work
- A right for night workers to receive free health assessments
- A right to eleven hours rest a day
- A right to a day off each week
- A right to an in-work rest break if the working day is longer than six hours
- A right to four weeks paid leave per year.

However, despite the legislation, a culture of working long hours is on the rise once more in the UK, after a decade of gradual decline (Ward, 2007). More than one in eight of the British workforce (one in six in London) now work more than forty-eight hours a week, the maximum allowed under the law

Form of Flexibility	Principles/Example at EIS
Staff head count • Increase or decrease staff levels in line with organisational demands (Ackers (1998) would refer to this as Numerical).	If a world class programme for a sport moves its training centre location the EIS will offer either: relocation to staff or if this is not taken up; a change in the service providers support portfolio or an offer of a vacant position in another region or as a last resort redundancy.
Staff roles • Organisational demands on the organisation may mean re-training and alternate working practices are necessary to fulfil the job requirements (Ackers (1998) would refer to this as functional).	EIS staff can also provide support across the nine EIS regions in terms of sharing major support projects (e.g. camp and competition cover, maternity / sick leave, technical projects – particularly where equipment is very expensive and where technical expertise is critical e.g. biomechanics). Some staff in the EIS are also multi-skilled (e.g. deliver physiology and strength and conditioning or athlete support manager and psychology) which enables various sports needs to be met. However, there is a move towards more specialisation of service providers in their disciplines working with one sport.
Monetary • The focus is on paying the market rate in line with local and regional variations or linking to organisational performance or a person's contribution (Ackers (1998) would refer to this as Financial).	To 'make the best better' EIS require the best service providers to meet elite athlete needs. Competitive pay structures enable the EIS to employ the best people for the job required. However, the EIS is also a national company funded with public money and subsequently it has to ensure parity across regional teams and appropriate performance related pay progression.
Contracts • Employing variable contracts where the employee can be dismissed or pay reduced (Ackers (1998) would refer to this as Distancing/Locational).	The EIS does not necessarily operate short-term contracts. Staff are employed on permanent contracts which are subject to funding levels being maintained and UK Sport can only commit funding over a 4 year Olympic cycle. Hence, the further the post is recruited into an Olympic cycle the earlier the post is reviewed within the overall spend for the EIS going into the next Olympic cycle. The majority of posts are now also part NGB funded and hence are subject to NGB staff strategies as well. Contractors are employed to provide short term / part-time cover or transient cover where future athlete migration is likely, or to grow a service initially and for succession planning for entry level positions.

Figure 24.5   Types of flexible working and practice at EIS.

unless workers agree to waive that limit (Labour Force Survey, 2007). The UK's working hours are among the longest in Europe. Despite a steady fall in long-hours working since 1997, the latest figures reverse that trend. They show that 93,000 more people now work more than forty-eight hours a week compared to 2006, taking the total to 3.2 million (Ward, 2007). The increase represents a rise from 12.8 per cent to 13.1 per cent of the workforce.

Given the demands placed by NGBs and élite athletes to service their needs, the EIS has had to look very carefully at its HRM practices in the light of the legislation highlighted above. Some sports demand a twenty-four hour service from EIS staff. Others are away overseas and want EIS service providers to travel with their athletes because of their professionalism, expertise and the relationship staff have with the athletes. Similar to other service industries, élite sport is not 9am to 5pm, Monday to Friday, and consequently, managing élite service providers can be a complex task requiring an integrated and flexible approach to optimize athlete performance. One EIS service element that plays a key role in supporting élite athletes trying to maximize their performance in their sport coupled with a busy lifestyle is known as 'Performance Lifestyle'.

PERFORMANCE LIFESTYLE

Earlier career transition research by Lavelle and Wylleman (2000) demonstrates that a need does exist to support athlete transitions, and there has been a worldwide development of programmes to assist athletes. From its rudimentary beginnings in 1985 with the establishment of an education centre at one of the USA's Olympic centres, through to the introduction of the ACE (Athlete Career and Education) programme in Australia and New Zealand in 1996 based on research and evaluation, athlete welfare programmes now flourish around the world. The International Athletes Service Forum held in the UK in 2006 entertained numerous different countries who offer support programmes for athletes.

In the UK, support to élite athletes began back in 2000, where UK Sport set up their own network of ACE advisers throughout the Home Country Sport Institutes, along with some professional sports. UK Sport franchised the ACE model from Australia, and all advisers underwent the postgraduate Diploma in Counselling offered on line at Victoria University. This enabled advisers to provide support to athletes in the areas of integrated planning, educational guidance, career planning, transitional support and employment opportunities, whilst gaining a recognized qualification.

In July 2001, an evaluation of athletes' experiences of sport, education and work and the role of the ACE UK programme was undertaken by UK Sport (North, 2001). The findings indicated that athletes' (n = 561) views of ACE were very positive. However, only 63 per cent of athletes had used the service, with only 35 per cent being 'high users' (that is, initial assessment plus the development of a specific action plan). Recommendations from the survey focused upon additional resources, adviser training (a more robust and vocationally pertinent scheme), adviser specialisms (expertise in careers, education and so on), and the development of better employment networks. It became apparent in the intervening years that the ACE franchise was quite restricting in the developments for advisers and the programme in the UK. Hence UK Sport established their own programme and called it 'Performance Lifestyle'.

The Performance Lifestyle programme orchestrated by UK Sport came into existence in 2004 based around the four home countries athletes' needs. In the UK more and more professional sports – for example tennis, rugby union and league and cricket – in addition to the traditional 'amateur' sports, are now signing up to the Performance Lifestyle premise. They realize that their athletes need support through transitions in their life in order to balance their sport, education and lifestyle. This indicates the growing realization by sports organizations that athletes need support to cope with their demanding lifestyles.

The EIS employs a number of athlete support managers who deliver the Performance Lifestyle programme to athletes across England; depending on athlete numbers, this varies from one to two advisers per EIS region. Whereas more tangible services – such as medicine, physiotherapy – are seen by NGBs as critical to maximizing the performance of athletes, this has not always been the case with Performance Lifestyle. Therefore, much work has been done by UK Sport and EIS to promote the value of the service to NGBs, coaches and athletes via workshops and training camps and utilizing advisers alongside current and ex-athletes who have benefited from the service.

Coaches and athletes often ask what is Performance Lifestyle? It is for high achievers, those athletes who want to get the most out of life and produce the best in everything they do. It is for athletes who know the many aspects of their life often impact on each other, and each one needs to be carefully planned and managed if all their goals and aspirations are to be achieved. For élite athletes to maintain a performance lifestyle they have to fit many aspects of their life alongside their intensive training programme.

The overall aims of the Performance Lifestyle programme are as follows:

- To give athletes the necessary skills to cope with the special demands of being an élite performer
- To better prepare athletes for their life after sport.

Underlying the Performance Lifestyle and worldwide programmes is the hybrid approach that incorporates education support, life skills development and career and education counselling. It is delivered by accredited advisers (either on a one-to-one or group basis), and provides the most comprehensive athlete welfare programme (Lavelle and Wylleman, 2000) given all the demands placed on élite athletes. The next chapter will consider how it works in practice.

25

An Athlete-Centred Approach to Performance Lifestyle

by John Porteous

THE ROLE OF A PERFORMANCE LIFESTYLE ADVISER

As stated in the last chapter, Performance Lifestyle was defined as being for high achievers (UK Sport, 2009), those athletes who want to get the most out of their life and produce the best in everything they do. It is for athletes who know that the many aspects of their life often impact on each other and each one needs to be carefully planned and managed if all their goals and aspirations are to be achieved. For élite athletes to maintain a performance lifestyle they have to fit many aspects of their life alongside their intensive training programme.

The overall aims of the Performance Lifestyle programme are as follows:

- To give athletes the necessary skills to cope with the special demands of being an élite performer
- To better prepare athletes for their life after sport

Performance Lifestyle advisers know that the ultimate aim of any World Class Pathway athlete (that is, Lottery funded) is to be standing on the podium in the Olympic Games, World Championships or major international sporting event: this is the pinnacle of success. Whatever one's sport, the focus on performance is paramount and vital if the aim identified above is to be achieved. However, maximizing performance can prove problematic to certain athletes due to the many demands in their lives.

Élite athletes are not dissimilar from many leading business figures. They have numerous competing demands on their time, and therefore they have to be extremely good at managing this resource as well as knowing their priorities. Competing demands may be seen as distractions, but athletes can develop and use coping skills and resources to maintain a

Figure 25.1   The Performance Lifestyle Advisor will offer 1:1 support to the athlete. (Courtesy of David Griffiths).

balanced lifestyle (that is, sport + education/work + social, and so on). Therefore, by managing their lives outside their sport, there is an extremely good chance that their sport performance will improve.

The athlete-centred support system is further enhanced by Performance Lifestyle advisers who operate within the Home Country Sport Institutes (HCSI) and certain professional sports (for example, cricket and rugby union). At present there are forty-five Performance Lifestyle advisers across the HCSI and professional sports in the UK. The advisers work with nominated athletes on the World Class Pathway to ensure they have a balanced lifestyle and can maximize their sport performance.

Performance Lifestyle is a personalized support service specifically designed to help each athlete create the unique environment necessary for their success. Trained and accredited athlete advisers recognize that the sport programme is the main focus for competing athletes, and provides guidance on how to maximize that focus while still fulfilling other important commitments such as career, family, social or financial. The approach is to work closely with coaches and support specialists as part of an integrated team to minimize potential concerns, conflicts and distractions, all of which can be detrimental to performance, and at worst, may end a sport career prematurely.

First, today's high performance athlete needs a high degree of self-management and professionalism. Performance Lifestyle advisers can support athletes with time management, budgeting and finance, dealing with the media, sponsorship (for example, see the resource at www.sponsorship.uksport.gov.uk) and negotiation/conflict management.

Second, advice is available for athletes on finding suitable jobs and deciding on a future career. Some common situations are:

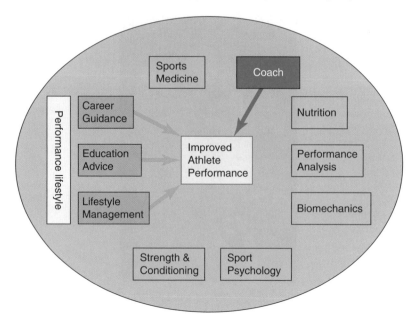

Figure 25.2   Improving athlete performance and integrated service. (Courtesy of John Porteous)

- A job to supplement income and fit around training demands
- Work placements to give a taste of possible career options
- Planning for a second career after sport.

Athlete advisers develop links with local employers to promote the range of skills and experiences athletes can bring to the workplace.

Finally, some athletes will be trying to combine study with their sport, while others may think about taking further qualifications and training in preparation for life after sport. Guidance is available on:

- Part-time or professional courses
- Gaining flexibility in an existing study programme
- Making the right education choices to fit into sporting demand (research tool at www.sportandstudy.net).

These three key performance areas (lifestyle support, education guidance and careers and employment advice) form part of a continuous circle. Quite often one area in an athlete's life can impact on another, which in turn has the potential to impact on an athlete's sporting performance. Similarly, these key performance areas are also associated with key sporting transitions identified by Lavalle and Wylleman (2000); these will be considered later, in Chapter 26.

As indicated earlier, the advice offered by Performance Lifestyle advisers may be in a one-to-one session, or as a workshop to a squad. The latter may involve coaches and parents to educate and inform the athlete's support network. Confidentiality (which will be considered later) is paramount in building rapport and a relationship between the adviser and the athlete, therefore information will only be shared if the athlete gives their permission.

Service Integration and Maximizing Performance

Performance Lifestyle has a role alongside sports medicine, nutrition, sports science, performance analysis, biomechanics, sport psychology and strength and conditioning as a core support service. Ideally, all these services need to be integrated to improve athlete performance, as demonstrated in the illustration. Naturally, the coach is a key element in this integrated approach, and, as with all core support services, they need to 'buy into' the concept of the service.

Clearly, many core support services can be objectively measured in relation to their contribution to maximizing athlete performance; however, this may not be so easy with Performance Lifestyle. Therefore, perhaps the best way a coach can view the service is to ensure that the time they have with their athletes is used in the most efficient way. For example, to quote one Olympic coach:

> When my athlete steps into the competition I don't want them to be thinking about anything else but the competition. If work is a distraction for them in any way I want it sorted out well before the competition takes place.

Similarly, an athlete may always be tired when they reach training because of manual work or educational commitments. Again, this means that their time at training is not maximized. The coaches need their athletes to focus totally on the training session, and therefore the adviser needs to work with the athlete to consider alternative or more flexible work or educational arrangements.

A Performance Lifestyle adviser can focus on athlete performance by supporting them in developing the skills needed to manage the special demands they face. Also, they can maximize athletes' time by working with them to remove the distractions and barriers to training and competition. Figure 25.3 is a case study of an athlete who will benefit from Performance Lifestyle and an integrated service.

BUILDING RAPPORT WITH ATHLETE AND COACH

Building rapport with an athlete, their coach and their support network is paramount if the Performance Lifestyle adviser is to assist the athlete in maximizing their performance. Naturally this will take time, and will also depend on the athlete, the situation, the stage in the process, the coach and the number of people in the support network. The adviser may use different styles or approaches. These include:

- Leading
- Advising
- Counselling
- Facilitating
- Mentoring
- Challenging.

Sport History	• World Class Potential athlete with recent success at the World Championships
Education History	• First year of a Sports Science degree at Loughborough University
Potential problem areas	• Moving from home to university • Change of coach • Conflict between training and competition commitments and education • Coping with new training demands • Media attention and recent success • Wants to pursue a degree alongside increased demands from sport • Financial issues after breaking his laptop and about to leave for a training camp
Integrated Service	• Work closely with significant others • Coach and performance director • University tutors/academic counsellor • Strength and conditioning coach and sports scientists

Figure 25.3   Case study – swimmer aged twenty.

The illustration [above] outlines in more detail the styles or approaches an adviser might adopt, together with some of the context and content surrounding each one. Rapport will be developed over time as the relationships grow. It may well be influenced by the style adopted by the adviser, together with their ability to listen to the athlete and coach. Listening can help to build rapport, confidence and trust, and to establish a clear relationship.

The style or approach utilized by an adviser will be influenced by the situation, the rapport they have with the athlete and/or coach, their experience in their role, and the confidence they have in their athlete. Ultimately advisers want their athletes to be 'self helpers' who can analyse, reflect and then motivate themselves to move forwards in their lives. However, the athlete may need to be challenged, and this is a key attribute of an adviser, based upon their experience and the rapport they have with their athlete.

Building rapport with an athlete and their coach can take considerable time, and the adviser may have to put in time 'track side' or 'pool side' to understand the environment in which the coach operates and the athlete trains. Furthermore, time is important when the adviser is meeting the athlete and coach for the first time. Naturally, the relationship is going to take time to evolve, and it will be dependent on the adviser's 'micro' communication skills. These, together with the styles and approaches mentioned earlier, will shape the rapport that an adviser develops with their athletes and coaches.

Micro skills include active listening, reflection, paraphrasing, summarizing and encouraging. Active listening is a key attribute for a Performance Lifestyle adviser. It goes beyond straightforward listening – meaning

Style/Approach	Context/Content
Leading	• Directing • Moving in a particular direction • Desired outcome • Adviser led • Passive for athlete
Advising	• Range of solutions • 'What if' scenarios • Analysis of the pro and cons • Guiding behaviour • Different level of involvement • Will depend on adviser knowledge
Counselling	• Explore reasons for situation • Non-judgemental • Empathetic • Athlete-centred • Listening • Need to know boundaries (knowledge & time)
Facilitating	• Common ground for discussion • Helping and supporting rather than leading • Open questions
Mentoring	• All skills mentioned above • 'Sounding board' • Feedback
Challenging	• Out of comfort zone • Need to know athlete • Developing self-help skills • Encourage autonomy and confidence • Mentor becoming redundant

Figure 25.4   Performance Lifestyle adviser styles and approaches.

simply focusing on something, contextualizing and tuning in: it involves an adviser being non-judgemental, showing respect to their athlete and coach, and it is more than just words as there needs to be empathy involved.

COMMUNICATION SKILLS

In working with athletes, coaches and their support networks, Performance Lifestyle advisers need to have excellent communication skills. Whether this is verbal or non-verbal communication, it is the essence of their work, and they must ensure they do it efficiently and effectively. As a result, their training and accreditation programme focuses upon developing their communication skills.

There are several counselling, communication and coaching models currently in use today. The Performance Lifestyle Programme adopts

Egan's (2007) 'The Skilled Helper' model, although the GROW (Goal, Reality, Options and Will (wrap-up)) model from Whitmore (2004) is gaining in popularity. The next two sections will consider Egan's model in more depth, followed by its application in two athlete case studies.

Egan's Model: The Skilled Helper

Egan (2007) identifies that theoreticians, researchers and practitioners agree that the relationship between client (athlete) and helper (adviser) is important. Egan also states that there are significant differences as to how this relationship should be characterized and played out in the helping process. Kelly (1994) stresses the *relationship itself*, whereas Reandeau and Wampold (1991) highlight the *work* that is done through the relationship; finally Horvath and Symonds (1991) focus on the *outcomes* to be achieved through the relationship.

It is more than likely that adviser–athlete sessions will try to encompass some, or all of these three approaches, in what Greenson (1967) referred to as the *working alliance*. Both the adviser and the athlete may work collaboratively. The relationship can be a forum for relearning, where the adviser may not cure athlete problems, but the relationship can be therapeutic. For example, an adviser may challenge an athlete about his/her educational likes and dislikes, which may have engaged him/her in the process of really addressing the issue. Finally, the idea that one kind of perfect relationship or alliance fits all athletes is a myth. Effective advisers use a mix of styles, skills and techniques tailored to the kind of relationship that is right for each athlete (Lazarus, 1993).

The model that Egan used is outlined in Figure 25.5.

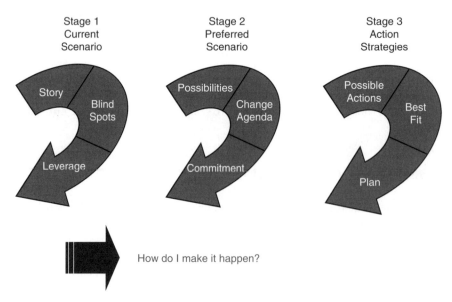

Figure 25.5   From Egan, The Skilled Helper, *8E. © 2007 Wadsworth, a part of Cengage Learning, Inc. reproduced by permission. www.cengage.com/permissions.*

It can be clearly seen that effective advisers will make things happen by moving the athlete from the current scenario (where are they now?) to the preferred scenario (where do they want to be?) via some action strategies (how are they going to get there?). However, it is worth mentioning that this is not a step-by-step process, and advisers will have to return to various stages of the model with the athlete as they progress. Underlying all the stages of the model is the adviser's ability to communicate, listen, ask questions, paraphrase, summarize, challenge, and so forth.

Stage One: Current Scenario
This stage is where the athlete currently is with their life, education or work. At the initial meeting between the adviser and the athlete (or indeed coach and athlete), it is all about getting the athlete to 'tell their story'. This may be easy when the athlete is open and giving, but at the first session no rapport will have been established and the athlete may be reluctant to talk. Furthermore, some younger athletes are 'quiet', and the adviser will have to focus the conversation on what the athlete is most confident in talking about. They may also have to use some tools (for example, 'Bears' cards or 'Views from the Veranda' cards) to encourage the athlete to talk.

Where athletes are reluctant to talk, the adviser may suspect some 'blind spots' that need further exploration. These could be problems or just areas for future discussion. The adviser may have to reframe – find another angle on – the area or topic in order to move the discussion forwards. The importance of the adviser being non-judgemental in this instance cannot be over-emphasized.

Finally, the adviser will look for 'leverage' to the next stage by identifying areas for further discussion. This could be as simple as asking the athlete 'what they want to do about' a certain thing. For example, it could be a need for a change in working patterns to enable attendance at new training and coaching sessions.

Stage Two: Preferred Scenario
This stage begins with the adviser focusing on the 'possibilities' for the athlete. This may be done via a brainstorming session looking at the advantages and disadvantages of the situation, either between the adviser and the athlete or the athlete on their own. The purpose of this is to get the athlete to focus on their priorities, their expectations and their ideal situation. In order to reach a 'change agenda' the adviser may have to challenge the athlete to persuade them to reflect on how much the reality of their situation is in line with their dreams.

The final element of this stage is getting the athlete to commit to change. The adviser needs to ensure that the athlete has fully explored the implications of any change, what it will require to see it through, and if it will achieve the desired goal.

Stage Three: Action Strategies
Once the adviser is sure there is commitment to change from the athlete, then it is time to look at some action strategies. The adviser will need to

persuade the athlete to look at their alternative strategies and plans to ensure they are realistic. This may be achieved by reframing the alternatives and examining the consequences. Choosing the best 'fit' for the athlete needs some positive realism, as well as the option being athlete-centred and athlete-specific alongside their sport.

Ideally, athletes need to work out a timeframe for their plan. This should be written down, with identified smaller interim tasks that they can tick off as they progress. As with all good plans and intentions, the 'goal posts' can move, and sporting success, loss of funding or injury might mean having to amend the plan, or that a new focus is needed.

Implications of Egan's Model

Egan's model may appear straightforward, but there is the potential for the athlete and the coach to become side-tracked by the story telling. However, it is athlete-centred in that it is flexible (as is the GROW model), and it allows advisers to go back and forth to previous stages, which encourages reinforcement of thoughts and actions. It also has no time boundary, despite the end goal being to find a solution.

Stage of the model	Interpretation	Skills to use	Useful questions
Tell the story	What is influencing somebody? What is in their life? Current scenario Priorities Where now? Influences	Active listening Counselling skills Paraphrasing Empathising Probing Body language Silence	Open questions Tell me about .... How's it been going? How? Why? What are you up to at the moment? How are things?
Blind spots	Something they don't think is important/ they don't want to talk about 'It's not an issue' Ostrich effect Athlete reluctant to talk Black holes – areas/ topics that you suspect contain problems Are you the right person to tell?	Build relationships/ rapport Listening skills No judgements Probing (appropriately) Hunches Paraphrasing reframing	It sounds like ... From what you've said ... Do you want to talk about ... You mentioned ... What about ...?
Leverage	Which bit do you want to deal with first? What will make a difference? Identifying areas for further discussion Passport to next stage	Summarising Clarification Challenging Use technique for giving feedback – 'good, bad, good' List the key points to highlight the first to sort	What's the first thing ...? What's the next thing ...? What is the easiest/ most difficult to change? Have I got this right ...? I think you said ...? Have you thought about ...?

(... continued)

Possibilities	Ideal situation Priorities Expectations Targets – SMART Ideal situation	Dreams Reduce barriers Brainstorm Encourage challenge	What if …? Imagine that … If you were … Why? What was it that you liked …?
Change agenda	Which ones fit? Re-establish parameters Fitting dreams into reality Separating what is fixed from what is not	Pro/con analysis Clarification Challenging Summarising	If … how would that affect …? What is the timescale for …? How realistic is that …?
Commitment	Do you think you will do it? Implications of change What will it require? Will it achieve the goal?	Scaling & repeat Clarify Paraphrase Reframe	How do you feel about …? Are you happy with …? Do you think you could make this …? Anything else we need to consider?
Possible actions	Alternatives Be realistic	Examine consequences Reframe	How would you tackle …? How will that help …? What could you do about …?
Best fit	Athlete-centred Athlete-specific Work out timeframe	Pro/con analysis Positive realism Break down into bite sized chunks	What is the best fit for you? What does the analysis say …?
Action	Plan Get athlete to write it down if necessary Achieve	Small tasks they can tick off Clarify Summarise	So what are you going to do …? So what happens now …?

Figure 25.6   Adaption of Egan's model (2007): making the model make sense to you. From Egan, The Skilled Helper, *8E. © 2007 Wadsworth, a part of Cengage Learning, Inc. reproduced by permission. www.cengage.com/permissions*

The accompanying illustration outlines the stages an adviser-athlete session would follow, and tries to make sense of Egan's model by interpreting each stage and showing the skills and questions an adviser might use.

Athlete Case Studies in Relation to Egan's Model

Figure 25.7 includes the review notes from two adviser-athlete sessions. The athletes are referred to as A and B in order to ensure confidentiality. The initial meeting, as demonstrated in these two sessions, between adviser (counsellor, helper) and athlete (client) is crucial to the continuation of the relationship. In a short period of time, a variety of counselling techniques were employed to facilitate the telling of athlete A and B's stories. Throughout the sessions the athletes provided verbal and non-verbal messages to the adviser about their problems. In return, the adviser also provided information and messages that set the tone of the meeting. These signals from the adviser probably gave the athletes an insight into the adviser (through self-disclosure) and their beliefs and values.

Name: Athlete A   Session no: 1

Type of session/key issues

- First meeting with the athlete.
- Educational advice post GCSE's.
- Issues related to **A**'s English language GCSE paper.
- Sixth Form College induction coming up and what to investigate and question.
- Forward planning and time management.

Rapport gained with the athlete

- Overall, good but with **A**'s mother being present this may have detracted from the session (i.e. whilst questions were initially targeted at **A**, mother was always keen to add further comments).
- Explored **A**'s educational and sporting background and in particular recent exploits in **A**'s sport.
- Explained adviser role within EIS and what it would be feasible to do at this session and latterly.

Style of questioning used

- Initially, open questions (i.e. what, how, why, when etc.) to get **A** to tell the story.
- This was followed with probing and closed questions to explore comments, gain understanding and to confirm statements.
- If appropriate, also wanted to challenge some of **A**'s comments to make sure **A** was clear in thinking about A level choices and where to go to study them.

Communication skills displayed

- Appropriate body language used (e.g. eye contact, positive sitting style without being aggressive).
- Note taking to ensure all the main points were recorded. Informed **A** that this would be done and **A** was quite happy.
- Smiling and enthusiastic to ensure a relaxed atmosphere.
- The Lounge room at the National Badminton Centre, Milton Keynes was good and adviser and **A** had it to themselves. It may have been otherwise had it been busy.
- Used language that could be understood by the athlete.
- Asked questions direct to **A** first to ensure **A** gave responses and ideas.

Action points agreed

- Adviser to send information on the routes into teacher training for **A**.
- **A** to meet with College staff to outline sport commitments and to ensure support mechanisms in place.

(... continued)

- **A** to start researching universities and to contact adviser when more information needed.
- **A**'s mother to speak to the school regarding English Language examination.
- **A** to contact adviser with any further questions and issues.

General comments

- Overall, a very positive session.

Learning Points

- If appropriate and possible, adviser to try to ensure the next session is with just the athlete.
- Make the athlete state the action points (ideally write them down) at the end of the session.

Name: Athlete B   Session no: 1

Type of session/key issues

- First meeting with the athlete.
- Educational advice on **B**'s current AS/A2 level study. Currently at college but not enjoying the environment and whilst likes one subject not really motivated for the other two.
- **B** wanted to discuss future aims and to get some advice on studying in America, the UK (at university) or working in the fire service.

Rapport gained with the athlete

- Very easy as athlete **B** is a talkative, sociable and likeable person.
- There was a commercial being shot at Crystal Palace involving **B**'s sport and **B** gave me an insight into it and explained **B**'s sport background in extensive detail.
- Even though **B**'s mother was present the session focused upon **B** and **B**'s mother remained very much in the background.

Style of questioning used

- Open questions (i.e. what, when, how and why) to get **B** to tell the story.
- **B** needed to be challenged about why **B** did not like two of the AS level subjects. This proved useful for the adviser to discover **B**'s thoughts and motivations towards the subjects.
- Further questioning explored **B**'s future educational and career aims, again challenging **B** with regard to why **B** liked certain things, what research **B** had done and where **B** wanted to be based with respect to **B**'s sport and education/work.

Communication skills displayed

- Appropriate body language was used with regard to eye contact, non verbal mannerisms and sitting positively.
- Verbal communication was conveyed in an enthusiastic, positive and non-judgemental way.
- Summarising was used when moving from one aspect to the next.
- Normalising, was also used to explain to **B** how other athletes in other sports feel and act, but also that **B** is unique in being an elite athlete.
- Note taking was agreed from the outset and **B** was happy with this arrangement.

(... continued)

Action points agreed
• **B** to research local college for resit options and new courses for September. • **B** to research university options for UK and USA with a view to combining sport and education. • **B** to keep in touch with adviser about progress and any future questions.
General comments
• Good session, but whilst athlete **B** 'talked a good game' adviser was not sure **B** will deliver on action points.
Learning Points
• Look at ways of ensuring **B** will follow through on the action points. Therefore, adviser will telephone in one month's time to review.

Figure 25.7   Athlete case studies.

Respect, Empowerment and Genuineness

Egan (2007) refers to three basic values of respect, empowerment and genuineness, which the adviser will now examine as part of the athlete sessions. The adviser had an enormous amount of *respect* for these élite-level athletes and what they had already achieved in their sport. As a result of this respect the adviser sought to ensure that the athlete received the best possible help, and this was a clear strength of both sessions. It is also important for the adviser to have respect for the competence of the athlete. This was reflected in the adviser agreeing with both athletes that they would leave the session with action points to complete.

The adviser had a wealth of work experience, and through this period always had high expectations of his students and athletes. This belief had followed him into this current role, together with a belief that the athlete had the ability to solve their own problems. *Empowerment* is one of the keys to the helping relationship, and whilst the adviser was trying to be non-judgmental in both of these athlete sessions, this was not in fact the case with athlete B. This was one of the weaknesses of the session, in that action points were agreed, but the adviser felt that the athlete's 'words were louder than the actions would be'. Therefore, the adviser needs to trust athletes more during and following initial sessions, to evaluate whether actions will be followed. Similarly, the adviser needs to ensure that the athlete states or writes down what actions they are going to take following the session.

Finally, *genuineness* was evident throughout both athlete sessions. This comes from taking an honest interest in the athlete and their situation. The adviser felt that this was both a strength and a weakness of the sessions. In both cases the athlete's mother was present. The adviser felt that athlete A was inhibited by this situation, and the mother spoke quite a lot of the time despite questions being specifically directed towards the athlete. Athlete B's mother spoke very little, and the athlete was more proactive in engaging in conversation. Therefore, the adviser needs to think seriously about conducting the session primarily with the athlete. This will mean asking both parties if they are happy with this scenario, and then speaking separately with the parent afterwards. If they are not happy, then it must be made clear that the dialogue is primarily with the athlete.

The Adviser's Techniques

As outlined earlier, advisers may use a variety of styles in their job when conducting athlete sessions. Throughout these two sessions the adviser tried to facilitate the telling of the athlete's story by employing a variety of techniques. The adviser also offered some advice on educational options, and challenged the athletes on particular issues. A strength of the session with athlete B was the summarizing of information before moving on to the next issue. Similarly, in both sessions the adviser visibly tuned into the athletes and what they were saying to demonstrate attention, interest and closeness (Egan, 2007).

Silence is an excellent means of stimulating thought from an athlete, and to a certain extent to put pressure on the athlete to move the story along. Two good examples were evident in these athlete sessions:

> To Athlete A:
>
> 'What questions will you be asking at your induction course for your new college?'
>
> To Athlete B:
>
> 'What are your reasons for liking Photography A level?'
>
> 'What are your reasons for disliking Sports Studies A level?'

In the first instance, athlete A thought long and hard, and although the adviser felt that the athlete was thinking, they were obviously not going to continue. The adviser therefore prompted A to fill the silence, with suggestions such as 'Are there examples of current élite athletes at the college?' 'Is there a likely timetable for your subjects?'

Using questions: the adviser used a significant variety of questions to elicit the athlete's stories, with a number of open questions (for example, 'How did you find...', 'What reasons for...', 'Tell me about...') which appeared to provide some longer answers. Unfortunately in athlete A's case these came more from the mother. These were also interspersed with closed questions to clarify information or to glean simple factual information (such as date of birth, confirmation of training days and time).

The adviser also used a number of transitional questions that return the focus to an earlier part of the discussion. For example:

> To Athlete A:
>
> 'You mentioned sport science. What other areas might you want to look at?
>
> To Athlete B:
>
> 'You mentioned the Fire Service. What do you need to gain entry to the Fire Service?'

The reason why the adviser asked transitional questions was because he/she had not been able to gather sufficient information on the first attempt at each particular section of the story. Furthermore, it was also a result of the athlete mentioning one thing whilst talking about another, and this is an area the adviser needs to work on to ensure that all issues or 'blind spots' (Egan, 2007) are covered. While it may appear to the athlete that in doing this the session is not moving forwards, it is essential that all issues are covered in sufficient depth to check understanding and to gain clarity. Summarizing and paraphrasing are useful skills the adviser can use in this instance. This was more in evidence in the session with athlete B, and it is something that the adviser needs to develop constantly.

Active listening: this latter point about checking understanding is closely related to the issue of active listening on the behalf of the adviser. One of the strengths of the session with athlete B was the ability to actively listen, using attending skills and listening noises (smiling, nodding the head in agreement, key words to support athlete – 'yes' and 'really').

The whole issue of listening is one the adviser needs to develop further. As Egan (2007, p. 92) identifies: 'One must muse on what is missing.' In other words, what key elements is the athlete leaving out? Therefore, having frameworks for listening can help the adviser spot key things that are missing. In telling their story, athletes often leave out their feelings and behaviour, and the adviser needs to listen and note what the athlete puts in and what they leave out.

Use of empathy: empathy also demonstrates one of the adviser's values – respect – and helps to keep the story moving along. Whilst the adviser did well in this respect, he/she could still look to improve their skills by listening for core messages (identified above) and gearing their responses to the client. Furthermore, they need to develop the skills of reframing and normalizing and to use them more with athletes, although normalizing was clearly evident with athlete B.

In both athlete sessions the adviser identified a number of potential blind spots (such as the issue of time, motivation to study, and starting a new college). A strength of both sessions was the adviser's ability to sufficiently challenge the athletes; this is probably a result of the adviser's previous experiences in higher education. The adviser did not suffer from what Egan (2007, p. 180) refers to as the 'MUM effect', where they are reluctant to ask challenging questions and therefore hinder the development of the athlete.

Information sharing: when there is a shortage of information, this can result in making a problem worse or leading to poor assessment and management of the issue (Egan, 2007). The adviser used information sharing with both athletes. This was clear from athlete A regarding potential universities for sport science or teacher training, and for athlete B who thought he wanted to study at university in America. By encouraging and challenging the athletes to work out where to acquire this information, and also providing them with other sources, the athletes moved closer to tackling their problems.

Both athletes needed help with planning, and in particular that help was needed with career and education planning. Their desire to make the correct choices – which study subjects, university, courses to select – and to effectively balance their sport with their studies, was one of several clear sources of leverage.

Information gathering: as Egan (2007) proposes, the first stage towards decision making is the gathering of information. As the session drew to a close, the adviser was trying to persuade both athletes to commit to conducting some research and information gathering (using for instance web sites, school staff and university/college prospectuses). Analysis and making choices would come later, but it did become clear what these choices might be (for example, which subjects to drop/continue, courses to study, universities to attend and professions to work towards). The adviser was able to draw upon experience to point out to the athletes that these choices were inter-related – that is, the type of profession dictates the course of study.

Summing up: although the adviser felt that progression through the first three steps of stage one (Egan's model) had occurred, he was initially less confident about progression into the latter stages. However, on later reflection of the session, he recognized that some elements of the later stages (for instance, discussing possibilities) had been touched upon. Most advisers will struggle to incorporate all stages of the model in the first session with the athlete, therefore this adviser was not unduly concerned.

Available tools: likewise, there are many tools available to an adviser when working with athletes. These include Bears cards, Views from the Verandah cards, Value cards and Strength cards. While these tools may not have been totally appropriate in an initial session (since adviser did not know the athlete that well), they could have helped the adviser in telling the story (for example, Bears cards or Views from the Verandah). This may be something the adviser needs to take into consideration for future sessions. However, the adviser did use the weekly planner with athlete A, when looking at how her sporting, educational and social commitments combined in a typical week.

In Conclusion

The adviser was relatively satisfied with these two sessions. Early counselling theory refers to there being three distinct styles – Client Centred, Narrative Therapy and Strength Based – but in fact the Skilled Helper (Egan, 2007) uses a combination of all three to build the relationship with the athlete. The adviser demonstrated good questioning techniques, with some summarizing, paraphrasing, empathizing and information giving. Challenging both athletes was evident, but in future sessions the adviser would have to address the issue of parental presence. The adviser needed to work on active listening, and in particular 'what was not being said', together with the skills of reframing and normalizing. Furthermore, additional work with resources and tools would enhance the athlete experience and help them develop.

BOUNDARIES AND CONFIDENTIALITY

As Barnard (2008) highlights, the relationship between counsellor (Performance Lifestyle adviser) and client (athlete) is a special one: it is built around trust and support, and offers clients a place free from judgment. This may not be the case when the athlete is talking with their coach or their parents. Therefore, it is important that boundaries and support mechanisms are in place to ensure the athlete's needs can be met.

The relationship between the Performance Lifestyle adviser and the athlete must always be professional. It should be formal, and the adviser must remain as objective as possible. If this were not the case – if they were friends – then the boundary might be lost and the relationship compromised. In addition, the adviser is not there to tell the athlete what to do. Advisers work towards developing athlete self-awareness, because athletes

Stage	Activities
Pre-support	• Selling transition awareness and services to sports • What is transition? What are the key issues and research? What are the main transition issues? • Directed to coaches, high performance managers, sport national governing bodies, educational staff etc.
Letter	• From sport to athlete outlining the process (i.e. national governing body has a clear transition policy)
Intake and induction support	• Sport led educational session involving key people • To include: 'How to live the life of an elite athlete' and 'How to balance sport, education and lifestyle' etc. • Role of the performance lifestyle adviser
Ongoing support during sport career	• Psychological assessment – at risk athletes – personal development programme • Development of referral and support networks • Workshop programme for elite athletes (e.g. education, life skill development etc.) • Activities written into athlete agreement (e.g. see performance lifestyle adviser etc.)
De-selection and/or retirement from sport	• Sport needs to inform athlete and adviser when they come off the WCPP • Performance lifestyle and other services (e.g. medicine, physiotherapy, strength and conditioning) should continue for twelve months • Retired athlete network • Referral services available (e.g. counselling)

Figure 25.8   The perfect support system.

are 'experts' themselves and are capable of making decisions. For example, the last thing an athlete wants to hear from an adviser is a totally unrelated story about themselves in response to the athlete's story.

Ideally the athlete should always feel safe in their relationship with the adviser and with the environment (where the counselling session takes place). Therefore a designated space for meeting athletes is important, together with starting and finishing sessions on time.

Finally, Performance Lifestyle advisers need to recognize their own limitations, and in the event of being unable to help further, should refer athletes to more appropriate support agencies, where the athlete can get more relevant help and advice.

While bearing in mind the boundaries within which Performance Lifestyle advisers operate, they should also be aware of the confidentiality of their athlete discussions: what they talk about is confidential and should remain so, unless the athlete might be in danger of harming themselves.

This issue of confidentiality is often hard for the coach to comprehend. The coach sometimes wants to know what is going on, but for various reasons the content cannot be divulged. For example, the athlete issue may be about their own coach and they want to talk it through with an impartial and objective person (the adviser). Ultimately the athlete may have to discuss it with their coach to move forwards, but the 'possibilities and action for change' (in relation to Egan's model) will come from their counselling session with the adviser.

FUTURE DEVELOPMENTS

While there has been a definite growth in Performance Lifestyle and ACE (athlete, career and education) advisers across the world over the last few years, the service is not without its challenges. Advisers are having to face up to the task of convincing some national governing bodies of sport, performance directors, coaches and athletes that the service will have an impact on them and their sport performance. As mentioned before, whereas other services, such as physiotherapy and strength and conditioning, can be measured in terms of their impact, Performance Lifestyle is more subjective and focuses on the softer skills. However, if the athlete turns up for training or competitions with their mind full of 'distractions' then they are not going to perform.

One exciting development within the English Institute of Sport is the appointment of an adviser with a specific remit to find flexible employment opportunities for the men's and women's hockey squads. This post is funded by hockey, and has been identified as crucial to retain élite hockey players within the sport. It may prove to be a model that could be useful to other national governing bodies of sport in the future.

Likewise, the 'perfect support system' outlined in the Figure 25.8 may be an ideal towards which Performance Lifestyle advisers can strive. This system would ensure a good working relationship between the athlete, coach and adviser, with the ultimate aim of improving athlete performance. This premise of a 'perfect support system' will be further discussed in relation to athlete coping skills in the next chapter on transitions.

Furthermore, UK Sport is working to develop the credibility and professionalism of Performance Lifestyle advisers. To achieve this goal, UK Sport is revamping its accreditation process for advisers to make it more robust. It is also revising the professional competencies for an adviser, together with looking at models from other professional organizations (for example, BASES – the British Association of Sport and Exercise Scientists).

Finally, in trying to ensure a support network for élite athletes from the 'playground to the podium', the development of advisers along the pathway is emerging. In specialist sports colleges there are Junior Athlete Education (JAE) advisers; in further and higher education there are the Talented Athlete Life Skills (TALS) advisers who look after TASS athletes. Finally, there are Performance Lifestyle advisers for World Class Pathway athletes. To ensure a smooth transition for athletes along this pathway, collaboration and communication between advisers at all levels will be essential if athletes are to maintain a balanced lifestyle and achieve their sporting success.

26

Key Athlete Transitions

by John Porteous

TRANSITION THEORY AND RESEARCH

The Olympic and Paralympic Games staged in Athens, Greece and Beijing, China were a magnificent spectacle. They also produced a significant medal tally for Team GB. Achieving selection is one thing, but ensuring a successful transition from junior to élite athlete and to Olympian is quite another. Success and failure bring with them their own issues. For example, the new diving sensation, Tom Daley (Beijing, 2008), has many more requests from the television and the media. How will he balance his time between his sport and education? The silver medallist mixed badminton players (Athens, 2004) Nathan Robertson and Gail Emms now have a higher media profile. What preparation have they undertaken or received to cope with their new-found status?

There has also been a lot of speculation in the media about the question of 'retirement' from élite sport following the 2008 Olympic and Paralympic Games – and in particular whether our Olympians will carry on to London 2012. Furthermore, it is not only athletes having to make these difficult decisions, but also their coaches – and not only in terms of making athlete selections, but also in respect of reviewing their own coaching strategy for the next four years.

At the other end of the spectrum, budding 'start/development' athletes will no doubt have been inspired to pursue their Olympic dream and participate in London 2012. Just like their current counterparts, they face many transitions along the way, since to possess talent is one thing, but to combine all the demands placed upon an élite athlete, maintain a balanced life, and achieve Olympic, Paralympic, World Championship or Commonwealth success is quite another. Furthermore, having reached the pinnacle in your sport, what happens next? How do élite athletes make that career transition?

In the sport psychology field, the concept of transitions over the last ten years has become a major area of study; early research (Hallden, 1965, and Mihovilovic, 1968), on the other hand, focused on how athletes coped with

Figure 26.1   Victoria Pendleton achieves a Gold Medal for Great Britain in Beijing, 2008. (Courtesy of Northumbria University)

	Transition
Sport	• Deselection • Moving between squads (e.g. development to senior level, change of training partners and change of coach) • Change in sports programme model (e.g. part to full-time, decentralised to centralised) • Move from squad to individual basis (and vice versa) • Change in seniority or role in squad • Gain or loss in benefits (e.g. funding and sponsorship) • Retirement from sport • Career ending injury
Personal	• Change in relationship with others (e.g. partner, family, work colleague or sport personnel) • Experience of major loss (e.g. death or illness of family member) or gain (e.g. partner or child) • Financial concerns • Sexuality issues
Career/education	• Change in employment status (e.g. movement between unemployment to part or full-time employment) • Change in employment position (e.g. new role/duties) • Retirement – move between study and work • Move from primary to secondary to tertiary education
Recognition	• Changes brought about by success or failure • Increased public attention (e.g. positive and negative media coverage)
Relocation	• Movement throughout the UK and overseas

Adapted from Hay (2004)

Figure 26.2 Common transitions.

retirement from élite competition or professional sport. More recent research (Lavallee and Wylleman, 2000) has indicated that the termination of an athlete's career is more than a single event, it is in fact a transitional process. They have also gone on to highlight the importance of several transitional phases and events occurring during the athlete's career. This 'development or holistic' approach (Wylleman, 2004), which includes both athletic and non-athletic transitions, will be considered in the next section. Therefore, before considering the various transitions an athlete may face in their life, let us first establish exactly what a transition is. Schlossberg (1981, p. 5) defined transition as:

> An event or non-event which results in a change in assumptions about oneself and the world and thus requires a corresponding change in one's behaviour and relationships.

Generally, all athletes from time to time will have to change their behaviour to cope with new demands and stresses. Many coaches can recall an instant where an athlete is not himself/herself while at a training session. As a one-off this may be fine, but over a sustained period of time it may become evident to the coach that something else significant is happening in the athlete's life that is dramatically affecting their ability to concentrate and perform. The athlete may have been experiencing a transition. As Figure 26.2 indicates, there are numerous athlete transitions during a full sporting career.

These transitions may be described as normative and predictable (as the move from primary to secondary to tertiary education) or non-normative and non-predictable (a career-ending injury). How an athlete copes with their transition(s) will be dependent on a number of factors:

- Preparation (before the transition, if possible – accept change is inevitable, learn about transitions, plan ahead and identify significant other to help)
- Characteristics of the individual (age, sex and health)
- Perceptions of the transition (role change, onset and duration)
- Characteristics of the pre- and post-transition environment (internal support systems and institutional support)
- Support after the event (possible responses both positive and negative, and de-brief after the event).

(Adapted from Hay (2004) and Schlossberg (1981))

It is clear from these factors that the athlete may need advice and assistance from their coach, Performance Lifestyle adviser and support network before, during and after the transition(s). This is very important when one reflects on the number of key transitions (*see* Figure 26.2) in an athlete's life, when they occur, and the demands placed on élite athletes from within and outside their sport.

According to Lavallee and Wylleman (2000), and as already identified above, all these sporting transitions have the potential to be positive or negative. The reasons for this are multi-faceted, because it is rarely one single factor that will result in a smooth or arduous transition: emotional, social, personal and academic factors may figure to a greater or lesser extent for each individual athlete. Furthermore, research has demonstrated a series of theoretical perspectives, conceptual models, environmental factors and individual characteristics that combine to either help or hinder the athlete's evolution.

Early Transitional Theory

As already stated, early transitional research focused upon retiring athletes, and as a result considered this transition to be a singular event. More recent research is concentrating on transitions throughout the athlete's life, and views it much more as a process. Both have relevance in enabling athletes, coaches, performance lifestyle advisers and support staff to understand the reasons behind transition and to assist in developing support mechanisms to cope.

In relation to theoretical perspectives, early theorists tried to make parallels with career transitions in sports with the processes of ageing, death and dying, and finally, models of human adaptation to transition. The first of these refer to the social gerontological models that concentrate on a mutual interaction between society and the aged. These models try to explain lives and activities of those who appear to age successfully. Furthermore, a number of perspectives exist within social gerontology linking ageing with sport retirement.

Social gerontology does provide some understanding to athletic retirement. However, there are a number of problems associated with the perspective, as highlighted above. The theory fails to appreciate that in most cases athletes will have a post-retirement career. Furthermore, as stated earlier and implied in Figure 26.2, transitional issues also happen at an earlier age. Finally, the theories suggest that transition is always a negative experience, and as indicated this is not always the case.

The second set of theories applicable to sport retirement falls under the banner of thanatological models. 'Social death' (Kalish, 1966) suggests that an athlete is treated as dead even though they are alive. In other words, they are isolated and ostracized at the end of their athletic career. However, this is purely descriptive in nature, and not every athlete will go through all the stages. Just as 'dying' is individualistic, so is retirement from sport.

Again, the thanatological models are inadequate when applied to sport. They used non-sport populations for their research, but they are useful tools in understanding the career transition process. Like social gerontology, they presume that retirement is a negative experience for the athlete, they see it as a singular event, and they provide a limited perspective as they do not focus on the life-span development of the athlete.

The theoretical perspective then shifted to that of 'transition models'. Unlike the former models, Human Adaptation Model (Schlossberg, 1981) is viewed as a process and allows for both positive and negative adjustment. It is believed that in this model (outlined above, in association with Hay, 2004) the characteristics of the individual (sex, age and health), the perceptions of the transition (role change, onset and duration) and the characteristics of the pre- and post-transition environment (internal support systems and institutional support) all interact. However, as Taylor and Ogilvie (1994) identified, the models still lacked operational detail of the various aspects of the change process for athletes. As a result the focus shifted from one particular transition (athletic retirement) towards a more holistic view of sporting involvement (Wylleman, Alfermann and Lavallee, 2002).

THE DEVELOPMENT MODEL (WYLLEMAN, 2004)

The focus on a life-span perspective of athletic development may have originated alongside talent development (Bloom, 1985) and the Long Term Athlete Development Model (Balyi and Hamilton, 2004). Both models include stages of initiation, development and mastery of a sport. However, while these perspectives could be linked to athlete transitions, it is likely that the research of Stambulova (1994 and 2000) is more pertinent to transitions across an athletic career. Stambulova's work outlined an athletic career consisting of predictable stages and transitions, including:

- The beginning of sports specialization
- The transition to intensive training in the chosen sport
- The transition to high achievement and adult sports
- The transition from amateur to professional sports
- The transition from culmination to the end of the sports career
- The end of the sports career.

Based on this previous research, it confirmed that athletes do encounter different stages and transitions throughout their sporting career. It was also identified that athletes have both athletic and non-athletic (academic, psychological and professional) transitions to deal with (Wylleman, De Knop, Ewing and Cumming, 2000). Therefore Wylleman (2004) developed his Development or Holistic Model, as outlined in the illustration below.

The model highlights that as an athlete matures, they are not only developing in terms of their sport, but also in terms of education and work, physical maturity, and the relationships with those around them. Whenever an athlete moves from one phase to another horizontally, a transition event takes place, with the additional possibility that a number of transitions can occur at the same time, vertically.

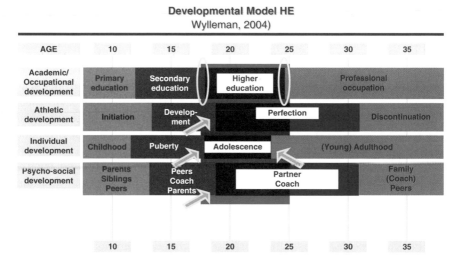

Figure 26.3   Development Model by Wylleman (2004). (Courtesy of Steven Pope, ICPE & FIT)

There are many critical transition periods, but certainly around the age of eighteen the athlete may experience a number of key changes dependent upon their sport. First, they could be moving from secondary education to higher/further education (as seen in Figure 26.3). This provides the athlete with a whole host of considerations, such as getting into their chosen institution, the impact of travel, home-based versus relocation, access to good training facilities/club, and access to a coach. At this age the athlete may also be progressing from development to performance squads (or junior to senior), and this will place a whole new remit of demands upon the athlete (for example, new training requirements, new competition structure, training camps and so on).

At eighteen an athlete will be moving from puberty into the later stages of adolescence and early adulthood, and the stage of individual development will affect their ability to cope with the increase in training. The athlete will also be coming to terms with forming their own identity (that is, athlete versus student), and moreover, the athlete may want to be an 'athlete' but this conflicts with the need to study. Similarly, the athlete may be establishing more permanent relationships with a partner, and this can lead to added pressure in an already busy schedule. The circles and arrows on the model by Wylleman (2004) highlight transitional stages where an athlete will need support.

Athlete Case Study

James is a golfer, who up until the age of fifteen years had competed quite successfully at club, county and national events. Then in his sixteenth year all that changed, and with some impressive performances during that year he was selected for the England Under 16s and then fast-tracked straight into the Under 18 squad for the next two years. His golf improved, but so did his expectations. He was part of the national squad, and there was more travelling to training camps both in England and overseas, and added pressure – put on himself and from the English Golf Union (EGU) – to perform as a squad member and to be selected for international matches. James's coach, with whom he had worked for six years, was local and this alliance continued alongside his work with the EGU coaches.

He also had to balance his increased commitment to golf with his academic studies, as well as trying to have a social life. He had performed outstandingly well in his GCSEs and was now studying for three A levels. He wanted to go to America on a golf scholarship, and this also meant studying for his SAT (Standard Attainment Test) tests to gain access to an American university. His school and parents were very supportive, ensuring he had as much flexibility as possible in his day to accommodate his studies, golf practice and time away for competitions and international tournaments.

James was very mature for his age and took most things in his stride; but he was a perfectionist, and became frustrated when his performance did not meet his personal standards, and he sometimes failed to communicate his true feelings and emotions. In his second year in the England squad he put in some poor performances, culminating in a serious illness when he missed two key months of the season. In hindsight, maybe James tried to achieve too much athletically and academically? Nevertheless, he did achieve three A levels, and he gained a place as a golf scholar alongside an undergraduate degree at an American university.

Application of the Case Study to the Development Model

Using the chronological age on the Development Model to present a profile for James across each level of development, the following information is revealed:

- James is in the development level of his athletic development
- Psychologically he is at the adolescent level
- The key people in his life should be peers, coach and parents
- He is at secondary school, moving into higher education.

In terms of his athletic development, while James is a junior international golfer, he is still developing his skills at the game. Perhaps the 'pressure' and 'perfectionism' came from striving to move into the mastery stage? His initial selection for England Under 16 and 18 had not proved a problem and he had coped well with the transition. However, as time progressed his performance had dipped, so perhaps he was not ready to cope with the mastery level at that time.

At the psychological level he is an adolescent, so he may have had issues surrounding his athletic identity. For example, is he an élite golfer, is he a golfer-student, or is he just 'one of the lads' in his local town? His coaches at the EGU, his local coach and his parents need to take account of his athletic identity and work together in developing a balanced plan for his future.

On a social level, James has a good relationship with his 'home' coach and his parents. These relationships have influenced his athletic development in significant ways, although little is known about his relationships with other squad members and his peers. Both sets of coaches could envisage that James might need and want to relate more with his peers from within as well as outside golf – although this would be difficult, as the EGU squad members lived all across the country. His parents could explore ways in which James could spend more time with his school peers.

Finally, to date James has combined golf and school quite successfully. He is a hard worker and well organized, and it seems from his ambition to go to university in America that he is keen to pursue higher education alongside his golf. However, it is worth considering whether his golfing demands both locally, nationally and internationally leave him enough rest to do his school work, and to recover from his golf commitments.

In Summary

The case study above highlights a few key transitions, both normative and non-normative, that James encountered. As a coach or an athlete adviser it is important to recognize all the levels of Wylleman's (2004) 'Development Model', as they may be interacting and occurring at the same time. Questions need to be asked, and the athlete's support network needs to work together to assist and empower the athlete through these transitions so they can continue to maximize their performance.

PERFORMANCE LIFESTYLE INTERVENTIONS

The research and case study above highlight the fact that athletes face a significant number of transitions throughout their sporting life. As Wylleman (2004) has highlighted in his 'Development Model', there may be a number of reasons for these transitions. Therefore, a coach and/or a Performance Lifestyle adviser need to be aware of these transitions and the considerations an athlete may have to make in order to adjust to the transition. The quality of adjustment to these transitions will depend on the coping strategies employed by the athlete, Performance Lifestyle adviser and coach. Integrating the key development stages with athletic development may assist all parties to help the athlete pursue their sport while understanding the internal and external changes they are encountering.

Elms (2004) highlights a number of coping strategies that the adviser and/or athlete can utilize to help them cope with the transition. First, understanding internal and external influences involves asking questions concerning an athlete's needs, interests, values, skills and traits; this can help establish where athletes are heading, and why. Second, good communication needs to be effective, open and honest. Third, making effective decisions is essential, but this will depend on having the right information available.

Fourth, the key to supporting athletes through transition is identifying and using their support network: this may include their coach, guidance teacher/tutor, family and friends, medical officer, Performance Lifestyle adviser and team manager. It is important to agree and identify the roles and responsibilities of each provider in the network.

Figure 26.4   School to Higher Education is a key transition for the athlete to manage. (Courtesy of Team Northumbria)

Finally, integrated and periodized planning can assist athletes in taking responsibility for their daily, weekly and monthly actions and decisions. This could involve a day and weekly planner with sport, academic and social 'things to do' clearly outlined. Similarly, a monthly and annual calendar would allow an athlete to include key sport dates along with subject choice dates, UCAS (University and College Application System) application and examination dates.

Helping athletes through the range and stages of transitions as per Wylleman's model requires athletes and coaches to be aware of these stages, and to understand and be able to plan for them. Major and normative transitions (such as examinations) can usually be planned for in advance, but due to the nature of sport there could be a reactive element for non-normative transitions (such as injury). Athletes need to plan and be educated about taking responsibility for their actions, which may initially involve their support network, but as they develop they will be empowered to make their own decisions. An interdisciplinary approach may also be appropriate to help an athlete with a transition.

Figure 26.5 outlines this approach for an injured athlete. After exploring the athlete case, a Performance Lifestyle adviser may need to work with a number of service providers (doctor, nutritionist, physiotherapist and psychologist) to ensure the athlete has all the necessary information to make his/her decisions. Presuming the athlete is returning to competitive action in the future, then collaboration with the coach will be essential.

Coping Strategies and Performance

Research by Douglas and Carless (2006) looked into the personal, lifestyle and environmental factors that affect sporting performance. They found the factors included education, employment, funding, communication styles and technology; these can be seen in Figure 26.5.

Potential Issues	Possible Solutions
Loss of funding	Investigate part-time job or flexible job opportunities
Change in dietary requirements	Provide menus/ideas – refer to nutritionist
Coping with new training demands or rehabilitation demands	Time management/daily planning See physiotherapist
Increased free time	Investigate new hobbies or study opportunities
Making doctor, physiotherapy or massage appointments	Resolve possible transportation issues
Low morale	Listening, boosting morale – refer to psychologist (if appropriate)

Figure 26.5   An interdisciplinary approach and the injured athlete.

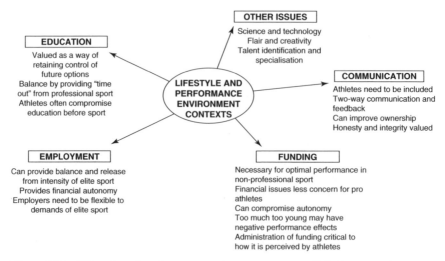

Figure 26.6   Lifestyle and performance environment contexts (UK Sport 2006).

These factors are very closely linked to some of the transitional issues and stages already mentioned in this chapter. If the athlete is to maximize their performance, then knowledge and understanding of these factors and the associated transitions will be crucial. There is also a need for the athlete and their support network to develop the coping strategies. As highlighted earlier in the chapter (Hay, 2004 and Schlossberg, 1981), a coach may be able to assist the athlete through their transitions by educating themselves and planning and preparing before the transition, and supporting their athlete after the transition.

Therefore, the importance of the coach, parents, teachers and partners cannot be over-emphasized. The communication loop between the athlete, their adviser and these key people will play a crucial role in ensuring athletes cope with the numerous transitions in their life.

One clear example of a sports organization that provides athletes with various coping strategies is the English Institute of Sport (EIS). They appointed a National Education Adviser to work with their Performance Lifestyle advisers across England, with a particular remit of providing educational advice and support to élite athletes going into higher and further education. The National Education Adviser develops tools, tactics, guides and educational resources to assist advisers and their athletes. As Porteous (2004) identified, the athlete will need to cope with induction, distractions, the pressure and relocation. This is where the athlete's support network and the role of the Performance Lifestyle adviser and coach can be invaluable.

The National Education Adviser delivered educational workshops for various sports and their athletes in order for them to be proactive in planning their educational transition from school to university or college. This pre-planning is very important in making the transition as smooth as possible for the athlete. To assist this process the National Education Adviser developed a new web site (www.sportandstudy.net 2009) in partnership with UK Sport and TASS (Talented Athlete Scholarship Scheme) to facilitate the process.

As identified earlier, there are numerous demands placed on élite athletes moving from school to university or college: educational (career), social (peers, partners, family and so on) and through their sport (competitions, camps and so on). The coping strategies introduced by the EIS reflect the numerous transitions an élite athlete faces in their educational cycle, as purported by Wylleman (2004). Furthermore, this transitional 'process' through education also reflects Schlossberg's (1981) transitional models of human adaptation by stressing the importance of the pre- and post-transitional environment.

The development of a 'perfect' support system (see Chapter 25) is the ultimate goal for sports organizations in assisting élite athletes through their numerous transitions. Coping resources need to focus on controlling the controllable negative adjustment factors associated with the transition process, and increasing the positive adjustment factors (Lavallee and Wylleman, 2000). The welfare programmes need to involve the sport's national governing body with a clear transition policy, working closely with Performance Lifestyle advisers, coaches and others in the athlete's support network. This will ultimately minimize negative adjustment factors and ensure the transition is as positive as possible for the athlete.

COACH SUPPORT TO KEY EDUCATION TRANSITIONS

The importance of education and qualifications cannot be overstated in today's world. Increasingly, the transferable skills and attributes associated with life-long learning are essential to succeed in one's chosen career. Athletes are no different, but they may need to balance their sport with their long-term career aspirations. Coaches are increasingly recognizing that athletes need a balanced lifestyle and need to plan for life after sport.

For example, a coach may wish to know what their athlete's future aspirations are, what type of career they seek, whether they want to go to university or college: starting the research phase early enough – in years ten, eleven or twelve in school – is paramount in order to plan for the future. Furthermore, flexibility within the athlete's training programme will assist and accommodate unforeseen changes in these plans.

In education, as previously identified, there are many transitions that the athlete and coach are likely to encounter. These may be from primary to secondary education, secondary to higher or further, full-time to part-time, class-based to distance learning, and may also include failure to achieve and relocation. Below are some examples of how a coach may help to prepare, plan and support their athlete in going to university and whilst at university, strategies which link clearly with the work of the EIS and Elms (2004) mentioned earlier.

First, if an athlete has aspirations of going to university or college, then his/her A levels (or equivalent) examination time (revision plus examination timetable) is very important. A clear calendar of events needs to be mapped out to see where any 'hot spots' may exist between sporting and educational commitments. Furthermore, clear communication pathways need to be in place between the school, the athlete, parents and coach. Similarly, sufficient time needs to be built into the training and competition programme to accommodate an athlete researching his/her options for university or college; this may include open days, visits, UCAS conventions, and talking direct with the university or sport personnel. Course selection is another key issue, because the athlete will be studying for three or four years and they are going to have to balance study with their sport.

Finally, crucial issues around university selection will be location, accommodation and training facilities, and factoring in coaching, travel and course commitments with sport commitments. Getting to know the environment, together with an understanding of the processes, will be essential for the athlete to make a smooth transition.

Likewise, when at university athletes will be faced with a multitude of distractions. The coach could relate his/her experiences to the athlete, or use other suitable athletes to meet and talk with first year university athletes. Similarly, there will be new pressures faced by the athlete, and time management, planning, prioritizing, saying 'no' and negotiating are essential skills so that the athlete can cope with the pressure of combining sport and education at university. Coaches can empower their athletes to develop these transferable skills in the pre-university years, or ensure workshops are available for them at university.

COACH SUPPORT TO ATHLETE RETIREMENT

Lavallee (2004) believes that for an athlete to make a smooth transition from their sport into retirement they should consider these factors during their sport career. Coaches are recognizing more and more that not only do athletes need a balanced life whilst competing, they also need to plan ahead for their career after sporting retirement. This holistic approach may enable an athlete to perform better in training and competition without this sort of distraction. Furthermore, coaches are not necessarily career specialists, and this is where knowledge, awareness and use of Performance Lifestyle advisers, either from the Home Country Institutes or national governing body can play a significant role in helping the athletes.

Some athletes will cope well with retirement from sport, others will not, and coaches need to realize that there are a number of factors that may help the latter. These may be related to whether the retirement was voluntary or involuntary, how the athlete views themselves (their identity), and their own coping resources. Pre-transition planning between the coach, Performance Lifestyle adviser and athlete is very useful as a coping strategy: it allows the athlete to consider their identity, maintain a balanced lifestyle and have a focus for post sport.

Finally, coaches can empower their athletes to become more aware of the transferable skills they have learned in sport, which could be applicable to the world of work. Alongside this, the athlete's Performance Lifestyle adviser can help them to develop a career profile (which would include values, likes/dislikes, personality traits and so on), identify career pathways and facilitate work experience or job shadowing. They can also help their athlete to develop a 'CV', and prepare them for job applications and interviews. All these facets can help to make the transition out of sports as smooth as possible, whilst maintaining the athlete's current performance.

27

Applying Management Principles in Sports Coaching

by Claire Bruce

THE PRINCIPLES OF MANAGEMENT

The word 'management' is dynamic, and encapsulates numerous processes and practices; it is widely accepted as a professional discipline that transcends industry and the three sectors (public, private and voluntary). The Management Standards Centre (MSC: 2008), an organization supported by the Charted Management Institute (CMI) and the Department for Education and Skills (DfES) draws together well the distinct purpose that defines management practice:

> The key purpose of management and leadership is to... provide direction, gain commitment, facilitate change and achieve results through the efficient, creative and responsible deployment of people and other resources. (www.management.standards.org.2009)

The practice of managing has always existed, and is documented and described in varying detail throughout history (managing resources to harvest crops, engage with religious movements, in battle and so forth). It was the Industrial Revolution that witnessed the most significant developments regarding the practice of resource management and efficiency/performance improvements, and it was these that brought about the significance of the role of 'the manager' within organizations as we accept them today in the twenty-first century. In management literature it is broadly accepted that the varying approaches to management can be illustrated in five primary categories (Watt, 2003):

Classical: managers are specialists in specific areas of an organization, who rely on core knowledge – in a sports coaching context an example would be the various squad coaching roles that exist: rugby union backs, forwards and kicking coaches.

Behavioural: identifies the need to understand individuals within the process of management and their specific requirements – in a sports coaching context an example would be the role of a head coach, such as a football coach taking the strategic overview of squad, first team, reserves, and academy player dynamics.

Science: focuses on scientific approaches to resolving issues relating to practice so that improved efficiency is achieved – in a sports coaching context an example would be the utilization and integration of sports science methods and research: physiological testing or biomechanical movement analysis to improve athlete performance.

Systems: utilizes specialists as the parts of a system that requires managing, where all the parts come together to achieve the required output/s – in a sports coaching context an example would be the trend towards bespoke athlete support services: TASS athletes utilizing lifestyle mentoring, injury rehabilitation, health and nutrition athlete support services.

Contingency: requires the manager to be dynamic and open to changing practice according to what the operational environment demands – in a sports coaching context this could be the approach adopted by a club coach to guide a team through a cup, league or national competition during a season.

However, there is a lack of clarity relating to which is the 'best' or 'better' approach to adopt when managing, with various management writers subscribing to the differing approaches in varying degrees. Peter Drucker, quite possibly the most enduring of management writers, states as one of his core principles of management that managing organizations is concerned with balancing a variety of needs and goals within multiple contexts (Drucker, 1954), underlining the very essence of management in contemporary society, this being the need for adaptability.

The pace of development in the sports industry, both economically and socially, has increased at a significantly rapid rate during the past eight years (post millennium) within the United Kingdom (UK). Within this development, sports coaching has experienced a significant change in direction since 2000, with the realization that high quality élite sports coaches are a limited resource in the UK sports industry. Such resource challenges have been linked to having a potential impact upon the realization of Great Britain's goal (Keen, 2005) of achieving fourth and first in the London 2012 Olympic, a Paralympic medals table (BOA, 2008), and more critically undermines competitive sustainability across sport in the UK on the world stage. With such high stakes embedded in élite sports performance and delivery, the current role of the sports coach has been drawn into the spotlight and opened up for intense professional and media scrutiny.

Central government policy direction in sport lies within the areas of élite sport, health, education and social/cultural inclusion, and from this it is clear to see that the sports industry now is wide and varied in striving to satisfy a multitude of needs, wants and desires. Indeed, Smith and Stewart (1999, p. 11) capture this thought well when they state 'Sport means different things to different people'. In 2007 Mintel described the sports industry as one of the most rapidly expanding markets in the UK, and such a statement is wholly relevant when considering the increasing level of priority the sports industry is now demanding on both national and global political, social and economic agendas (Hylton and Bramham, 2008). The structure of sport in the UK today is highly complex, and it is within this tall, mechanistic structure that delivery of current government sport policy is centred, in three key agencies:

- UK Sport, Élite Sport Delivery System
- Sport England, Community Sport Delivery System
- Youth Sport Trust, School Sport Delivery System.

It is through a combination of these three agencies and the Department of Culture, Media and Sport (DCMS) that sport in the UK is governed and managed, and importantly where the principles of management combine with the role of the sports coach in contemporary sport. Before we continue and consider management functions and skills, it is important to have an understanding of the key concepts that impact on management and coaching practice in the sports industry:

- Managing does not take place in isolation: partnerships and multi-agency and cross-sector/industry practice are essential
- Facilitating the most effective use of available resources underpins delivery in sport management
- The environment (both internal (micro) and external (macro)) in which a sports manager operates impacts significantly on the achievement of goals
- High quality interpersonal skills when managing in sport are critical to nurturing innovation and realizing potential.

Boddy (2008, p. 10) states 'A manager is someone who gets things done with the aid of people and other resources', and Sports Coach UK (SCUK) states that a sports coach is focused on developing people in order to improve performance (Miles, 2004). These are important statements to reflect upon when considering how managers and sports coaches realize a balanced, adaptable approach to improving performance through practice. Success and the delivery of outputs are both highly reliant on the ability of both individuals and organizations to operate effectively across all functions of management while utilizing highly developed management skills – subjects covered in the next sections of this chapter.

FUNCTIONS OF MANAGEMENT

In 1967 Henri Fayol established what he considered to be the six functions of management: planning, organizing, leading, co-ordinating, controlling and staffing (human resources). Since this point, the search for the definitive list of what academics and practitioners believe to be the most important management skills has continued (Cole, 2004; Boddy, 2008; Hannagan,

2008) with numerous revised attempts published seemingly each year. However, for the purpose of this text we will draw upon the two management functions of planning and controlling in order to highlight explicit links between management and sports coaching. Staffing (human resources) will be covered in the following management skills section, and leading in a later chapter in this section.

Planning

Sports managers must have a strategic plan: without a plan how do they know the business they are in, what direction to take and how to get there? In sports coaching the same questions can be applied; without a plan how does an athlete/team/squad/coach:

- Understand the environment they are competing within?
- Understand what training, development and support is required to ensure they are competitive?
- Acknowledge how they are going to realize their goals?

Crisfield, Cabral and Carpenter (2005) observe that lack of long-term planning in sports coaching practice creates disjointed learning impacting upon the achievement of goals and athlete/team performance. The word 'strategy' is synonymous with planning and has long been used by organizations, with each establishing their own clear thoughts about what strategy means to them. Johnson, Scholes and Whittington (2005, p. 9) state, 'Strategy is likely to be concerned with the long-term direction of an organization', and it is an important element of strategy to understand that it is primarily concerned with a long-term timescale (one to five years). However, Beech and Chadwick really crystallize for sports managers what is meant by strategy when they observe:

> Strategy, then, is a plan that sport managers create and hold based on their knowledge of the culture, resources, capabilities and purpose of their own organization (2004, p. 215).

It is widely acknowledged that in order for the planning or organizational strategy to be effective it must be part of a cyclical process in which specific components of organizational strategy have to be created. These components are a mission statement, aims, objectives and a continuous review process (Smith and Stewart, 1999). This cyclical planning process, and the integral stages of the planning process, are distinctly identifiable with the coaching process.

In this sports coaching model the same stages used in management planning are drawn upon, indicating essentially the same processes of strategic planning practice. The importance of creating a clearly defined structure to a planning process cannot be emphasized strongly enough, a structure underlined by a mission statement that not only defines the business the organization is in, but one that illustrates the core values of the people who operate within it. In the sports industry, sports coaching now has a clearly identifiable strategic direction within each of the three

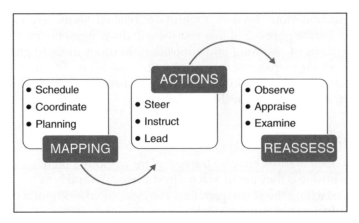

Figure 27.1   The Sport Coaching Process.

sport delivery systems, and therefore contributes significantly to the strategic direction and delivery points across élite, community and school sport in the UK.

Control as a Management Practice

The process of control as a management practice is focused on the establishing of three primary activities:

- Setting goals and standards that are adopted throughout the organization
- Creating systems that enable consistent and valid performance measurement
- Establishing processes that contain contingency planning, enabling corrective action to be implemented when necessary.

Sport is defined by how well athletes/teams perform and the quality of their performances (Lyle, 1999), which has little relevance and context unless the performance is analysed against predetermined measurements of control. Crisfield *et al.* (2005) identify the importance of performance measurement within a sports coaching context when they observe that sports coaches must '… analyse and evaluate performance (their own and that of their performers) to gauge and direct progress' (2005, p. 5). Without a reference point to compare to, the industry of sport becomes dramatically less attractive, and in many cases meaningless. Organizations, no matter what sector/industry, need to measure performance, and by doing so gain feedback that can be used to strive for further success and improvements in competitiveness.

The DCMS game plan document published in 2002 sets out the Labour Government's strategic direction for sport in the UK, and defines in specific detail the key performance measures that need to be implemented by 2020. Strategic planning supports the evaluation of government interventions throughout sport policy in the UK. The measurement of performance

Figure 27.2   The sports industry is dynamic and diverse. (Courtesy of David Griffiths)

provides managers with a 'formal mechanism of control within sports businesses' (Beech and Chadwick, 2004, p. 255), and it is through this that communication of control processes is permeated to as wide an audience as possible.

In general, the sports industry is traditionally very poor at monitoring and evaluating, and the DCMS (2002, p. 168) openly states:

> Monitoring and evaluation is key to assessing the progress being made in delivering sport … but it is weak, with poor lines of account-ability and a focus on short-term results and outputs.

Monitoring and evaluation in sport is critical in order to determine good practice from which benchmarks can be set and lessons learnt. Crisfield *et al.* (2005) identify that a systematic process of evaluation that supports the sports coach in the practice of monitoring and evaluation is essential, a process clearly identifiable within broader management practice. However, it is important to understand that the dynamic and diverse context of the sports industry, and the increasingly high pace at which it operates, does not currently create an environment in which managers are empowered to reflect upon practice, a key skill required in sports coaching (Crisfield *et al.*, 2005). The following section will draw upon the key skill of human resource management, and will identify the importance of human resource skills for both managers and sports coaches.

HUMAN RESOURCE MANAGEMENT SKILLS

The development of a highly skilled workforce throughout the width and depth of industry is of primary importance not only to organizations competing in increasingly boundary-less geographical markets, but also for central government. The MSC observes that '... upgrading the skills of managers is fundamental to the government's aim to raise UK productivity and competitiveness ...' (http://www.management-standards.org, 2008).

It is this mission of striving to develop highly competent professionals across all industry that distinct parallels can be drawn with the current priorities that exist within sports coaching:

- Coaching is as much about people as teaching technical skills and techniques
- Coaching is focused on performance improvements across all levels of participation
- Coaching is concerned with challenging people, which offers development opportunities and realizes potential.

In addition, Chelladurai (2006) crystallizes the specific human resource management (HRM) challenges that exist within the sports industry by making reference, first, to the predominant provision of services, and second, to the reliance on a mix of volunteer and paid employees.

The managing of people in a place of work has been traced back to the English Industrial Revolution – though at that time the emphasis was on the managing of personnel as opposed to human resources. This subtle change in wording from personnel to human resources brought with it a significant alteration in how employees within organizations were viewed

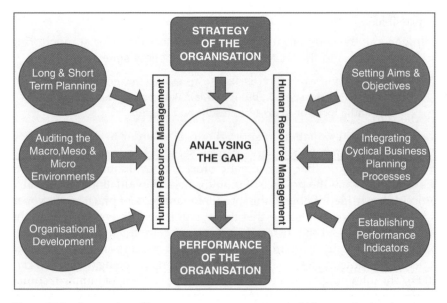

Figure 27.3   Integration of human resource management within organizational strategy.

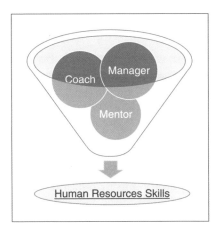

Figure 27.4   Multiple roles of the sports coach.

(Torrington, Hall and Taylor, 2008) and consequently managed. With this in mind, it is important to define human resource management (HRM): 'HRM is a strategic approach to managing employment relations' (Bratton and Gold, 2003, p. 7); this provides a broad context for HRM.

In general, it is recognized that changes in business and labour market conditions are reflected in shifts in human resource management. The important element to understand is that HRM is an essential component of business planning, and in order to generate the most effective impact, HRM needs to be aligned with the strategic direction of the organization (Jamrog and Overholt, 2004). Reinforcing this point of HRM working as a cohesive part of organizations' wider strategy is animated clearly in Figure 27.3, p. 456).

'This model emphasises the importance of the two-way relationship between business and HR strategies' (Johnson *et al.*, 2005, p. 456). In sport this synergy of HRM and organizational strategic goals can be seen in the role that many professional sport team managers and coaches perform. In the sports industry today professional sports clubs rely significantly on private sector investment that is aligned closely with the commercial viability of the club/team brand. This in itself highlights the broadening of the role and responsibilities demanded from sports coaches, both on strategic business and interpersonal levels; this is illustrated in the accompanying diagram (*see* Figure 27.3).

This model establishes the dynamic HRM requirements integral to the role of a sports coach within the sports industry today, and McQuade (2003, p. 1) reinforces this perspective when she states 'As a coach you will fulfil a number of roles ...'. In this model the three roles reflect:

Manager: focused on the wider business/organizational landscape that is reflected within strategic planning and performance evaluation.

Coach: an expert within a specific field providing specialist knowledge and development for all level performers.

Mentor: serves as a role model and provides guidance and support on both professional and personal development levels (Pastore, 2003).

Previously in this chapter we have outlined the links that exist between management principles, management functions and HRM skills within sports coaching. It is clear that the approach adopted to manage or coach within a sports setting is distinctly reliant on the context within which the action or practice is taking place – that is, in a period of national economic downturn for either professional sport teams, community sport initiatives, or for sports volunteers. Each of these contexts will demand differing approaches and importantly a balance of HRM skills, and also the ability of the practitioner to be adaptable in relation to environmental change. The following section will outline the key principles of change management and the impacts they have on sports management and coaching practice.

THE ROLE OF CHANGE MANAGEMENT

The fast pace at which industry and society in general moves today has significantly altered how we live our lives; the reality of a twenty-four-hour society is certainly in existence (Torkildsen, 2005). It follows that if we are living our lives so differently, then organizations also have many challenges in relation to the constantly changing environments in which they operate. Change within organizations takes place for many reasons; Amis and Slack (2004, p. 158) observe:

> Within the sports industry, increasing commercialization, alterations to geopolitical boundaries, technological advances and greater competition in the market place have resulted in pronounced changes to many organizations, often over very short periods of time.

Academics and practitioners offer multiple views on what they believe are the most critical elements impacting on change within organizations (Beech and Chadwick, 2004; Mullins, 2005; Slack and Parent, 2006). In addition to this it is important to acknowledge that change within organizations is driven by both internal (micro) and external (macro) forces of change (Bloisi, Cook and Hunsaker, 2003). However, when identifying the drivers of change factors, it is possibly easier for sports managers and coaches to refer to the PESTEL model (Beech and Chadwick, 2002, p. 220):

- **Political:** direction of sport policy within sports coaching
- **Economic:** availability of public funding and private sponsorship to support development and delivery
- **Social:** defining the needs of user groups within the parameters of individual social contexts
- **Technological:** integration of updated and new working practice or equipment to support competitiveness

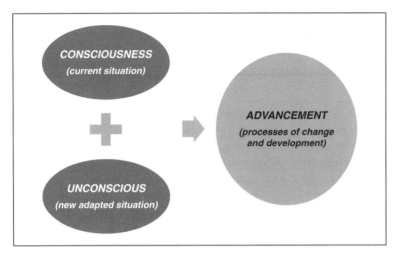

Figure 27.5   Interpreting the change process.

- **Environmental:** impacts across local, national and international priorities and current agendas
- **Legal:** legislation and the adoption of new parameters relating to practice.

What is evident within the concept of change is that it occurs in all organizations, driven from a multitude of sources brought about by multiple factors. It is then a clear challenge for sports managers and coaches to ensure organizations are strategically placed to handle change, either proactively as anticipated change (integration of new training methods), or reactively with forced change (adoption of new health and safety working practices), whatever the situation demands. Karl Lewin (1951) developed a useful model when taking on change, as shown in Figure 27.5.

This uses interpretation to symbolize the realization for change and acceptance that the current situation cannot be maintained; following this stage advancement is the process where the actions necessary to change are developed. Finally, the unconsciousness process is the capturing of the change solutions and integration into the organization through appropriate support mechanisms. This structured approach to implementing change as a management process has distinct resonance with the period of change that sports coaching has experienced within the UK since 1986, and the stages of change from the National Coaching Foundation to a full rebrand as Sports Coach UK in 2001.

Change within an organization is unlikely to be successful if not everyone in the organization is involved or agrees with the change process. It is clearly then the responsibility of the sports manager and coach to embrace change, and to market change within an organization as an exciting challenge rather than a negative experience. Gill (2003) observes that the difficult and sometimes delicate issue of change will only succeed if effective leadership is employed to handle the change process. It is highly unlikely that sports coaches will never encounter change within the context of their practice. The nature of the sports industry today, with multiple policy directions, delivery systems and funding streams, illustrates the complex environment (Parkhouse, 2001) in which sports managers and coaches operate.

The priority when encountering change is to ensure that it results in a positive strategic output for the organization, team, athlete or indeed the coach. For this to become a reality, strategic planning and the control processes within it must be developed in such a way that managers and coaches are able to adapt and cope with change when and where it occurs.

28

Competition Preparation and Management

by Anita Navin

Any coach will readily admit that success in competition is a result of effective planning leading up to and during the event. The demands of competition should not be underestimated, as there are often weekly matches, back-to-back fixtures, tournaments or week-long fixtures in the competition phase. Effective planning and preparation by the coach, support staff and indeed the athlete is essential for success.

EFFECTIVE SUPPORT TEAMS

Élite performance structures involve a support team, and roles between the various personnel must be clarified, accepted and firmly communicated between the support team and athletes. The ability to plan, pay attention to detail, be fully committed and possess high levels of motivation would be characteristics essential for any individual adopting a support team role. While there are varying roles and staff that make up the support team, the following staff feature in an élite competition environment:

- Head coach
- Assistant coach
- Physiotherapist
- Doctor
- Team manager
- Nutritionist
- Strength and conditioning coach.

The head coach is primarily responsible for the coordination of the support group, and must ensure that all individuals work together as a cohesive unit to create a positive climate to best support the athlete. The support group should engage in setting their personal and group goals regarding non-playing issues, and create a collective identity based upon the standards and expectations of the group. Remaining united for task accomplishment is essential for maximum productivity, and the group should build rapport and communicate a unity of purpose.

Effective leadership is essential, and the head coach must develop positive working relationships with the support staff; this is often achieved through structured and regular communication methods. For example, daily meetings while on a competition tour, which are short and focused, will contribute to the success of any competition programme, and the dissemination of a daily schedule would promote positive communication networks. The short daily meeting on a tour should also offer a period of time for support staff to communicate any issues requiring attention.

An effective coach will also prepare fully for the competition by assigning roles to staff, analysing the opposition, delivering appropriate training sessions prior to the competition, selecting the squad and team, goal setting, and communicating the game plan.

Roles

The majority of accredited clubs produce clear role descriptions and codes of conduct for the staff and volunteers in the club. However, each competition will have different administrative and domestic arrangements, and it is in the remit of the head coach to ensure that roles are clarified for all staff attending the competition. Prior to the competition day several domestic issues need to be finalized, for example travel arrangements, accommodation, umpiring, scoring, and management roles whilst on the bench. The team manager will often take ownership of the domestic issues, and through liaison with the relevant staff and head coach, will draw up a competition schedule. This schedule will be printed and handed to players, parents and support staff so that the timings and meeting points are all clearly documented.

The management of the bench during the competition must be addressed, and the bench players will often be assigned a specific role and responsibility. Roles assigned to the bench players could be any of the following: handing court players drinks during a time out, putting the balls into the bag after any warm-up, leading the bench players to warm up with five minutes remaining in the quarter, and also collating any match statistics based on tasks set by the coach.

Analysing the Opposition

A coach is expected to assess the strengths and weaknesses of the opposition and to note any individual, unit and team tactics and strategies. The coach must then apply this information into the training sessions leading up to the event, looking at methods that could be implemented to counteract the strengths and capitalize on the weaknesses of the opposition.

An effective coach will assess the strategies employed and the technical strengths of each opposing player. For example, typical questions a netball coach might seek to find the answer for when addressing the opposition are outlined below:

Goal keeper: Does she have good elevation? Can she mark a moving shooter effectively?

Goal defence: Is she a tight stage one defender? Does she follow a rotating shooter, or zone the circle?

Wing defence: Does she commit for the interception? Is she beaten on a dodge or a straight sprint?

Centre: Does she front-cut a defender? Is she a main feeder of the shooters?

Wing attack: Does she attack the top of the circle edge? Does she use different set-ups at the centre pass?

Goal attack: Does she receive many centre passes? Does she use base line runs to enter the circle?

Goal shooter: Does she move, or play a holding game? Does she offer for the ball out of the circle?

The coach must also assess the style of play adopted by the team, and an example of the questions to ask of the opposition could be:

- What styles of defence are used through the court (zone or man to man)?
- Do they use the overlap player to support attacking play?
- Do they front-cut, or rely on overhead passing?
- What defending strategies are used at the centre pass and back line throw-in?
- Do players switch roles through the court?

Training Sessions and Selection

The pre-competition training must prepare players for the match, and the various team combinations must be practised. A coach will build up a firm understanding of the combinations that work effectively through communication patterns, player strengths and decision making. The coach must work through the skills and tactics that need to be implemented in the forthcoming match, and in doing this must assess the strengths and weaknesses of each player in relation to the intended game plan. A coach will select the squad and start seven players based upon their ability to implement the game plan that will counteract the strengths of the opposing players.

The coach must ensure that the players selected have the ability to make accurate decisions under pressure, and it is advantageous if they are flexible in their thoughts and actions.

The information below demonstrates how a Junior Super League coach has assessed an opposing goal shooter and subsequently selected a goal keeper to try and counteract the strengths of this key attacking player. The information noted below represents the findings from an assessment of the opposing goal shooter:

- A very static player who plays a holding game
- Moves out of the circle to receive but is not fast

- Is intimidated by the defender jumping when shooting
- Likes to receive a bounce pass from an attacking player on the circle edge.

As a result of the above assessment the following goal keeper was selected:

- Has quick feet and is able to reposition when marking a shooter
- Can intercept short passes to a shooter by reaching low and using a long arm span
- Has excellent elevation and a well timed jump when marking the shot.

A developmental level coach working with talented players will often prioritize the value of the competition and may decide to use such an event for individual player development. In this instance the coach may decide that all players in the squad will be exposed, and will highlight that it is a game of low priority in terms of winning. This is where developing players can link with more experienced players in the squad, and also begin to experience higher intensity match play. The effective coach will communicate the intentions of the competition to ensure all players are well informed. Occasionally players join a squad at the higher level to experience the bench procedures and overall pressures encountered when a large crowd is present.

Goal Setting

The goal-setting process has been covered in more detail in Chapter 19; however, competition goals should be devised as a result of the following actions:

- Discussions with individual players in training sessions
- Discussions with the squad in the final training session
- Coach observations of the opposition
- Coach observations and analysis of her own squad in previous matches.

A coach must ensure that not only outcome goals but performance and process goals are set for any competition. By incorporating all three types of goal, each individual player is able to evaluate their performance accurately, irrespective of the result.

The following goals were set by a coach leading into a Talent League netball match:

Outcome Goal

- To win the match.

Performance Goals

- Achieve a 90 per cent success rate from the centre pass to shooting opportunity
- Achieve an 80 per cent success rate of centre pass to goal scored

Figure 28.1   Process and performance goals are crucial in achieving the outcome. (Courtesy of Jeanette Pointon)

- Gain six interceptions in the mid court per quarter
- Wing attack and centre to achieve an 80 per cent success rate for passing to a shooter.

Process Goals
Release the ball from a balanced position having assessed the options available:

- Two forward options must be available for the ball carrier
- Effectively mark the player at the second stage of defence
- Tight man-to-man for the first five minutes of each quarter.

To ensure good practice a coach should also set process goals for individuals: for example, if there is a squad member who constantly seeks out and delivers a diagonal pass that is intercepted, a goal could be 'to use the straight line option or the square pass to an overlapping player'.

Communicating the Game Plan

A coach must present the game plan during the squad meeting, and this is usually one hour prior to the match warm-up. The information covered in this meeting will simply reinforce the key issues covered in the training sessions, and will reinforce the tactical methods to be implemented. The coach should focus clearly on the positive aspects of previous performances, ensuring that all players emerge from the meeting confident and motivated. Using a facilitative style through questioning will encourage players to take ownership of the plan and remain focused on the discussions. The game plan should be communicated concisely, and the use of visual aids to represent formations or defending set-ups will often support this process.

Effective routines will ensure that both players and support staff remain focused on their role. Ultimately the players should feel well supported, organized and fully focused on the competition itself. Due to effective planning, organization, and the presence of systematic preparation by the coach, all players should feel confident of a positive competition outcome.

COMPETITION ROUTINES

A coach will encourage all individual players to develop their own competition routine; this represents a set of personalized activities including travel, contingency planning, goal setting, psychological preparation, warm-up routines and evaluation. Any player and coach will begin planning for the competition well in advance of the day to ensure that they are well organized and focused.

The coach should work with all individual players to support them in formulating their own individual routine for the competition. Key questions a coach will ask the players in formulating their plan include:

- How much sleep do you need the night before the event?
- What food do you prefer to eat leading into the event?
- What routine do you have for packing your kit bag?
- How will you travel to the meeting point?
- When do you like to go over the game plan in your mind?
- How do you cope with family and friends leading up to the day?
- Do you have set individual exercises you like to do in the warm-up?
- How do you control your anxiety?

An example of a preparation routine for a coach might be as follows:

- Complete an analysis of the opposition
- Review the referees/umpires for the match, noting trends
- Prioritize and structure the team and individual goals
- Allow time on the competition day to collect your thoughts (one hour)
- Engage in self-talk reviewing past successes, calmness when in a crisis, and rehearse key words and actions
- When the competition begins, enjoy the experience; if judgements and the mind become cloudy, find a sign on the court to refocus on
- Resist any disturbances that take away your focus on the competition
- If and when nervous, employ some breathing techniques.

MANAGING THE SUBSTITUTES

Substitutes may at times lose motivation and become demotivated as a result of limited involvement in competition. It is vital the coach ensures that each individual is clear about their role in the team, and in this process it is essential that they communicate clearly what the individual must improve on or add to their game in order to have more involvement. A coach can prevent conflict if the rationale for substitutions is communicated to players and individual feedback given where performance requires attention. An effective coach will utilize the following methods to avoid conflict with those performers not playing a fully active part in any competition:

- Communicate intentions clearly with regard to selection
- Ensure the squad are aware of the importance and demands placed upon a reserve
- Utilize reserves and allocate a clear role for them during competition
- Brief reserves prior to entering the game, and allow them sufficient time for warming up wherever possible
- Encourage a performer who may not feature in the competition to set goals that do not relate to the performance in competition, but focus on targets in the training environment.

EFFECTIVE CONFLICT MANAGEMENT

Conflict is a natural occurrence of any group faced with competition and the associated pressures and athlete selection issues. How the coach or members of the support group manage conflict will determine whether this is beneficial or destructive. Effective conflict management will enhance the functioning of a group, as positive strategies will improve productivity and working relationships, lead to constructive problem solving, and often promote positive change. Conflict can be destructive and can at times divert the athlete and staff from the goals set for the competition, it can deplete resources, especially time, affect an individual's psychological well-being, and overall inhibit team performance. How we manage conflict will determine whether it is beneficial or detrimental to performance. Five conflict management styles exist: these are referred to as forcing, avoiding, accommodating, collaborating and compromising, and are applied as follows:

Style	Example
Forcing	The athlete will complete the task
Avoiding	Leave the athlete alone
Accommodating	Athlete's preference adopted
Collaborating	Athlete and staff work out the problem together
Compromising	'Split the difference'

PROJECTING SELF-CONFIDENCE IN COMPETITION

Managing staff and performers in a competition environment can place significant demands on the coach, and it is vital that the coach displays a confident approach at all times. There is a belief that a coach who is not confident will transmit such a mental state to others. Any coach should consider the following hints for success:

- Communication should not be high pitched as this is deemed to convey anxiety in competitive environments. Utilizing a lower-pitched tone is more credible and can add conviction to your message
- A soft voice can convey an element of uncertainty, so ensure that all can hear the message being communicated
- Eye contact is a measure of control and sincerity. A coach who lacks confidence will often not look an individual in the eye, and this can be associated with a lack of confidence
- Posture is critical, and being upright with head and shoulders back will instantly convey a positive and controlled approach to the event
- A smile will convey to others that you are in control.

Following any competition it is vital that a review and evaluation takes place. All support staff should be encouraged to contribute, and outlined below are the areas which should be considered in this process:

- **Effective leadership:** Has the coach managed the co-ordination of support staff effectively? Was a positive motivational climate created?
- **Performance feedback:** Have staff been given the chance to feed back on each other's performances in their role?
- **Appreciation and satisfaction:** Do team members feel satisfied and valued within the support team?
- **Group cohesion:** Have all roles in the support team been effectively integrated?
- **Task cohesion:** Are the support team united in their message, approach and commitment in relation to task accomplishment?
- **Balance between work and free time:** Have the support staff planned for, and taken some time out, during the competition in order to rest?
- **Coping skills:** Have the support staff received training to note the various methods for conflict management?

SUMMARY

This chapter has highlighted the key role of the coach in managing not only the performers but a network of support personnel. A coach must therefore be able to plan, co-ordinate and best integrate a range of specialist support. There will be instances where support is minimal and a coach must operate in isolation, which ultimately places more pressure on the performance coach.

In summary, the ability of a coach to manage the performer and a support team is challenging, but it is essential that all individuals have a sound understanding of their responsibilities (role clarity) and accept (role acceptance) and execute them effectively (role performance).

PART 5: PROFESSIONAL ISSUES IN COACHING

29

Sports Equity: Policy to Practice

by Dr Lesley Fishwick

CULTURAL CONTEXT OF SPORT COACHING IN THE UK

Participating in sport – be it playing, coaching, officiating or watching – does not occur in isolation, as sport is intricately linked to society and takes place within a specific cultural context. The United Kingdom can be characterized as a highly competitive, capitalistic, patriarchal, product-oriented culture in which a win-at-all-cost ethic is occurring with increasing frequency. Recent debates about cheating in sport reflect these societal characteristics. Incidents such as diving in football, the bloodgate scandal in rugby, and doping allegations in cycling and tennis, provide ample evidence that social values, beliefs and biases held by participants and coaches permeate the playing fields and sports arenas.

To play within or beyond the rules is likely to be part of a conscious decision-making process made by coaches, which results in specific behaviours on the field of play. Unconscious decisions made by coaches based on taken-for-granted assumptions also have consequences in terms of hindering some groups from even reaching the field of play. In the UK an emphasis on particular values such as competition and winning over other values, combined with a focus on élite performance and 'traditional' team games, excludes some social groups more than others. As a result most sports operate within a male, White, middle-class environment that marginalizes other minority groups.

Shaw (2007) persuasively argues that negative stereotypical views concerning the abilities and interests of minority groups are strongly held in many sport organizations, and enable some sport practitioners to argue that women/Black/disabled/older/gay and lesbian athletes are not interested, are not good enough, or do not have the natural propensity to participate. These taken-for-granted beliefs impact on sporting opportunities for those groups excluded by these stereotypes.

It is for these reasons that it is important for coaches to be self-reflective of the role they play in perpetuating injustice through their sporting beliefs and practices. The focus of this chapter is to critically examine the role coaches may inadvertently play in perpetuating cultural stereotypes, and the impact that this has in terms of placing barriers of participation for different groups.

PATTERNS OF INEQUALITY IN SPORT

In some cases there is evidence that some of the barriers are being dismantled, as successful Paralympians and Black premiership footballers have visible profiles in the media. Further signs of achieving equality are key sport events such as Wimbledon finally responding to pressure and awarding equal prize money for men and women. Despite these gains, however, there is much more compelling evidence that social influences such as gender, ethnicity and class continue to act as barriers to participation. Nationwide surveys consistently demonstrate disparities between specific groups. The elderly, the disabled, many women, certain ethnic groups and the unwaged are less likely to participate in sport. The most extensive participation survey ever conducted in the UK, the Active People Survey (2006), reveals the following disparities across different socio-demographic groups in terms of participation in sport:

- Males: 23.7 per cent (4.7 million); females: 18.5 per cent (3.8 million)
- Sixteen to twenty-four years: 32.7 per cent
- Thirty-five to forty-four years: 24.7 per cent
- Fifty-five to sixty-four years: 16.0 per cent
- Seventy-five to eighty-four years: 6.0 per cent
- People with a limiting longstanding illness or disability 8.8 per cent; those without: 23.3 per cent
- Black and other ethnic minority groups: 18.6 per cent
- Adults of white origin: 21.2 per cent
- Black Caribbeans who regularly participate: 17.5 per cent
- Asians: 17 per cent
- Lowest socio-economic groups: 16.3 per cent
- Highest socio-economic group: 25.1 per cent.

The continued lower participation rates for women, the elderly, ethnic minorities, people with a disability and the lower social classes brings into focus the gaps between policy and practice. The Department for Culture, Media and Sport (DCMS) clearly states that everybody should have the opportunity to participate in sport and physical activity regardless of sex, age, race or disability. The Council of Europe Charter makes an even stronger statement, outlining that 'sport is the inalienable right of every person and should be kept free of any kind of discrimination on the ground of religion, race, sex, politics or social status'. The policy rhetoric advocates sport is for everyone, but the reality is very different. The participation patterns indicate that discrimination is still occurring, and as a result everyone does not have equal access to sporting opportunities.

The evidence of discrimination and subsequent inequality is even stronger when considering who gains employment within the coaching profession. There is a vast amount of research documenting that women are under-represented in coaching roles (Carpenter and Acosta, 2005; West *et al.*, 2001; and Fishwick, 1990). In the UK, the statistics indicate that at all levels of coaching less than 25 per cent of coaches are women (Heuze, 2005). At the élite level, only one coach in ten on the British Olympic team in 1996 was female, and at the 2004 Games in Athens this had reduced even further, as only twelve of the 116 coaches that accompanied the British squad were women (Heuze, 2005).

There is further concern of inequalities in the systems, structures and career pathways offered to coaches across other social groups. For example, there is a growing recognition that the increasing success of Black footballers has not been translated into future employment opportunities in terms of former players progressing through the coaching ranks and becoming football managers.

SEXISM, HOMOPHOBIA AND RACISM IN SPORT

Patterns of inequalities in participation and in employment opportunities are a clear example of how sport is directly influenced by society. Hylton and Bramham (2008) note that where prejudice, discrimination, power differentials and social exclusion prevail in wider society, they will also be manifest in sport. Sport reproduces rather than merely reflects the patterns of inequality in society (Coakley and Pike, 2009); consequently there is much evidence that sport is riddled with sexism, homophobia and racism, and coaches can inadvertently contribute to this discrimination.

One of the clearest examples is the way sport often divides the sexes and perpetuates distorted definitions of masculinity and femininity. Schempp and Oliver (2000, p146) argue that most of the differences between boys and girls' skill performances are attributable to social, not physical differences. They argue that coaches can unconsciously perpetuate myths and use social and cultural differences as reasons for denying access or opportunity. Schempp and Oliver (2000, [p. 147]) also warn that homophobia is rife as often when boys or girls participate outside their gender-labelled activities their sexual orientation is either questioned or assumed.

In a similar vein, Schempp and Oliver (2000, [p. 148]) find that coaches may hold racist beliefs and attitudes that can lead to exaggerated and inaccurate assumptions regarding physical ability and work ethics linked to ethnic groups. These examples clearly indicate that in sport as well as everyday life there are social groups who experience discrimination because of any combination of age, social class, gender, religion, sexuality, disability and ethnicity. For these reasons Hylton and Bramham (2008) argue that it is incumbent on those working in sport to make their practice as equitable as possible.

Figure 29.1   Coaching practice must be equitable. (Courtesy of David Griffiths)

SPORT EQUITY POLICIES AND SPORTS EQUITY ALLIANCE

In recent years, sports organizations in the UK have increasingly been called upon to address equal opportunities issues, and outline the degree to which they have recognized and provided for the needs of individuals in communities (Penney, 2002). The most recent policy document is the Equality Standard: A Framework for Sport (2004), developed by the UK's sport governance bodies with input from Sportscotland, the Sports Council of Wales, the Sport Council for Northern Ireland and Sport England. The work of a coach is highly likely to be governed within this framework, as Shaw (2007) indicates that the Equality Standard is the product of a long-running initiative to professionalize and formalize sports delivery in the UK. Sport England's definition of sports equity crucially draws attention to the need to change the culture and structure of sport:

> Sports equity is about fairness in sport, equality of access recognizing inequalities and taking steps to address them. It is about changing the culture and structure of sport to ensure that it becomes equally accessible to all members of society, whatever their age, ability, gender, race, ethnicity, sexuality or social/economic status. (Sport England, 2004, p. 4)

The standard is a guide towards achieving equality, which is defined as the state of being equal – treating individuals equally, which is not necessarily the same as treating them the same. Shaw (2007) provides an insightful analysis and critique of the Equality Standard. She notes that the standard acknowledges that the need for equality may require unequal effort, and that despite many claims of sport organizations to have 'open door' policies, in practice this is not the case for many minority groups. The major critique offered by Shaw (2007) is to the audit-based nature of the policy, as she argues that increasing numbers does nothing to achieve equity if the structure and culture of sport organizations remain the same. She offers that what is needed is to examine the delivery and structure of sport in a meaningful way that is neither tokenism nor surveillance, and this can only be achieved as the product of long integration and education programmes.

Education programmes for coaches will gain by associating with key organizations striving towards equality in sport. Courses such as Clubmark relay important messages that sports equity is about recognizing and removing barriers faced by people involved in, or wanting to be involved in sport. A positive step forwards in recent years has been the formation of the Sports Equity Alliance, which acts as one voice on collaborative work on sports equity. These organizations demonstrate that increasing opportunities, promoting awareness, campaigning and influencing policy are all essential elements of changing the culture and structure of sport to achieve equity.

Women's Sports and Fitness Foundation is the UK's lead organization for women and sport. Their key aims are, first, to improve, increase and promote opportunities for women and girls in sport, and, second, to campaign for change at all levels of sport through raising awareness and influencing policy.

Similarly, the organization Sporting Equals works with key national umbrella organizations and sports governing bodies to develop policy and practices to promote racial equality. Their key activities focus on, firstly, administering the Sport for Communities Project, providing grants to increase participation in sport by ethnic minorities, migrants and refugees, and secondly on developing a standard for local authority sport and leisure services, promoting racial equality through sport.

The umbrella body for a number of England's major disability sports organizations is the English Federation of Disability Sport (EFDS). It is the national body responsible for developing sport for disabled people in England.

These organizations demonstrate that coaches are not alone in having a critical role to play in sport development by making sport inclusive. Coaches employed in schools, sport colleges and sport clubs have much to gain in terms of developing pathways in participation and élite pathways that are inclusive in practice as well as policy. The following section addresses key issues facing sport practitioners striving to achieve sports equity, and then offers a vision of inclusive coaching.

A VISION FOR INCLUSIVE COACHING

Coaches being willing to question taken-for-granted assumptions is one of the most effective weapons in the battle against inequalities in sport. Self-reflection is a central aspect of the coaching role. In this context, coaches who are critically reflective of the community in which they operate, so they can recognize inequalities and be willing to take steps to address them, will make progress towards enabling the full involvement of disadvantaged groups in every aspect of sport. There is no 'quick fix' solution. The challenge is for the coaching profession to consider new strategies for learning and to re-evaluate approaches to coaching practice. This will require coaches to acquire and take seriously an awareness of the effects of gender, race, disability and other distinctive social characteristics on coaching. Coaches must be prepared to confront existing prejudices and myths concerning who participates in sport, and to reflect on whose participation is valued.

The next step is to acknowledge how unjust social practices can result if sport coaches unwittingly discriminate against certain groups by stereotyping and labelling certain social groups. The key here is the notion of difference. Recognition and appreciation of the many dimensions to 'difference' between individuals is key to avoiding simplistic categorizations of 'all women', for example, that can lead to damaging stereotypical images. There is a need to move towards understanding the complexities of difference, and in particular the diversities within identified groups. The provision of coaching courses with the caveat 'everyone welcome' does not ensure that all potential participants will be able to access the activities on offer. To be inclusive, coaching practice needs to consider the different needs and interests of various groups. For example, research demonstrates that some women feel more comfortable in single sex contexts and are much more likely to participate when women-only sessions are provided on this basis (Penney, 2002).

As well as considering the type of coaching courses to provide, much thought also needs to be given as to how to publicize the courses. Key factors to consider include how to contact hard-to-reach groups, where the courses are being advertised, who is likely to see the publicity and, more importantly, who is unlikely to see the advert and will therefore be excluded. If the publicity is only written in English, this excludes some ethnic minorities. Contacting outreach organizations can be beneficial in terms of engaging minority groups. There are even potential shortcomings of well intentioned developments such as including disabled athletes in showcase events, but then not providing any subsequent opportunities for disabled athletes to participate in future sessions.

In general, publicity and subsequent provision of coaching sessions tend to reach only those who play sport. This maintains the status quo, but does little to encourage change and attract those who traditionally have not been welcomed into the sporting arena. Achieving equitable practice is complex, and Bagilhole (1997) outlines three dimensions of equality that are highly relevant to coaching practice:

- Equality of opportunity – there is recognition here that all social groups need equal access to facilities and services
- Equality of condition – here it is acknowledged that even when access is open there may be material and cultural disparities that need to be considered. These may revolve around travel, cost, religion, physical access, timing and environment

- Equality of outcome – here the impact of historical disadvantage is considered. Action is taken to privilege marginalized groups; this is sometimes referred to as positive action.

Frequently sport providers focus on the more obvious issues of cost of participation, transport to facilities, and timing of sessions. These issues need to be considered, but there are also much more subtle and just as powerful dynamics that must be addressed, such as the use of inclusive language. This includes avoidance of gendered terms and phrases such as 'man of the match' (most valuable player), 'man to man' (one to one), and 'linesman' (referee's assistant). Characteristics associated with potential participants also form barriers. For example, many sports are traditionally dominated by males, and are often off-putting for many females. Coaches can unknowingly contribute to perpetuating this image by making overt comments such as 'Don't throw like a girl'. There is literature available to help coaches develop gender-inclusive strategies: the following guidelines are provided by Linnes and Stidder (2003):

- In mixed-sex coaching sessions be sensitive when asking boys and girls to demonstrate
- Involve boys and girls equally in principal roles
- Give equal amounts of time and attention to boys and girls
- Do not allow boys to dominate
- Challenge forms of discriminatory behaviour, such as ridicule and harassment
- Do not prioritize boys for the best training and match times
- Encourage more appointments of women at élite levels
- Encourage more appointments of female coaches of all-boys teams
- Provide coaching experiences to male and female trainees with respect to same sex, opposite sex, and mixed sex coaching groups
- Display posters of male and female participants in non-stereotypical activities
- Avoid the use of gendered terms or phrases.

A similar level of attention is needed to re-evaluate how traditional approaches to coaching can exclude certain groups based on ability. For example, traditionally even participation coaches have tended to unconsciously cater to the élite end of the spectrum, thereby excluding participants who are not so able. If a participation coach spends most of their sessions paying attention to skill development, this will minimize the opportunities to participate informally, for fun with friends of varied abilities. Structuring these sessions differently will make coaching more accessible to participants of all abilities, and this may also lead to developing opportunities for more integration rather than segregation of disabled participants.

Inclusive strategies must take into account coaching practices, coaching behaviours and language, coaching pathways and structures. Coaches can be proactive and commit to challenge matters such as racism, sexism and homophobia in a sport context. Proactive behaviour can at times feel uncomfortable, yet to do nothing and to remain silent promotes injustice.

For example, during a tournament spectators may shout inappropriate comments from the sideline, so what guidelines are built into a coaching code of conduct to help coaches deal with these situations appropriately? In these situations there is also the added pressure of the coach as a role model, and their silence being seen to endorse inappropriate behaviour. Providing training on how to challenge sexism, racism or homophobia needs to be an integral part of coach education programmes.

ACHIEVING SPORTS EQUITY DEPENDS ON EVERYONE

The main message from this chapter is that achieving sports equity depends on everyone. Key governmental departments and agencies have developed policies and identified specific target groups such as women, young people, disabled people, elderly and ethnic minorities in recognition that different people do not have the same opportunities to participate in sport. For policies to work in practice, sport providers have to respond to different needs and interests of various groups. It is imperative for sport coaches to reflect on what achieving sports equity means in reality, and to ensure their practices are 'inclusive'. Given that everyone holds biases and prejudices, it is unlikely that reading a chapter in a book will overturn ingrained values and beliefs. However, as Schempp and Oliver (2000) note, by learning to identify biases, coaches can deconstruct their foundations, examine potential consequences and find alternatives. In this way, coaching practice can continually strive to become fair and just.

Supporting Coach Development Through Mentoring

by Frederic Pivotti

COACH DEVELOPMENT AND CONTINUAL LEARNING

The development of a coach and expert coaching practice is a continuous process that occurs over a long period of time and passes through several stages of development.

Stages of Coach Development

There are several models available from research, which describe and explain the developmental stages that coaches pass through from beginner to expert. Each stage represents a specific level of development, and can be described according to the coach's behaviour that typically occurs at that level:

Stage 1: The Beginner Coach
- Learns the rules and tries to manage the job
- Participants are busy, happy and good (but are not necessarily learning)
- Establishes overall routines so as not to get lost in everyday practice
- Lacks a sense of control and responsibility over the effect of own behaviour (external attribution: blames the participants and other external factors)
- Practice and experience is the best teacher (use of coaching cycle; observe/learn from others).

Stage 2: The Competent Coach
- Becomes more task- and learner-centred
- Sees and connects similarities and principles; transfer of learning
- Develops strategic knowledge to ignore/bend the rules of the job and adapt to the situation

- Experiments with different decisions and their effect
- Is guided by goals and long-term plans
- Contingency planning: plan B, C, D and so on.

Stage 3: The Proficient Coach
- Develops a feel for subtleties in the learning environment that have a crucial effect on events taking place (recognizes when something is not working, recognizes opportunities)
- Addresses the cause rather than the symptoms
- Extends beyond the technical/mechanical to the psychological/pedagogical
- Adapts, rather than making the participants/athletes adapt
- Has a stronger sense of personal responsibility towards the failure/success of participants/athletes
- Can predict outcomes
- Learns more from sources outside the sport/discipline.

Stage 4: The Expert Coach
- Has an extensive integrated knowledge (from multi-discipline sources)
- Uses intuition and intuitive decision making based on situational factors
- Uses an extensive, detailed planning process
- Behaves automatically (applies effective coaching skills without thinking)
- Attends to the atypical and individual
- Has problem-solving strategies
- Is self-monitoring.

Research has identified that it takes at least ten years to become an expert in anything, whether it is as an athlete, a musician or a coach. Hence, any long-term coach development model that tries to describe and explain the development of a coach will have to take into consideration the ten-year period it will take to evolve from beginner to expert, with each phase taking approximately two to three years to complete.

Long-Term Coach Development Models

There are several models available that describe or explain long-term coach development. The following model describes the development of the coach from the stage when he/she was a participant or athlete.

Athlete/Participant Phase
The development of a coach starts from the time he/she was involved in (the) sport as an athlete or participant. The different coaching environments, and also the relationships with, and examples set by the coaches encountered during active participation in the sport, will shape the early views and intrinsic beliefs of a coach very early on in the initial stages of development. These initial views and beliefs will become very intrinsic and will

require a great deal of challenging in further coach development activities. The better the experience and examples received from coaches and coach environments as a participant/athlete, the better the quality of the initial coach development period will be.

Coach Education Phase

The coach education phase is the period in coach development when coaches are enrolled in a formal coach education programme consisting of formal courses that lead to formal qualifications. The coach education phase can partly overlap with the participant/athlete phase if beginner coaches start going through their first qualification level(s) when they are still actively involved as participants/athletes. This can have a positive impact on early established beliefs. This phase can also partly overlap with the coach experience phase, allowing coaches to gain relevant experience in between qualification levels.

Coach Experience Phase

In the experience phase, coaches take up coaching practice within a specific context and learn to apply knowledge and skills in real coaching situations. This experience will allow the coach to continue to develop and establish solid coaching routines and effective coaching behaviour. It is in this phase that mentoring and continuous professional development occur.

Coach Support/Development Phase

Finally, a coach can continue to develop by taking on responsibility for a team of coaches, becoming a supporter for other coaches, and functioning as a mentor, a coach educator and a motivator. In this way he/she contributes towards the development of other coaches, and shares with them their knowledge, skills and experience.

A different way of looking at the long-term development of coaches is to consider their evolution in the concerns they have with regard to themselves as coaches (self), what they coach (task), and who they are coaching (learners). Research suggests that the concern for the learner only appears later in the development process.

Beginner coaches tend to be concerned with their own self: they want to do well, be liked by the others, and be accepted as a coach. They are initially less concerned with the tasks or the learners. The beginner coach is very self-centred.

Gradually, concerns will evolve and the learning tasks will become more and more a concern Is what we are trying to get across technically correct? Is this the best possible drill? The evolving coach becomes more task-centred.

Eventually the focus of concern will shift further and start including the learners. Are they actually learning? Are the approach and the learning task design suitable for their needs and stage of learning? The developing coach becomes learner-centred.

The Coach Education Process

Coach education programmes are designed to take novice coaches through a number of qualification levels in order to develop their coaching expertise, and should be aligned with the stages of coach development. They should gradually integrate the what, the how and the why of coaching, and allow coaches to practise and gain experience. Eventually there will be a formal assessment to see if the coaches meet a certain level of competence against criteria linked to the level of qualification. The UK Coaching Certificate has introduced four levels of qualification, each of them roughly linked to a stage of coach development:

Level 1   Assistant coach
Level 2   Independent coach
Level 3   Advanced coach
Level 4   Expert/master coach.

Any coach education course runs more or less along the following lines:

- **Information:** promotion of the course offered to target group, clarifying prerequisites, course aims and learning outcomes, course process and potential areas of employment
- **Enrolment:** checking prerequisites (age, previous qualification, fees), confirmation of enrolment, allocation of pre-course tasks, distribution of resource packs
- **Course:** contact days with a trained tutor, and preparatory homework tasks in between course days
- **Post course guided learning:** period of mentored learning under the wings of an already qualified, experienced coach or a trained mentor to enhance further development in preparation of the assessment
- **Assessment:** formal assessment of coaching competence against set criteria by a trained and qualified assessor
- **Certification:** formal notification that all the qualification requirements have been met, and official awarding of the qualification by the awarding body.

Continuous Professional Development (CPD)

The formal coach education process of taking coaches through different levels of qualification is but one area in the long-term development process of coaches. In between qualification levels, and after reaching the highest qualification level, there is a need for continuous professional development (CPD). The aim of CPD is to recap and further extend the knowledge, skills and experiences gained at a certain level of qualification. CPD should be tailored to the development needs of the coaches and should take into account the specific context in which daily coaching practice occurs. CPD can consist of attending generic coaching workshops, sport specific technical/methodological workshops, coaching and sport science conferences, consultation of resources such as books, articles, websites, discussion groups, and so on. There should be a system in place to record the CPD that coaches are attending via a CPD portfolio and an IT-based tracking system.

Knowledge, Skills and Context Learning

Coaching expertise is a combination of knowledge (things you know), skills (things you are able to do) and context (experience with the specific environment in which coaching practice occurs). Coach development will accordingly focus on activities that allow the acquisition of more background knowledge and deeper understanding (theory), practical training to further develop the required skills in order to develop effective coaching behaviour (skills), and in-service training to familiarize coaches with the specific context in which they operate (context learning). Knowledge, skills and context will expand increasingly and become more and more integrated as a higher level of coaching expertise is reached.

In addition, knowledge, skills and context can be tailored towards the specific role the coach will fulfil within the participant pathway: either introducing novice participants into the sport and coaching the foundations of the sport (foundation pathway coach); coaching participants that engage in the sport in a recreational capacity with a life-time perspective towards enjoyment, social contacts and health reasons (participation pathway coach for specific age groups from children to adults); or coaching participants who engage in competitive sport at a lower or higher performance level (competition and high-performance pathway coach). The differentiation into more specific coaching roles linked to a variety of participation pathways has recently been introduced in the coach education structures as part of the UK Coaching Framework, and will result in more articulate pathways for coach development, coach education and CPD, known as the 4 by 4 model.

Figure 30.1   Context learning is critical in developing coach expertise. (Courtesy of Team Northumbria)

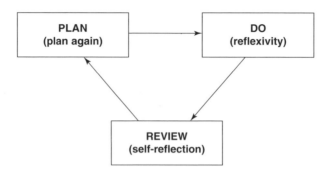

Figure 30.2 The reflective coaching cycle with 'plan – do – review', an indication of reflexivity and self-reflection as part of the process.

Coach Reflexivity and Self-Reflection

The long-term development of a coach does not only occur through the intervention of other people during the formal coach education process or CPD. Coaching is an activity consisting of preparation, delivery and evaluation in a cyclic process called the coaching cycle, and every coach can play a pivotal role in their own development through the application of reflective practice. There are two types of reflective practice, depending on where they occur in the coaching cycle: coach reflexivity occurs during delivery of the prepared activity, while self-reflection occurs after delivery in order to feed into the preparation of the next delivery.

Reflexivity Strategies

Following planning and preparation, coaches are required to reflect 'on their feet' while delivering their session in order to steer the session alongside the prepared plan, or to decide to change from the original plan in order to accommodate variables that occur during the session roll-out. This process is called reflexivity. For the coach, it all comes down to the ability to constantly observe and monitor what is going on, evaluate that against planned session aims and outcomes, anticipate the impact of learning activities, and make decisions with regard to the next steps, time management and the focus of the learning activities.

Self-Reflection Strategies

Following the delivery of a session, coaches are expected to evaluate and review their session. This is called self-reflection, and there are different ways of doing this. Coaches can use a column or box on their session plan to make notes against the initial preparation, the actual session roll-out and the session goals. Alternatively, they could use a specific self-reflection form containing a selection of items (technical, organizational, learning, how to coach) depending on the development action plan of the coach. The results of the self-reflection process should inform the preparation of the following sessions. It is important that self-reflection is recorded via a portfolio or a reflective journal that can be reviewed from time to time.

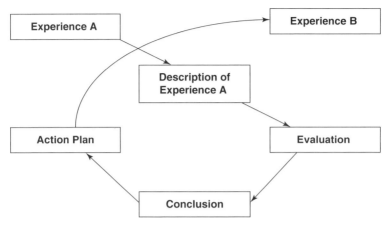

Figure 30.3   The reflective cycle. (Courtesy of The National Coaching Foundations)

Learning to Learn Strategies

Coach education programmes often have a limited effect on the coaching behaviour of coaches because they were traditionally focused on extending knowledge and passing on information without linking it to changed coaching behaviour. One of the aims of the UK Coaching Certificate is actually making sure coach education programmes result in a behavioural change of coaches. Hence, coach education programmes will increasingly incorporate elements of reflective practice and the development of reflective skills as part of the course process, course learning aims and assessment criteria. The development of reflective practice is one way for coaches to develop 'learning to learn' skills, and for coaches to take a greater responsibility towards their own learning in order to make permanent changes in their coaching behaviour.

Reflective practice goes back to the ability to analyse a problem, decide on what information is needed in order to resolve it, and then have the skill to gather the information, structure it in a way that it can be applied to the problem, apply it and finally evaluate the effectiveness of the solution. Reflective skills/practice and learning to learn strategies are not exclusively aimed at coaches, they are important to any person in a learning situation thus are also applicable to athletes and participants in sport. The overall process of self-reflection can be described as a loop.

THE ROLE OF MENTORING AND MENTORS

The name 'mentor' goes back to the time of the ancient Greeks. Mentor was an old friend of Odysseus. To him Odysseus entrusted his household when he joined the coalition that sailed against Troy. Athena, the Goddess of Wisdom, assuming several times the shape of Mentor, became the guide of Odysseus' son Telemachus, giving him prudent counsel. Since then, wise and trusted advisers have been called 'mentors'.

What is Mentoring?

Mentoring is a process during which learning (change in coaching behaviour) would be expected to take place, which would in some way be initiated or triggered by a mentor and would ultimately enhance the person's ability to function as a coach as a result of that process. The mentee usually has the following expectations toward the mentoring process:

- Acquire new knowledge and information
- Receive feedback on their coaching performance
- Be offered advice, guidance or ideas
- Be provided with support in their development as coaches
- Establish changed coaching behaviour (be a better, more effective coach).

In order to achieve this, there should be a knowledge/experience differential between mentor and mentee. In addition to this, mentors should be trained in order to effectively facilitate, support and manage behavioural change in coaches. Hence, effective mentoring programmes should have an element of mentor training that will help establish clear goals and outcomes for the mentee.

The Mentoring Process

The mentoring process between mentor and mentee will roll itself out alongside the long-term development stages that coaches go through. Mentoring usually takes place in a post-course period. Ideally, the mentoring process should be integrated in the coach education process and should run alongside course dates and the post-course learning process leading up to the assessment. In addition, the mentoring process can extend beyond the point of gaining qualification and become part of the ongoing development process and CPD in between qualification levels.

The nature of the mentoring process will change with the stages of coach development. The prior focus for gain will be on the enhancement of knowledge. Reflective practice leading to changes in coaching behaviour will occur further in the mentoring process and will become an increasing focus as the level of coaching expertise increases. There will also be a shift in the content of knowledge as the coach progresses through the stages of coach development. Less experienced coaches see the acquisition of technical and sport-specific knowledge to be the main priority, whilst established coaches see the focus as more on the generic aspects of coaching and more advanced sports science knowledge. With regard to gaining feedback on their coaching behaviour, there will be an evolution as to how mentees want the feedback to be presented. Less experienced coaches will place emphasis on direct feedback as a means to get answers to their questions and solutions to problems, where more established coaches will put more emphasis on the need for support and will see themselves more as active engagers rather than passive recipients.

Mentees should be guided by their mentor towards finding answers for themselves, rather than simply being told what to do. They should be made to think about it, and be assisted in working it out for themselves. Mentors have a guiding role, but initially there will be a need from the mentee for more formal instruction. From there, the mentor support should evolve towards more active guidance. More established coaches will find it beneficial to go outside their discipline or sport for mentoring, and can receive support from more than one mentor.

Role of the Mentor

The main role of the mentor is to support the mentee in becoming more and more self-reflective, that way taking in hand their own learning and development that results in changed coaching behaviour. The role of the mentor will change depending on the stage of learning of the mentee: see boxed text.

The role of the mentor will also change during the different steps in self-reflection:

- During coaching activity: objective observer/listener
- During evaluation: objective listener/probing
- During analysis: challenging
- During conclusion: clarifying/source of knowledge/objective feedback
- During planning: adviser/building confidence.

STAGE OF LEARNING	MENTOR ROLE
Modelling stage, in which the mentees are developing an idea of the perfect model that reflects best practice as a reference for own practice	Mentor provides a perfect model and is being observed by the mentee
Competency stage, in which the mentees extend levels of competence by gaining more and more experience through practice	The mentor 'coaches' the mentee and offers support to gain more experience and become more competent
Reflection stage, in which the mentees becomes increasingly involved in self-reflection on their own coaching practice	The mentor becomes more a facilitator supporting the mentee through the self-reflection process, challenging the mentee with questions
Autonomy stage, in which the mentees becomes increasingly autonomous in shaping their own development	The mentor becomes a partner and co-enquirer. They collaborate as colleagues and stimulate each other in their learning and development

Mentoring Skills and Qualities

Based on the different aspects of their role, mentors will need to acquire certain skills in order to help facilitate the learning of the mentee. Those skills will include effective communication skills (observation skills, active listening, questioning skills, the ability to build rapport and give feedback) and learning facilitation skills (planning learning aims and tasks, analysing learning styles, questioning).

On top of those skills, there are also a number of qualities mentors should have in order to be effective. Mentors should have empathy, patience, objectivity, time, knowledge, experience, credibility, flexibility, the ability to challenge and a good sense of humour.

Mentor/Mentee – Interaction

Learning and behavioural change can only occur in a relation of thrust and respect between mentor and mentee. Hence, mentees should have an input in the selection of their mentor, and the relationship between mentor and mentee should be a positive one, however, also one where critical dialogue is possible on the frontiers of the comfort zone of the mentee, without resulting in too much pressure or conflict. The relationship should remain protected from barriers such as distrust, suspicion, fear of criticism, complacency and fear of rejection or unbalanced ownership. The mentor-mentee relationship should be part of an evaluation process: the mentee should be able to give feedback to the mentor, and the mentor should be able to learn something from the mentee as well.

Mentoring in Practice

Mentoring practices in the field can vary from very informal to very formal. Formal and informal mentoring practices occur throughout all levels of participation, from grass roots up to excellence.

Mentoring at Grass Roots Level

Coaching programmes that run at local level within a community context of clubs, schools, leisure centres or local authorities usually involve (young) volunteers, teachers or parents who help out with sports delivery at introductory or recreational level. Those volunteers sometimes have access to more informal coach education workshops where they become familiar with the basics of sports delivery and then support coaching under (direct) supervision of experienced, officially qualified coaches who offer them guidance and help them gain a more structured experience base as beginner coaches. This type of mentoring practice is usually informal in nature.

When new coaches enter the first ladder of the coach education programme, the course process usually contains a formal or informal element of mentoring outside the course contact hours. In some cases there is a structured logbook with tasks to complete, or the coach is asked to keep a personal log of their mentoring experience. Mentors are usually experienced, more highly qualified coaches; however, there is an increasing demand that mentors should undergo some sort of mentoring training when they formally take up a role as a mentor.

Figure 30.4   Young volunteers benefit from informal coach mentoring in the local author-ity. (Courtesy of Team Northumbria)

Mentoring at grass roots level usually occurs within the context of the club, school or leisure centre of the local authority, where the higher qualified coaches take care of the lower qualified and beginner coaches. Local delivery hubs have the opportunity to recognize mentoring more formally as an essential component to enhance the development and delivery quality of their workforce if they decide to recognize the role of mentors and allocate resources to support mentoring activities.

Mentoring at Performance Level
Competitively orientated coaching programmes that run in sports clubs usually involve a higher level of qualification from both mentors and mentees, which might not be available in the clubs at that point in time. Coaches will have to go outside their own club environment to be able to work with a more experienced coach or mentor in a different club. In some instances, governing bodies provide a mentoring scheme across clubs linked to their performance coaching structure. Mentoring activities are built into regional training days or weekends where experienced coaches are linked up with less experienced coaches as mentors, that way integrating mentoring practice into coaching practice to provide a plat-form for continuous professional development for coaches. Again, some sort of recording of aims, activities, outcomes and action plans will be required in a formal (structured logbook) or informal (personal journal, portfolio) way.

Most coach education programmes at performance level have a built-in formal mentoring period as part of the preparation towards the assess-ment that allow coaches to develop over a longer period of time outside the course days. It is of benefit to the mentees if coaches that function as mentors have gone through a formal mentoring training that allow them to separate their mentoring role from their coaching role. More and more governing bodies are designing and putting in place mentoring workshops, training programmes and qualifications to support the development of mentoring within their sport.

Mentoring at Excellence Level

At the highest performance level, mentoring practices usually contain an element of cross-sport scope, a sports science focus and an individualized 'one-to-one' approach. Coaches collaborate with peers who work at a comparable performance level in a different sport. Mentors (usually professionally trained via some sort of mentoring qualification) are brought in from outside the sport. External agencies responsible for high performance programme development and support sometimes offer mentoring support as part of their service package. The Sportscoach UK has piloted one-on-one mentoring programmes that are based on 360 degree performance management tools as applied in professional settings outside sport and aspects of life-style analysis taken from personal counselling practices.

Mentoring practices at grass roots, performance and excellence level have only recently started to develop in a more structured way, and will no doubt continue to do so in the future.

The Coaching Profession and Career Pathways

by Frederic Pivotti

The professionalization of sport coaching first of all impacts on the professional standards upheld within sport coaching itself. In addition, there is an evolution towards coaching as a route for professional employment. In 2006, the British government launched a policy plan called the UK Coaching Framework to actively move sport coaching towards a professional regulated vocation.

THE UK COACHING FRAMEWORK (UKCF)

Government policy makers have come to realize that coaching is the central factor to develop, sustain and increase participation in sport. Quality coaching leads to better performances and increased success in sport; it also supports key social, economic and health objectives. Good coaches help to improve technical, tactical, physical, mental and lifestyle skills, contributing to personal and social development across all levels of society. In order to increase the quality of coaching, the UK Coaching Framework was developed as a framework to install integrated coaching systems across sport. The UKCF is a reference point for developing coaching in the UK with the intention to be world leading by 2016.

The framework ensures both the development and the delivery of the coaching system, taking into account policies, strategies and priorities of devolved administrations and Home Country Sports Councils. The governing bodies play a lead role in the sport-specific delivery within the context of their relationships with Home Country Sports Councils and UK Sport. Sportscoach UK leads on the development of the coaching system while being overseen by a UK Coaching Strategy Group. All organizations involved in both the development and delivery of coaching in the UK have been asked to sign up to the UKCF and to use it as a reference point to align their efforts and resources to the objectives outlined in it.

Central to the effective UK Coaching system are the coaches in person. Their dedication, enthusiasm, expertise and experience are strongly valued qualities that need to be promoted, supported and valued. There is a need to further enhance the quality and quantity of coaching available to participants and performers, and to put in place clear, viable career structures for coaches. To support this, the creation of an effective, professionally regulated vocation for coaching that recognizes the needs of volunteers and part/full-time paid coaches is an essential step forwards to developing coaching as a profession. The process will take account of different contexts within governing bodies and home nations.

In 2008, Sportscoach UK published a UK Coaching Framework vision document that describes a three-seven-eleven year action plan for the development of coaching in the UK. The document describes the vision of the UKCF '... to create a cohesive, ethical, inclusive and valued coaching system where skilled coaches support all participants in sport at each stage of their development in sport' (Smith, 2008, p.11). The UKCF action plan consists of three phases:

2006–2008   Building the foundations – three years
2006–2012   Delivering the goals – seven years
2006–2016   Transforming the system – eleven years.

The UKCF action plan consists of five strategic action areas supported by twelve specific actions.

Strategic Action Area 1: The UK Coaching System

Specific Action 1: The UK coaching model: develop an inclusive model for coaching that provides clear direction and a strategic framework for coaching policy and practice in the UK. It integrates the long-term participant development models with long-term coach development models, CPD, licensing and support and management systems for coaching and coaches. (Smith, 2008, p. 47)

Specific Action 2: Participant pathways: set out and implement a clear, comprehensive and inclusive model for the long-term development of sport participants across the UK. This should be based on sound understanding of long-term participant development, participant skills/capabilities, and the participation contexts and pathways and their implication on coaching practice. (Smith, 2008, p. 48)

Specific Action 3: Coach pathways: set out and implement clear, comprehensive and inclusive models for the long-term development of coaches across the UK. This implements servicing the needs of coaches against the background of the long-term development strategies, maximizes the impact of coaches, and clarifies coaching contexts, roles and pathways. (Smith, 2008, p. 49)

Specific Action 4: Coaching strategies: set out and implement inclusive sport-specific coaching strategies at UK, national, regional and local levels, linked to long-term participant and coach development models, strategic and operational delivery plans, system delivery and capacity, alignment of goals and structures, and develop skills set of key management personnel at the various levels. (Smith, 2008, p. 50)

Strategic Action Area 2: Front Line Coaching

Specific Action 5: Active, skilled and qualified coaches: recruit and retain qualified coaches with the skills to coach inclusively at each phase of the participant pathway. The workforce should have role descriptions and employment/deployment systems, clear and viable pathways and recognition, reward and valuing. (Smith, 2008, p. 51)

Specific Action 6: Coaching in education: maximising the role of coaching in the education sector, complementing the expertise of PE teachers and other professionals within the education sector via primary/secondary schools, HE, FE and school networks, employment and deployment of coaches. (Smith, 2008, p.53)

Strategic Action Area 3: Support for Coaches

Specific Action 7: Coaching support and system delivery: establish accessible and effective education, delivery systems and resources to underpin the long-term development of coaches and the coach education workforce in the context of the UK Coaching Certificate and effective CPD programmes. This should be linked to governing body networks and partnerships, web-based support, learning resources, direct delivery, CPD opportunities, media campaigns, license and registration, coaching bursaries, forums and networks, and mentoring systems. (Smith, 2008, p. 55)

Specific Action 8: Targeted development of coaches: establish appropriate systems to identify, train, qualify and support quality coaches for specific sport populations. This should commence with coaches of high-performance athletes, talent-ID athletes, children and coaches of disabled people. (Smith, 2008, p. 58)

Specific Action 9: Coaching qualifications and Continued Professional Development (CPD): develop coaching qualifications, CPD and specialist qualifications linked to the pathway phase/target group/disability. Commence with inclusive coaching of primary-aged children. (Smith, 2008, p. 59)

Strategic Action Area 4: A Professionally Regulated Vocation

Specific Action 10: Licensing and registration: set out and implement the steps needed to establish coaching as a professionally regulated vocation recognizing volunteer and part/full-time roles. These steps should include agreed quality standards, reflect the need of coaches, and be underpinned by a licence system and a CPD system. (Smith, 2008, p. 60)

Specific Action 11: Profile and recognition of coaching: conduct a sustained, long-term campaign to raise the profile and recognition of coaching at all stages via coaching scholarships and support systems. (Smith, 2008, p. 62)

Strategic Action Area 5: Research and Development

Specific Action 12: Research and development: implement an ongoing research and development programme into participant and coach pathways, coaching quality and expertise and coaching interventions, programmes and resources in sport and disability sport in line with UKCF priorities, and in strong collaboration with NGBs, HE sector and other relevant agencies. (Smith, 2008, p. 63)
Perceived outcomes of the UKCF are to:

- Enhance the quality of coaching at all stages
- Provide active skilled and qualified coaches to meet demand.

This will lead to sustained and increased participation, and improved performances in sport, underpinned by clear career structures for coaches within a professional regulated vocation.

The four key pillars for building the coaching system and underpinning the UKCF are as follows:

- Capacity for the deployment and employment of coaches
- Capacity of governing bodies of sport and other relevant organizations to design, deliver and quality assure inclusive coaching and coach education systems on a local, regional, national and UK-wide basis
- Education and CPD for coaches
- Capacity and alignment of funding, policy and other complementary support agencies.

COACHING AS A PROFESSION

Developing coaching as a profession is a process that aims to establish a professional structure for coaching very similar to the one developed in other regulated professions and similar industries.

For coaching, whether in a participation or a performance context, to become a regulated profession, the industry of sport needs to develop clear skill profiles that are incorporated within industry-specific qualifications, and are linked to minimal operating standards, licence to practise, and quality assurance arrangements.

Licence to Practise

Licences are used to uphold a certain level of quality towards people practising a specific profession. Licences are not permanent and are only valid for a limited period of time during which the licence holder is considered to be fully competent and to meet all the necessary requirements in order to do a certain job. Licences allow an industry to add additional requirements towards people practising the profession and to guarantee they continuously upskill themselves in order to be up to date with the latest standards of best practice within the industry.

Some sports already have a licence system, others do not, but it is one of the aims of the UKCF to establish (the principles of) a licensing and registration scheme across the sports coaching industry in the UK. Existing licences vary, and usually consist of one or more of the following aspects:

- Recent, up-to-date coaching qualification at the appropriate level for the job
- Membership to the governing body or a professional body that regulates the sport context
- Insurance
- Criminal Records Bureau (CRB) check
- Safeguarding and Protecting Children and Health and Safety training
- First aid
- Minimal CPD requirements and updating.

Licences are registered by a central administration (usually the governing body or the professional agency regulating the sport) which keeps all the information relevant to the licence of a coach in a database system. Where a coach qualification is obtained for ever and in principle cannot be taken away, a licence is a temporary pass for qualified people to practise as a coach as long as they meet a minimum set of additional requirements. The combination of licence requirements has to guarantee that the minimal operating standards (MOS) for a given profession in a given industry are upheld during practice.

Minimal Operating Standards (MOS)

Minimal Operating Standards describe the standards to which coaching practice needs to adhere, in order to be considered good practice. Any coaching behaviour below that standard will be considered poor practice and will not be allowed to continue to occur. Minimal Operating Standards are a shared set of criteria within the industry and the professions, and are linked to a list of applications:

- Qualification learning aims and assessment criteria
- CPD and updating requirements
- Competency descriptors and job applications
- Job evaluations and employee development action plans
- Mentoring programmes.

MOS are part of the quality assurance system for the industry. They allow for people practising the profession to be measured against a set of objective criteria in order to determine the quality level of their practice as good or poor, and to make interventions where needed. MOS are not static: they evolve over time with the sector. Every now and then they are reviewed, re-discussed and adapted, that way driving forwards the concepts of good practice within the industry and profession.

For an overview of the National Occupational Standards for Sports Coaching (proposal September 2009), see the boxed text.

Overview of the National Occupational Standards for Sports Coaching (proposal September 2009)

Level 1

Standard 1.1	Help to plan and prepare a session
Standard 1.2	Help to provide equipment for activities
Standard 1.3	Help to give good levels of service to participants and customers
Standard 1.4	Help to deal with accidents and emergencies
Standard 1.5	Lead an activity within a session

Level 2

Standard 2.1	Plan a series of coaching sessions
Standard 2.2	Prepare the coaching environment
Standard 2.3	Deliver a series of coaching sessions
Standard 2.4	Monitor and evaluate coaching sessions
Standard 2.5	Deal with accidents and emergencies

Level 3

Standard 3.1	Analyse participants' current and potential performance needs and aspirations
Standard 3.2	Plan annual coaching programmes
Standard 3.3	Manage safe and effective coaching programmes
Standard 3.4	Manage the delivery of effective coaching programmes
Standard 3.5	Develop participant performance through effective coaching
Standard 3.6	Monitor and evaluate effective coaching programmes
Standard 3.7	Manage and develop coaching practice

Each of the three levels also has a set of knowledge and understanding specifications which outline the background that coaches should have at the various operational levels.

Quality Assurance

The aim of developing a professional regulated vocation for coaching is to increase and assure standards of quality within the profession in order for coaches to do the best job possible. This goes back to the vision of the UKCF as described by Smith (2008, p. 11):

> (To) create a cohesive, ethical, inclusive and valued coaching system where skilled coaches support children, players and athletes at all stages of their development in sport, and to guarantee the best possible coach for each participant at every stage of the participation pathway.

The quality of coaching and coaches can be measured in very different ways, both direct and indirect. Traditionally, the quality of coaching programmes has been measured indirectly using quantitative methods such as increase in participation numbers, lower drop-out rates, number of performers within certain levels of performance, ranking and number of bronze, silver and gold medals. Indirect measurement of quality is far easier than directly measuring quality; however, quality assurance has started to emerge on the sport field over the last decade. Several sports have started to develop quality labels for sports clubs, and have introduced customer satisfaction questionnaires as part of marketing reviews, all trying to provide information about the quality of coaching delivery in a more direct way. Quality research within the sports industry is still in full development, and is slowly starting to incorporate aspects of coaching quality in the equation. This tendency is very likely to continue to develop in the future for the different roles, pathways and careers in coaching.

CAREER OPPORTUNITIES AND PATHWAYS

Coaching as a vocational profession refers to coaches being involved in the practical delivery of coaching sessions linked to various participation pathways within the context of employment. However, in a wider sense, additional career opportunities revolving around the emergence of coaching posts have come to exist.

There are various organizations that have started to employ coaches to deliver coaching sessions to participants on a professional basis. Posts could be linked to sports clubs, schools, leisure centres, local authorities and private companies. Coaching jobs either link to introducing participants in grass roots activities within a local community context on a regular basis, or as part of a periodic series of sessions, or a holiday sports camp. There is an increasing opportunity for coaches to achieve employment within competitive sports clubs to develop young and/or adult athletes on a regular basis. Collaboration between local and national governments also results in employment opportunities for community sport coaches who can be allocated to a diversity of coaching programmes depending on detected needs. National governing bodies also recruit coaches to deliver coaching to national teams and squads within the context of excellence programmes. It is anticipated that the number of coaches in professional employment will continue to increase in the future.

In addition to coaches being employed to deliver coaching sessions, there is a network of jobs emerging to support the development of coaching and to offer support to coaches. These jobs sit within the various providers of coaching opportunities: local authorities, leisure centres, educational sectors and governing bodies. They all employ coaching development officers, coach education co-ordinators, coach managers or coach educators in one or other capacity. More and more institutes of higher and further education are venturing into this emerging field of employment, and offering students programmes in the area of sports development, sports management and leisure facility management as an offshoot from the traditional physical education qualifications.

It is anticipated that the number of qualifications, career opportunities and pathways within sport will continue to develop and diversify over time.

References

CHAPTER 1

Abraham, A. and Collins, D., 'Examining and extending research in coach development' *Quest* (Volume 50, 1998, pp. 59–79).

Allen, J. B. and Howe, B., 'Player ability, coach feedback and female adolescent athletes' perceived competence and satisfaction' *Journal of Sport and Exercise Psychology* (Volume 20, 1998, pp. 280–299).

Arai, S. M., 'Empowerment: from the theoretical to the personal' *Journal of Leisurability* (Volume 24 (1) 1997, pp. 3–11).

Becker A. J. and Wrisberg, C. A., 'Effective coaching in action: observations of legendary collegiate basketball coach Pat Summitt' *The Sport Psychologist*, (Volume 22, 2008, pp. 197–211).

Boardley, I. D., Kavussanu, M., and Ring, C., 'Athletes' Perceptions of Coaching effectiveness and Athlete-Related Outcomes in Rugby Union: An investigation Based on the Coaching Efficacy Model' *The Sport Psychologist*, (Volume 22, 2008, pp. 269–287).

Bowes, I. and Jones, R. L., 'Working at the Edge of Chaos: Understanding Coaching as a Complex, Interpersonal System' *The Sport Psychologist*, (Volume 20, 2006, pp. 235–245).

Claxton, D. B., 'A systematic observation of more or less successful high school tennis coaches' *Journal of Teaching in Physical Education* (Volume 7, 1988, pp. 302–310).

Cote, J., Yardley, J., Hay, J., Sedgewick, W. and Baker, J., 'An exploratory examination of the Coaching Behaviour Scale for Sport' *Avante* (Volume 5, 1999, pp. 82–92).

Cross, N. and Ellice, C., 'Coaching effectiveness and the coaching process: Field Hockey revisited' *Scottish Journal of Physical Education* (Volume 25, 1997, pp. 19–33).

Feltz, D. L., Chase, M. A., Moritz, S. E. and Sullivan, P. J., 'A conceptual model of coaching efficacy: preliminary investigation and instrument development' *Journal of Educational Psychology* (Volume 91, 1999, pp. 765–776).

Gallimore, R. and Tharp, R. G., 'What a Coach can Teach a Teacher, 1975–2004: Reflections and Reanalysis of John Wooden's Teaching Practices' *The Sport Psychologist* (Volume 18, 2004, pp. 119–137).

Gilbert, W. and Trudel, P., 'Analysis of coaching science research published from 1970–2001' *Research Quarterly for Exercise and Sport* (Volume 75, 2004, pp. 388–400).

Jackson, B., Knapp, P. and Beauchamp, M. R., 'The Coach-Athlete Relationship: A Tripartite Efficacy Perspective' *The Sport Psychologist* (Volume 23, 2009, pp. 203–232).

Kidman, L., *'Athlete Centred Coaching'* (Innovative Print, NZ, 2005)

Lacy, A. C. and Darst, P. W., 'Evolution of a systematic system: the ASUOI observation instrument' *Journal of Teaching in Physical Education* (Volume 3, 1984, pp. 59–66).

Lent, R. W. and Lopez, F. G., 'Cognitive ties that bind: a tripartite view of efficacy beliefs in growth-promoting relationships' *Journal of Social and Clinical Psychology* (Volume 21, 2002, pp. 256–286).

Lyle, J., *'Sports Coaching Concepts: A framework for coaches' behaviour'* (Routledge, 2002).

Mallet, C. and Cote, J., 'Beyond winning and losing: Guidelines for Evaluating High Performance Coaches' *The Sport Psychologist* (Volume 20, 2006, pp. 213–221).

Markland, R. and Martinek, T. J., 'Descriptive analysis of coach-augmented feedback given to high school varsity female volleyball players' *Journal of Teaching in Physical Education* (Volume 7, 1988, pp. 289–301).

Myers, N. D., Vargas-Tonsing, T. M. and Feltz, D. L., 'Coaching efficacy in inter-collegiate coaches: Sources, coaching behaviour and team variables' *Psychology of Sport and Exercise* (Volume 6, 2005, pp. 129–143).

Smith, R. E., Smoll, F. L. and Hunt, E. B., 'A system for the behavioural assessment of athletic coaches' *Research Quarterly* (Volume 48, 1977, pp. 401–407).

Smoll, F. L. and Smith, R. E., 'Leadership behaviours in sport: A theoretical model and research paradigm' *Journal of Applied Social Psychology* (Volume 19, 1989, pp. 1522–1551).

Smoll, F. L. and Smith, R. E., 'Conducting sport psychology training programmes for coaches: Cognitive-behavioural principles and techniques': in J. Williams (ed.) *Applied sport psychology: Personal growth to peak performance* (4th edition) (Mountain View, USA, 2001).

Tharp, R. G. and Gallimore, R., 'What a coach can teach a teacher' *Psychology Today* (Volume 9, 1976, pp. 75–78).

Weinberg and Gould *Foundations of Sport and Exercise Psychology* (4th edition) (Human Kinetics, USA, 2007).

Williams, J. M., Jerome, G. J., Kenow, L. J. and Rogers, T., 'Factor Structure of the Coach Behaviour Questionnaire and its Relationship to Athlete Variables' *The Sport Psychologist* (Volume 17, 2003, pp. 16–34).

CHAPTER 2

Bandura, A. *Psychological Modelling: Conflicting Theories* (Lieberton, 1974).

Bandura, A., 'Self-Efficacy: Toward a unifying theory of behavioural change' *Psychological Review* (Volume 84, 1977, pp. 191–215).

Barrett, K., 'A hypothetical model of observing as a teaching skill' *Journal of Teaching in Physical Education* (Volume 3, 1983, 1, pp. 23–25).

Lyle, J. *Sports Coaching Concepts: A Framework for Coaches' Behaviour* (Routledge Publishers, 2002).

Martens, R. M., *Successful Coaching 3rd edition* (Human Kinetics Publishers, 2004).

McCullagh, P., Weiss, M. R. and Ross, D., 'Modelling considerations in motor skill acquisition and performance: An integrated approach' In K. Pandolf (ed) *Exercise and Sports Science Reviews* (Volume 17, 1989, pp. 275–513) (Baltimore, Williams and Wilkins).

Rink, J. E., *Teaching Physical Education for Learning* (1993, Mosby).

Weinberg, R. S. and Gould, D., *Foundations of Sport and Exercise Psychology* Leeds (Human Kinetics Publishers, 2003).

CHAPTER 3

Arai, S. M., 'Empowerment: from the theoretical to the personal' *Journal of Leisurability* (Volume 24, 1997, No. 1, pp. 3–11).

Argyris, C., 'Empowerment: the emperor's new clothes. *Harvard Business Review* (Volume May – June, 1998, pp. 98–105).

Bandura, A. *Social Foundations of Thought and Action: A Social Cognitive Theory* (Englewood Cliffs, NJ: Prentice-Hall, 1986).

Bayham, W. C. *Zapp! The Lightning of Empowerment* (Pittsburgh, PA: Development Dimensions International Press, 1988).

Beckhard, R. *Organisation Development: Strategies and Models* (Reading, MA: Addison-Wesley, 1969).

Blinde, E. M., Taub, D. E. and Han, L., 'Sport Participation and Women's Personal Empowerment: Experiences of the College Athlete', *Journal of Sport and Social Issues* (Volume 17, 1993, No. 1 pp. 47–60).

Blinde, E. M., Taub, D. E. and Han, L., (1994) 'Sport as a Site for Women's Group and Societal Empowerment: Perspectives from the College Athlete', *Sociology of Sport Journal* 11(1), pp. 51–9.

Capozzoli, T. K., 'Managers and leaders: a matter of cognitive difference' *Journal of Leadership Studies* (Volume 2, 1995, No. 3, pp. 20–29).

Cassidy, T., Jones, R., Potrac, P., *Understanding Sports Coaching: The Social, Cultural and Pedagogical Foundations of Coaching Practice* (Oxon: Routledge, 2004).

Davis, W. E. and Broadhead, G. D., *Ecological Task Analysis and Movement* (Champaign, Illinois: Human Kinetics, 2007).

Deci, E. L. and Ryan, R. M., (eds) *Handbook of Self-Determination Research* (Rochester, NY: University of Rochester Press, 2002).

Deci, E. L., Eghrari, H., Patrick, B. C., and Leone, D., 'Facilitating internalisation: the self-determination theory perspective' *Journal of Personality* (Volume 62, 1994, pp. 119–142).

Gibson, C. H., 'A concept analysis of empowerment' *Journal of Advance Nursing* (Volume 16, 1991, No. 3, pp. 354–61).

Gill, R., *Theory and Practice of Leadership* (London: Sage, 2006).

Hawks, J. H., 'Empowerment in nursing education: concept analysis and application to philosophy, learning and instruction' *Journal of Advance Nursing* (Volume 17, 1992, No. 5, pp. 609–18).

Hogg, J. M., *Mental Skills for Swim Coaches* (Edmonton, Al: Sport Excel Publishing, 1995).

Hollembeak, J. and Ambrose, A. J., 'Perceived coaching behaviours and college athletes' intrinsic motivation: a test of self-determination theory' *Journal of Applied Sport Psychology* (Volume 17, 2005, pp. 20–36).

Hoyle, E., *The Politics of School Management* (London: Hodder & Stoughton, 1986).

Jones, R. L., 'Applying empowerment in coaching: Some considerations' in L. Kidman (ed) *Developing Decision Makers: An empowerment approach to coaching* (Christchurch, NZ: Innovative, 2001).

Jones, R. L., *The Sports Coach as Educator: Re-conceptualising Sports Coaching* (Oxon: Sage, 2006).

Kanter, R. M., 'Power failure in management circuits' *Harvard Business Review* (Volume 57, 1979, No. 4, pp. 65–75).

Kidman, L., *Developing Decision Makers: An Empowerment Approach to Coaching* (NZ: Wyatt and Wilson, 2001).

Kidman, L., *Athlete-Centred Coaching: Developing Inspired and Inspiring People* (NZ: Innovative, 2005).

Krane, T. D., Marks, M. A., Zaccaro, S. J., and Blair, V., 'Self-efficacy, personal goals, and wrestlers' self-regulation' *Journal of Sport & Exercise Psychology* (Volume 18, 1996, pp. 36–40).

Krazmien, M. and Berger, F., 'The coaching paradox' *International Journal of Hospitality Management* (Volume 16, 1997, No. 1, pp. 3–10).

Lather, P., *Getting Smart: Feminist Research and Pedagogy with/in the Postmodern* (London: Routledge, 1991).

Lindgren, E., Patriksson, G., and Fridlund, B., 'Empowering young female athletes through a self-strengthening programme: a qualitative analysis' *European Physical Education Review* (2002; 8; pp. 230–248).

Lowe, P., 'Empowerment; management dilemma, leadership challenge' *Executive Development* (Volume 7, 1994, No. 6, pp. 23–24.

Lyle, J., *Sports Coaching Concepts: A Framework for Coaches' Behaviour* (London: Routledge, 2002).

McClenland, D. C., *Power: The Inner Experience* (New York: Irvington Press, 1975).

Mills, P. K., and Ungson, G. R., 'Reassessing the limits of structural empowerment: organisational constitution and trust as controls' *Academy of Management Review* (Volume 28, 2003, No. 1, pp. 143–153).

Morgan, M. J., 'Winning with initiative' *Strategies* (Volume 17, 2004, No. 3, pp. 31–32).

Nutbeam, D., 'Health Promotion Glossary' *Health Promotion International* (Volume 13, 1998, No. 14, pp. 349–64).

Quinn, R. E., and Spreitzer, G. M., 'The road to empowerment: seven questions every leader should consider' *Organisational Dynamics* (Volume 26, 1997, No. 2, pp. 37–49).

Rink, J. E., French, K. E., and Tjeerdsma, B. L., 'Foundations for the learning and instruction of sport and games' *Journal of Teaching in Physical Education* (1996, 15, pp. 399–417).

Seaborn, P., Trudel, P., and Gilbert, W., 'Instructional content provided to female ice hockey players during games' *Applied Research in Coaching and Athletics Annual* (1998, 13, pp. 119–141).

Stamatis, D. H., *Six Sigma and Beyond* (Florida: CRC Press, 2002).

Tannenbaum, A. S., *Control in Organisations* (New York: McGraw-Hill, 1968).

Turney, P. B. B., 'Beyond TQM with workforce activity-based management' *Management Accounting* (1993, September, pp. 28–31).

Usher, P., 'Empowerment as a powerful coaching tool' *Coaches' Report* (Volume 4, 1997, No. 2, pp. 10–11).

Wallace, M., 'Sharing leadership of schools through teamwork: a justifiable risk?' *Educational Management and Administration* (Volume 29, 2001, No. 2, pp. 153–167).

Whitmore, J., *Coaching for Performance: Growing People, Performance and Purpose* (London: Nicholas Brealey, 2002).

CHAPTER 4

Atkinson, J., *An Introduction to Motivation* (Van Nostrad, New York, 1974).

Ames, C., 'Classrooms: Goals, Structures and Students' Motivation' *Journal of Educational Psychology* (Volume 84,1992, No. 3, pp. 261–271).

Beck, R., *Motivational Theories and Principles, 4th edition* (Prentice Hall, 2000).

Carpenter, P. and Morgan, K., 'Motivational Climate: Personal Goal Perspectives and Cognitive and Affective Responses in Physical Education Classes' *European Journal of Physical Education* (Volume 4, 1999, pp. 31–44).

Deci, E. and Ryan, R., *A Motivational Approach to Self-Integration in Personality* in Dienstber, R. (editor) *The Nebraska Symposium on Motivation: perspectives on Motivation* (Volume 38, 1991, pp. 237–288).

Duda, J. L., 'Relationship between Task and Ego Orientation and the Perceived Purpose of Sport among High School Athletes' *Journal of Sport and Exercise Psychology* (Volume 11, 1989, pp. 318–335).

Duda, J. L., and Hall, H., *Achievement Goal Theory in Sport: Recent Extensions and Future Directions* in Singer, R., Hausenblas, H., and Janelle, C. (editors) *Handbook of Sport Psychology, 2nd edition* (Wiley 2001, pp. 417–443).

Epstein, J., *Family Structures and Student Motivation: A Developmental Perspective* cited in Roberts, G. C. *Motivation in Sport and Exercise* (Human Kinetics Publishers, 1992).

Gill, D., *Psychological Dynamics of Sport and Exercise* (Human Kinetics, 2000).

Heider, F., *The Psychology of Interpersonal Relations* (Wiley, 1958) cited in Weinberg, R. S., and Gould, D. *Foundations of Sport and Exercise Psychology* (Human Kinetics Publishers, 2007).

Honey, P., and Mumford, A., *Learning Styles Questionnaire* (Peter Honey Publications, 2006).

McClelland, D., *The Achieving Society* (New York Free Press, 1961) cited in Weinberg, R. S., and Gould, D. *Foundations of Sport and Exercise Psychology, 4th edition* (Human Kinetics Publishers, 2007).

Newton, M., and Duda, J. L., 'The interaction of motivational climate, dispositional goal orientations and perceived ability in predicting indices of motivation' *International Journal of Sport Psychology* (Volume 30, 1999, pp. 63–82).

Nicholls, J. G., 'Achievement Motivation: Conceptions of Ability, Subjective Experience, Task Choice and Performance *Psychological Review* (Volume 91, 1984, pp. 328–346) cited in Roberts, G. C. *Motivation in Sport and Exercise* (Human Kinetics Publishers, 1992).

Ntoumanis, N., and Biddle, S. J. H., 'A review of motivational climate in physical activity' *Journal of Sports Sciences* (Volume 17, 1999, pp. 643–665).

Roberts, G. C., *Motivation in Sport and Exercise* (Human Kinetics Publishers, 1992).

Sage, G., *Introduction to motor behaviour: a neurophysiological approach (2nd edition)* (Addison-Wesley 1977), cited in Weinberg, R. S., and Gould, D. *Foundations of Sport and Exercise Psychology, 4th edition* (Human Kinetics Publishers, 2007).

Scanlan, T. K., *Social evaluation and the competition process: A developmental perspective*, cited in Weinberg, R. S., and

Gould, D. *Foundations of Sport and Exercise Psychology, 4th edition* (Human Kinetics Publishers, 2007).

Smith, S. L., Fry, M. D., Ethington, C.A., and Li, Y., 'The Effect of Female Athletes' Perceptions of their Coaches' Behaviours on their Perceptions of the Motivational Climate *Journal of Applied Sport Psychology* (Volume 17, 2005, pp. 170–177).

Treasure, D., 'Perceptions of the Motivational Climate and Elementary School Children's Cognitive and Affective Response' *Journal of Sport and Exercise Psychology* (Volume 19, 1997, pp. 278–290).

Weiner, B., 'An Attribution Theory of Achievement Motivation and Emotion' *Psychological Review* (Volume 92, 1985, pp. 548–573).

Weinberg, R. S., and Gould, D., *Foundations of Sport and Exercise Psychology, 4th edition* (Human Kinetics Publishers, 2007).

CHAPTER 7

Bailey, R., *Teaching Physical Education: (Kogan Page, 2000).*

Black, K. and Haskins, D., Including all Children in Top Play and BT Top Sport, *Primary PE Focus,(1996)* – Winter pp. 9–11.

Fitts, P. M. and Posner, M. I., *Human Performance* Belmont (1967).

Gentile, A. M., A working model of skill acquisition with application to teaching *Quest Monograph, XV11(1972),* pp. 3–23.

Honey, P. and Mumford, A., *Using your Learning Styles* Peter Honey Publications (1986).

Schmidt, R. A. and Wrisberg, C. A., *Motor Learning and Performance* (Human Kinetics, 2000).

CHAPTER 8

Bailey, R., *Teaching Physical Education:* (Kogan Page, 2000).

Hardy, C., Student misbehaviours and teacher's responses in physical education lessons – *Learning and Teaching in Physical Education* Falmer Press, London.

Lambirth, A. and Bailey, R. P., Promoting a positive learning environment, *Teaching Physical Education 5-11 (2000)* Continuum, London.

Hellison, D. R. and Templin, T. J., *A Reflective Approach to Teaching Physical Education* Human Kinetics, USA.

Cohen, L., Mannion, L. and Morrison, K., *A Guide to Teaching Practice* Routledge, London.

CHAPTER 9

Bailey, R., *Teaching Physical Education: (Kogan Page, 2000).*

Schmidt, R. A. and Wrisberg, C. A., *Motor Learning and Performance (Human Kinetics, 2000).*

Vickers, J. N., *Decision Training: A New Approach To Coaching (CABC, 1996).*

CHAPTER 14

Bandura, A., 'Self Efficacy: Toward a Unified Theory of Behavioural Change'. *Psychological Review* (1977, 84, pp. 191–215).

Blair, A., Hall, C. and Leyson, G., 'Imagery Effects on the Performance of Skilled and Novice Soccer Players'. *Journal of Sports Sciences* (1993, 11, pp. 95–101).

Bull, S. J., 'Reflections on a 5-Year Consulting program with the England Women's Cricket Team'. *The Sport Psychologist* (1995, 9, pp. 148–163).

Bull, S. J., Albinson, J. G. and Shambrook, C.J., *The Mental Game Plan.* (Sports Dynamics, 1996).

Butler, R. J., *Sports Psychology in Action.* (Butterworth Heinemann, 1996).

Butler, R. J. and Hardy, L., 'The Performance Profile: Theory and Application'. *The Sport Psychologist* (1992, 6, pp. 253–264).

Butler, R., Smith, M. and Irwin, I., 'The Performance Profile in Practice' *Journal of Applied Sport Psychology* (1993, 5, pp. 48–63).

Collins, D., Morriss, C. and Trower, J., 'Getting it Back: a Case Study of Skill Recovery in an Elite Athlete'. *The Sport Psychologist,* (1999, 13, pp. 288–298).

Cropley, B., Miles, A., Hanton, S. and Niven, A., 'Improving the Delivery of Applied Sport Psychology Support Through Reflective Practice'. *The Sport Psychologist* (2007, 21, pp. 475–494).

Dane, G. A. and Wrisberg, C.A., 'The Use of Performance Profiling Techniques in a Team Setting: Getting the Athletes and Coaches on the 'Same Page' *The sport Psychologist*, (1996, 10, pp. 261–277).

Davidson, R. J. and Schwartz, G. E., 'The Psychobiology of Relaxation and Related States: A Multi-Process Theory' in Mustofsky, D. (Ed.) *Behavioural Control and Modification of Physiological Activity*. Engelwood Cliffs, N.J. Prentice-Hall, 1976).

Feltz, D. L., Short, S. E. and Sullivan, P. J., *Self Efficacy in Sport: Research Strategies for Working with Athletes, Teams and Coaches*. (Human Kinetics, 2008).

Filby, W. C. D., Maynard, I. W. and Graydon, J. K., 'The Effect of Multiple Goal Strategies on Performance Outcomes in Training and Competition. *Journal of Applied Sport Psychology* (1999, 11, pp. 230–246).

Gallmeier, C. P., 'Putting on the Game Face; The Staging of Emotions in Professional Hockey'. *Sociology of Sport Journal* (1987, 4, pp. 347–362).

Gallwey, W. T., *Inner Game of Tennis*. (New York: Bantam Books, 1982).

Gould, D., Hodge, K., Paterson, K. and Gianni, J., 'An Exploratory Examination of Strategies used by Elite Coaches to Enhance Self-Efficacy in Athletes'. *Journal of Sport and Exercise Psychology* (1989, 11, pp. 128–140).

Green, L. B., 'The Use of Imagery in the Rehabilitation of Injured Athletes'. *The Sport Psychologist* (1992, 8, pp. 126–142).

Hardy, L. and Fazey, J. A., *Mental Preparation for Performance*. (National Coaching Foundation, Leeds, 1986).

Hardy, L., and Fazey, J. *Mental Training* (National Coaching Foundation, Leeds, 1990).

Hardy, L., Jones, G. and Gould, D., *Understanding Psychological Preparation for sport: Theory and Practice of Elite Performers*. (Chichester, Wiley, 1996).

Hill, K. L., *Frameworks for Sport Psychologists Enhancing Sport Performance*. (Human Kinetics, Champaign Ill., 2001).

James, B. and Collins, D., (1995). Creating an Impression: The Processes of Psychological Support to a National Squad. *Journal of Sport and Exercise Psychology* (1995, 17, S12).

Jones, G., 'The Role of Performance Profiling in Cognitive Behavioural Interventions in Sport'. *The Sport Psychologist* (1993, 7, pp. 160–172).

Jones, G. J. and Hardy, L., *Stress and Performance in Sport*. (Wiley, 1993).

Jones, G. J. and Swain, A., 'Intensity and Direction as dimensions of competitive state anxiety and relationship with competitiveness'. *Perceptual and Motor Skills* (74, pp. 467–472).

Kirschenbaum, D. S., 'Self- Regulation and Sport Psychology, Nurturing and Emerging Symbiosis.' *Journal of Sport Psychology* (1984, 6, pp. 159–183).

Krane, V., 'A Practical Model for Examining the Anxiety- Athletic Performance Relationship – Zone of Optimal Functioning Hypothesis'. *The Sport Psychologist* (1993, 7, pp. 113–126).

Leary, M. R. 'Self-Presentational Processes in Exercise and Sport'. *Journal of Sport and Exercise Psychology* (1992, 14, pp. 339–351).

Leary, M. R. *Self-Presentation: Impression Management and Interpersonal Behaviour*. (Dubuque, IA: Brown & Benchmark, 1995).

Mace, R., *With Netball in Mind*. (Sports Council, 1994).

Maynard, I. M., MacDonald, A. L. and Warwick-Evans, L., 'Anxiety in Novice Rock Climbers. A further test of the matching hypothesis in a field setting. *International Journal of Sport Psychology* (1997, 28, pp. 67–78).

McNair, D., Lorr. M. and Droppleman, L. *Profile of Mood State Manual*. (San Diego: Educational and Testing Service, 1971).

Munroe, K. J., Giacobbi, P. R. Jr, Hall, C. and Weinberg, R., 'The Four Ws of Imagery Use: Where, When Why and What'. *The Sport Psychologist* (2000, pp. 119–137).

Nideffer, R. M., *Athletes' Guide to Mental Training*. (Human Kinetics, 1985).

Partington, J. and Orlick, T., 'The Sport Psychology Evaluation Form'. *The Sport Psychologist* (1987, 1, pp. 309–317).

Poczwardowski, A., Sherman, C. P. and Ravizza, K., 'Professional Philosophy in Sport Psychology Service Delivery: Building on Theory and Practice. *The Sport Psychologist* (2004, 18, pp. 445–463).

Sinclair, G. D. and Sinclair, D. A. 'Developing Reflective Performers by Integrating Mental Management Skills with the Learning Process'. *The Sport Psychologist* (1994, 8, pp. 13–27).

Weinberg, R. S. and Gould, D., *Foundations of Sport and Exercise Psychology*. (Human Kinetics, 1995, 2003).

Williams, J. M. (Ed.) *Applied Sport Psychology: Personal Growth to Peak performance*. (Mayfield Publishing Co., 1993, 2nd Edition).

CHAPTER 19

Abbott, A., Button, C., Pepping, G. & Collins, D., (2005). Unnatural selection: Talent identification and development in sport. *Nonlinear Dynamics, Psychology, and Life Sciences*, 9, pp. 61–88.

Abbott, A., Collins, D., Martindale, R. and Sowerby, K., (2002). *Talent Identification and Development: an academic review* (Edinburgh: sportscotland).

Abernethy, B., Côté, J. and Baker, J., (2002). *Expert decision-making in team sport* (Canberra, Australian Institute of Sport).

Balyi, I., and Hamilton, A., (2000). Key to Success: Long-term Athlete Development. *Sport Coach* (Canberra, Australia). 23, pp. 10–32.

Bouchard, C., Shephard, R. J., and Stephens, T. (Eds) (1993) *Physical Activity, Fitness & Health: A consensus statement* (Champaign, IL: Human Kinetics).

Cimons, M., (1999). Youth movement: children and teens vulnerable to sports injury. Runners's World, 34(4), 42.

Côté, J., (1999). The influence of the family in the development of talent in sport. *The Sport Psychologist*, 13, pp. 395–417.

Côté, J, and Fraser-Thomas, J., (2007). Youth involvement in sport. In P.R.E. Crocker (Ed.), *Introduction to sport psychology: a Canadian perspective* (pp. 266–294) (Toronto: Pearson Prentice Hall).

Csikszentmihalyi, M., Rathunde, K. and Whalen, S., (1993). *Talented teenagers: The roots of success and failure* (Cambridge: Cambridge University Press).

Deakin, J. M. and Cobley, S., (2003). An examination of the practice environments in figure skating and volleyball: a search for deliberate practice (pp. 90–113). In J. Starkes and K. A. Ericsson (Eds) *Expert performance in sports: advances in research on sport expertise* (Champaign, IL, Human Kinetics).

English Sports Council (1998). *The Development of Sporting Talent, 1997*. (London: English Sports Council).

Ericsson, K. A., Krampe, R. T., and Tesch-Römer, C., (1993). The role of deliberate practice in the acquisition of expert performance. *Psychological Review*, 100, pp. 363–406.

Green, M., (2007). Policy transfer, lesson drawing and perspectives on elite sport development systems. *International Journal of Sport Management and Marketing*, 2, pp. 426–441.

Helsen, W. F., Starkes, J. L. and Hodges, N. J. (1998). Team sports and the theory of deliberate practice. *Journal of Sport and Exercise Psychology*, 20, pp. 12–34.

Hoare, D., (1995). Talent Search. The National Talent Identification and Development Program, *Coaching Focus*, 13, pp. 10–12.

Houlihan, B., (2000). Sporting Excellence, Schools and Sports Development: The Politics of Crowded Policy Spaces, *European Physical Education Review*, 6, pp. 171–193.

Kay, W., (2003). Physical Education, R.I.P.? *The British Journal of Teaching Physical Education*, 34, pp. 6–10.

Kirk, D., (2004). Framing Quality Physical Education: the elite sport model or Sport Education? *Physical Education and Sport Pedagogy*, 9, pp. 185–195.

Kirk, D., (2005). Physical Education, youth sport and lifelong participation: the importance of early learning experiences, *European Physical Education Review*, 11, pp. 239–255.

Kirk, D., Brettschneider, W. and Auld, C. (2007). Junior sport models representing best practice nationally and internationally (pp. 83–99). In S. Hooper, D. Macdonald, and M. Phillips, (Eds.) *Junior Sport Matters: Briefing Papers for Australian Junior Sport.* (Belconnen: Australian Sports Commission).

Kirk, D. and Gorely, T. (2000). Challenging Thinking about the Relationship between School Physical Education and Sport Performance, *European Physical Educational Review*, 6, pp. 119–134.

Lee, M. J. (2004). Values in Physical Education and Sport: A conflict of interests. *British Journal of Teaching Physical Education*, 35, pp. 6–10.

Miller, P. and Kerr, G., (2002). Conceptualising Excellence: past, present, and future. *Journal of Applied Sport Psychology*, 14, pp. 140–153.

Morley, D., Cobley, S. and Bailey, R. P., (2005). Talent Development in Physical Education: the pupils' voice. Paper presented to British Educational Research Association conference, University of Glamorgan, Cardiff.

Ollis, S., McPherson, A. and Collins, D. (2006). Expertise and Talent Development in Rugby Referees. *Journal of Sports Sciences*, 24, pp. 309–22.

Peltola, E., (1992). Talent Identification. *Sport Psychology Bulletin*, 3, pp. 10–11.

Penney, D., (2000). Physical Education, Sporting Excellence and Educational Excellence. *European Physical Educational Review*, 6, pp. 135–150.

Rowley, S. R. W., (1992). *Training of Young Athletes (TOYA) and the Identification of talent*. London: Sports Council.

Schmidt, B., (2006). *Constructing a Pyramid of Progression for Talent in Dance*. (Coventry: National Academy for Gifted and Talented Youth).

Siedentop, D., (2002). Junior Sport and the evolution of sport cultures, *Journal of Teaching in Physical Education*, 21, pp. 392–401.

Sport England (2002). *Annual report 2001– 2002, Part 1* (London: Sport England).

Sport England (2004). *The Framework for sport in England. Making England an active a successful sporting nation: A vision for 2020.* (London: Sport England).

Stafford, I. (2005). *Coaching for Long-Term Athlete Development* (Leeds: sports coach UK).

Youth Sport Trust (2008). Junior athlete Education programme. Available at: www. youthsporttrust.org. (Accessed 14/01/08).

Weiss, M. R. and Chaumeton, N., (1992). Motivation orientations in sport (pp. 61–99). In T. Horn (Ed.), *Advances in sport psychology* (Champaign, IL: Human Kinetics).

CHAPTER 20

Alicke, M. D., LoSchiavo, F. M., Zerbst, J. and Shaobo, Z. (1997) The Person Who Outperforms me is a Genius: Maintaining perceived competence in upward social comparison. *Journal of Personality and Social Psychology*, 74 (4) pp. 781–789.

Armstrong, N. and Macmanus, A., (1994). Children's fitness and physical activity- A challenge for Physical Education. *The British Journal of Physical Education, Spring*, pp. 20–26.

Bailey, R. P., Wellard, I. and Dismore, H., (2005). *Girls' participation in physical activities and sports: Benefits, patterns, influences and ways forward*. Geneva: World Health Organisation.

Bailey, R., Morley, D. and Dismore, H., (2009). Talent development in physical education: a national survey of policy and practice in England, *Physical Education & Sport Pedagogy*,14:1, pp. 59–72.

Balyi, I., and Hamilton, A., (2000). Key to Success: Long-term Athlete Development. *Sport Coach* (Canberra, Australia). 23, pp. 10–32.

Barnes, S., (2009). Grabbing that fun-size piece of the action, *The Times*, 6 June.

Bloom, S., Bullion, P. and Caldwell, B., (1998). World View: An Integrated Districtwide Model for School Change. *Phi Delta Kappa*, Vol. 78, Number 5, pp. 411–412.

Bowe, R., Ball, S. J. and Gold, A., (1992). *Reforming Education and Changing Schools.* London: Routledge.

Burton, A. and Miller, D., (1992). *Movement Skill and Assessment*. Ch; IL: Human Kinetics.

Cale, L., (2000). Physical activity promotion in secondary schools, *European Physical Education Review*, 6(1), 71–90.

Cale, L. and Harris, J. (2009). Fitness testing in physical education—a misdirected effort in promoting healthy lifestyles and physical activity? *Physical Education and Sport Pedagogy*, 14,1, pp. 89–108.

Côté, J., and Hay, J., (2002). 'Children's involvement in sport: a developmental analysis'. In, J. M. Silva & D. Stevens (eds) *Psychological Foundations of Sport*. Boston, MA: Allyn and Bacon.

Council of Europe (CoE) (2001). Recommendation No. R. (92) 13 REV of the Committee of Ministers of Members States on the Revised European Sports Charter. Strasbourg: CoE.

DfES / DCMS (2003). *Learning Through PE and Sport* (London, DfES/DCMS).

DCMS (2005a). *Living life to the full*. London: DCMS.

DCMS (2005b). *Business Plan 2005*. London: DCMS.

DfEE (1999). *National Curriculum for Physical Education*. London, DfEE.

DCSF (2008). *National Curriculum for Physical Education*. London, DCSF.

Dickens, J. (2008). Future of English football relies on re-structuring of youth Development. Available at: http://keskisuomi.palloliitto.fi/mp/db/file_library/x/IMG/23787/file/Futisseminaari_Horst_Wein_M.pdf. [Accessed 20 April 2009].

English Sports Council (1998), *The Development of Sporting Talent, 1997*. London: English Sports Council.

ESP (Education and Special Projects) (2009) Multi-skills Training Award (Level 3). Award information available at: http://www.espplay.co.uk [Accessed 4 Jul 09].

Gallahue, D. and Ozmun, (2006) *Understanding Motor Development: Infants, Children, Adolescents, Adults, 6th Ed.*, New York, McGraw-Hill.

Hargreaves, A., (1995). Renewal in the Age of Paradox. *Educational Leadership*, Number 52, Vol. 7, pp. 14–19.

Harris, J., (1995). Physical education—a picture of health?, *The British Journal of Physical Education*, 26(4), pp. 25–32.

Hamilton, M., Pankey, R. and Kinnunen, D., (2002). Constraints of Motor Skill Acquisition: Implications for teaching and learning. Education Resources Information Centre, ED471196. [Available at: www.eric.ed.gov. Accessed 23 Mar 09].

Hands, B., (2002). How can we best measure Fundamental Movement Skills? ACHPER Interactive Health and Physical Education Conference. University of Tasmania, Launceston Campus, 3–6 July 2002.

Horn, T. S. and Weiss, M. R., (1991). A Developmental Analysis of Children's Self Ability Judgements in the Physical Domain, *Pediatric Exercise Science*, 3, pp. 310–326.

Jess, M. and Collins, D. (2003). Primary Physical Education in Scotland: the future in the making. *European Journal of Physical Education*, 8 (2) pp. 103–118.

Kirk, D., (1992). *Defining Physical Education: the Social Construction of a School Subject in Postwar Britain* (London, Falmer).

Law, M. P., Cote, J., and Ericsson, K. A., (2007). Characteristics of expert development in rhythmic gymnastics: A retrospective study. *International Journal of Sport and Exercise Psychology*, 5, pp. 82–103.

Lazerson, M., (1997). Who Owns Higher Education? The Changing Face of Governance. *Change: The Magazine of Higher Education*, Vol. 29, Number 2, pp. 10–15.

Lewin, K., (1947). *Group Decisions and Social Change*. Troy, MO: Holt, Rinehart & Winston.

Lerner, R. M., Fisher, C. B., and Weinberg, R. A., (2000). Toward a science for and of the people: promoting civil society through the application of developmental science. *Child Development*, 71, pp. 11–20.

Marsh, H. W., (1993). Physical Fitness Self-concept: Relations to field and technical indicators of physical fitness for boys and girls aged 9–15. *Journal of Sport and Exercise Psychology*, 15, pp. 184–206.

Maulding, W. and Styron, R. A., (2005). Restructuring an Educational Leadership Program Using Action Research. *Journal of Scholarship & Practice*, 1, 4, pp. 8–12.

McKenna, J., (2008). Playgrounds as Three-Stage Evaluation of ESP-Made Playground Markings in Derby Schools, Summer 2008. Accessed online: http://www.espplay.co.uk/products/cpd-products.html

Mills, G., (2003). Action Research. Columbus, Ohio: Merrill Prentice Hall Publishing Co.

Morley, D., Cobley, S. and Bailey, R. (2005). Talent Development in Physical Education: the pupils' voice. Paper presented to British Educational Research Association conference, University of Glamorgan, Cardiff.

Morley, D., Tremere, R. and Bailey, R. P., (2005). Utilising a Case Study Methodology to Describe and Evaluate Talent Development Strategies in Physical Education. Paper presented to the British Educational Research association annual conference. University of Glamorgan.

Morley, D., Tremere, R. and Bailey, R., (2005). Multi-skilling talented children in PE and sport. Paper presented to the British Educational Research association annual conference. University of Glamorgan.

Morley, D. and Bailey, R., (2006). *Meeting the needs of your most able pupils: Physical Education and Sport*. David Fulton: London.

Morley, D. and Webb, V., (2009). A A 'Fit for Purpose' approach to skills development in Rugby Football League, UK Coaching Summit, Glasgow, 27–29 Apr.

Newell, K. M., (1986). Constraints on the development of coordination. In Wade M, Whiting HTA (editors): Motor Development in Children: Aspects of Coordination and Control (pp. 341–360). Dordrecht, Germany: Martinus Nijhoff.

Okely, A. D., Booth, M. L., and Patterson, J. W., (2001). Relationship of physical activity to fundamental movement skills among adolescents. *Medicine in science and sport exercise,* 33 (11) pp. 1899–1904.

Peltola, E., (1992). Talent Identification. *Sport Psychology Bulletin*, 3 (5), pp. 10–11.

Penney, D., (1998). School subjects and structures: reinforcing traditional voices in contemporary "reforms" of education, *Discourse: Studies in the Cultural Politics of Education*, 19 (1) pp. 5–18.

Penney, D., (1999). Physical Education: In changing times is it time for a change? *British Journal of Physical Education*, 30 (4) pp. 4–6.

Penney, D., (2000). Physical Education, Sporting Excellence and Educational Excellence. *European Physical Educational Review*, 6, pp. 135–150.

Penney, D. and Evans, J., (1999). *Politics, Policy & Practice in Physical Education*. London: E & FN Spon.

Penney, D. and Harris, J., (1997). Extra-curricular Physical Education: More of the same for the more able? *Sport, Education and Society*, 2 (1) pp. 41–54.

Qualifications and Curriculum Authority (2007). Physical Education: Programme of study for key stage 3 and attainment target. London: QCA.

Raedeke, T. D. and Smith, A. L., (2004). Coping Resources and athlete burnout: An examination of stress-mediated and moderation hypotheses. *Journal of Sport and Exercise Psychology*, 26, pp. 525–541.

Rowley, S. R. W., (1992). *Training of Young Athletes (TOYA) and the Identification of talent*. London: Sports Council.

Seefeldt, Haubenstricker and Reuchlien., (1979). Cited in Graham, G., Holt/Hale, S. and Parker, M. (2001). *Children Moving: A Reflective Approach to Teaching Physical Education*, 4th Ed., Mountain View: Mayfield Press.

Sparkes, A., (1988). The micropolitics of innovation in the Physical Education curriculum. In, J. Evans (ed.) *Teachers, Teaching and Control in Physical Education*. London: The Falmer Press.

Sports Council for Wales (1995). *The pattern of play: Physical Education in Welsh Secondary schools:1990–1994*. Cardiff: The Sports Council for Wales.

Smith, R. E., (1986). *Journal of Sport Psychology*, 8, pp. 36–50. Toward a cognitive-affective model of athletic burnout.

Sports Coach UK (2008). *The UK Coaching Framework: executive summary. A 3-7-11 Year Action Plan*. Coachwise: Leeds.

Sports Coach UK (2009). *The UK Coaching Framework: The Coaching Workforce 2009-2016*. Coachwise: Leeds.

Stafford, I. (2005). *Coaching for Long-term Athlete Development: To improve participation and performance in sport*. Leeds: The National Coaching Foundation.

Strachan, L., Côté, J., and Deakin, J., (2009). "Specializers" Versus "Samplers" in Youth Sport: Comparing Experiences and Outcomes. *The Sport Psychologist*, 23, 1, pp. 77–92.

Stringer, E., (2004). *Action Research in Education*. Columbus, OH: Pearson, Merrill, Prentice Hall.

Vereijken, B. and Bongaardt, R., (1999). *Complex motor skill acquisition. In Psychology for physical educators* (edited by Y. Vanden Auweele, F. Bakker, S. Biddle, M. Durand and R. Seiler). pp. 233–256. Champaign, Ill. Human Kinetics.

Wenger, Etienne and Richard McDermott, and William Snyder (2002). *Cultivating communities of practice: a guide to managing knowledge*. Cambridge, Mass.: Harvard Business School Press.

Wenger, Etienne (2007). 'Communities of practice. A brief introduction'. *Communities of practice* [http://www.ewenger.com/theory/. Accessed January 14, 2009].

Whitson, D. J. and Macintosh, D., (1990). The scientization of physical education: discourses of performance, Quest, 42(1), pp. 40–51.

Williams, G., (2009). Payments to Physical Education teachers for extra-curricular activities? *Physical Education Matters*, 4, 1, pp. 24–28.

Young, M. F. D., (1998). *The curriculum of the future: From the 'New Sociology of Education' to a critical theory of learning*. London: Falmer Press.

Youth Sport Trust (2009). Multi-skills Academies: Programme Information Sheet. Available from: http://gifted. youthsporttrust.org/page/msas/index. html. [Accessed 20 Jun 09].

Youth Sport Trust (2009b). Selecting Young People for Multi-skill Academies: Information and Guidance. Available from: http://gifted.youthsporttrust.org/page/msas/index.html. [Accessed 20 Jun 09].

CHAPTER 22

Côté, J., (1999). The influence of the family in the development of talent in sport. *The Sport Psychologist*, 13, pp. 395–417.

Côté, J, and Fraser-Thomas, J., (2007). Youth involvement in sport. In P.R.E.

Crocker (Ed.), *Introduction to sport psychology: a Canadian perspective* (pp. 266–294). Toronto: Pearson Prentice Hall.

Create Development (2009). Raising The Bar. Available online from www.createdevelopment.org.uk [Accessed 14 Nov 09].

Csikszentmihalyi, M., Rathunde, K., and Whalen, S., (1993). *Talented teenagers: The roots of success and failure*. Cambridge: Cambridge University Press.

ESP (Education and Special Projects) (2009) Multi-skills Training Award resources. Available from: www.esplay.co.uk [Accessed 14 Nov 09].

Holt, N. and Morley, D., (2004). Gender differences in Psychological Factors Associated with Athletic success during childhood. *The Sports Psychologist*. 18 (2) pp. 138–153.

Rowley, S. R. W., (1992). *Training of Young Athletes (TOYA) and the Identification of talent*. London: Sports Council.

CHAPTER 30

Casidy T., Jones R. and Potrac P. *Understanding Sports Coaching*, (Routledge: 2004).

Galvin, B (Editor) *A Guide to Mentoring Sports Coaches* (Sports Coach UK, 2005).

Jones, R (Editor) *The Sports Coach as Educator* (Routledge: 2006).

Reference "Coaching as a profession" Skills Active, 2009, Sports Coaching National Occupational Standards, www.skillsactive. com/coachingNOS Smith, C (Ed), 2008, The UK Coaching Framework, Leeds: sportscoach UK.

References "The coach as a professional" Casidy T, Jones R, Potrac P, 2004, Understanding Sports Coaching, London: Routledge.

Jones, R (Ed), 2006, The Sports Coach as Educator, London: Routledge.

Martens R, 2004, Successful Coaching, Leeds: Human Kinetics.

The National Coaching Foundation, 2005, Code of Practice for Sports Coaches, Leeds: sportscoach UK.

The National Coaching Foundation, 2005, The Successful Coach, Leeds: sportscoach UK.

CHAPTER 31

Casidy T., Jones R. and Potrac P., *Understanding Sports Coaching*, (Routledge: 2004).

Jones, R (Editor) *The Sports Coach as Educator* (Routledge: 2006).

Sports Coach UK *The Coaching Framework* (Coachwise: 2008).

Reference "Coaching as a profession" Skills Active, 2009, Sports Coaching National Occupational Standards, www.skillsactive.com/coachingNOS

Smith, C (Ed), 2008, The UK Coaching Framework, Leeds: sportscoach UK.

References "The coach as a professional" Casidy T, Jones R, Potrac P, 2004, Understanding Sports Coaching, London: Routledge.

Jones, R (Ed), 2006, The Sports Coach as Educator, London: Routledge.

Martens R, 2004, Successful Coaching, Leeds: Human Kinetics.

The National Coaching Foundation, 2005, Code of Practice for Sports Coaches, Leeds: sportscoach UK.

The National Coaching Foundation, 2005, The Successful Coach, Leeds: sportscoach UK.

Index